D0842839

RETOOLING FOR AN AGING AMERICA

BUILDING THE HEALTH CARE WORKFORCE

Committee on the Future Health Care Workforce for Older Americans
Board on Health Care Services

INSTITUTE OF MEDICINE
OF THE NATIONAL ACADEMIES

THE NATIONAL ACADEMIES PRESS
Washington, D.C.
www.nap.edu

THE NATIONAL ACADEMIES PRESS   500 Fifth Street, N.W.   Washington, DC 20001

NOTICE: The project that is the subject of this report was approved by the Governing Board of the National Research Council, whose members are drawn from the councils of the National Academy of Sciences, the National Academy of Engineering, and the Institute of Medicine. The members of the committee responsible for the report were chosen for their special competences and with regard for appropriate balance.

This study was supported by contracts between the National Academy of Sciences and AARP; Archstone Foundation (Contract No. 07-01-07); The Atlantic Philanthropies (Contract No. 14984); The California Endowment (Contract No. 20062172); The Commonwealth Fund (Contract No. 20070140); The Fan Fox and Leslie R. Samuels Foundation, Inc.; The John A. Hartford Foundation, Inc. (Contract No. 2006-0133); The Josiah Macy, Jr. Foundation (Contract No. B06-07); The Retirement Research Foundation (Contract No. 2006-278); and Robert Wood Johnson Foundation (Contract No. 57803). Any opinions, findings, conclusions, or recommendations expressed in this publication are those of the author(s) and do not necessarily reflect the view of the organizations or agencies that provided support for this project.

Library of Congress Cataloging-in-Publication Data

Retooling for an aging America : building the health care workforce / Committee on the Future Health Care Workforce for Older Americans, Board on Health Care Services.
    p. ; cm.
    Includes bibliographical references and index.
    ISBN-13: 978-0-309-11587-2 (hardcover)
    1. Older people—Medical care--United States. 2. Caregivers—United States. 3. Geriatricians—Supply and demand--United States—Forecasting. I. Institute of Medicine (U.S.). Committee on the Future Health Care Workforce for Older Americans.
    [DNLM: 1. Health Services for the Aged—manpower—United States. 2. Aged—United States. 3. Caregivers—United States. 4. Health Manpower—trends—United States. WT 31 R438 2008]
    RA564.8.R48 2008
    618.97′023—dc22

                                        2008024225

Additional copies of this report are available from the National Academies Press, 500 Fifth Street, N.W., Lockbox 285, Washington, DC 20055; (800) 624-6242 or (202) 334-3313 (in the Washington metropolitan area); Internet, http://www.nap.edu.

For more information about the Institute of Medicine, visit the IOM home page at: **www.iom.edu.**

The serpent has been a symbol of long life, healing, and knowledge among almost all cultures and religions since the beginning of recorded history. The serpent adopted as a logotype by the Institute of Medicine is a relief carving from ancient Greece, now held by the Staatliche Museen in Berlin.

Suggested citation: IOM (Institute of Medicine). 2008. *Retooling for an aging America: Building the health care workforce.* Washington, DC: The National Academies Press.

"Knowing is not enough; we must apply.
Willing is not enough; we must do."
—Goethe

INSTITUTE OF MEDICINE
OF THE NATIONAL ACADEMIES

Advising the Nation. Improving Health.

THE NATIONAL ACADEMIES
Advisers to the Nation on Science, Engineering, and Medicine

The **National Academy of Sciences** is a private, nonprofit, self-perpetuating society of distinguished scholars engaged in scientific and engineering research, dedicated to the furtherance of science and technology and to their use for the general welfare. Upon the authority of the charter granted to it by the Congress in 1863, the Academy has a mandate that requires it to advise the federal government on scientific and technical matters. Dr. Ralph J. Cicerone is president of the National Academy of Sciences.

The **National Academy of Engineering** was established in 1964, under the charter of the National Academy of Sciences, as a parallel organization of outstanding engineers. It is autonomous in its administration and in the selection of its members, sharing with the National Academy of Sciences the responsibility for advising the federal government. The National Academy of Engineering also sponsors engineering programs aimed at meeting national needs, encourages education and research, and recognizes the superior achievements of engineers. Dr. Charles M. Vest is president of the National Academy of Engineering.

The **Institute of Medicine** was established in 1970 by the National Academy of Sciences to secure the services of eminent members of appropriate professions in the examination of policy matters pertaining to the health of the public. The Institute acts under the responsibility given to the National Academy of Sciences by its congressional charter to be an adviser to the federal government and, upon its own initiative, to identify issues of medical care, research, and education. Dr. Harvey V. Fineberg is president of the Institute of Medicine.

The **National Research Council** was organized by the National Academy of Sciences in 1916 to associate the broad community of science and technology with the Academy's purposes of furthering knowledge and advising the federal government. Functioning in accordance with general policies determined by the Academy, the Council has become the principal operating agency of both the National Academy of Sciences and the National Academy of Engineering in providing services to the government, the public, and the scientific and engineering communities. The Council is administered jointly by both Academies and the Institute of Medicine. Dr. Ralph J. Cicerone and Dr. Charles M. Vest are chair and vice chair, respectively, of the National Research Council.

www.national-academies.org

PAUL C. TANG, Vice President, Chief Medical Information Officer, Palo Alto Medical Foundation; Consulting Associate Professor of Medicine (Biomedical Informatics), Stanford University
JOSHUA M. WIENER, Senior Fellow and Program Director of Aging, Disability, and Long-Term Care, RTI International

Study Staff

ROGER HERDMAN, Director, Board on Health Care Services[1]
MICHELE ORZA, Acting Director, Board on Health Care Services[2]
MEGAN McHUGH, Study Director[3]
TRACY HARRIS, Study Director
BEN WHEATLEY, Program Officer
MICHELLE BRUNO, Research Associate
REDA URMANAVICIUTE, Administrative Assistant
MICHAEL PARK, Senior Program Assistant

---

[1]Starting October 2007.
[2]Through October 2007.
[3]Through November 2007.

Reviewers

This report has been reviewed in draft form by individuals chosen for their diverse perspectives and technical expertise, in accordance with procedures approved by the National Research Council's (NRC's) Report Review Committee. The purpose of this independent review is to provide candid and critical comments that will assist the institution in making its published report as sound as possible and to ensure that the report meets institutional standards for objectivity, evidence, and responsiveness to the study charge. The review comments and draft manuscript remain confidential to protect the integrity of the deliberative process. We wish to thank the following individuals for their review of this report:

KATHLEEN C. BUCKWALTER, The John A. Hartford Center of Geriatric Nursing Excellence, The University of Iowa
SARAH GREENE BURGER, The Hartford Institute for Geriatric Nursing, College of Nursing, New York University
CHRISTINE K. CASSEL, American Board of Internal Medicine
STEVEN L. DAWSON, PHI
DON DETMER, American Medical Informatics Association
WALTER H. ETTINGER, University of Massachusetts Memorial Medical Center
NATHAN HERSHEY, University of Pittsburgh, Professor Emeritus
ULA HWANG, Department of Emergency Medicine and Geriatrics, Mount Sinai School of Medicine
JUDY R. LAVE, Pennsylvania Medicaid Policy Center, Graduate School of Public Health, University of Pittsburgh

BRIAN W. LINDBERG, Consumer Coalition for Quality Health Care

MARILYN MOON, American Institutes for Research

JOSEPH G. OUSLANDER, Division of Geriatric Medicine and Gerontology, Wesley Woods Center of Emory University

ROBYN I. STONE, Institute for the Future of Aging Services, Association of Homes and Services for the Aging

DONALD H. TAYLOR, JR., Benjamin N. Duke and Trinity Scholarship Program and Terry Sanford Institute of Public Policy, Duke University

Although the reviewers listed above have provided many constructive comments and suggestions, they were not asked to endorse the conclusions or recommendations nor did they see the final draft of the report before its release. The review of this report was overseen by **NEAL VANSELOW,** Tulane University, Professor Emeritus, and **EDWARD B. PERRIN,** School of Public Health, University of Washington, Professor Emeritus. Appointed by the NRC and the Institute of Medicine, they were responsible for making certain that an independent examination of this report was carried out in accordance with institutional procedures and that all review comments were carefully considered. Responsibility for the final content of this report rests entirely with the authoring committee and the institution.

Foreword

The retirement of the baby boom generation is rapidly approaching. Between 2005 and 2030, the number of adults aged 65 and older in the United States will almost double. This dramatic shift in the age distribution of America's population will place accelerating demands upon the U.S. health care system.

For the health care workforce, the challenges presented by the aging of America are multifaceted. The sheer volume of older adult patients threatens to overwhelm the number of physicians and other professionals who will be available, unless more is done to ensure an adequate supply. Specific skill sets are required to treat older patients, and our country is unlikely to have enough geriatricians to meet the needs. The vast majority of older adults have chronic illnesses that take them to multiple providers each year, and the management of chronic illness depends on better coordination and team-based care.

The Institute of Medicine's (IOM's) Committee on the Future Health Care Workforce for Older Americans, chaired by John W. Rowe, was formed to probe these challenges and to set out a course of action that will improve our nation's readiness to care for an aging population. The committee conducted a thorough analysis of the forces that shape the health care workforce, including education, training, modes of practice, and the financing of public and private programs.

During the course of its work, the committee sought to answer a number of questions that will be crucial in determining our readiness to meet the health care needs of a rapidly aging society, including: what is the best use of the paid health care workforce and informal caregivers in meeting the needs of older adults? What new roles or new types of providers might be necessary to facilitate efficient, high-quality care? How should the health care workforce be educated and trained to deliver high-value care to older adults, and how should this training be financed? And, what will strengthen the recruitment and retention of the needed workforce?

This year marks the 30th anniversary of the first IOM report on the workforce for geriatric patients, *Aging and Medical Education* (1978). While the aging of the U.S. population as a whole has been projected for decades, we are now on the cusp of this change. The actions called for in this report to bolster the health care workforce will take years to reach their full effect. We can no longer afford to delay these changes that will ultimately help ensure that all older Americans will receive adequate health care.

Harvey V. Fineberg, M.D., Ph.D.
President, Institute of Medicine
April 2008

Preface

In 2007, the Institute of Medicine convened the Committee on the Future Health Care Workforce for Older Americans to recommend steps to improve health care for the growing number of adults over age 65. The committee envisions a future health care system in which the health needs of the older population are addressed comprehensively, services are provided efficiently, and older patients are encouraged to be active partners in their own care.

In the near future, the nation will be aging dramatically, primarily due to increases in life expectancy and the aging of the baby boom generation. Together, these factors will contribute to the largest-ever proportion of older adults, increasing from 12 percent of the U.S. population in 2005 to almost 20 percent by 2030. The 78-million member baby boom generation born between 1946 and 1964 begins turning 65 in 2011. While a large segment of this group will maintain health and independent functioning well past the age of 65, reaching traditional retirement age is generally accompanied by an increasing number of personal health challenges. More than three-fourths of adults over age 65 suffer from at least one chronic medical condition that requires ongoing care and management. Currently, 20 percent of Medicare beneficiaries have five or more chronic conditions.

Caring for the elderly population poses a unique set of challenges. In addition to geriatric syndromes, such as falls and malnutrition, which often lead to acute health care problems, older adults also suffer from a range of cognitive impairments that can impact their ability to perform as active participants in their own care. Moreover, older adults are complex because they often suffer from a range of ailments, including chronic conditions such as hypertension and congestive heart failure, which require ongoing care and active management from multiple providers simultaneously.

The Medicare program has tested various methods for improving its fee-for-service financing system, which is broadly regarded as promoting fragmented care delivery. The imminent increase in the number of complex patients will require further innovations in financing and care delivery as the need for more effectively coordinated care becomes more pressing. The health care system as a whole must do better in ensuring that complex older patients are provided with care that is streamlined and coherent, and the committee supports various approaches to promote this, including the improvement of education and training, increases in recruitment and retention, and the development of new models of care.

The health care workforce in general receives very little geriatric training and is not prepared to deliver the best care to older patients. Geriatric care has not attracted health care professionals in sufficient numbers in the United States and clearly more professionals specializing in geriatrics will be needed to meet the needs of the coming elderly population both because of their clinical expertise as well as their role in educating and training the rest of the health care workforce in geriatric principles. Since virtually all health care workers care for older adults to some degree, the geriatric competence of all providers must also be improved more generally, through significant enhancements in educational curricula and training programs.

Meeting the demand that is expected in coming years will require expansion of the roles of many members of the health care workforce, including technicians, direct-care workers and informal caregivers, all of whom already play significant roles in the care of older adults. Patients, as well as their families and friends, also need to be considered essential parts of the health care team and learn how to be active and effective participants in the care plan. As the roles and responsibilities of individual members of the health care workforce change, the Medicare system will need to be flexible in paying for innovative models of care and perhaps emerging types of providers that have new designations and training requirements. Interdisciplinary models that support collaboration among multiple types of providers will be essential in improving care delivery for older adults.

This report calls for fundamental reform in the way that care is delivered to older adults and puts forth a plan to help ensure that the health care workforce is sufficient in both size and skill to handle the needs of a new generation of older Americans. These changes are urgently needed to prepare for a sizeable demographic shift that threatens to overwhelm present and future capacity.

John W. Rowe, M.D.
Chair
April 2008

Acknowledgments

Retooling for an Aging America: Building the Health Care Workforce benefited from the contributions of many individuals. The committee takes this opportunity to recognize those who so generously gave their time and expertise to inform its deliberations.

The committee benefited from presentations made by a number of experts. The following individuals shared their experiences and perspectives during public meetings of the committee: Marcia K. Brand, Health Resources and Services Administration (HRSA); Eric Coleman, University of Colorado Health Sciences Center; Steven Dawson, PHI; Steven DeMello, HealthTech; Federico Girosi, RAND; Stephen Goss, Social Security Administration; Jennie Chin Hansen, University of California, San Francisco; Charlene Harrington, University of California, San Francisco; Barbara Harvath, HealthTech; Jeanie Kayser-Jones, University of California, San Francisco; Bruce Leff, Johns Hopkins University Schools of Medicine and Public Health; Sharon A. Levine, Boston University School of Medicine; David B. Reuben, University of California, Los Angeles; Michèle J. Saunders, The University of Texas Health Science Center at San Antonio; Robyn I. Stone, Institute for the Future of Aging Services, American Association of Homes and Services for the Aging; Alice Wade, Social Security Administration; Gwen Yeo, Stanford University School of Medicine; and Dan Zabinski, MedPAC.

The committee commissioned several papers to provide background information for its deliberations and to synthesize the evidence on particular issues. We thank the following individuals for their contributions to these papers: Chad Boult, Johns Hopkins Bloomberg School of Public Health;

Lisa B. Boult, Johns Hopkins University School of Medicine; Ariel Green, Johns Hopkins University School of Medicine; The Health Technology Center (HealthTech); Wendy King, Stanford University School of Medicine; R. Tamara Konetzka, University of Chicago; Bruce Leff, Johns Hopkins University School of Medicine; Mark Mather, Population Reference Bureau; James T. Pacala, University of Minnesota Medical School; Claire Snyder, Johns Hopkins University School of Medicine; Jennifer L. Wolff, Johns Hopkins Bloomberg School of Public Health; and Gwen Yeo, Stanford University School of Medicine.

We extend special thanks to the following individuals who were essential sources of information, generously giving their time and knowledge to further the committee's efforts: Dana Goldman, RAND; Seth Landefeld, University of California, San Francisco; Linda Martin, Institute of Medicine; and Joan Weiss, HRSA. We also thank Robert Pool, copyeditor.

Finally, the committee gratefully acknowledges the assistance and support of individuals instrumental in developing this project: Jeane Ann Grisso, Robert Wood Johnson Foundation; Sarah Handley, The Atlantic Philanthropies; Marilyn Hennessy, The Retirement Research Foundation; Linda Hiddemen, American Geriatrics Society; Gavin Hougham, The John A. Hartford Foundation, Inc.; Marvin A. Kauffman, The Fan Fox and Leslie R. Samuels Foundation, Inc.; Mary Jane Koren, The Commonwealth Fund; Mary Ellen Kullman, Archstone Foundation; Christopher Langston, The John A. Hartford Foundation, Inc. (formerly of The Atlantic Philanthropies); June E. Osborn, formerly of the Josiah Macy, Jr. Foundation; Corinne H. Rieder, The John A. Hartford Foundation, Inc.; Laura Robbins, The Atlantic Philanthropies; John Rother, AARP; George E. Thibault, Josiah Macy, Jr. Foundation; Julio Urbina, The Fan Fox and Leslie R. Samuels Foundation, Inc.; Dianne Yamashiro-Omi, The California Endowment; and Nancy Zweibel, The Retirement Research Foundation.

Contents

Summary

In 2011 the first baby boomers will turn 65, ushering in a new generation of older Americans. The 65-and-older population of the future will be markedly different from previous generations, with higher levels of education, lower levels of poverty, more racial and ethnic diversity, and fewer children. Their most striking characteristic, however, will be their numbers. The aging of the baby boom population, combined with an increase in life expectancy and a decrease in the relative number of younger persons, will create a situation where older adults make up a much larger percentage of the U.S. population than has ever before been the case. Between 2005 and 2030 the number of adults aged 65 and older will almost double, from 37 million to over 70 million, accounting for an increase from 12 percent of the U.S. population to almost 20 percent. While this population surge has been foreseen for decades, little has been done to prepare the health care workforce for its arrival.

Older Americans use considerably more health care services than younger Americans and their health care needs are often complex. The health care system often fails to deliver high-quality services in the best manner to meet their needs. Indeed, the education and training of the entire health care workforce with respect to the range of needs of older adults remains woefully inadequate. Recruitment and retention of all types of health care workers is a significant problem, especially in long-term care settings. Unless action is taken immediately, the health care workforce will lack the capacity (in both size and ability) to meet the needs of older patients in the future.

To address major shortages, steps need to be taken immediately to increase overall workforce numbers and to use every worker efficiently (i.e., to each individual's maximum level of competence and with an increased flexibility of roles). Additionally, the entire health care workforce, including both formal and informal caregivers, need to have the requisite data, knowledge, and tools to provide high-quality care for older patients. To improve the ability of the health care workforce to care for older Americans, the committee proposes a three-pronged approach:

- Enhance the competence of all individuals in the delivery of geriatric care
- Increase the recruitment and retention of geriatric specialists and caregivers
- Redesign models of care and broaden provider and patient roles to achieve greater flexibility

STUDY CHARGE AND SCOPE

This year marks the 30th anniversary of the first report published by the Institute of Medicine (IOM) on the health care workforce for older patients, *Aging and Medical Education*. That report and others have called for an expansion of geriatric training, but so far the geriatric discipline has grown little in numbers or in stature. This current report builds upon the IOM's broader work in the area of quality. In 2001, the IOM's *Crossing the Quality Chasm* noted that a major challenge in transitioning to a 21st-century health system is preparing the workforce to acquire new skills and adopt new ways of relating to patients and to each other.

The IOM charged the Committee on the Future Health Care Workforce for Older Americans with determining the health care needs of Americans over 65 years of age and analyzing the forces that shape the health care workforce for these individuals (Box S-1).

This study considers a range of care settings and health care team members, including professionals, direct-care workers, informal caregivers, and patients. The committee focused on a target date of 2030—by which time all baby boomers will have reached age 65—because it allows enough time to achieve significant goals, yet it is not so far in the future that projections become highly uncertain or advances in health care treatment or technologies change the medical landscape too greatly. Although the target year of 2030 may not seem to imply a sense of urgency, the contrary is true, as the preparation of a competent health care workforce and widespread diffusion of effective models of care will require many years of effort.

TODAY'S OLDER AMERICANS

The health status of older Americans has improved over the past several decades. Today, older adults (defined here as those 65 and older) live longer

---

BOX S-1
Statement of Task

This study will seek to determine the health care needs of the target population—the rapidly growing and increasingly diverse population of Americans who are over 65 years of age—then address those needs through a thorough analysis of the forces that shape the health care workforce, including education, training, modes of practice, and financing of public and private programs.

Starting with the understanding that health care services provided to older Americans should be safe, effective, patient centered, timely, efficient, and equitable, the committee will consider the following questions:

1. What is the projected future health status and health care services utilization of older Americans?
2. What is the best use of the health care workforce, including, where possible, informal caregivers, to meet the needs of the older population? What models of health care delivery hold promise to provide high-quality and cost-effective care for older persons? What new roles and/or new types of providers would be required under these models?
3. How should the health care workforce be educated and trained to deliver high-value care to the elderly? How should this training be financed? What will best facilitate recruitment and retention of this workforce?
4. How can public programs be improved to accomplish the goals identified above?

---

and have less chronic disability than those in previous generations. Still, almost all Medicare spending is related to chronic conditions. Many older adults also experience one or more geriatric syndromes—clinical conditions that do not fit into discrete disease categories (e.g., falls and malnutrition). Older adults also tend to experience more mental health conditions (e.g., depression and anxiety). Many community-dwelling older adults need assistance with one or more activities of daily living (ADLs), such as bathing, and dressing, or with instrumental activities of daily living (IADLs), such as shopping for groceries and preparing meals. Severely disabled adults—that is, those who have difficulty with three or more ADLs—generally require more intensive care if they are to remain in the home.

Older adults receive health care in many different settings and are particularly high-volume users. Although older adults make up only about 12 percent of the U.S. population, they account for approximately 26 percent of all physician office visits, 47 percent of all hospital outpatient visits with nurse practitioners, 35 percent of all hospital stays, 34 percent of all prescriptions, 38 percent of all emergency medical service responses, and

90 percent of all nursing-home use. Just over 60 percent of disabled older adults living in the community obtain some long-term care services, most commonly in the form of help with personal care and household chores. The vast majority of these services are provided by informal caregivers, typically a spouse or child.

OLDER AMERICANS IN THE FUTURE

The future elderly population will be different from today's older adults in a number of ways. The demographic characteristics of older Americans will differ from previous generations in terms of their race, family structure, socioeconomic status, education, geographic distribution, and openness regarding their sexual orientation. All of these factors can affect health status and utilization of services. Trends in illness and disability will influence the need for services among the future older adult population, though the direction and the magnitude of the effects cannot be predicted with certainty. Declines in smoking rates, for example, could lead to a decreased need for health care services, but that decrease could be offset by increased utilization associated with high rates of obesity. Medical advances and technologies may extend or improve life for older patients. In the future, more health care may be provided remotely, and older adults may be better able to monitor their conditions and communicate with health care providers from home. Finally, older adults in the future may simply have different preferences for care than their predecessors.

Changes in Medicare or Medicaid policies could also have a significant effect on service utilization by older adults—and, given that a severe cost crisis in the Medicare program is widely expected, such changes are likely. While a full consideration of likely health expenditures is beyond the scope of the committee's charge, committee members were mindful of financial realities during the course of their deliberations. Whether or not the current patterns of health status and utilization continue, one prediction is certain: the future elderly population will have a greater collective need for health care services than those who have come before it.

BUILDING THE CAPACITY OF THE HEALTH CARE WORKFORCE

With few exceptions, all types of health care workers need to be educated and trained in the care of older adults. First, while efforts to educate and train the formal (i.e., paid) workforce in geriatrics have improved, they remain inadequate in both scope and consistency. Second, much of the care for older adults falls to informal caregivers, yet these unpaid workers receive very little preparation for their responsibilities. Finally, the management of chronic illness requires daily decision making, and patients often lack the knowledge or the skills to be effective members of their own health care team. To the extent that patients are better able to manage their conditions, they will be less likely to depend upon members of the already limited health care workforce.

Besides being inadequately prepared in geriatrics, the current workforce is not large enough to meet older patients' needs, and the scarcity of workers specializing in the care of older adults is even more pronounced. Among direct-care workers, nursing assistants provide 70 percent to 80 percent of the direct-care hours to those older adults who receive long-term care, but their shortage is well documented. Older adults account for about one-third of visits to physician assistants (PAs), but less than 1 percent of PAs specialize in geriatrics. Less than 1 percent of both pharmacists and registered nurses are certified in geriatrics. In 1987 the National Institute on Aging predicted a need for 60,000 to 70,000 geriatric social workers by 2020, yet today only about 4 percent of social workers—one-third of the needed number—specialize in geriatrics.

These shortages will only be worse in the future. By 2030 the United States will need an additional 3.5 million formal health care providers—a 35 percent increase from current levels—just to maintain the current ratio of providers to the total population. The Bureau of Labor Statistics predicts that personal- and home-care aides and home health aides will represent the second- and third-fastest growing occupations between 2006 and 2016, which will exacerbate current shortages. As of 2007, there were 7,128 physicians certified in geriatric medicine and 1,596 certified in geriatric psychiatry. According to one estimate, by 2030 these numbers will have increased by less than 10 percent; others predict a net loss of these physicians because of a decreased interest in geriatric fellowships and the decreasing number of physicians who choose to recertify in geriatrics. According to the Alliance for Aging Research, by 2030 the United States will need about 36,000 geriatricians. It may well not be possible to reach this goal, but the projection underscores the need for immediate and dramatic increases in the numbers of workers who care for older patients in order to close the gap between current supply and future demand. All segments of the health care workforce face significant barriers to recruitment and retention, but in the case of the older-adult health care workforce there are additional obstacles, including negative perceptions about working with older patients, concerns about physically and emotionally demanding working conditions, and misgivings about the financial disadvantages of such work. These issues merit persistent attention and the development of an evidentiary basis to monitor the progress made in increasing the capacity of this future workforce.

> Recommendation 1-1: Congress should require an annual report from the Bureau of Health Professions to monitor the progress made in addressing the crisis in supply of the health care workforce for older adults.[1]

While increasing the supply of workers is important, numbers alone will not solve the impending crisis. Current models of care delivery often fail to provide the best care possible to older adults, and they often do not promote the most efficient use of existing workers. While a number of innovative models have been developed to address these shortcomings, most have not been widely adopted. In short, to meet the health care needs of the next generation of older adults, the geriatric competence of the entire workforce needs to be enhanced, the number of geriatric specialists and caregivers needs to be increased, and innovative models need to be developed and implemented such that the workforce is used more efficiently and the quality of care is improved (Box S-2).

Enhancing the Competence of All Providers

The geriatric competence of virtually all members of the health care workforce needs to be improved through significant enhancements in educational curricula and training programs and then assessed through career-long demonstrations of this competence. There are a number of challenges to the geriatric education and training of health care workers, including a scarcity of faculty, variable curricula, and a lack of training opportunities. Furthermore, both education and training need expanded content in order to address the diversity of health care needs among older adults.

Professionals

For professionals, one notable way in which training is inadequate is the lack of exposure to settings of care outside of the hospital. Since 1987 hospitals have been allowed to count the time that residents spend in settings outside the hospital for graduate medical education funding purposes, but many residents still do not spend significant amounts of time in these alternative settings. Because most care of older patients occurs outside the hospital, the committee concluded that preparation for the comprehensive care of older patients needs to include training in non-hospital settings.

---

[1]The committee's recommendations are numbered according to the chapter of the main report in which they appear. Thus, Recommendation 1-1 is the first recommendation in Chapter 1.

BOX S-2
Recommendations

Recommendation 1-1: Congress should require an annual report from the Bureau of Health Professions to monitor the progress made in addressing the crisis in supply of the health care workforce for older adults.

Enhancing Geriatric Competence

Recommendation 4-1: Hospitals should encourage the training of residents in all settings where older adults receive care, including nursing homes, assisted-living facilities, and patients' homes.

Recommendation 4-2: All licensure, certification, and maintenance of certification for health care professionals should include demonstration of competence in the care of older adults as a criterion.

Recommendation 5-1: States and the federal government should increase minimum training standards for all direct-care workers. Federal requirements for the minimum training of certified nursing assistants (CNAs) and home health aides should be raised to at least 120 hours and should include demonstration of competence in the care of older adults as a criterion for certification. States should also establish minimum training requirements for personal-care aides.

Recommendation 6-2: Public, private, and community organizations should provide funding and ensure that adequate training opportunities are available in the community for informal caregivers.

Increasing Recruitment and Retention

Recommendation 4-3: Public and private payers should provide financial incentives to increase the number of geriatric specialists in all health professions.

Recommendation 4-3a: All payers should include a specific enhancement of reimbursement for clinical services delivered to older adults by practitioners with a certification of special expertise in geriatrics.

Recommendation 4-3b: Congress should authorize and fund an enhancement of the Geriatric Academic Career Award (GACA) program to support junior geriatrics faculty in other health professions in addition to allopathic and osteopathic medicine.

Recommendation 4-3c: States and the federal government should institute programs for loan forgiveness, scholarships, and direct financial incentives for professionals who become geriatric specialists. One such mechanism should include the development of a National Geriatric Service Corps, modeled after the National Health Service Corps.

Recommendation 5-2: State Medicaid programs should increase pay and fringe benefits for direct-care workers through such measures as wage pass-

continued

BOX S-2
Continued

throughs, setting wage floors, establishing minimum percentages of service rates directed to direct-care labor costs, and other means.

Redesigning Models of Care

Recommendation 3-1: Payers should promote and reward the dissemination of those models of care for older adults that have been shown to be effective and efficient.

Recommendation 3-2: Congress and foundations should significantly increase support for research and demonstration programs that

- promote the development of new models of care for older adults in areas where few models are currently being tested, such as prevention, long-term care, and palliative care; and
- promote the effective use of the workforce to care for older adults.

Recommendation 3-3: Health care disciplines, state regulators, and employers should look to expand the roles of individuals who care for older adults with complex clinical needs at different levels of the health care system beyond the traditional scope of practice. Critical elements of this include

- development of an evidence base that informs the establishment of new provider designations reflecting rising levels of responsibility and improved efficiency;
- measurement of additional competence to attain these designations; and
- greater professional recognition and salary commensurate with these responsibilities.

Recommendation 6-1: Federal agencies (including the Department of Labor and the Department of Health and Human Services) should provide support for the development and promulgation of technological advancements that could enhance an individual's capacity to provide care for older adults. This includes the use of activity-of-daily-living (ADL) technologies and health information technologies, including remote technologies, that increase the efficiency and safety of care and caregiving.

Recommendation 4-1: Hospitals should encourage the training of residents in all settings where older adults receive care, including nursing homes, assisted-living facilities, and patients' homes.

After receiving formal training, the mechanisms used most often to ensure the general competence of health care workers are state- or jurisdiction-based licensure and national board certification. Often, neither licensure nor certification examinations have explicit geriatric content, or the content is inadequate to ensure competency in the area of geriatrics. Since educational curricula are often devised to prepare students for these examinations, the explicit inclusion of geriatrics in standardized examinations may encourage programs to enhance geriatric content.

Recommendation 4-2: All licensure, certification, and maintenance of certification for health care professionals should include demonstration of competence in the care of older adults as a criterion.

Direct-Care Workers

Similar mechanisms are needed to enhance the competence of the direct-care workforce in caring for older adults. Direct-care workers are the primary providers of paid hands-on care and emotional support for older adults, yet the requirements for their training and testing are minimal. Furthermore, even though patient care has become much more complex, the federal minimum of 75 hours of training for nurse aides has not changed since it was mandated in 1987 (although many states have higher numbers of required hours). Home health aides have similarly low requirements, and very little is done to ensure the competence of personal-care aides. The committee concluded that current federal training minimums are inadequate to prepare direct-care workers and that the content of the training lacks sufficient geriatric-specific content.

Recommendation 5-1: States and the federal government should increase minimum training standards for all direct-care workers. Federal requirements for the minimum training of certified nursing assistants and home health aides should be raised to at least 120 hours and should include demonstration of competence in the care of older adults as a criterion for certification. States should also establish minimum training requirements for personal-care aides.

Informal Caregivers

Informal caregivers—most often family members and friends of the patient—play an enormous role in the care of older adults, and there is growing awareness of the benefits of providing them with better training and improving their integration with the formal health care team. Informal caregivers often feel insufficiently prepared to assist with home-based technologies, medically oriented treatments, or even basic tasks such as lifting and feeding.

Recommendation 6-2: Public, private, and community organizations should provide funding and ensure that adequate training opportunities are available in the community for informal caregivers.

Increasing Recruitment and Retention

Professionals

Among most health care professions, the opportunities for advanced training in geriatrics are scarce or nonexistent and among the professionals who do have the opportunity to pursue advanced geriatric training, very few take advantage of these programs. Aside from their clinical expertise, specialists in geriatrics are needed because of their role in educating and training the rest of the workforce in geriatric issues. Resistance to entering geriatric fields may arise from significant financial issues.

Recommendation 4-3: Public and private payers should provide financial incentives to increase the number of geriatric specialists in all health professions.

The costs associated with extra years of geriatric training do not translate into additional income, and geriatric specialists tend to earn significantly less income than other specialists or even generalists in their own disciplines. In part, this income disparity is due to the fact that a larger proportion of a geriatric specialist's income comes from Medicare and Medicaid, which have low rates of reimbursement for primary care activities in general. Moreover, reimbursements fail to fully account for the fact that the care of more frail older patients with complex needs is time consuming, leading to fewer patient encounters and fewer billings.

Recommendation 4-3a: All payers should include a specific enhancement of reimbursement for clinical services delivered to older adults by practitioners with a certification of special expertise in geriatrics.

Similar financial burdens affect the recruitment and retention of faculty in geriatrics. For example, in spite of their extra training, junior faculty in geriatric medicine have lower compensation than junior faculty in family medicine or internal medicine. The Geriatric Academic Career Awards (GACAs), awarded by the Bureau of Health Professions, have been instrumental in the development of academic geriatricians. Similar opportunities for geriatric faculty in other health professions are rare.

Recommendation 4-3b: Congress should authorize and fund an enhancement of the Geriatric Academic Career Award (GACA) program to support junior geriatrics faculty in other health professions in addition to allopathic and osteopathic medicine.

Many efforts to recruit and retain health professionals seek to relieve at least part of the financial burden associated with the personal cost of their education and training. The committee concluded that programs linking financial support to service have been effective in increasing the numbers of health care professionals who care for underserved populations and that they would serve as a good model for the development of similar programs to address the shortages of professionals in geriatrics.

Recommendation 4-3c: States and the federal government should institute programs for loan forgiveness, scholarships, and direct financial incentives for professionals who become geriatric specialists. One such mechanism should include the development of a National Geriatric Service Corps, modeled after the National Health Service Corps.

Direct-Care Workers

Recruitment and retention is especially dire among direct-care workers. They receive low wages and few benefits, they have high physical and emotional demands placed on them, and they are at significant risk for on-the-job injuries. These workers report high levels of job dissatisfaction resulting from poor supervision, a lower level of respect among colleagues, and few opportunities for advancement. Not surprisingly, then, there are high levels of turnover among these workers. Overall, the successful recruitment and retention of direct-care workers depends on a significant culture change to increase the quality of these jobs through improvements in the job environment and adequate financial compensation for their current and expanding roles.

Recommendation 5-2: State Medicaid programs should increase pay and fringe benefits for direct-care workers through such measures as wage pass-throughs, setting wage floors, establishing minimum percentages of service rates directed to direct-care labor costs, and other means.

Redesigning Models of Care

The U.S. health care system suffers from deficiencies in quality, and the health and long-term care services provided to older patients are no exception. Simply expanding the capacity of the current system to meet the rising needs of older adults would not address the serious shortcomings in the care of this population. The committee created a vision for the future that rests on three key principles:

- The health needs of the older population need to be addressed comprehensively.
- Services need to be provided efficiently.
- Older persons need to be active partners in their own care.

The committee's vision represents a vast departure from the current system, and implementation will require a shift in the way that services are organized, financed, and delivered. Several models have been shown to improve quality and patient outcomes, sometimes at a lower cost. Other newer models have not been adequately tested, but appear promising. After reviewing the available evidence on a variety of models of care for older adults, the committee determined that there is no single approach or best model that could be broadly adopted for all older patients. Older adults have diverse health care needs and a variety of models are necessary to meet those needs.

Identifying successful models of care is only the first challenge to improving the delivery of care to older adults. The models need to be replicated widely to reach the larger patient population. However, the dissemination of successful models has been slow and some of the interventions have been unsustainable due to a number of challenges, including an inadequate mechanism for reimbursement. Many of the models require the delivery of services that are not typically reimbursed under Medicare.

The committee concluded that a new method of reimbursement is needed to support the implementation of effective and efficient models of care.

Recommendation 3-1: Payers should promote and reward the dissemination of those models of care for older adults that have been shown to be effective and efficient.

The committee supports reimbursement for services that are not currently covered (e.g., interdisciplinary teams); provision of capital for infrastructure (e.g., health information technology); and the streamlining of administrative and regulatory requirements. Payers need to also eliminate existing impediments to the use of innovative models by older patients, such as Medicare's copayment disparity for mental health services.

The broad efforts to develop new models of care indicate not only a recognition that services for older adults need to be improved, but also a willingness among providers, private foundations, and federal and state policy makers to commit resources to learning about better ways to finance and deliver care. The committee supports the continued development of newer models, especially in areas that have traditionally been overlooked or for more effective use of the workforce.

> Recommendation 3-2: Congress and foundations should significantly increase support for research and demonstration programs that
>
> - promote the development of new models of care for older adults in areas where few models are currently being tested, such as prevention, long-term care, and palliative care; and
> - promote the effective use of the workforce to care for older adults.

Delivering care within all of these new models will require adaptations by the workforce. For example, many successful models require providers of different disciplines to work collaboratively in interdisciplinary teams, but reimbursement for team care is currently lacking, and many providers are not trained to work effectively in teams. Also, several successful models of care require members of the health care team, including patients and their families, to take on new roles and assume greater levels of responsibility. Shifting various patient-care responsibilities (e.g., through job delegation) will be essential to create meaningful improvements in the efficiency of the health care workforce, but will require the training of many workers both in the skills needed to deliver more technical services, as well as the skills needed to be effective delegators and supervisors.

> Recommendation 3-3: Health care disciplines, state regulators, and employers should look to expand the roles of individuals who care for older adults with complex clinical needs at different levels of the health care system beyond the traditional scope of practice. Critical elements of this include
>
> - development of an evidence base that informs the establishment of new provider designations reflecting rising levels of responsibility and improved efficiency;
> - measurement of additional competence to attain these designations; and
> - greater professional recognition and salary commensurate with these responsibilities.

Finally, many new models incorporate the use of various technologies. Health information technologies, such as electronic health records, facilitate the sharing of information among providers and improve their ability to coordinate the complex care of older patients. Remote-monitoring technologies can efficiently extend the reach of health care professionals into the home. ADL technologies can extend the independent functioning of older adults and reduce the demands placed on direct-care workers and informal caregivers.

> **Recommendation 6-1:** Federal agencies (including the Department of Labor and the Department of Health and Human Services) should provide support for the development and promulgation of technological advancements that could enhance an individual's capacity to provide care for older adults. This includes the use of ADL technologies and health information technologies, including remote technologies, that increase the efficiency and safety of care and caregiving.

CONCLUSION

The United States today faces enormous challenges as the baby boom generation nears retirement age. The impending crisis, which has been foreseen for decades, is now upon us. The nation needs to act now to prepare the health care workforce to meet the care needs of older adults. If current reimbursement policies and workforce trends continue, the nation will continue to fail to ensure that every older American is able to receive high-quality care. The dramatically rising number of older Americans, along with changes in their demographic characteristics, health needs, and settings of care will necessitate transformations related to the education, training, recruitment, and retention of the health care workforce serving older adults. This in turn will require the commitment of greater financial resources, even at a time when program budgets will already be severely stretched.

The committee asserts, however, that throwing more money into a system that is not designed to deliver high-quality, cost-effective care would be largely a wasted effort. Instead, this report serves as an appeal for fundamental reform in the way that care is delivered to older adults. In doing so, it provides a vision for how the workforce can best be developed and organized to improve its capacity to deliver the care that a new generation of older adults will soon be needing.

1

Introduction

CHAPTER SUMMARY

By 2030 the number of adults in the United States who are 65 years old or older is expected to be almost double what it was in 2005, and the nation is not prepared to meet their social and health care needs. If current patterns of utilization continue, there will be a tremendous shortage of health care workers, and many of these providers will lack the appropriate geriatric training to provide high-quality care to these older adults. At the same time, Medicare and Medicaid budgets are facing tremendous cost pressures, with the Medicare hospital trust fund projected to be depleted by 2019. This impending crisis needs to be addressed immediately.

The Institute of Medicine (IOM) charged the Committee on the Future Health Care Workforce for Older Americans to identify models of care that hold promise to provide high-quality, cost-effective care to older adults, and to analyze the factors that shape the health care workforce, including education and training as well as recruitment and retention. While this report builds on other IOM studies on health care quality and the workforce, it is unique in that it defines the health care workforce broadly, including consideration of both the professional and direct-care workforces, as well as the roles of informal caregivers and patients.

The next generation of older adults will be like no other before it. It will be the most educated and diverse group of older adults in the nation's history (U.S. Census Bureau, 2008). They will set themselves apart from their predecessors by having fewer children, higher divorce rates, and a lower likelihood of living in poverty (He et al., 2005; U.S. Census Bureau,

2008). But the key distinguishing feature of the next generation of older Americans will be their vast numbers.

According to the most recent census numbers, there are now 78 million Americans who were born between 1946 and 1964 (U.S. Census Bureau, 2006). By 2030 the youngest members of the baby boom generation will be at least 65, and the number of older adults (defined in this report as ages 65 and older) in the United States is expected to be more than 70 million—or almost double the nearly 37 million older adults alive in 2005. The number of the "oldest old," those who are 80 and over, is also expected to nearly double, from 11 million to 20 million. In percentage terms, the portion of the U.S. population that is 65 or older is expected to rise from 12 percent to almost 20 percent.

The major reason for the growing number of older adults in the United States will be the aging of the baby boom generation, but increased longevity will also contribute. During the lifetime of the baby boomers, there has been a variety of improvements in personal health behaviors (e.g., smoking cessation) and advances in medical technologies (e.g., diagnostic imaging technologies and prescription drugs) (Cutler et al., 2007), and these changes have helped to increase life expectancy. For example, the widespread use of cholesterol- and hypertension-lowering medications contributed to a decline in the rate of deaths from cardiovascular disease (NCHS, 2006).

Although advances in longevity are to be applauded, increased life expectancy coupled with new treatments that convert once-fatal disease to lifelong conditions is giving rise to what some observers call "an epidemic of chronic disease" (Anderson and Horvath, 2004). The vast majority of older adults (80 percent) suffer from at least one chronic condition (e.g., dementia, diabetes, hypertension, heart disease) (Anderson, 2003), and chronic diseases are the leading causes of death for older adults in the United States (Kramarow et al., 2007). Chronic disease also brings an increased risk of major depression, which is associated with substantial disability (Moussavi et al., 2007) along with non-adherence to treatment of co-existing medical illness and increased utilization of health care resources (Ciechanowski et al., 2000). Unlike most infectious diseases or acute illnesses, chronic conditions may last for years, place limits on the activities of older adults, and require ongoing care (Anderson and Horvath, 2002). As a result, individuals with chronic conditions tend to use far more health services than others, and care of chronic conditions has fueled much of the increase in Medicare spending over the past two decades (MedPAC, 2007).

The nation needs to prepare to meet the social and health care needs of an older adult population of an unprecedented size. Additionally, as Americans live longer, the composition of the population that is 65 or older will also become more complex with varying characteristics and demands due to the inclusion of multiple generations of older adults (i.e., the 65-year-old adult will be much different from the 85-year-old adult). A necessary step is the development of a health care workforce (including health care professionals, direct-care workers and informal caregivers) sufficient in size and skill to serve this growing number of older adults.

Health services provided to older adults today are not as effective as they could or should be. The quality of care provided to older adults often falls short of acceptable levels for a variety of conditions (Wenger et al., 2003), and the proportion of recommended care that patients actually receive declines with age (Asch et al., 2006). One of the greatest challenges will be reorganizing the health care system and its workforce so that older adults have access to quality services at a cost that the country can afford. Care coordination and other health-management practices that may facilitate this have not been widely adopted. These practices involve restructuring how the health care workforce operates, but they provide an opportunity to reform service delivery so that the next generation of older adults will receive more effective health care services than their parents.

CHALLENGES TO IMPROVING CARE FOR OLDER ADULTS

In addition to having a higher prevalence of chronic disease, older adults have greater vulnerability to injury (e.g., falls) and to acute illness (e.g., pneumonia) and have more limitations on their activities of daily living (ADLs).[1] As a result, older adults use health services at far higher rates than the rest of the population. These high rates of health service utilization coupled with the large rise in the number of older adults can be expected to result in a dramatic increase in the demand for health and long-term care services in the coming decades. This escalation in demand for health care services will in turn create a number of challenges that will need to be addressed, including inadequate numbers of health care workers, the limited training of those workers in geriatric skills, the misalignment of the payment system, and scarce financial resources.

Shortages in the Supply of Health Care Workers

The rising demand for services places increasing pressure on the health care workforce to expand its capacity. The Bureau of Labor Statistics (BLS) reports that the aging of the population will make the health care industry a major source of overall projected employment growth in the United States between 2006 and 2016 (BLS, 2007b). Employment in the home health and the residential-care industries is rising particularly quickly (Table 1-1).

---

[1]Activities of daily living (ADLs) relate to personal care needs, including eating, bathing, using the toilet, dressing, and transferring from bed to chair.

TABLE 1-1 Health and Home-Care Jobs Among the Top 30 Fastest-Growing Occupations in the United States, 2006 to 2016

Occupation	Employment by Year (in Thousands)		Percent Increase (%)
	2006	2016	
Personal- and home-care aides	767	1,156	50.6
Home health aides	787	1,171	48.7
Medical assistants	417	565	35.4
Physical therapist assistants	60	80	32.4
Pharmacy technicians	285	376	32.0
Dental hygienists	167	217	30.1
Mental health counselors	100	130	30.0
Mental health and substance abuse social workers	122	159	29.9
Dental assistants	280	362	29.2
Physical therapists	173	220	27.1
Physician assistants	66	83	27.0

SOURCE: BLS, 2007a.

However, the population that has traditionally worked in those industries is expected to increase only slightly, and this increase will likely not be enough to satisfy the growing need for these types of workers, especially considering persistent challenges in recruitment and retention (DHHS and DOL, 2003).

Just over two-thirds of older adults will need some form of long-term care at some point in their lives (AAHSA, 2007; Kemper et al., 2005), and the dominant providers of long-term care services are families and friends, referred to as informal caregivers (also known as unpaid or family caregivers) (Johnson and Wiener, 2006). Estimates of the number of informal caregivers for older adults vary, but they most likely number in the tens of millions. The economic value derived by the collective involvement of informal caregivers has been estimated at hundreds of billions of dollars annually (Arno et al., 1999; ASPE, 2005; Gibson and Houser, 2007; Langa et al., 2001, 2002; LaPlante et al., 2002).

Unfortunately, the next generation of older adults may be less able to rely on informal caregivers because they have fewer children and higher divorce rates than their parents (Center for Health Workforce Studies, 2005; Johnson et al., 2007). And while the geographic dispersion of families has been generally constant over the past several decades (Wolf and Longino, 2005), it continues to limit the availability of informal care (Donelan et al., 2002). The lack of available informal caregivers may exacerbate the growing need for paid long-term care providers.

Health care professionals will have difficulty meeting the increased need for services for older adults. Shortages of nurses (Gerson et al., 2005; HRSA, 2004), certain types of physicians (AMA, 2005), pharmacists (HRSA, 2000), dentists (Ryan, 2003), and many others are already apparent, particularly in non-urban areas (Box 1-1). Enrollment in medical schools (AAMC, 2007b), nursing schools (AACN, 2006), pharmacy schools (AACP, 2006), and certain other institutions training health care professionals is on the rise, but in some fields, such as dentistry, student enrollment is stagnant (Luke, 2007). Overall, the workforce is not growing at a rate commensurate with the projected rise in need.

The shortage of geriatric specialists is even worse. This is important not only because of the need for specialist care, but also for the need for these specialists to train the entire workforce in geriatric principles. For the year 2000, the Alliance for Aging Research estimated that the United States needed about 20,000 geriatricians to provide adequate health care to older adults (Alliance for Aging Research, 2002). At the time, however, there were only 9,000 practicing geriatricians. The number of geriatric specialists is no better today. In fact, the number of geriatricians and geriatric psychiatrists has declined over the past decade, as many do not seek recertification (ADGAP, 2007b). In 1987, the National Institute on Aging predicted a need for 60,000 to 70,000 geriatric social workers, but today we still only have about one-third of that number (NIA, 1987). In fact, very few geriatric specialists exist among all types of health care professions. The estimated needs for the year 2030 are even more dire. As depicted in Figure 1-1, while it is projected that the United States will require 36,000 geriatricians, it will fall far short of that number.

BOX 1-1
Reports of Current or Projected
Health Care Workforce Shortages

- Twenty-nine of 38 states surveyed indicate that a shortage of direct-care workers is currently a "serious" or "very serious" issue (Harmuth and Dyson, 2005).
- There is currently a shortage of approximately 12,000 geriatricians; by 2030 the shortage will be about 28,000 (ADGAP, 2007a; Alliance for Aging Research, 2002).
- By 2025 there is projected to be a shortage of 100,000 physicians (AAMC, 2007a).
- The shortage of registered nurses overall is projected to be as high as 808,000 by 2020 (Auerbach et al., 2007; HRSA, 2002).

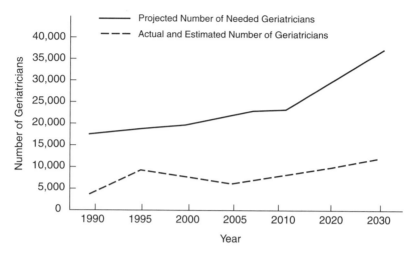

FIGURE 1-1 Projected number of needed geriatricians.
SOURCE: Alliance for Aging Research, 2002. Copyright 2002 by the Alliance for Aging Research.

One of the challenges to retention in many health professions is the aging of the workforce itself. As of January 2007, 23.3 percent of all active physicians were 60 or older (AAMC, 2007a), and by 2020 almost half of all registered nurses are expected to be over age 50 (AHA, 2007; Buerhaus et al., 2000). Large numbers of health care workers are also expected to retire just as the need for services increases. For example, more dentists are retiring now than are entering practice (Center for Health Workforce Studies, 2005). Based on current trajectories, many health professions will struggle just to replace the current workforce and will not be able to meet increases in demand.

Overall, the committee recognized the difficulty and inaccuracy associated with attempting to predict specific numbers of future health care workforce supplies. Instead, the committee chose to present some previously reported predictions of shortages in an attempt to highlight the relative scale of the needed increases in workers rather than determine a specific number needed for every profession. Box 1-1 highlights just a few of the current and future shortages.

Discussions of health care workforce shortages often focus solely on professionals,[2] but direct-care workers (i.e., nursing assistants, home health aides, and personal- and home-care aides) warrant at least equal consider-

---

[2]For the purposes of this report, the term "professional" is meant to imply a professional in a health care field.

ation. These workers, also known as paraprofessionals, provide hands-on care, supervision, and support to millions of older adults, particularly for long-term care. However, long-term care organizations struggle to recruit and, in particular, to retain workers to fill current positions (Harmuth, 2002). The annual turnover rate for certified nursing assistants is 71 percent (AAHSA, 2007), and 91 percent of nursing homes report that they do not have adequate staff to provide basic care (Lawlor, 2007). Home-care workers often stay with an agency for only a few months (PHI, 2003b). Although many direct-care workers find their work to be rewarding, the positions tend to be poorly paid with limited or no fringe benefits and to involve heavy workloads, unsafe working conditions, inadequate training, a lack of respect from supervisors, and few opportunities for advancement (PHI, 2003a; Stone and Wiener, 2001). Because of the low pay and frequently poor working conditions, long-term care employers compete for entry-level workers with other service industries, which may offer higher pay and better work environments (Wright, 2005).

Limited Provider Training in Geriatrics

Unfortunately, the size of the health care workforce is only a part of the problem. Another challenge is that the general health care workforce receives relatively little geriatric training and may not be prepared to deliver the best care to older patients. Not only do older patients have greater health care needs, but their conditions are often complex with multiple comorbidities. The average 75-year-old has three chronic conditions and uses more than four prescription medications; furthermore, 42 percent of those 85 and older have Alzheimer's disease (Alzheimer's Association, 2007). Some evidence indicates that patient outcomes improve when providers receive specialized training in the skills needed to care for older patients (Kovner et al., 2002). For example, studies show that patients treated by nurses prepared in geriatrics are less likely to be physically restrained, have fewer readmissions to the hospital, and are less likely to be transferred inappropriately from nursing facilities to the hospital (Evans et al., 1997; Naylor et al., 1999).

A very small percentage of professional health care providers specialize in geriatrics. Only 4 percent of social workers and less than 1 percent of physician assistants identify themselves as specializing in geriatrics (AAPA, 2007; Center for Health Workforce Studies, 2006). Less than 1 percent of both pharmacists (LaMascus et al., 2005) and practicing professional nurses (Alliance for Aging Research, 2002) are certified in geriatrics. For professionals who do not specialize, exposure to geriatric issues during training has generally improved in recent years, motivated in part by financial support from both public and private organizations. Still, many professionals tend to receive very little specific training in caring for older people, and the adequacy of the education and training varies widely. Thus, many providers delivering care to older adults have relatively little exposure to the complexities of aging patients.

Training is particularly important for direct-care workers, who interact closely with adults who tend to be very old and disabled, many of them with cognitive limitations. However, the training of direct-care workers is very limited. Federal requirements for training do exist for some types of direct-care workers, but they tend to be minimal. For example, home health aides and certified nurse assistants employed by nursing homes or home health agencies must have 75 hours of training (PHI, 2003b); by way of comparison, state laws often require more training for cosmetologists, dog groomers, and crossing guards (Direct Care Alliance, 2005). No federal requirements exist for workers employed directly by consumers or by agencies that provide non-skilled home services, although many states do set minimum training levels. The limited training that does occur tends to focus on discrete clinical tasks instead of core competencies for interpersonal communication or clinically informed problem-solving and decision-making skills that can guide caregivers in their interactions with clients. Finally, while some resources are available to support and educate informal caregivers, they generally receive no formal training (Wolff and Kasper, 2006), and older patients are often not educated on self-management principles.

Misaligned Payment Systems

Current Medicare and Medicaid policies do not encourage the delivery of the best care for older patients or the development of an adequate workforce. The Medicare program was originally designed to address acute illnesses, as these posed the major threats to health for older adults in the 1960s when the program was created. Under fee-for-service, a physician is paid based on the services performed during an in-person visit. However, current Medicare enrollees are more likely to need assistance with chronic illness and geriatric syndromes, which require ongoing monitoring and self-management. Medicare does not provide reimbursement for the time-consuming and ongoing education that patients need to better manage chronic conditions (Brown et al., 2007). Payment under fee-for-service is made regardless of the quality of those services and often pays more for newer and more complicated procedures, which may lead to overuse and misuse of services and procedures (IOM, 2007e).

Additionally, chronically ill patients typically receive services from multiple clinicians and across many sites, but Medicare does not provide reimbursement for providers to communicate and collaborate with one another (Guterman, 2007; IOM, 2003; MedPAC, 2006). It also does not pay for services provided by non-physicians, except under limited circumstances (Lawlor, 2007). Legislation to provide reimbursement to physicians, social workers, or others for medical care management has been proposed but not passed (Cigolle et al., 2005).

Although older adults are more likely to see a primary care physician than any other type of physician, Medicare payment levels serve as a deterrent to the practice of primary care. The Medicare reimbursement system allocates more generous payments for procedures and specialist services—a policy that some have suggested discourages physicians from entering primary care practice (ADGAP, 2007a; Guterman, 2007; LaMascus et al., 2005). Medicare does not have a risk adjuster to account for the additional time and complexity involved with treating frail, older patients. Patients with complex health care needs are more likely to be found in geriatricians' practices. Geriatricians and geriatric psychiatrists rely heavily on Medicare reimbursement for their income, and surveys indicate that they have lower incomes on average than almost every other type of physician (ADGAP, 2004), which may further discourage physicians from specializing in geriatrics.

Medicare's teaching and supervision guidelines for resident physicians also make it difficult to collect reimbursement for services provided in the home and in nursing-home settings, which may limit training opportunities outside of the hospital setting (Warshaw et al., 2002). For example, a faculty preceptor must accompany a resident to the setting in order for the clinician to receive reimbursement for the visit; few residency programs can accommodate this one-on-one teaching (Mold, 2003). The vast majority of Medicare graduate medical education (GME) support is directed to physician training, though some funding is available to hospitals for the training of nurses and other health care professionals (MedPAC, 2001).

Other problems exist with Medicaid. While states are working to expand home- and community-based long-term care services, a bias remains toward institutional settings, especially nursing homes (Wiener, 2007). As a result, beneficiaries often can receive only nursing home care, even when they would prefer community-based services. Additionally, nursing home providers contend that low Medicaid payments challenge their ability to provide high-quality care. The integration of services between Medicare and Medicaid for more than 7 million dually eligible individuals is especially difficult (Holahan and Ghosh, 2005; Tritz, 2005; Wiener, 1996). The lack of coordination between the programs often results in inefficiencies and fragmented services for the most vulnerable members of the older population. For example, while Medicare has a financial incentive to shift dually eligible patients into a Medicaid-funded long-term-care facility, Medicaid has an incentive to shift beneficiaries toward Medicare-funded hospital stays (Tritz, 2006).

Inadequate Financial Resources

Even if the workforce is adequate in size and training to meet the need for care of older adults in the future, simply continuing to operate under current patterns of care will put an extreme financial strain on health care budgets. Not only will enrollment in Medicare greatly expand in the future, but the cost per beneficiary will also rise if Medicare policy and patterns of care remain the same. The main factors contributing to rising health care costs overall include increases in the use of technology and greater service intensity (CBO, 2007b,c).

The Medicare program, the primary payer for services to older adults, spent about $10,200 per beneficiary in 2006, and that figure is projected to rise to $16,800 by 2016 (in 2006 dollars) (Federal HI and SMI Trust Funds Board of Trustees, 2007). Perhaps the most important signal is that the Hospital Insurance Trust Fund, which funds Medicare Part A, is projected to be exhausted by 2019 (see Table 1-2 for intermediate projections). This will result in a rapidly growing need for additional funding from taxes or a substantial increase in patient deductibles.

The Medicaid program finances much of long-term care for older adults and will face similar pressures, assuming no changes in policy or patterns of care. Projections show that Medicaid spending will grow 8 percent per year between 2007 and 2017 (CBO, 2007a). As a percentage of gross domestic product (GDP), Medicaid spending is projected to increase from 2.6 percent in 2006 to 4.1 percent in 2025 (Kronick and Rousseau, 2007). Medicaid spending accounts for approximately 16.5 percent of state budgets today, and is projected to rise to 19 percent by 2045. As state Medicaid spending rises, it competes with investments in other areas, such as education and transportation.

Future Medicare and Medicaid policy cannot be predicted, but financial

TABLE 1-2 Intermediate Projections for the Medicare Program, 2007, 2016, and 2030

	2007	2016	2030
Medicare enrollment	44 million	55 million	79 million
Medicare expenditures	$438 billion	$863 billion	NA
HI trust fund assets	$305 billion	$221 billion	$0
Medicare spending as a percentage of gross domestic product	3.2%	3.9% (2015)	6.5%
Number of workers per Medicare beneficiary	3.9 (2006)	3.2 (2015)	2.4

NOTE: NA = Not Available; HI = Hospital Insurance.
SOURCE: Federal HI and SMI Trust Funds Board of Trustees, 2007; Moon and Storeygard, 2002.

pressures to control costs will surely increase while spending continues to rise faster than economic growth. The Congressional Budget Office reports that if health care costs continue growing at the current rate, federal spending on Medicare and Medicaid will rise to 20 percent of the GDP by 2050, roughly the same share of GDP that the entire U.S. federal budget accounts for today (CBO, 2007b; Orszag and Ellis, 2007). It is unlikely that there will be adequate funds to support all desirable models of care for the future older population, and changes in benefits and taxes are likely to occur. Retirees are experiencing reductions in Medicare supplemental benefits provided by their prior employers, a trend that will likely continue (AHRQ, 2004; Zabinski, 2007). Moreover, many older adults in the future may not have the coverage or resources needed to pay out of pocket for some clinically indicated services.

In coming years the health care system as a whole will be faced with a number of pressing concerns, including children's health, obesity, emerging infections, HIV/AIDS, and other challenges that will compete for scarce public resources. While the committee recognizes the tensions that are likely to arise as policymakers are forced to prioritize among multiple need areas, it maintains that workforce shortages in the care of older adults (in terms of both size and competence) is a looming crisis that demands significant attention.

STUDY CHARGE AND APPROACH

The Institute of Medicine (IOM) formed the Committee on the Future Health Care Workforce for Older Americans in January 2007 to determine the best use of the health care workforce to meet the needs of the growing number of adults 65 and older (Box 1-2). To address this charge, the committee sought to describe promising models of health care delivery and the workforce that will be necessary in the future to serve the medically indicated, culturally conditioned, and satisfiable health care needs of the population of older adults, recognizing that any or all of these needs may be modified.

The committee met four times during the course of the 15-month study. It commissioned six technical papers (see Appendix B) and heard testimony from a wide range of experts (see Appendix C) during two public workshops. Staff and committee members also met with and received information from a variety of stakeholders and interested individuals. Support for the study was provided by 10 organizations: AARP, the Archstone Foundation, the Atlantic Philanthropies, the California Endowment, the Commonwealth Fund, the Fan Fox and Leslie R. Samuels Foundation, the John A. Hartford Foundation, the Josiah Macy, Jr. Foundation, the Retirement Research Foundation, and the Robert Wood Johnson Foundation.

BOX 1-2
The Committee on the Future Health Care
Workforce for Older Americans

Statement of Task

This study will seek to determine the health care needs of the target population—the rapidly growing and increasingly diverse population of Americans who are over 65 years of age—then address those needs through a thorough analysis of the forces that shape the health care workforce, including education, training, modes of practice, and financing of public and private programs.

Starting with the understanding that health care services provided to older Americans should be safe, effective, patient centered, timely, efficient, and equitable, the committee will consider the following questions:

1. What is the projected future health status and health care services utilization of older Americans?
2. What is the best use of the health care workforce, including, where possible, informal caregivers, to meet the needs of the older population? What models of health care delivery hold promise to provide high-quality and cost-effective care for older persons? What new roles and/or new types of providers would be required under these models?
3. How should the health care workforce be educated and trained to deliver high-value care to the elderly? How should this training be financed? What will best facilitate recruitment and retention of this workforce?
4. How can public programs be improved to accomplish the goals identified above?

Scope

In addressing the statement of task, the committee focused on the period of time from the present through 2030, by which point all baby boomers will have reached age 65. The year 2030 was also selected because it allows enough time to achieve significant goals, such as the establishment of a workforce with enhanced geriatric training, but it is not so far in the future that population projections are uncertain or that advancements in health care treatment or technologies are expected to change substantially. Although the choice of 2030 may not initially convey a sense of urgency, the contrary is true. The first baby boomers turn 65 in 2011, and it will require many years of effort to develop and train a health care workforce prepared to meet the needs of future older adults and to develop effective models of care and diffuse them widely. In order to achieve the committee's goals by the year 2030, immediate action needs to be taken.

The study focuses on primary health care (including both acute and chronic care) and long-term care services for older adults, defined here as those individuals ages 65 and older. Primary care is the provision of integrated, accessible health care services by clinicians who are accountable for addressing a large majority of personal health care needs, developing a sustained partnership with patients, and practicing in the context of family and community (IOM, 1996). Long-term care is broadly defined as an array of health care, personal care, and social services generally provided over a sustained period of time to persons with chronic conditions and with functional limitations (IOM, 2001b). While the committee primarily focused on the health care aspects of long-term care, it acknowledges that these services are often intertwined with personal care and, in particular, that many health care services are provided by the same workers who provide personal-care services.

The study considers a broad range of care delivery settings, including ambulatory clinics, hospitals, and the home and other long-term care settings. Older Americans from across the entire spectrum of health care status are included in the study, but the committee focused in particular on the care of individuals with chronic conditions, who account for the bulk of health care services and spending.

The committee defined the health care workforce broadly to encompass all personnel involved in the delivery of health care services, including health care professionals (physicians, nurses, physician assistants, social workers, oral-health care workers, pharmacists, allied health care workers, and so on), and direct-care workers (e.g., nurse aides, home health aides, and personal- and home-care aides). The committee recognized the significance of informal caregivers, not only because of the amount and breadth of services they provide to older adults but also because the availability of informal caregivers greatly affects the need for formal, or paid, services. The committee also acknowledged the importance of consumers playing an active role in their own care.

The committee also limited its consideration of models of care and workforce challenges to the United States. While the committee recognized that many unique efforts exist around the world, it concluded that the systems of care are too different and heterogeneous to warrant extensive examination of these systems in this report. Instead, the committee suggests that lessons learned from these international models in general may help to inform future research and development programs in the United States.

As seen in Box 1-2, the committee was charged with determining the health care needs of older adults. The committee recognizes that the term "need" can seem to be somewhat ambiguous and open-ended. An individual asked to list his or her needs without regard to price might, for instance, evince an almost unending desire for various services. It is for this reason that economists generally use the term "demand," which refers to the services an individual would be willing to pay for at a particular price. In economic terms, "need" and "demand" are quite different things.

In the context of health care services for older adults, however, "need" is understood to be "clinical need," which is what a medical or social services professional believes is appropriate care for an individual, given his or her medical condition. And since the public and private third-party payment system uses "clinical need" to determine which services will be paid for, in practice the distinction between demand and clinical need is much smaller. In this report most of the estimates concerning the "demand" for aging services and for a workforce to provide such services are in reality estimates based on clinical need.

Similar considerations apply to the term "supply." The committee recognizes, for example, that the supply of health care workers available to take care of older adults will depend on the expected wages or compensation paid to workers providing aging services. Thus baseline estimates of the workforce that will be available to provide aging services in the future are based on straightforward projections of the current compensation package for such workers. Several of the committee's recommendations to increase the "supply" of personnel focus on increasing the compensation package in order to attract more workers into the aging-services field. Therefore when the committee speaks of supply and demand or supply and clinical need, it does so with the recognition that all of these terms require an appreciation for the prices paid for the services and the wages paid to workers. The level of economic analysis needed to fully address these projections is beyond the scope of this report.

While the committee concluded that a full consideration of likely health expenditures was beyond the scope of its charge, committee members were mindful of financial realities during the course of their deliberations. The committee also focused their attention on those aspects of the health care system that are unique or especially important to the care of older adults. For example, while the committee explicitly recognized the importance and influence of health information technology, care coordination, and financing, it curtailed its discussion of these types of challenges that may apply to the health care workforce and system of care delivery as a whole. The committee concluded that fuller discussion of these general issues was beyond the scope of its charge.

Previous Work

This year marks the 30th anniversary of the IOM's first report on the geriatric workforce, *Aging and Medical Education* (IOM, 1978), which raised national awareness of the challenges posed by the aging of the U.S. population. That report, as well as several that followed, called for expansion of geriatric training opportunities and offered a number of recommendations for action. Over the past 30 years, opportunities for geriatric training for professionals have expanded. For example, the John A. Hartford Foundation established centers of excellence in geriatric medicine and geriatric psychiatry based on recommendations from a 1987 IOM report, *Academic Geriatrics for the Year 2000* (Rowe et al., 1987), and that foundation also devotes significant financial and career support for geriatric nursing and social work (Warshaw and Bragg, 2003). Still, the geriatric discipline has failed to thrive in numbers and stature, and the level of geriatric training among most providers remains too limited. Many recommendations from previous IOM committees and other committees have had limited impact.

What makes this current effort different is the broad nature of the study. It expands the scope of analysis well beyond physicians to consider all formal and informal health care providers for older adults. It focuses not only on the size and skills of the workforce but also on the models of care—that is, on the ways in which health care services are provided to older adults. We have known for decades that as the baby boom generation aged it would challenge the capacity of the health care system (IOM, 1978; NIA, 1987); that time is now upon us.

This current effort also builds upon the IOM's broader work in the area of quality. The landmark report, *Crossing the Quality Chasm* (IOM, 2001a), described quality care as being safe, timely, efficient, effective, equitable, and patient centered. However, there are strong indications that the current system of care fails the older adult population in significant ways along all of these dimensions of care. The report specifically noted that a major challenge in transitioning to a twenty-first-century health system will be preparing the workforce to acquire new skills and adopt new ways of relating to patients and each other.

Since that report, the IOM has addressed workforce issues in a number of areas—in emergency care (IOM, 2007b,c,d), public health (IOM, 2007f), pharmacy (IOM, 2007a), mental health and substance abuse (IOM, 2006), cancer care (IOM, 2005a), rural health (IOM, 2005b) and many others. This report addresses workforce needs for older adults comprehensively, across the spectrum of health services.

OVERALL CONCLUSIONS

After reviewing the evidence, the committee concluded the following:

1. *The future health care workforce will be woefully inadequate in its capacity to meet the large demand for health services for older*

adults if current patterns of care and of the training of providers continue.

2. *In all of the health professions where efforts to promote geriatric specialization have been undertaken, these efforts have been mostly insufficient to produce a larger number of geriatric leaders.*

3. *Informal caregivers provide a large amount of long-term care services to families and friends, and will continue to be a significant part of the health care workforce.*

4. *The structure of public programs precludes both the effective delivery of care to many older adults and the development of an appropriate workforce.*

5. *Immediate and substantial action is necessary by both public and private organizations to close the gap between the status quo and the impending needs of future older Americans.*

The nation is responsible for ensuring that older adults will be cared for by a health care workforce prepared to provide high-quality care. If current Medicare and Medicaid policies and workforce trends continue, the nation will fail to meet this responsibility. This report is not simply a call for more Medicare and Medicaid spending. Throwing more money into a system that is not designed to deliver high-quality, cost-effective care or to facilitate the development of an appropriate workforce would be a largely wasted effort. Rather, this report serves as a call for fundamental reform. If such reform is to occur, it will require both timely information and ongoing reexamination.

The committee concluded that more needs to be done to ensure that bold and appropriate actions are set in motion.

An important first step is to provide a reliable evidentiary basis to help focus attention.

Recommendation 1-1: The committee recommends that Congress should require an annual report from the Bureau of Health Professions to monitor the progress made in addressing the crisis in supply of the health care workforce for older adults.

This report needs to include regular reexamination of the health care needs of older Americans so that workforce redesign strategies may be properly adjusted. This report may also include monitoring of accomplishments toward national goals and milestones and needs to be inclusive of the entire workforce with consideration for the interaction between the informal and formal workforces.

The urgency for action cannot be overstated. Even with aggressive implementation of reform, it will take years to reshape the workforce and change delivery models. Deliberate workforce planning for the baby boom generation should have begun years ago; the greater the delay, the more difficult it will be to properly care for the nation's future older adults.

OVERVIEW OF THE REPORT

Chapter 2 begins with a review of the current data and projections of the composition and health status of the older population. Using current condition-specific rates of utilization of health services and available estimates of future health care service utilization, the committee provides a picture of the future demand for health services by older adults. These estimates include several important assumptions that may prove incorrect. Notably, they assume that Medicare's benefits package will remain stable and that current patterns of utilization and service delivery will continue. These projections need to be viewed with caution. Baby boomers differ from preceding generations with respect to levels of education, wealth, and their access to health care services. These factors may yield a generation of older adults whose demand for health care resources differs from their parents. At the same time, cost pressures under Medicare and Medicaid may lead to policy changes aimed at improving the efficiency of care, including efforts to reduce overutilization of health services. The net effect of these changes cannot be predicted.

Concluding that the current approach to care for the next generation of older adults is neither well-organized nor financially sustainable, the committee presents a discussion of models of care in Chapter 3. The committee identified a number of models that have been created to improve patient outcomes and to reduce utilization or cost. To date these models have not been widely used, and the chapter discusses many of the challenges to their dissemination. In addition, the chapter considers the implications of these models for workforce training and care provision as well as the role that cross-disciplinary training and evidence-based practice will likely play in workforce training in the future. The remainder of the report considers additional changes that will be needed to transform our health care workforce in order to better serve older patients and implement new models of care.

Chapter 4 focuses on health care professionals. In spite of expected increases in need for geriatric services, the number of geriatric specialists remains too low. While there have been improvements in the education and training of the workforce in geriatrics, these efforts have failed to ensure that all professionals who treat older adults have the necessary knowledge and skills to provide high-quality care. The chapter concludes with an examination of the challenges involved in the recruitment and retention of professionals in geriatric specialties. Many of the strategies to increase recruitment and retention depend on overcoming financial barriers, such as lower salaries and high costs of education.

Chapter 5 describes the direct-care workforce. These workers supply a major portion of the formal services provided to older adults, including assistance with ADLs and with instrumental activities of daily living (IADLs).[3] Direct-care workers have difficult jobs, and they are typically very poorly paid. As a result, turnover rates are high and recruitment and retention of these workers is a persistent challenge. Chapter 5 discusses a range of alternatives for bolstering the direct-care workforce, including measures to increase pay and benefits. In addition, the chapter recommends improvements in the education and training of these workers to ensure that they have the core competencies required to meet the specific care needs of older patients.

Chapter 6 discusses the role that informal caregivers play in providing direct-care services to older adults. These individuals are integral members of the patient's overall care team. The chapter discusses the need to promote the knowledge and skills of these caregivers in order to enhance their capabilities and strengthen their role as members of the workforce. The chapter also focuses on the central role that patients play in the care process and as members of the care team. Finally, the chapter describes the emergence of new technologies that are likely to preserve and extend the capabilities of older patients, thereby increasing their independence and reducing their reliance on direct-care workers and informal caregivers.

REFERENCES

AACN (American Association of Colleges of Nursing). 2006. *Student enrollment rises in U.S. nursing colleges and universities for the 6th consecutive year.* http://www.aacn.nche. edu/06Survey.htm (accessed July 9, 2007).

AACP (American Association of Colleges of Pharmacy). 2006. *Interest in pharmacy continues to rise as more students apply, enroll and graduate from schools of pharmacy.* http:// www.aacp.org/site/tertiary.asp?TRACKID=&VID=2&CID=1257&DID=7613 (accessed July 9, 2007).

AAHSA (American Association of Homes and Services for the Aging). 2007. *Aging services: The facts.* http://www.aahsa.org/aging_services/default.asp (accessed July 9, 2007).

AAMC (Association of American Medical Colleges). 2007a. *2007 state physician workforce data book.* Washington, DC: AAMC.

AAMC. 2007b. *U.S. medical school enrollment projected to increase by 17 percent.* http:// www.aamc.org/newsroom/pressrel/2007/070212.htm (accessed July 9, 2007).

AAPA (American Academy of Physician Assistants). 2007. *2007 AAPA physician assistant census report.* Alexandria, VA: AAPA.

---

[3]Instrumental activities of daily living (IADLs) refer to activities needed to remain independent, including shopping for groceries, preparing hot meals, using the telephone, and managing money.

ADGAP (Association of Directors of Geriatric Academic Programs). 2004. Financial compensation for geriatricians in academic and private practice. *Training & Practice Update* 2(2):1-7.

ADGAP. 2007a. Fellows in geriatric medicine and geriatric psychiatry programs. *Training & Practice Update* 5(2):1-7.

ADGAP. 2007b. Geriatrics in psychiatry residency programs. *Training & Practice Update* 5(1):1-7.

AHA (American Hospital Association). 2007. *TrendWatch chartbook 2007: Trends affecting hospitals and health systems, April 2007*. Chicago, IL: AHA.

AHRQ (Agency for Healthcare Research and Quality). 2004. *Employer-sponsored health insurance: Trends in cost and access*. Rockville, MD: AHRQ.

Alliance for Aging Research. 2002. *Medical never-never land: Ten reasons why America is not ready for the coming age boom*. Washington, DC: Alliance for Aging Research.

Alzheimer's Association. 2007. *Alzheimer's disease facts and figures*. Chicago, IL: Alzheimer's Association.

AMA (American Medical Association). 2005. *AMA announces physician shortage*. Chicago, IL: AMA.

Anderson, G. 2003. Chronic care. *Public Health & Policy* 3(2):110-111.

Anderson, G., and J. Horvath. 2002. *Chronic conditions: Making the case for ongoing care*. Baltimore, MD: Johns Hopkins University.

Anderson, G., and J. Horvath. 2004. The growing burden of chronic disease in America. *Public Health Reports* 119:263-270.

Arno, P. S., C. Levine, and M. M. Memmott. 1999. The economic value of informal caregiving. *Health Affairs* 18(2):182-188.

Asch, S. M., E. A. Kerr, K. Joan, J. Adams, C. M. Setodji, S. Malik, and E. A. McGlynn. 2006. Who is at greatest risk for receiving poor-quality health care? *New England Journal of Medicine* 354(11):1147-1156.

ASPE (Assistant Secretary for Planning and Evaluation, U.S. Department of Health and Human Services). 2005. *Informal caregiving: Compassion in action*. http://aspe.hhs.gov/search/daltcp/reports/Carebro2.pdf (accessed January 15, 2005).

Auerbach, D. I., P. I. Buerhaus, and D. O. Staiger. 2007. Better late than never: Workforce supply implications of later entry into nursing. *Health Affairs* 26(1):178-185.

BLS (Bureau of Labor Statistics). 2007a. *Fastest growing occupations, 2006-2016* (November 2007 Monthly Employment Review). http://www.bls.gov/emp/emptab21.htm (accessed December 17, 2007).

BLS. 2007b. Occupational employment projections to 2016. *Monthly Labor Review Online* 130(11):86-125. http://www.bls.gov/opub/mlr/2007/11/art5full.pdf (accessed December 17, 2007).

Brown, R., D. Peikes, A. Chen, J. Ng, J. Schore, and C. Soh. 2007. *The evaluation of the Medicare coordinated care demonstration: Findings for the first two years*. Washington, DC: Mathematica Policy Research, Inc.

Buerhaus, P. I., D. O. Staiger, and D. I. Auerbach. 2000. Implications of an aging registered nurse workforce. *Journal of the American Medical Association* 283(22):2948-2954.

CBO (Congressional Budget Office). 2007a. *Fact sheet for CBO's March 2007 baseline: Medicaid*. http://www.cbo.gov/budget/factsheets/2007b/medicaid.pdf (accessed September 11, 2007).

CBO. 2007b. *Health care and the budget: Issues and challenges for reform*. Testimony by Director Peter R. Orszag before the Senate Committee on the Budget. June 21, 2007.

CBO. 2007c. *The long-term outlook for health care spending: Sources of growth in projected federal spending on Medicare and Medicaid*. Washington, DC: Congressional Budget Office.

Center for Health Workforce Studies. 2005. *The impact of the aging population on the health workforce in the United States.* Rensselaer, NY: School of Public Health, University at Albany.

Center for Health Workforce Studies. 2006. *Licensed social workers serving older adults, 2004.* Rensselaer, NY: School of Public Health, University at Albany.

Ciechanowski, P. S., W. J. Katon, and J. E. Russo. 2000. Depression and diabetes: Impact of depressive symptoms on adherence, function, and costs. *Archives of Internal Medicine* 160(21):3278-3285.

Cigolle, C. T., K. M. Langa, M. U. Kabeto, and C. S. Blaum. 2005. Setting eligibility criteria for a care-coordination benefit. *Journal of the American Geriatrics Society* 53(12): 2051-2059.

Cutler, D. M., E. L. Glaeser, and A. B. Rosen. 2007. *Is the US population behaving healthier? Working paper 13013.* Cambridge, MA: National Bureau of Economic Research.

DHHS and DOL (U.S. Department of Health and Human Services and U.S. Department of Labor). 2003. *The future supply of long-term care workers in relation to the aging baby boom generation.* Washington, DC: U.S. Department of Health and Human Services.

Direct Care Alliance. 2005. *Issue brief 3: A poorly trained paraprofessional workforce.* http:// www.directcarealliance.org/sections/pubs/IssueBrief3.htm (accessed July 17, 2007).

Donelan, K., C. A. Hill, C. Hoffman, K. Scoles, P. H. Feldman, C. Levine, and D. Gould. 2002. Challenged to care: Informal caregivers in a changing health system. *Health Affairs* 21(4):222-231.

Evans, L. K., N. E. Strumpf, S. L. Allen-Taylor, E. Capezuti, G. Maislin, and B. Jacobsen. 1997. A clinical trial to reduce restraints in nursing homes. *Journal of the American Geriatrics Society* 46(6):675-681.

Federal HI and SMI Trust Funds Board of Trustees. 2007. *2007 annual report of the boards of trustees of the Federal Hospital Insurance and Federal Supplementary Medical Insurance Trust Funds.* Washington, DC.

Gerson, J., T. Oliver, C. Gutierrez, and U. Ranji. 2005. *Addressing the nursing shortage.* Washington, DC: Kaiser Family Foundation.

Gibson, M. J., and A. Houser. 2007. *Valuing the invaluable: A new look at the economic value of family caregiving.* Washington, DC: AARP.

Guterman, S. 2007. *Enhancing value in Medicare: Chronic care initiatives to improve the program.* Testimony before the U.S. Senate Special Committee on Aging. May 9, 2007.

Harmuth, S. 2002. The direct care workforce crisis in long-term care. *North Carolina Medical Journal* 63(2):87-94.

Harmuth, S., and S. Dyson. 2005. *Results of the 2005 national survey of state initiatives on the long-term care direct-care workforce.* New York: The National Clearinghouse on the Direct Care Workforce and the Direct Care Workers Association of North Carolina.

He, W., M. Sengupta, V. A. Velkoff, and K. DeBarros. 2005. *65+ in the United States: 2005.* Washington, DC: U.S. Census Bureau.

Holahan, J., and A. Ghosh. 2005. *Dual eligibles: Medicaid enrollment and spending for Medicare beneficiaries in 2003.* Washington, DC: The Henry J. Kaiser Family Foundation.

HRSA (Health Resources and Services Administration). 2000. *The pharmacist workforce: A study of the supply and demand for pharmacists.* Rockville, MD: HRSA.

HRSA. 2002. *Projected supply, demand, and shortages of registered nurses: 2000-2020.* Rockville, MD: HRSA.

HRSA. 2004. *What is behind HRSA's projected supply, demand, and shortage of registered nurses?* Rockville, MD: HRSA.

IOM (Institute of Medicine). 1978. *Aging and medical education.* Washington, DC: National Academy Press.

IOM. 1996. *Primary care: America's health in a new era.* Washington, DC: National Academy Press.

IOM. 2001a. *Crossing the quality chasm: A new health system for the 21st century.* Washington, DC: National Academy Press.

IOM. 2001b. *Improving the quality of long-term care.* Washington, DC: National Academy Press.

IOM. 2003. *Fostering rapid advances in health care: Learning from system demonstrations.* Washington, DC: The National Academies Press.

IOM. 2005a. *From cancer patient to cancer survivor: Lost in transition.* Washington, DC: The National Academies Press.

IOM. 2005b. *Quality through collaboration: The future of rural health.* Washington, DC: The National Academies Press.

IOM. 2006. *Improving the quality of health care for mental and substance-use conditions.* Washington, DC: The National Academies Press.

IOM. 2007a. *Adverse drug event reporting: The roles of consumers and health care professionals: Workshop summary.* Washington, DC: The National Academies Press.

IOM. 2007b. *Emergency medical services at the crossroads.* Washington, DC: The National Academies Press.

IOM. 2007c. *Emergency medical services for children: Growing pains.* Washington, DC: The National Academies Press.

IOM. 2007d. *Hospital-based emergency care: At the breaking point.* Washington, DC: The National Academies Press.

IOM. 2007e. *Rewarding provider performance.* Washington, DC: The National Academies Press.

IOM. 2007f. *Training physicians for public health careers.* Washington, DC: The National Academies Press.

Johnson, R. W., and J. M. Wiener. 2006. *A profile of frail older Americans and their caregivers.* Washington, DC: The Urban Institute.

Johnson, R. W., D. Toohey, and J. M. Wiener. 2007. *Meeting the long-term care needs of the baby boomers: How changing families will affect paid helpers and institutions.* Washington, DC: The Urban Institute.

Kemper, P., H. Komisar, and L. Alecxih. 2005. Long-term care over an uncertain future: What can current retirees expect. *Inquiry* 42:335-350.

Kovner, C. T., M. Mezey, and C. Harrington. 2002. Who cares for older adults? Workforce implications of an aging society. *Health Affairs* 21(5):78-89.

Kramarow, E., J. Lubitz, H. Lentzner, and Y. Gorina. 2007. Trends in the health of older Americans, 1970-2005. *Health Affairs* 26(5):1417-1425.

Kronick, R., and D. Rousseau. 2007. Is Medicaid sustainable? Spending projections for the program's second forty years. *Health Affairs* 26(2):w271-w287.

LaMascus, A. M., M. A. Bernard, P. Barry, J. Salerno, and J. Weiss. 2005. Bridging the workforce gap for our aging society: How to increase and improve knowledge and training. Report of an expert panel. *Journal of the American Geriatrics Society* 53(2):343-347.

Langa, K. M., M. E. Chernew, M. U. Kabeto, A. R. Herzog, M. B. Ofstedal, R. J. Willis, R. B. Wallace, L. M. Mucha, W. L. Straus, and A. M. Fendrick. 2001. National estimates of the quantity and cost of informal caregiving for the elderly with dementia. *Journal of General Internal Medicine* 16(11):770-778.

Langa, K. M., S. Vijan, R. A. Hayward, M. E. Chernew, C. S. Blaum, M. U. Kabeto, D. R. Weir, S. J. Katz, R. J. Willis, and A. M. Fendrick. 2002. Informal caregiving for diabetes and diabetic complications among elderly Americans. *The Journals of Gerontology Series B: Psychological Sciences and Social Sciences* 57:S177-S186.

LaPlante, M. P., C. Harrington, and T. Kang. 2002. Estimating paid and unpaid hours of personal assistance services in activities of daily living provided to adults living at home. *Health Services Research* 37(2):397-415.

Lawlor, E. 2007. Imagining Medicare's next generation. *Public Policy & Aging Report* 16(3): 3-8.

Luke, G. G. 2007. *Career choice & workforce trends in the health professions: Trends in dental education 2006.* Paper presented at AAMC Professional Development Conference, Scottsdale, AZ. January 14, 2007.

MedPAC (Medicare Payment Advisory Commission). 2001. *Medicare payment for nursing and allied health education.* Washington, DC: MedPAC.

MedPAC. 2006. *Report to the Congress: Increasing the value of Medicare.* Washington, DC: MedPAC.

MedPAC. 2007. *Report to the Congress: Promoting greater efficiency in Medicare.* Washington, DC: MedPAC.

Mold, J. W. 2003. General internists and family physicians: Partners in geriatric medicine? *Annals of Internal Medicine* 139(7):594-597.

Moon, M., and M. Storeygard. 2002. *Solvency or affordability? Ways to measure Medicare's financial health.* Washington, DC: Henry J. Kaiser Family Foundation.

Moussavi, S., S. Chatterji, E. Verdes, A. Tandon, V. Patel, and B. Ustun. 2007. Depression, chronic disease, and decrements in health: Results from the world health surveys. *The Lancet* 370:851-858.

Naylor, M. D., D. Brooten, R. Campbell, B. S. Jacobsen, M. D. Mezey, M. V. Pauly, and J. S. Schwartz. 1999. Comprehensive discharge planning and home follow-up of hospitalized elders: A randomized clinical trial. *Journal of the American Medical Association* 281(7):613-620.

NCHS (National Center for Health Statistics). 2006. *Health, United States, 2006. Special excerpt: Trend tables on 65 and older population.* Hyattsville, MD: Centers for Disease Control and Prevention.

NIA (National Institute on Aging). 1987. *Personnel for health needs of the elderly through the year 2020.* Bethesda, MD: U.S. Department of Health and Human Services.

Orszag, P. R., and P. Ellis. 2007. The challenge of rising health care costs—a view from the Congressional Budget Office. *New England Journal of Medicine* 357(18):1793-1795.

PHI (Paraprofessional Healthcare Institute). 2003a. *Long-term care financing and the long-term care workforce crisis: Causes and solutions.* Washington, DC: Citizens for Long Term Care.

PHI. 2003b. *Training quality home care workers.* Bronx, NY: National Clearinghouse on the Direct Care Workforce.

Rowe, J. W., E. Grossman, E. Bond, and Institute of Medicine Committee on Leadership for Academic Geriatric Medicine. 1987. Academic geriatrics for the year 2000. *New England Journal of Medicine* 316(22):1425-1428.

Ryan, J. 2003. *Improving oral health: Promise and prospects.* Washington, DC: National Health Policy Forum.

Stone, R. I., and J. M. Wiener. 2001. *Who will care for us? Addressing the long-term care workforce crisis.* Washington, DC: The Urban Institute.

Tritz, K. 2005. *A CRS series on Medicaid: Dual eligibles.* Washington, DC: Congressional Research Service.

Tritz, K. 2006. *Integrating Medicare and Medicaid services through managed care.* Washington, DC: Congressional Research Service.

U.S. Census Bureau. 2008. *Statistical abstract of the United States: 2008.* Washington, DC: U.S. Census Bureau.

Warshaw, G. A., and E. J. Bragg. 2003. The training of geriatricians in the United States: Three decades of progress. *Journal of the American Geriatrics Society* 51(7s):S338-S345.

Warshaw, G. A., E. J. Bragg, R. W. Shaull, and C. J. Lindsell. 2002. Academic geriatric programs in US allopathic and osteopathic medical schools. *Journal of the American Medical Association* 288(18):2313-2319.

Wenger, N. S., D. H. Solomon, C. P. Roth, C. H. MacLean, D. Saliba, C. J. Kamberg, L. Z. Rubenstein, R. T. Young, E. M. Sloss, R. Louie, J. Adams, J. T. Chang, P. J. Venus, J. F. Schnelle, and P. G. Shekelle. 2003. The quality of medical care provided to vulnerable community-dwelling older patients. *Annals of Internal Medicine* 139(9):740-747.

Wiener, J. M. 1996. Managed care and long-term care: The integration of financing and services. *Generations* 20(2):47-53.

Wiener, J. M. 2007. It's not your grandmother's long-term care anymore! *Public Policy & Aging Report* 16(3):28-35.

Wolf, D. A., and C. F. Longino, Jr. 2005. Our "increasingly mobile society"? The curious persistence of a false belief. *Gerontologist* 45(1):5-11.

Wolff, J. L., and J. D. Kasper. 2006. Caregivers of frail elders: Updating a national profile. *Gerontologist* 46(3):344-356.

Wright, B. 2005. *Direct care workers in long-term care.* Washington, DC: AARP.

Zabinski, D. 2007. *Medicare in the 21st century: Changing beneficiary profile.* Presentation at March 2007 Meeting of the Committee on the Future Health Care Workforce for Older Americans, Washington, DC.

2

Health Status and Health
Care Service Utilization

CHAPTER SUMMARY

Older adults use far more health care services than do younger groups. Although older adults vary greatly in terms of health status, the majority of them have at least one chronic condition that requires care. Older adults also vary in their demographic characteristics, which leads to differences in their demand for and utilization of health services. Projections of the utilization of health and long-term care services often suffer from important methodological limitations, but all projections indicate that the demand for services for older adults will rise substantially in the coming decades, which will put increasing pressure on Medicare and Medicaid budgets and on the capacity of the health care workforce to deliver those services.

Over the coming decades, the total number of Americans ages 65 and older will increase sharply. As a result, an increasing number of older Americans will be living with illness and disability, and more care providers and resources will be required to meet their needs for health care services. In order to design effective models of care delivery and prepare a health care workforce to serve this future population, one needs to understand both the projected health status of this population and the demand for health services under the current system. Such an understanding will help identify what changes will need to be made in the health care workforce (in terms of its size, distribution, and training) to fulfill its looming charge.

This chapter begins with an overview of the current health status and health services utilization patterns of older adults. Older adults today encounter a number of health challenges as they age and, on average, use a relatively large volume of health care services. However, the older adult population is quite heterogeneous, with individual members displaying an array of health statuses and needing a variety of services. Box 2-1 presents some hypothetical examples to illustrate the diversity of the current older population by describing several typical older adult profiles.

The chapter continues with a review of projections of the future health status and utilization patterns of older adults as well as a description of the assumptions and limitations of those projections. Although it is difficult to predict with accuracy the number and types of health services that will be demanded by older adults, it is clear that the total volume of health and long-term care services needed in the future will be much greater than the volume provided today.

The chapter concludes with a brief discussion of the implications of these projections. If current patterns continue, the financial and human resources required to meet the projected demand for services will be strained well beyond today's supply.

THE HEALTH AND LONG-TERM CARE
NEEDS OF OLDER ADULTS

The health status of older Americans has improved over the past several decades (Crimmins, 2004). Older adults today have greater longevity and less chronic disability than did those of previous generations (Federal Interagency Forum on Aging Related Statistics, 2006; Manton et al., 1997, 2007). While these improvements appear to be related in part to declines in smoking rates and better control of blood pressure (Cutler et al., 2007), the causation has not been conclusively proven. Studies also show improvements in the reported physical functioning of older adults, such as the ability to lift, carry, walk, and stoop (Freedman et al., 2002), as well as declines in limitations in instrumental activities of daily living (IADLs), such as shopping for groceries, preparing hot meals, using the telephone, taking medications, and managing money. The evidence for declines in limitations in activities of daily living (ADLs), such as eating, bathing, dressing, using the toilet, transferring (such as from bed to chair), and walking across the room is less strong (Freedman et al., 2004a). Finally, the percentage of older adults who self-report their health as "fair" or "poor" has declined (Martin et al., 2007). Despite these improvements, however, older adults still do have high rates of chronic disease and disability, particularly as compared to younger adults (Table 2-1), and disease prevalence has risen as longevity has increased (Crimmins, 2004).

It is important to note that if one looks just at aggregate data, such as those on disease prevalence (Table 2-1), it obscures important differences in

BOX 2-1
Typical Profiles of the Older Adult Population

Mrs. S is a 75-year-old divorced woman who is retired from her job as an executive secretary and now lives in a retirement community where she plays golf three times a week. She lives without assistance and frequently drives 45 minutes to babysit for her daughter's children. Mrs. S had breast cancer 20 years ago, which was treated with a mastectomy, and now has hypertension, which is treated with a diuretic. She sees her primary care physician twice a year and her oncologist once a year.

Mr. Y is an 82-year old man who lives in an apartment with his wife. He has diabetes with peripheral neuropathy, hypertension, coronary artery disease, and chronic obstructive pulmonary disease. He continues to drive and has been assuming many of the instrumental activities of daily living because of his wife's failing health; she has moderate dementia. Mr. Y sees a primary care physician every three months, a pulmonary specialist twice a year, a cardiologist once a year, and a diabetes educator once a year. He participated in pulmonary rehabilitation following a hospitalization for pneumonia 3 months ago. His primary care physician recently gave him the name of a social worker to consult with about possibilities for getting additional support in the home (e.g., a homemaker and an attendant to help bathe and dress his wife) and community-based resources (e.g., adult day health programs, caregiver support).

Mrs. M is a 97-year-old woman who has had severe Alzheimer's disease for 8 years. She recognizes her son and speaks to him, but her speech has no meaningful content other than to indicate when she is uncomfortable. Over the past decade she has gotten progressively more immobile, and she stopped walking 3 years ago. She has been cared for at home by her son, who retired to be able to care for his mother. Mrs. M takes no medications. Her course has been punctuated by recurrent complications of immobility including pressure sores, contractures, and recurrent pneumonias. She sees her primary care physician every 2 months but also has several emergency department visits per year, occasional hospitalizations, and periodic care from home health for wound care.

Mr. R is an 88-year-old man who is widowed. His medical problems include heart failure, hypertension, polymyalgia rheumatica, and prostate cancer. He has been living in a nursing home since falling and sustaining a hip fracture 1 year ago. Although he can ambulate with a walker, he is dependent in several activities of daily living. He has a niece who visits approximately once a month. Prior to his relocation to the nursing home, he saw several specialists, but none of them make nursing home visits. His primary care physician sees him every 3 months as well as in between these routine visits when an acute problem arises. None of his specialist physicians sees him in the nursing home.

NOTE: These are hypothetical examples developed for illustrative purposes and are not actual patient summaries.

TABLE 2-1 Indicators of Health Status, by Age Group, 2006 (Percent)

	Ages 18 and Over	Ages 65-74	Ages 75 and Older
Prevalence of Chronic Disease			
Hypertension	22.9	52.9	53.8
Chronic joint symptoms	25.2	42.7	44.2
Heart disease	10.9	26.2	36.6
Any cancer	7.1	17.2	25.7
Diabetes	7.7	18.6	18.3
Stroke	2.6	7.6	11.2
Asthma	7.3	7.8	6.1
Chronic bronchitis	4.2	5.6	6.7
Prevalence of Disability/Limitations			
Trouble hearing	16.8	31.9	50.4
Vision limitations, even with glasses or contacts	9.5	13.6	21.7
Absence of all natural teeth	8.0	22.8	29.4
Any physical difficulty	14.6	30.2	48.1
Overall Health Status			
Self-assessed health status as fair or poor	12.1	22.5	27.5

NOTE: Does not contain information on the institutionalized adult population.
SOURCE: Pleis and Lethbridge-Çejku, 2007.

the health status among subgroups of older adults. Many older adults are actually in very good health, for example—44 percent of adults in the 65-74 age range and 35 percent of adults 75 and older report their health status to be "very good" or "excellent" (Pleis and Lethbridge-Çejku, 2007). And a sizable minority, approximately 20 percent, have no chronic illnesses (AOA, 2006; CDC and Merck Company Foundation, 2007). These healthier older adults tend to be community-dwelling individuals who require only preventive and episodic health services.

On the other hand, a large majority of older adults (approximately 82 percent) have at least one chronic disease that requires ongoing care and management, with hypertension, arthritis, and heart disease being the most common (Table 2-2). These chronic conditions damage older adults' quality of life, they contribute to a decline in functioning, and they have become the primary reason why older adults seek medical care (Hing et al., 2006). In fact, Medicare beneficiaries with more than one chronic condition visit an average of eight physicians in a year (Anderson, 2003). An analysis of Medicare expenditures shows that the 20 percent of Medicare beneficiaries with five or more chronic conditions account for two-thirds of Medicare spending (Partnership for Solutions National Program Office, 2004). Data from the 2001 Medical Expenditure Panel Survey show that almost all

TABLE 2-2 Chronic Disease Prevalence, Cost, and Physician Use Among Medicare Beneficiaries

	Number of Chronic Conditions				
	0	1	2	3	4 or more
Percent of all Medicare beneficiaries, 1999	18%	17%	22%	19%	24%
Average Medicare expenditures, 1999	$211	$1,154	$2,394	$4,701	$13,973
Percent that sees more than 10 different physicians per year, 2003	6%	18%	40%	61%	Not available

SOURCE: MedPAC, 2006; Wolff et al., 2002.

Medicare spending and 83 percent of Medicaid spending is for the provision of services to individuals with chronic conditions.

In addition, many older adults experience one or more geriatric syndromes, clinical conditions common among older adults that often do not fit into discrete disease categories. Examples include delirium, depression, falls, sensory impairment, incontinence, malnutrition, and osteoporosis. The syndromes tend to be multifactorial and result from an interaction between identifiable patient-specific impairments and situation-specific stressors (Flacker, 2003; Inouye et al., 2007). Geriatric syndromes are prevalent conditions even among community-dwelling older adults and can have a substantial effect on older adults' quality of life (Cigolle et al., 2007). Estimates of incontinence, for example, range from 17 percent to 55 percent in older women and from 11 percent to 34 percent in older men. Almost half of older men and 34 percent of older women (ages 65 and older) report trouble hearing.

Although estimates vary across surveys, data from the 2002 Health and Retirement Study indicate that 27 percent of community-dwelling adults ages 65 and older (8.7 million people) need assistance with one or more ADLs or IADLs (Johnson and Wiener, 2006). Approximately 6 percent of older adults living in the community (2.0 million people) are severely disabled, reporting difficulty with 3 or more ADLs (Johnson, 2007). This group of older adults requires more intensive care in the home, particularly personal-care services.

Approximately 6.5 percent of older adults live in a long-term care facility. The majority, approximately 1.45 million, live in nursing homes, and approximately 750,000 live in other residential-care settings that provide some long-term care services (Spillman and Black, 2006). Those over age 85 are much more likely to live in a long-term care setting than younger older adults. In fact, those over age 85 are four times as likely to live in a nursing home as those aged 75 to 84 (Jones, 2002). On average, older adults living in nursing homes and residential care facilities tend to have more severe disabilities than older adults living in their own private homes, although more disabled older adults live in the community than in long-term care settings. Residents of long-term care facilities often have the additional need for symptom management and palliative care, that is, for noncurative care that is focused on alleviating physical symptoms and addressing psychological, social, and spiritual needs (Moon and Coccuti, 2002).

Approximately 80 percent of deaths in the United States occur among older adults (Kung et al., 2008). The leading causes of death among older adults are diseases of the heart, malignant neoplasms, cerebrovascular diseases, chronic lower respiratory diseases, and Alzheimer's Disease (NCHS, 2007). Studies indicate that older adults follow different trajectories of dying (IOM, 1997). Some have normal functioning but then die suddenly. Others die after a distinct terminal phase of illness, such as occurs with many types of cancer. Still others have a slower decline with periodic crises before dying from complications, as is the case with stroke or dementia. On average, about one-fourth of Medicare outlays occur in the beneficiary's last year of life, with 38 percent of beneficiaries spending at least some time in a nursing home and 19 percent using hospice services (Hogan et al., 2001). About half of Medicare patients who die from cancer use hospice services in the last year of life. Deciding whether to use palliative care or curative treatment for illness during these times is a very personal choice and depends on the individuals being affected (Moon and Coccuti, 2002).

Mental Health Conditions

Vulnerability to mental health conditions tends to increase as older adults age and become more likely to encounter stressful events, including declines in health and the loss of loved ones. Approximately 20 percent of adults ages 55 and older have a mental health condition, the most common being anxiety disorders (e.g., generalized anxiety and panic disorders), severe cognitive impairment (e.g., Alzheimer's disease), and mood disorders (e.g., depression and bipolar disorder) (AOA, 2001). Cognitive impairment with no dementia (CIND) has been described as the intermediate state between normal cognitive function and dementia, a chronic illness characterized by a decline in memory and other cognitive functions. The prevalence of dementia increases with age, escalating from about 5 percent among individuals aged 71 to 79 to about 37 percent among those aged 90 and older (Plassman et al., 2007). In 2007, 42 percent of adults 85 years or older had Alzheimer's disease (Alzheimer's Association, 2007), although estimates have varied somewhat. Additionally, suicide rates for men 65 and older are higher than any other age group and are more than twice the national rate for all persons (NCHS, 2007).

Mental health conditions are also more prevalent among community-dwelling older adults with ADL and IADL limitations. In 2002 approximately 31 percent of persons with disabilities and 45 percent of severely disabled persons reported depressive symptoms, and 15 percent of older adults with disabilities and 25 percent of severely disabled older adults had cognitive impairments (Johnson and Wiener, 2006). The prevalence of mental health conditions is even higher among nursing home residents. In 2005 nearly half of nursing home residents had dementia, and 20 percent had other psychological diagnoses (Houser et al., 2006).

One reason for these trends may be that mental and physical health are interrelated (New Freedom Commission on Mental Health, 2003). While the direction of causality between the two remains unclear, the correlation between them has been well documented. Persons with dementia and CIND have more serious comorbidity than those without cognitive impairment (Lyketsos et al., 2005). Physically disabled adults report higher rates of mental health conditions. People with depressive symptoms often experience higher rates of physical illness, health care utilization, disability, and an increased need for long-term care services (Federal Interagency Forum on Aging Related Statistics, 2006; Ormel et al., 2002). In addition, depression in later life is associated with poor health habits and diminished adherence to treatment for co-existing medical disorders. Among older adults, the combination of heavy alcohol or substance use with depressive symptoms has been shown to be associated with high risk for suicidal ideation and poor physical well-being (Bartels et al., 2006a,b).

CURRENT UTILIZATION OF HEALTH CARE SERVICES

Older adults have much higher rates of health services utilization than do non-elderly persons. Although they represent about 12 percent of the U.S. population, adults ages 65 and older account for approximately 26 percent of all physician office visits (Hing et al., 2006), 35 percent of all hospital stays (Merrill and Elixhauser, 2005), 34 percent of prescriptions (Families USA, 2000), and 90 percent of nursing home use (Jones, 2002). Utilization data for several acute-care services are displayed in Table 2-3.

On average, older adults visit physicians' offices twice as often as do people under 65, averaging 7 office visits each year and totaling approximately 248 million visits in 2005 (NCHS, 2007). Older adults are more likely to visit a physician's office for a chronic problem or for a pre- or post-surgery visit, but they are less likely than younger persons to seek preventive care. In 2004 the most common reasons for older adults to make office visits were all related to chronic conditions: hypertension, malignant

TABLE 2-3 Health Services Utilization by Age Group, 2005

	All Ages	Ages 65-74	Ages 75 and Over
Number of physician office visits per 100 persons	329	647	768
Number of preventive care visits per 100 persons[a]	51.0	50.6	48.1
Number of injury-related visits per 100 persons[a]	36.5	60.0	73.6
Number of hospital outpatient visits per 100 persons (not including ED)	31	41	38
Number of ED visits per 100 persons	40	37	60
Number of days of hospital care per 100 persons	55.4	139.8	259.4
Average hospital length of stay	4.8 days	5.3 days	5.7 days

NOTE: Data are for non-institutionalized persons. ED = Emergency Department.
    [a]Data are for 2004.
SOURCE: Hing et al., 2006; NCHS, 2007.

neoplasms (i.e., cancer), diabetes, arthropathies and related disorders (i.e., problems with joints), and heart disease (Hing et al., 2006). Older adults frequently made visits to internal and family-medicine physicians, but more than half of their visits were to specialists (NCHS, 2007). Older adults also tend to visit multiple physicians. In 2003 half of Medicare patients visited between two and five different physicians, 21 percent visited six to nine physicians, and 12 percent visited ten or more different physicians (MedPAC, 2006).

Although there are many specialists for which older adults constitute a large percentage of visits (e.g., 35 percent for internal medicine, 30 percent for neurology), older adults account for only 9 percent of visits to psychiatrists (ADGAP, 2007). The stigma associated with seeking mental health services presumably contributes in part to this low utilization, but limited coverage by Medicare for psychiatric services is also a reason (Manderscheid, 2007). Medicare requires a 50 percent copayment for outpatient mental health services as compared with only 20 percent for most other outpatient services.

Older adults also receive a considerable amount of ambulatory care at hospital outpatient departments. Older adults accounted for more than 13 million visits to hospital outpatient departments in 2004, not including visits to emergency departments (EDs); the reasons for these visits were similar to those for visits to office-based physicians (Middleton and Hing, 2006).

Older adults account for a disproportionate share of emergency services. In fact, the rate of use of emergency medical services (EMS) by older adults is more than four times that of younger patients, and older adults account for 38 percent of all EMS responses (Shah et al., 2007). Between 1993 and 2003 ED visits by patients between the ages of 65 and 74 increased by 34 percent, and adults over age 65 had the greatest increase in visit rate of all age groups (Roberts et al., 2008). In 2004 older adults made 15.7 million visits to EDs, which accounted for 14 percent of all ED visits. More than one-third of older adult ED patients arrived by ambulance, using ambulance transport at more than double the rate of ED patients as a whole (McCaig and Nawar, 2006). Despite older adults' higher rates of using emergency services, many EDs are not prepared to address the unique needs of older patients (Hwang and Morrison, 2007; Wilber et al., 2006). These EDs do not have the expertise, equipment, or policies to provide optimal care for older patients.

Once they have been treated, older adults are more likely to have an overnight hospital stay and also more likely to have multiple overnight hospitalizations. In 2002 older adults accounted for more than 13 million inpatient discharges. The most common inpatient diagnoses included coronary atherosclerosis (hardening of the heart arteries and other heart disease), congestive heart failure, and pneumonia (Merrill and Elixhauser, 2005).

Forty-two percent of older adults receive some post-acute care services after discharge from the hospital. Approximately 27 percent of older adults are discharged to another institution, such as a skilled nursing facility (SNF) or rehabilitation center; another 15 percent receive home health care (AHRQ, 2007). Medicare covers up to 100 days (20 days of full coverage and 80 days of partial coverage) in a SNF after a hospitalization of at least three consecutive days (MedPAC, 2007b). The average length of SNF stays covered by Medicare in 2005 was 26 days (MedPAC, 2007a). Overall, almost 3 million Medicare beneficiaries received home health services in 2006, including skilled nursing, physical therapy, speech-language pathology services, aide service, and medical social work (MedPAC, 2007a). Medicare provides home health care to homebound beneficiaries needing part-time (fewer than 8 hours per day) or intermittent (temporary but not indefinite) skilled care to treat their illness or injury. Personal care and other non-skilled needs are not covered by Medicare.

Older adults are especially vulnerable as they transition between types of care. A lack of coordination among providers in different settings can lead to fragmentation of care, placing older adults at risk for absence or duplication of needed services, conflicting treatments, and increased stress (Parry et al., 2003). For example, medication changes, which are a common cause of adverse drug events, are not unusual in the transition from hospital to long-term care settings such as nursing homes and private home settings (Boockvar et al., 2004; Foust et al., 2005; Levenson and Saffel, 2007). Incomplete procedures during hospital discharge may also be linked to unnecessary rehospitalizations (Halasyamani et al., 2006; Kripalani et al., 2007). This type of fragmented care can also result from a lack of coordination among providers who concurrently care for older adults in different settings, exemplifying the failure of the health care system to meet the standards of quality (most notably safety, efficiency, and patient-centeredness) as described in the IOM's *Crossing the Quality Chasm* (IOM, 2001). Coordination of care and the use of interdisciplinary teams, is discussed in more detail later in this report.

Long-term care services include health and personal services provided to chronically disabled persons over an extended period of time. Estimating the total amount of long-term care services received by older adults is difficult because utilization data are not often collected in a consistent manner across settings or care providers. Just over 60 percent of disabled older adults living in the community obtain some long-term care services, most commonly basic personal-care services and help with household chores, averaging about 177 hours per month (Johnson and Wiener, 2006). Informal caregivers provide the vast majority of these services. Approximately 5.7 million older adults received some unpaid services in 2000 (Johnson et al., 2007). Only about 18 percent of long-term care services provided to disabled older adults in their homes are delivered by formal paid sources. Medicaid accounts for about 41 percent of total long-term care expenditures (including non-elderly persons), while Medicare and out-of-pocket costs each account for 22 percent of expenditures (Kaiser Commission on Medicaid Facts, 2007).

As noted earlier, while approximately 1.45 million older adults live in nursing homes, another 750,000 older adults live in alternative residential care facilities, which provide housing and services outside nursing homes for those unable to live independently (Spillman and Black, 2006). In fact, assisted-living facilities have been the most rapidly expanding form of residential care for older adults (Maas and Buckwalter, 2006). At the same time, the percentage of older adults living in nursing homes declined from 21 percent to 14 percent between 1985 and 2004, consistent with the preferences of older adults to live in the community (Alecxih, 2006b). While the Veterans Health Administration (VHA) allots 90 percent of its long-term care resources toward nursing homes, about 56 percent of formal long-term care service recipients receive community-based care (Kinosian et al., 2007).

In 2005 about 870,000 Medicare beneficiaries received hospice care, accounting for $7.92 billion in total Medicare payments (OIG, 2007). Twenty-eight percent of these beneficiaries received some hospice care in a nursing facility.

In addition to their increased needs for assisted housing and other types of care, older adults account for a disproportionate share of prescription and over-the-counter medications (ACCP, 2005). They consume 34 percent of all prescriptions dispensed and account for about 40 percent of every dollar spent on prescriptions (Families USA, 2000). According to physician office records and hospital outpatient records, the most common medications used by older adults in 2004-2005 included anti-hypertensives (133.3 drugs per every 100 older adults), cholesterol control drugs (128.1), non-narcotic analgesics for pain relief (104.7), and diuretics for high blood pressure and heart disease (95.4) (NCHS, 2007). In 2002, prior to the implementation of Medicare Part D, the average Medicare enrollee aged 65 and older filled 32 prescriptions (including refills), but that number rose dramatically for individuals with greater numbers of chronic conditions. On average, enrollees with three or four chronic conditions filled an average of 44 prescriptions per year, and those with five or more filled 60 prescriptions per year (Federal Interagency Forum on Aging Related Statistics, 2006).

Besides the traditional forms of health care discussed so far, surveys on the use of complementary and alternative medicine (CAM) estimate that anywhere from 30 percent to 88 percent of older adults use some form of CAM. Studies often vary in terms of which forms of CAM are examined. According to data from the National Health Interview Survey, prayer for health is among the most common forms of CAM practiced among older adults (Barnes et al., 2004). Data from the Health and Retirement Study, which did not examine prayer, found that the most common forms of CAM used by older adults included dietary supplements (65 percent) and chiropractic services (46 percent), though personal practice (breathing exercises and meditation), massage therapy, and herbal supplements were also commonly used (Ness et al., 2005).

There are also a number of different types of providers, such as nurse practitioners, social workers, psychologists, dentists, and pharmacists, for which utilization data have not been discussed in this section. Visits to these providers are typically not captured by national surveys of older adults, but the numbers are likely to be considerable.

DIFFERENCES BY DEMOGRAPHIC CHARACTERISTICS

The data presented above mask important differences in the health status of and the health care service use by older adults in various demographic categories, including sex, race, and socioeconomic status. For example, women and men face different challenges in maintaining their health and have different patterns of service utilization. Men have higher rates of heart disease, cancer, diabetes, and emphysema and have more inpatient hospital stays than women (Robinson, 2007). On the other hand, women have higher rates of osteoporosis, arthritis, asthma, chronic bronchitis, and hypertension, and women are more likely to report depressive symptoms (Federal Interagency Forum on Aging Related Statistics, 2006). Because women have longer life expectancy than men and greater age-adjusted disability rates (NCHS, 2007), women are more likely to live alone, and they use more post-acute care services and long-term care services than men.

Much research has been conducted on the disparities in health status between non-Hispanic whites and others. According to an analysis by Hayward and Heron that studied adults of all ages, Native Americans between the ages of 30 and 34 have a disability rate of 12 percent, but the disability rate does not become that high among blacks until around age 37, not until ages 50 to 54 for whites and Hispanics, and not until age 60 for Asian Americans (Hayward and Heron, 1999). Their data for both sexes combined indicate that Asian Americans exhibit the lowest rates of disability, the longest life expectancy, and the fewest years lived in poor health; black populations have the shortest life expectancy, and a high proportion of those years are lived with a chronic health problem. Black populations have higher prevalence rates of stroke, diabetes, and hypertension than white populations (IOM, 2004). Whites, however, are more likely to report cases of cancer and chronic lung disease.

To examine these issues among older populations, the committee commissioned a paper to explore the topic. That paper reported many examples of disparities among older adults of differing ethnic backgrounds. For the most part, illness and poor health were more common among minority groups (those not classified as non-Hispanic white) than among non-Hispanic whites. The 2000 Census found, for example, that approximately 49 percent of Hispanic older adults and 53 percent of non-Hispanic black older adults reported a limitation or disability, versus 40 percent of non-Hispanic white respondents (Freedman et al., 2004b). Older non-Hispanic white adults (40 percent) and Asians (35 percent) are more likely to report being in excellent or good health than are older Hispanics (29 percent), American Indians/Alaskan Natives (28 percent) or African Americans (25 percent) (AOA, 2006).

Although minorities tend to be in poorer health than non-minorities, they also tend to use health services less frequently (AHRQ, 2006; Damron-Rodriguez et al., 1994). A review by Gornick found that African American beneficiaries used fewer preventive and health-promotion services (e.g., influenza and pneumococcal vaccines) than white beneficiaries, used fewer diagnostic tests (e.g., colonoscopy), and underwent more surgical procedures associated with poor management of chronic disease (e.g., lower limb amputations) (Gornick, 2003). Despite their less frequent use of many acute-care services, African Americans tend to use nursing homes at higher rates than white older adults, reversing a historical trend (NCHS, 2007). They are also more likely to experience preventable adverse events or complications of care from hospitalization (AHRQ, 2005).

Some of the disparities in health status and utilization by race and ethnicity may be attributable to differences in income. An inverse relationship exists between mortality and income (McDonough et al., 1997), and older adults living below the poverty level are more likely to have multiple chronic conditions than those at higher income levels (NCHS, 2007). Among older adults who require medical attention, wealthier individuals are more likely to use health care services than are lower-income individuals (Chen and Escarce, 2004). And while today's older adults are wealthier than previous generations, their increased life expectancy may lead to less economic self-sufficiency in their later years than previous generations, leading to worse health status for the oldest of adults.

Socioeconomic factors may play an even larger role than race and ethnicity with regard to differences in the use of preventive services (Leatherman and McCarthy, 2005). For example, low-income older adults are less likely to receive a mammogram, colonoscopy, or influenza vaccination than are high-income older adults. Similarly, the use of preventive services is more common among those with supplemental coverage than among dually eligible older adults. Still, the vast literature detailing the relationship between cultural background and health shows that cultural disparities in health status and utilization persist after controlling for other factors, such as income level (AHRQ, 2005; IOM, 2002). All of these differences demand examination of whether the health care system for older Americans is equitable according to the standards set by the IOM report *Crossing the Quality Chasm* (IOM, 2001).

Income, gender, and race and ethnicity are but a few of the demographic characteristics that influence health status and health utilization. Research has also identified differences based on marital status, level of education, geographic location, and other factors (Freedman et al., 2004b; Johnson and Wiener, 2006; Martin et al., 2007; Schoeni et al., 2005). For example, Medicare beneficiaries with limited English proficiency are less likely to have access to a consistent source of care and less likely to receive important preventive care than Medicare beneficiaries who speak English fluently. Married older adults are less likely to report a limitation or disability than those who are widowed, divorced, or never married, and rates of limitations and disabilities decline with years of education. Studies have also found differences in health status and utilization based on geography. Older adults living in rural areas are more likely to rate their health as "fair" or "poor" than are those in urban areas, and those in rural areas have higher rates of chronic illness, disability, and mortality (Brand, 2007). The geographic distribution of older adults also affects workforce needs because different regions have differing needs for geriatric services. In 2006 older adults accounted for 12.5 percent of the total U.S. population, but this percentage ranged from 6.8 percent of the population in Alaska to 16.8 percent of the population in Florida. (See Chapter 4 for more on the effect of geographic distribution on the professional health care workforce.)

Finally, certain subgroups of older adults may have particular health needs. For example, veterans are twice as likely to commit suicide as the general population (Kaplan et al., 2007). Posttraumatic stress disorder and traumatic brain injury are sources of high morbidity for veterans returning from the present-day conflicts in Iraq and Aghanistan as well as for Persian Gulf War-era veterans (Rosenheck and Fontana, 2007; Warden, 2006). As these veterans age, they will likely have persistent and unique health care needs.

PROJECTIONS

This section begins with a brief review of population projections, perspectives on future technology and preferences for care, and simple projections of health status and utilization. Next is an examination of three relatively complex models that were developed by RAND, the Lewin Group, and the Urban Institute to simulate future health status and health care utilization. Many of the projections discussed in the following sections focus on future dates other than the 2030 target date chosen by the committee, but the projections still serve the overall purpose of presenting a picture of the expected need for services and expected utilization rates if patterns of care for older adults continue on the current trajectory.

The Elderly Population

Between 2005 and 2030 the population of older adults is expected to almost double, from almost 37 million to 70 million (U.S. Census Bureau, 2000), although the need for health services may not rise in direct proportion. During that time, a number of factors are likely to alter the future health status and patterns of utilization among older adults, making projections of health status and utilization uncertain. As discussed previously, health status and utilization patterns vary according to certain demographic characteristics, and the future older adult population will look somewhat different from today's older adults (Box 2-2).

It has been estimated that minority groups will make up a much larger proportion of older adults in the future. The current population aged 65 and older is less diverse than the population currently aged 40 to 64 (Table 2-4), implying that older adults in 2030 will be a more diverse group than older adults today. One projection has the percentage of minorities in the oldest-old population increasing from 14 percent in 2000 to nearly 50 percent by 2100 (Wolf, 2001). As the proportion of minority populations increases over time, especially those minorities with higher prevalences of certain chronic diseases, the growing diversity among the older population is bound to influence the types of services demanded and the subsequent

---

**BOX 2-2
A Profile of the Future Medicare Population**

The Medicare Payment Advisory Committee (MedPAC), recognizing that future Medicare beneficiaries will likely have different characteristics than today's beneficiaries, conducted a project to develop a profile of these future Medicare beneficiaries. With input from an expert panel and a literature review, MedPAC staff identified several important changes in beneficiaries' characteristics that can be expected to occur in the coming decades: increases in the proportions of obese beneficiaries, of beneficiaries with chronic conditions, and of beneficiaries who are racial or ethnic minorities; a decline in the proportion of beneficiaries with disabilities; a decline in the proportion with employer-sponsored insurance to supplement Medicare; fluctuations in the proportion of beneficiaries age 85 and older (increasing through 2010, decreasing through 2030, and increasing thereafter); an increase in the level of beneficiaries' formal education; and a decreased reliance on adult children as a source of care. MedPAC also noted that Medicare beneficiaries' incomes have grown more slowly than health costs and that disparities in incomes across beneficiaries have increased. These changes are likely to affect future beneficiaries' demand for care and to influence the types of services most appropriate for future beneficiaries.

As a result, MedPAC staff identified several changes to the program that could be put into place in order to better serve future beneficiaries. Those changes included facilitation of care coordination, expanding the use of information technology and comparative effectiveness analysis, greater promotion of healthy lifestyles, and modifying cost sharing to have a single deductible for Medicare parts A and B and to stop loss protection.

SOURCE: Zabinski, 2007.

---

rates of utilization. (See Chapter 4 for more on the effects of diversity on the workforce.)

Additionally, the educational attainment of older adults is increasing. Better-educated older adults tend to have lower levels of disability, and they may be more likely to make beneficial changes in their lifestyles, to have better access to care, and to comply with physicians' instructions (Freedman and Martin, 1998). However, this may not fully reflect the capacity of older adults to navigate today's complex health care system. Age itself also plays an important role. The oldest older adults (ages 85 and older) have the highest per capita utilization of health services, and that population is expected to increase from 5 million to 9 million between 2005 and 2030. Other demographic characteristics, such as net worth, family structure, and geographic distribution, may similarly affect health status and the utilization of services.

TABLE 2-4 Diversity Among the U.S. Resident Population Ages 40+, 2006

	Ages 40-64		Ages 65+	
	Numbers (in Thousands)	Percentage of All Residents Aged 40-64	Numbers (in Thousands)	Percentage of All Residents Aged 65 and Older
Total population	97,346	100%	37,261	100%
White alone	80,130	82.3%	32,444	87.1%
Black alone	11,172	11.5%	3,169	8.5%
Asian alone	4,151	4.3%	1,178	3.2%
Hispanic or Latino origin	10,184	10.5%	2,400	6.4%

NOTE: The total population includes races in addition to white, black, and Asian, so these three groups do not total 100 percent. Hispanic or Latino origin was determined separately from race, and so the categories are not mutually exclusive.
SOURCE: U.S. Census Bureau, 2008.

Demographic trends also have implications for the sites where care is needed. A growing percentage of older adults prefer to receive long-term care services in home and community-based settings, increasing the demand for care in these alternative settings. The delivery of long-term care will become especially complex as varying options for housing for older adults develop leading to demands for services in multiple sites.

In addition, sites of care for special populations will be affected by the aging trend. For example, in 2006, 3.7 percent of inmates in state and federal prisons and local jails were over age 55. By 2030 one-third of prisoners will be over the age of 55 (Enders et al., 2005). Also, in the next decade the number of veterans over the age of 85 enrolled in the VHA is expected to increase by 700 percent, and the utilization of long-term care services is expected to increase by 20 to 25 percent, with special need for community-based services (Kinosian et al., 2007). As Persian Gulf War-era veterans and veterans currently returning from Iraq and Afghanistan get older, their mental and physical impairments may persist, increasing the need for the care of older adults within the VHA system. The VHA has a remarkable history regarding the availability of a variety of geriatric care programs, including nursing home care, home care, palliative care, and acute care services for older adults; however, an influx of older veterans will surely strain this well-developed system.

Finally, members of the future older adult population may bring a different stock of health capital to their older years than the current cohort of older adults has done. Disability rates among older adults have been declining in recent decades (Freedman et al., 2002; Manton et al., 1997, 2006), in part due to the educational gains among older adults discussed previously (Freedman and Martin, 1999). Educational gains are expected to continue, although at a slower rate. On the other hand, the recent trend of increases in disability at younger ages, although small and starting from a very low level, may have negative implications for the future elderly population (Lakdawalla et al., 2004). Some studies suggest that the gains in mortality from reductions in smoking and better control of blood pressure might be reversed in the coming years by high rates of obesity (Cutler et al., 2007; Olshansky et al., 2005). Another study found that baby boomers on the verge of retirement are in poorer health than pre-retirees 12 years ago (Soldo et al., 2006). Trends in illness and disability will influence the need for health services among the future older adult population, though the direction and magnitude of their effects are not entirely clear. Still, even if disability rates among older adults continue to decline, the size of the future older adult population is so large that, overall, the total need for services can be expected to increase (Johnson et al., 2007).

Health Status

Many efforts to project the future incidence or prevalence of disease assume that the health status of individuals in a given age-sex category will remain constant, and, therefore, the projections depend only on changes in the age and sex composition of the population (Goldman et al., 2004). This assumption may prove incorrect in the future. Nonetheless, for many health conditions this type of projection offers the best available estimates. Examples of such projections include the following:

- The proportion of older adults with self-reported, doctor-diagnosed arthritis will rise from 34 percent in 2005 to 48 percent in 2050 (Fontaine et al., 2007).
- The prevalence of diabetes among older adults will rise from 5 million in 2005 to 10.6 million in 2025 and to 16.8 million in 2050 (Boyle et al., 2001).
- 7.7 million people will have Alzheimer's disease in 2030, up from 4.9 million in 2007 (Alzheimer's Association, 2007).

Assuming no change in current prevalence rates for disability, 26 million of the 75 million older adults alive in 2040 will have limitations in at least one IADL, 16 million will have at least one ADL limitation, and 3 million will be institutionalized (Waidmann and Liu, 2000).

The Health Care Marketplace

Changes in the health marketplace will likely influence the demand for services as well. A number of medical advances and technologies may be introduced in the coming decades (e.g., intraventricular cardioverter defibrillators, continuous blood sugar monitors, pacemakers to control atrial fibrillation, treatment of acute stroke, and cancer vaccines) that could extend or improve life for older patients and, depending on the technology, increase or decrease the total demand for health services (AHA, 2007; Goldman et al., 2004). More care may be provided remotely, and older adults may be better able to monitor their conditions and to communicate with health care providers from home. Additionally, more or different options for care may offer better matches to patient preferences. For example, an increase in the availability of assisted-living options may result in fewer older adults living in nursing homes (Stone, 2000).

Furthermore, in the future older adults may have different preferences for care than older adults have had up to this point. Some data indicate that the physician visit rates for the baby boom generation are higher than for previous generations (AAMC, 2007). Baby boomers may have greater expectations about care or may treat their illnesses more aggressively than did their parents. Market research suggests that most baby boomers expect to be healthier in their retirement than their parents were, and one-quarter of them believe that a cure for cancer will be found before they retire (Del Webb Corporation, 2003).

Finally, future changes in coverage, cost sharing, and reimbursement policies could have a significant effect on access to care for older adults, but it is not possible to predict exactly what these changes might be. For example, the projected rise in Medicare and Medicaid spending may lead policymakers to consider new ways to improve efficiency in the programs, such as the use of health care rationing (Aaron et al., 2005). Researchers from Dartmouth estimated that nearly 20 percent of total Medicare expenditures provide no benefit in terms of patient survival or quality of life (Skinner et al., 2001); these expenditures might be cut to improve efficiency. Or, if all regions of the country could lower their spending levels to be commensurate with the lowest-spending regions, Medicare could potentially save 30 percent per year (Fisher et al., 2003). Policy makers are currently exploring the expanded use of comparative effectiveness research (Jacobson, 2007). Many of the new services provided to older adults today have little or no evidence showing that they are more effective than established treatments, and it is difficult for patients and providers to make informed decisions (MedPAC, 2007b). Policy makers may also explore the potential of alternative payment mechanisms, such as bundled payments, to provide incentives for providers to deliver care more efficiently.

Health Services Utilization

A number of projections have been developed to estimate the future demand for care from certain types of health care providers using age-, sex-, and race-specific utilization patterns. However, these projections forecast demand from all patients, not just older adults, and in most cases they assume that current utilization patterns will continue in the future, though some efforts also include projections under alternative scenarios in which practice or utilization patterns shift. For example, projections include the following:

- The need for critical care services will rise, increasing the need for intensivists[1] from 1,880 in 2000 to 2,600 by 2020 if current patterns of care continue. If utilization of critical-care physicians rises by one-third (which is, some suggest, a more appropriate level of use), approximately 4,300 intensivists would be required by 2020 (HRSA, 2006a).
- Visits to oncologists for cancer are projected to increase from about 40 million to almost 60 million between 2005 and 2020 if current patterns of care continue. A 2 percent increase in the percentage of patients who see an oncologist and a 2 percent increase in the average visit-rates in the first 12 months post-diagnosis would result in 70 million visits in 2020 (AAMC, 2007).
- If trends in emergency department visits among patients between the ages of 65 and 74 continue at current rates, the number of visits by these individuals would almost double from 6.4 million to 11.7 million by 2013 (Roberts et al., 2008).

Perhaps the most sophisticated models that project demand for health services from health professionals are those maintained by the National Center for Health Workforce Analysis at the Health Resources and Services Administration (HRSA). The Physician Aggregate Requirements Model (PARM) and Nursing Demand Model (NDM) project demand for services and providers based on current and forecasted patterns of health care use, staffing patterns, and insurance coverage. They consider provider-to-population ratios for population segments defined by age, sex, metropolitan/non-metropolitan location, and type of insurance. An assumption for the baseline scenario is that these ratios are fixed (i.e., there is a constant insurance probability for each population group defined by age and sex). These ratios are then applied to population projections to estimate future demand (HRSA, 2003, 2006b).

Under a baseline scenario in which there is no change in per capita health care utilization patterns, provider productivity, or provider staffing patterns, changes in population characteristics would drive a 30 percent increase in hospital inpatient days, a 20 percent increase in outpatient visits,

---

[1]HRSA defines intensivists as "physicians certified in critical care who primarily deliver care to patients in an intensive care unit" (HRSA, 2006a).

and a 17 percent increase in emergency department visits between 2000 and 2020. During that same period, nursing home residents would increase by 40 percent, home health visits by 36 percent, and visits to physicians' offices by 23 percent. This rise in demand would result in a 33 percent increase in the requirements for physicians and similarly large increases in demand for other health professions: 28 percent for nurses, 18 percent for physical therapists, 20 percent for optometrists, 28 percent for podiatrists, 30 percent for licensed practical nurses, and 33 percent for nurse aides (HRSA, 2003). The PARM and NDM can be adjusted to produce estimates under different scenarios, such as an increase in the productivity of health care providers in the future.

These projections represent the aggregate rise in demand from all patients, not just older adults. However, the changes are largely driven by the growth of the elderly population, particularly since the non-elderly population is growing at a much slower rate. The committee identified only a few efforts that provide projections of the future health status and health services utilization specifically for older adults. Three of those efforts are highlighted in the next section: RAND's Future Elderly Model is designed to develop projections of disability and chronic disease and the use of acute care services; the Lewin Group's Long-Term Care Financing Model projects the use of long-term care and expenditures; and the Urban Institute's DYNASIM3, coupled with data from the Health and Retirement Study, produces projections for disability and paid and unpaid long-term care.

RAND's Future Elderly Model

The Centers for Medicare and Medicaid Services (CMS) contracted with RAND to develop a model that would incorporate demographic characteristics in generating estimates of the future health care needs of Medicare beneficiaries as well as the expenditures on these beneficiaries. Every year the Office of the Actuary in CMS issues a report containing an overview and projections of current and future Medicare spending (Federal HI and SMI Trust Funds Board of Trustees, 2007). These projections incorporate long-term trends in age-specific mortality rates (Goldman et al., 2004), but they do not attempt to make any other assumptions about future health trends (Singer and Manton, 1998). CMS has successfully predicted the number of future Medicare beneficiaries, but it has encountered more difficulty predicting program expenditures; thus the impetus for the RAND project.

RAND's Future Elderly Model (FEM) takes a comprehensive look at the health status and utilization patterns of participating older adults and allows for alternative projections based on various assumptions (Girosi, 2007). The FEM is a microsimulation model that tracks Medicare-eligible individuals over time. The model begins with a sample of beneficiaries, ages 65 and older, from the 1998 Medicare Current Beneficiary Survey. The model ages that cohort year by year, simulating health and functional outcomes over time. These simulations require information on the risk of developing a new health condition (e.g., hypertension or diabetes) and entering a new functional state (ADL limitation, nursing home entrance, death) based on such risk factors as age, sex, race, education, obesity, and smoking. As the initial sample ages (rendering the model less representative of the entire older population), the sample is "replenished" each year with a new cohort of 65-year-olds using data from the National Health Interview Survey, which provides information on the health status of those individuals (Goldman et al., 2004, 2005).[2]

Baseline projections assume improvement in the mortality rate of 1.2 percent per year[3] and a 2 percent increase in obesity from 2004 to 2028, with a 0.5 percent increase thereafter. Results indicate a rise in the prevalence of many chronic conditions (e.g., high blood pressure, heart disease, diabetes, cancer, stroke) and ADL limitations by 2050, although the prevalence of lung cancer decreases slightly. The projections change as the assumptions are modified. Figure 2-1 shows the percentage change in prevalence for various conditions between 2004 and 2050 under the baseline scenario. All conditions, with the exception of lung cancer, are projected to increase. However, under an alternative scenario in which obesity is reduced (half of those who are obese are made overweight and half of those who are overweight are changed to a healthy weight), the prevalence of diabetes and lung cancer are reduced and the rates of increase for the other conditions and limitations (excluding stroke) are decreased in comparison to the baseline scenario. Under a scenario in which all older smokers quit, the rates of increase for most health conditions are also smaller than in the baseline scenario (except for cancer, which rises faster), and the prevalence of lung cancer falls.

The FEM also makes projections that take into account variations in utilization rates by age, health status, and socioeconomic class in the future elderly population. The baseline projections suggest increases in office visits, hospital days, and hospital stays of 155 percent, 170 percent, and 165 percent, respectively, between 2004 and 2050 (Table 2-5). The researchers further apportioned the change in utilization into two parts: the demographic effect, or changes in utilization related to a change in the demographic composition of the population; and the health effect, or changes

---

[2]See Goldman et al., 2004, for a thorough explanation of the methods and assumptions for the projections.

[3]During the 20th century mortality among older adults declined approximately 1 percent per year (Crimmins, 2004).

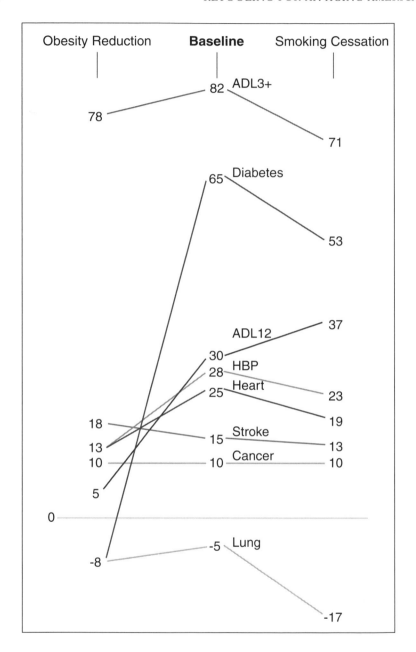

FIGURE 2-1 Percentage change in prevalence for various conditions projected for 2004-2050 under three scenarios: baseline, assuming obesity reductions, and assuming smoking cessation.
SOURCE: Girosi, 2007.

TABLE 2-5 Utilization Projections and Decomposition, Baseline Projections

	Percent Change (%)	Demographic Effect on Percent Change (%)	Health Effect on Percent Change (%)
Office visits	155	85	15
Hospital days	170	80	20
Hospital stays	165	85	15
Total expenditures	180	75	25

SOURCE: Girosi, 2007.

in per capital utilization due to changes in health. Demographic changes account for the vast majority of the increase in utilization.

Even under the alternative scenarios of obesity reduction and smoking cessation, utilization still rises considerably overall between 2004 and 2050 (Table 2-6). Still, reductions in obesity would save resources and reduce the overall increase in utilization compared to the baseline projection. Efforts to persuade Medicare beneficiaries to quit smoking would improve health but would also increase utilization because beneficiaries would live longer (Girosi, 2007).

The Lewin Group's Long-Term Care Financing Model

The Lewin Group developed a microsimulation model to estimate disability, use of long-term care (LTC) services, and LTC spending through the year 2050 for older adults. The model uses data from a number of sources including the Current Population Survey, Panel Study of Income Dynamics, the Employee Benefits Survey, and the Health and Retirement Survey to develop information on the individuals within the model, then uses prob-

TABLE 2-6 Utilization Projections and Decomposition Under Alternative Scenarios

	Obesity Reduction Scenario (%)			Quit Smoking Scenario (%)		
	Percent Change	Demographic Effect	Health Effect	Percent Change	Demographic Effect	Health Effect
Office visits	155	95	5	160	85	15
Hospital days	155	100	0	170	90	10
Hospital stays	155	100	0	170	90	10
Total expenditures	170	90	10	180	80	20

SOURCE: Girosi, 2007.

abilities to simulate events and transitions year by year, including family status, work history, retirement income and assets, disability and mortality, use of LTC services, and financing of LTC. Although the model is focused on individuals ages 65 and older, it uses data on younger groups to project characteristics of future cohorts of older adults (Kemper et al., 2005).

The model assumes, with some exceptions, that both individual behavior and current health policy (e.g., Medicaid benefits and eligibility requirements) will remain the same in the coming decades (Kemper et al., 2005). Based on current trends, the model projections assume that age-specific disability rates will continue to decline, that the use of assisted living will grow relative to nursing home use, that the cost of LTC services will rise faster than inflation, and that more workers will be offered LTC insurance by their employers.[4] Perhaps not surprising, the number of older adults with disability is projected to rise steadily through 2050, so that the number of older adults with any disability (IADL or ADL limitation) will rise from about 7 million in 2005 to more than 15 million by 2050. The projections for LTC spending are particularly striking, rising from $140 billion in 2005 to $570 billion by 2045 (Alecxih, 2006a).

Urban Institute Model

The Urban Institute and RTI International developed projections of the number of older adults with disabilities and of their use of long-term care services. First, the size and demographic characteristics of the older population were obtained from the Urban Institute's microsimulation model, DYNASIM3, which, like the Future Elderly Model, begins with a sample of individuals and families and "ages" those observations year by year, simulating such demographic events as births and deaths, immigration, marriage and remarriage, changes in living arrangements, and changes in disability. It also simulates economic events, such as retirement. Second, data from the Health and Retirement Study were used to develop models for the provision of paid and unpaid long-term care services as a function of disability, financial resources, children's availability, and other factors. Finally, three different disability projection scenarios are used to project future long-term care services. The model assumes that families weigh relative costs and benefits when making long-term care arrangements and that they would use less unpaid help from children and more paid help when the costs to children of providing informal care are high (Johnson et al., 2007).[5]

---

[4]See Kemper at al., 2005, for a thorough explanation of the methods and assumptions for the projections.
    [5]See Johnson et al., 2007, for a thorough explanation of the methods and assumptions for the projections.

Table 2-7 shows the results, detailing the percentage and number of older adults with disabilities in 2000 and in 2040 under the three different disability scenarios. Disability is defined as having any ADL or IADL limitation. The intermediate scenario, or the researchers' "best guess," assumes no particular future trend in disability rates; the variations in rates are small and depend on changing mortality rates and changes in the demographic characteristics of the population. The high scenario assumes that the older adult disability rate would increase by 0.6 percent per year from 2000 to 2014 and remain constant thereafter, similar to the rate of increase used in RAND's future elderly model. The low scenario assumes that older adult disability rates will decline 1 percent per year indefinitely, which is consistent with assumptions for earlier projections made by the Congressional Budget Office (Johnson et al., 2007).

Although disabled older adults are expected to decrease as a percentage of all older adults in both the low and intermediate disability scenarios, they are projected to increase in numbers under all scenarios because of the rapidly increasing size of the older adult population. In the intermediate scenario, for example, the number of disabled older adults more than doubles between 2000 and 2040. This increase would fuel the use of both paid and unpaid long-term care services. Under the intermediate scenario, an additional 5.5 million older adults would receive unpaid services and 3.1 million more would receive paid services in 2040 (Table 2-8). Even under the optimistic low scenario, several million more older adults would receive unpaid help and over a million more would receive paid care in 2040 than in 2000.

Despite the considerable growth in the absolute numbers of older adults receiving services, the percentage of the population receiving services

TABLE 2-7 Size of the Population with Disabilities, by Disability Scenario, 2000 and 2040

	Year 2000	Year 2040		
		Low	Intermediate	High
Percentage of Adults Ages 65+				
Any disability	30.3%	20.3%	28.0%	33.0%
1-2 ADL limitations	21.2%	14.2%	19.6%	23.1%
3+ ADL limitations	9.1%	6.1%	8.5%	9.9%
Number of Adults Ages 65+ (Millions)				
Any disability	10.0	15.1	20.9	24.6
1-2 ADL limitations	7.0	10.6	14.6	17.2
3+ ADL limitations	3.0	4.5	6.3	7.4

SOURCE: Johnson et al., 2007.

TABLE 2-8 Number of Older Adults Receiving Long-Term Care Services, by Disability Scenario, 2000 and 2040 (in Millions)

	Year 2000	Year 2040		
		Low	Intermediate	High
Any unpaid help	5.7	8.2	11.2	13.1
Unpaid help from children	2.8	3.7	5.0	5.8
Unpaid help from other sources	3.9	5.7	7.9	9.3
Paid home care	2.2	3.9	5.3	6.2
Nursing home care	1.2	2.0	2.7	3.1

SOURCE: Johnson et al., 2007.

is projected to remain steady or to decline (Figure 2-2). Nevertheless, in the intermediate scenario, the average number of paid help hours per month is projected to increase from 163 to 221 over the 40-year time period. The average number of hours of unpaid at-home care received from children would remain relatively constant, and the number of hours of unpaid help received from others would decline slightly (Johnson et al., 2007).

Limitations of Projections

The projections presented above are helpful in providing a general idea of the possible future health needs and health services utilization of older

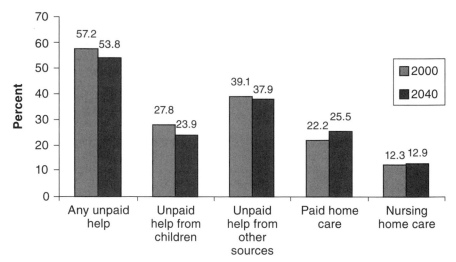

FIGURE 2-2 Percentage of older adults with disability receiving long-term care services, intermediate disability scenario, 2000 and 2040.
SOURCE: Johnson et al., 2007.

adults, but they do not describe a complete picture. Most of the projections rely heavily on data collected from large national surveys that ask about a limited number of illnesses and types of health services used. Although the Health Retirement Survey, the National Long-Term Care Survey, the Current Medicare Beneficiary Survey, and the National Health Interview Survey provide some limited data on geriatric syndromes, the simulation models often do not examine that data. Also, national surveys and datasets provide comprehensive information on physician visits and hospital stays but not on visits to other types of providers who deliver significant amounts of care services.

What all of the projections described above have in common is that they extrapolate data from the past in order to predict the future. Although it may be the best approach available in many cases, it is not without its limitations and certainly not without controversy (Olshansky, 2005). For example, one limitation of these projections is that they cannot predict changes in utilization patterns that result from changing patient demands. The models will project sizable increases in nursing-home use because of the growing number of older adults, even though the use rates have been falling.

Demographers and health service researchers regularly debate whether assumptions about future rates of disability or illness are inappropriately high or low; regardless of the precise assumptions used, however, the qualitative interpretations of the findings are clear and consistent. Even among the most optimistic projections in which the future cohort of older adults is healthier than today's, the growth in the absolute number of older Americans will result in a greater total volume of illness and disability and a greater collective need for services from the health care system. Estimates of the magnitude may vary, but again, even the most optimistic scenarios indicate that the change will be considerable—and, in particular, that it will be one that warrants a high level of attention and action today so that the system is better prepared by 2030.

IMPLICATIONS FOR FINANCIAL RESOURCES

Although an examination of health expenditures is beyond the scope of the committee's charge, a consideration of the tremendous growth expected in the use of health services would not be complete without turning some attention to its cost. In 1999 per capita health care spending for the population under age 65 was $2,793; for the older adult population it was $11,089, and for nursing home residents it was $44,520. The vast majority of health care costs for older adults was borne by Medicare (52 percent) and Medicaid (12 percent) (ASPE, 2005). In 2006 Medicare paid $406 billion in benefits (Federal HI and SMI Trust Funds Board of Trustees, 2007).

In 2003 Medicaid paid $263 billion in benefits, including $105 billion for dually eligible beneficiaries, the vast majority of whom are older adults, and $68 billion for other aged and disabled Medicaid beneficiaries (Holahan and Ghosh, 2005).

The 2007 report of the Federal Hospital Insurance and Supplemental Medical Insurance Board of Trustees contained a Medicare funding warning: The projected growth rates are not sustainable under current financing arrangements. The hospital insurance trust fund, which funds Medicare Part A, is projected to be exhausted by 2019 (Federal HI and SMI Trust Funds Board of Trustees, 2007). The financial outlook for Medicaid is hardly better. Medicaid is the second largest program in state budgets, growing faster than other state programs. Medicaid spending grew 9.5 percent in 2004, compared to a 3.4 percent growth in state revenue. States have implemented a number of measures designed to slow the rate of spending, including reductions in eligibility and benefits (Smith et al., 2004). The budgetary situation of these two programs is dismal, and policy changes will likely occur prior to 2030 in order to address them.

Although the committee did not consider policy options for addressing the financial viability of the two programs, committee members were mindful of the financial realities during the course of their deliberations. Insufficient funding for Medicare and Medicaid will place strains on the ability of health care professionals to provide quality health care services. It will also exacerbate issues of recruitment and retention—a particular concern in the case of providers qualified in geriatrics, whose presence in the field is already dreadfully low.

The financing of care is only part of the problem, however, and simply allocating more funding or resources will not fully address the deficiencies in the care of older adults.

CONCLUSION

Older Americans today have longer life expectancies than did previous generations of older adults. As the population ages, however, the actual numbers of older adults living with disability or illness are rapidly increasing. Many older adults live their extra years with higher rates of chronic health conditions that require vigilant care on the part of their health providers. As a result, older adults account for a disproportionate amount of the health care services delivered in the United States. Furthermore, because of the variety of physical and mental illnesses seen among older adults and the variety of care sites in which they receive services, the care of today's older adults is especially complex.

Future generations of older Americans may have different health care needs because of changes in the distribution of many demographic characteristics, including race, socioeconomic status, and geographic location, and also because of changes in personal preferences about how they care for their health and where they receive their health care services. It is difficult to make exact projections of these needs because of uncertainties regarding the effects of changes in demographics, lifestyle, and disease prevalence. Utilization patterns may also change markedly because of these effects and also because of changes in the health care marketplace and innovations in medical diagnostic and treatment modalities. While projections are difficult, one conclusion is certain—that the absolute growth in the number of older Americans will strain the current health care system if patterns of care remain the same.

If the health care workforce—already too low in numbers and competence levels to provide adequate care to the current population of older adults—is to be prepared for the coming spike in demand for services, serious reforms need to be considered. This will include redesign in the way that health care teams deliver their services. New models of care have been developed to improve the financing and organization of health care services for older adults. These models have a variety of implications for the workforce with respect to individual roles and responsibilities, scopes of practice, and payment rates. Chapter 3 examines a number of these new models as well as strategies to support their further development.

REFERENCES

AAMC (Association of American Medical Colleges). 2007. *Forecasting the supply of and demand for oncologists.* Washington, DC: AAMC.

Aaron, H. J., W. B. Schwartz, and M. Cox. 2005. *Can we say no? The challenge of rationing health care.* Washington, DC: Brookings Institution Press.

ACCP (American College of Clinical Pharmacy). 2005. Pharmacy practice, research, education, and advocacy for older adults. *Pharmacotherapy* 25(10):1396-1430.

ADGAP (Association of Directors of Geriatric Academic Programs). 2007. Geriatrics in psychiatry residency programs. *Training & Practice Update* 5(1):1-7.

AHA (American Hospital Association). 2007. *When I'm 64.* Chicago, IL: American Hospital Association.

AHRQ (Agency for Healthcare Research and Quality). 2005. *National healthcare disparities report.* Rockville, MD: AHRQ.

AHRQ. 2006. *Health care for minority women.* Rockville, MD: AHRQ.

AHRQ. 2007. Welcome to *HCUPnet.* http://hcupnet.ahrq.gov/ (accessed January 7, 2008).

Alecxih, L. 2006a. *Long term care financing in the U.S.* Paper presented at Alliance for Health Reform Briefing, Washington, DC. November 9, 2006.

Alecxih, L. 2006b. *Nursing home use by "oldest old" sharply declines.* Washington, DC: The Lewin Group.

Alzheimer's Association. 2007. *Alzheimer's disease facts and figures.* Chicago, IL: Alzheimer's Association.

Anderson, G. 2003. Chronic care. *Public Health & Policy* 3(2):110-111.

AOA (Administration on Aging). 2001. *Older adults and mental health: Issues and opportunities.* Washington, DC: U.S. Department of Health and Human Services.

AOA. 2006. *A statistical profile of older Americans aged 65+.* Washington, DC: U.S. Department of Health and Human Services.

ASPE (Assistant Secretary for Planning and Evaluation, U.S. Department of Health and Human Services). 2005. *Long-term growth of medical expenditures—public and private.* Washington, DC: ASPE.

Barnes, P. M., E. Powell-Griner, K. McFann, and R. L. Nahin. 2004. *Complementary and alternative medicine use among adults: United States, 2002.* Hyattsville, MD: National Center for Health Statistics.

Bartels, S. J., F. C. Blow, A. D. Van Citters, and L. M. Brockmann. 2006a. Dual diagnosis among older adults: Co-occurring substance abuse and psychiatric illness. *Journal of Dual Diagnosis* 2(3):9-30.

Bartels, S. J., K. M. Miles, T. E. Oxman, S. Zimmerman, L. A. Cori, A. S. Pomerantz, B. H. Cole, A. D. Van Citters, and N. Mendolevicz. 2006b. Correlates of co-occurring depressive symptoms and alcohol use in an older primary care clinic population. *Journal of Dual Diagnosis* 2(3):57-72.

Boockvar, K., E. Fishman, C. K. Kyriacou, A. Monias, S. Gavi, and T. Cortes. 2004. Adverse events due to discontinuations in drug use and dose changes in patients transferred between acute and long-term care facilities. *Archives of Internal Medicine* 164(5):545-550.

Boyle, J. P., A. A. Honeycutt, K. M. V. Narayan, T. J. Hoerger, L. S. Geiss, H. Chen, and T. J. Thompson. 2001. Projection of diabetes burden through 2050: Impact of changing demography and disease prevalence in the U.S. *Diabetes Care* 24(11):1936-1940.

Brand, M. 2007. *The future healthcare workforce for older Americans: Rural recruitment and retention.* Presentation at Meeting of the Committee on the Future Health Care Workforce for Older Americans, San Francisco, CA. June 28, 2007.

CDC (Centers for Disease Control and Prevention) and The Merck Company Foundation. 2007. *The state of aging and health in America 2007.* Whitehouse Station, NJ: The Merck Company Foundation.

Chen, A. Y., and J. J. Escarce. 2004. Quantifying income-related inequality in healthcare delivery in the United States. *Medical Care* 42(1):38-47.

Cigolle, C. T., K. M. Langa, M. U. Kabeto, Z. Tian, and C. S. Blaum. 2007. Geriatric conditions and disability: The health and retirement study. *Annals of Internal Medicine* 147(3):156.

Crimmins, E. M. 2004. Trends in the health of the elderly. *Annual Review of Public Health* 25(1):79-98.

Cutler, D. M., E. L. Glaeser, and A. B. Rosen. 2007. *Is the US population behaving healthier? Working paper 13013.* Cambridge, MA: National Bureau of Economic Research.

Damron-Rodriguez, J., S. Wallace, and R. Kington. 1994. Service utilization and minority elderly: Appropriateness, accessibility and acceptability. *Gerontology & Geriatrics Education* 15(1):45-64.

Del Webb Corporation. 2003. *Baby boomer report: Annual survey.* Bloomfield Hills, MI: Pulte Homes, Inc.

Enders, S. R., D. A. Paterniti, and F. J. Meyers. 2005. An approach to develop effective health care decision making for women in prison. *Journal of Palliative Medicine* 8(2):432-439.

Families USA. 2000. *Cost overdose: Growth in drug spending for the elderly, 1992-2010.* Washington, DC: Families USA.

Federal HI and SMI Trust Funds Board of Trustees. 2007. *2007 annual report of the boards of trustees of the Federal Hospital Insurance and Federal Supplementary Medical Insurance trust funds.* http://www.cms.hhs.gov/ReportsTrustFunds/downloads/tr2007.pdf (accessed January 29, 2008).

Federal Interagency Forum on Aging-Related Statistics. 2006. *Older Americans update 2006: Key indicators of well-being.* Washington, DC: U.S. Government Printing Office.

Fisher, E. S., D. E. Wennberg, T. A. Stukel, D. J. Gottlieb, F. L. Lucas, and E. T. L. Pinder. 2003. The implications of regional variations in medicare spending. Part 2: Health outcomes and satisfaction with care. *Annals of Internal Medicine* 138(4):288-298.

Flacker, J. M. 2003. What is a geriatric syndrome anyway? *Journal of the American Geriatrics Society* 51(4):574-576.

Fontaine, K., S. Haaz, and M. Heo. 2007. Projected prevalence of US adults with self-reported doctor-diagnosed arthritis, 2005 to 2050. *Clinical Rheumatology* 26(5):772-774.

Foust, J. B., M. D. Naylor, P. A. Boling, and K. A. Cappuzzo. 2005. Opportunities for improving post-hospital home medication management among older adults. *Home Health Services Quarterly* 24(1-2):101-122.

Freedman, V. A., and L. G. Martin. 1998. Understanding trends in functional limitations among older Americans. *American Journal of Public Health* 88(10):1457-1462.

Freedman, V. A., and L. G. Martin. 1999. The role of education in explaining and forecasting trends in functional limitations among older adults. *Demography* 36(4):461-473.

Freedman, V. A., L. G. Martin, and R. F. Schoeni. 2002. Recent trends in disability and functioning among older adults in the United States: A systematic review. *Journal of the American Medical Association* 288(24):3137-3146.

Freedman, V. A., E. M. Crimmins, R. F. Schoeni, B. C. Spillman, H. Ayakan, E. Kramarow, K. Land, J. Lubitz, K. G. Manton, L. G. Martin, D. Shinberg, and T. Waidmann. 2004a. Resolving inconsistencies in trends in old-age disability: Report from a technical working group. *Demography* 41(3):417-441.

Freedman, V. A., L. G. Martin, and R. F. Schoeni. 2004b. Disability in America. *Population Bulletin* 59(3):1-32.

Girosi, F. 2007. *Projections of health status and utilization for older Americans.* Presentation at Meeting of the Committee on the Future Health Care Workforce for Older Americans, Washington, DC. March 27, 2007.

Goldman, D. P., P. G. Shekelle, J. Bhattacharya, M. Hurd, G. F. Joyce, D. N. Lakdawalla, D. H. Matsui, S. J. Newberry, C. Panis, and B. Shang. 2004. *Health status and medical treatment of the future elderly.* Santa Monica, CA: RAND Corporation.

Goldman, D. P., B. Shang, J. Bhattacharya, A. M. Garber, M. Hurd, G. F. Joyce, D. N. Lakdawalla, C. Panis, and P. G. Shekelle. 2005. Consequences of health trends and medical innovation for the future elderly. *Health Affairs* 24(Suppl 2):W5-R5-W5-17.

Gornick, M. E. 2003. A decade of research on disparities in Medicare utilization: Lessons for the health and health care of vulnerable men. *American Journal of Public Health* 93(5):753-759.

Halasyamani, L., S. Kripalani, E. Coleman, J. Schnipper, C. van Walraven, J. Nagamine, P. Torcson, T. Bookwalter, T. Budnitz, and D. Manning. 2006. Transition of care for hospitalized elderly patients—development of a discharge checklist for hospitalists. *Journal of Hospital Medicine (Online)* 1(6):354-360.

Hayward, M. D., and M. Heron. 1999. Racial inequality in active life among adult Americans. *Demography* 36(1):77-91.

Hing, E., D. K. Cherry, and B. A. Woodwell. 2006. *National ambulatory medical care survey: 2004 summary. Advance data from vital and health statistics; no 374.* Hyattsville, MD: National Center for Health Statistics.

Hogan, C., J. Lunney, J. Gabel, and J. Lynn. 2001. Medicare beneficiaries' costs of care in the last year of life. *Health Affairs* 20(4):188-195.

Holahan, J., and A. Ghosh. 2005. *Dual eligibles: Medicaid enrollment and spending for Medicare beneficiaries in 2003.* Washington, DC: The Henry J. Kaiser Family Foundation.

Houser, A., W. Fox-Grage, and M. J. Gibson. 2006. *Across the states: Profiles of long-term care and independent living.* Washington, DC: AARP Public Policy Institute.

HRSA (Health Resources and Services Administration). 2003. *Changing demographics: Implications for physicians, nurses, and other health workers.* Washington, DC: HRSA.

HRSA. 2006a. *The critical care workforce: A study of the supply and demand for critical care physicians, report to Congress.* Rockville, MD: HRSA.

HRSA. 2006b. *Physician supply and demand: Projections to 2020.* Rockville, MD: HRSA.

Hwang, U., and R. S. Morrison. 2007. The geriatric emergency department. *Journal of the American Geriatrics Society* 55(11):1873-1876.

Inouye, S. K., S. Studenski, M. E. Tinetti, and G. A. Kuchel. 2007. Geriatric syndromes: Clinical, research, and policy implications of a core geriatric concept. *Journal of the American Geriatrics Society* 55(5):780-791.

IOM (Institute of Medicine). 1997. *Approaching death: Improving care at the end of life.* Washington, DC: National Academy Press.

IOM. 2001. *Crossing the quality chasm: A new health system for the 21st century.* Washington, DC: National Academy Press.

IOM. 2002. *Unequal treatment.* Washington, DC: The National Academies Press.

IOM. 2004. *Critical perspectives on racial and ethnic differences in health in late life.* Washington, DC: The National Academies Press.

Jacobson, G. A. 2007. *Comparative clinical effectiveness and cost-effectiveness research: Background, history, and overview.* Washington, DC: Congressional Research Service.

Johnson, R. W. 2007. *The burden of caring for frail parents.* Paper presented at testimony before the Joint Economic Committee, Washington, DC. May 16, 2007.

Johnson, R. W., and J. M. Wiener. 2006. *A profile of frail older Americans and their caregivers.* Washington, DC: The Urban Institute.

Johnson, R. W., D. Toohey, and J. M. Wiener. 2007. *Meeting the long-term care needs of the baby boomers: How changing families will affect paid helpers and institutions.* Washington, DC: The Urban Institute.

Jones, A. 2002. *The national nursing home survey: 1999 summary.* Hyattsville, MD: National Center for Health Statistics.

Kaiser Commission on Medicaid Facts. 2007. *Medicaid and long-term care services and supports.* http://www.kff.org/medicaid/upload/2186_05.pdf (accessed February 8, 2008).

Kaplan, M. S., N. Huguet, B. H. McFarland, and J. T. Newsom. 2007. Suicide among male veterans: A prospective population-based study. *Journal of Epidemiology and Community Health* 61(7):619-624.

Kemper, P., H. Komisar, and L. Alecxih. 2005. Long-term care over an uncertain future: What can current retirees expect? *Inquiry* 42:335-350.

Kinosian, B., E. Stallard, and D. Wieland. 2007. Projected use of long-term-care services by enrolled veterans. *Gerontologist* 47(3):356-364.

Kripalani, S., A. T. Jackson, J. L. Schnipper, and E. A. Coleman. 2007. Promoting effective transitions of care at hospital discharge: A review of key issues for hospitalists. *Journal of Hospital Medicine* 2(5):314-323.

Kung, H. C., D. L. Hoyert, J. Xu, and S. L. Murphy. 2008. *Deaths: Final data for 2005. National Vital Statistics Reports* 56(10). Hyattsville, MD: National Center for Health Statistics.

Lakdawalla, D. N., J. Bhattacharya, and D. P. Goldman. 2004. Are the young becoming more disabled? *Health Affairs* 23(1):168-176.

Leatherman, S., and D. McCarthy. 2005. *Quality of health care for Medicare beneficiaries: A chartbook*. Washington, DC: The Commonwealth Fund.

Levenson, S. A., and D. Saffel. 2007. The consultant pharmacist and the physician in the nursing home: Roles, relationships, and a recipe for success. *The Consultant Pharmacist* 22(1):71-82.

Lyketsos, C. G., L. Toone, J. Tschanz, P. V. Rabins, M. Steinberg, C. U. Onyike, C. Corcoran, M. Norton, P. Zandi, J. C. S. Breitner, and K. Welsh-Bohmer. 2005. Population-based study of medical comorbidity in early dementia and "Cognitive Impairment, No Dementia (CIND)." Association with functional and cognitive impairment: The Cache County Study. *American Journal of Geriatric Psychiatry* 13(8):656-664.

Maas, M. L., and K. C. Buckwalter. 2006. Providing quality care in assisted living facilities: Recommendations for enhanced staffing and staff training. *Journal of Gerontological Nursing* 32(11):14-22.

Manderscheid, R. W. 2007. *Testimony before the Subcommittee on Health*. Paper presented at House Committee on Ways and Means, Washington, D.C. March 27, 2007.

Manton, K. G., L. Corder, and E. Stallard. 1997. Chronic disability trends in elderly United States populations: 1982-1994. *Proceedings of the National Academy of Sciences* 94(6): 2593-2598.

Manton, K. G., X. Gu, and V. L. Lamb. 2006. Change in chronic disability from 1982 to 2004/2005 as measured by long-term changes in function and health in the U.S. elderly population. *Proceedings of the National Academy of Sciences* 103(48):18374-18379.

Manton, K. G., G. R. Lowrimore, A. D. Ullian, X. Gu, and H. D. Tolley. 2007. From the cover: Labor force participation and human capital increases in an aging population and implications for U.S. research investment. *Proceedings of the National Academy of Sciences* 104(26):10802-10807.

Martin, L. G., R. F. Schoeni, V. A. Freedman, and P. Andreski. 2007. Feeling better? Trends in general health status. *Journals of Gerontology B: Psychological Sciences and Social Sciences* 62(1):S11-S21.

McCaig, L. F., and E. W. Nawar. 2006. *National hospital ambulatory medical care survey: 2004 emergency department summary*. Hyattsville, MD: National Center for Health Statistics.

McDonough, P., G. J. Duncan, D. Williams, and J. House. 1997. Income dynamics and adult mortality in the United States, 1972 through 1989. *American Journal of Public Health* 87(9):1476-1483.

MedPAC (Medicare Payment Advisory Commission). 2006. *Report to the Congress: Increasing the value of Medicare*. Washington, DC: MedPAC.

MedPAC. 2007a. *Report to the Congress: Medicare payment policy*. Washington, DC: MedPAC.

MedPAC. 2007b. *Report to the Congress: Promoting greater efficiency in Medicare*. Washington, DC: MedPAC.

Merrill, C. T., and A. Elixhauser. 2005. *Hospitalization in the United States, 2002: HCUP fact book no. 6*. Rockville, MD: AHRQ.

Middleton, K. R., and E. Hing. 2006. *National hospital ambulatory medical care survey: 2004 outpatient department summary*. Rockville, MD: National Center for Health Statistics.

Moon, M., and C. Coccuti. 2002. *Medicare and end of life care*. Washington, DC: The Urban Institute.

NCHS (National Center for Health Statistics). 2007. *Health, United States, 2007*. Hyattsville, MD: U.S. Government Printing Office.

Ness, J., D. J. Cirillo, D. R. Weir, N. L. Nisly, and R. B. Wallace. 2005. Use of complementary medicine in older Americans: Results from the health and retirement study. *Gerontologist* 45(4):516-524.

New Freedom Commission on Mental Health. 2003. *Achieving the promise: Transforming mental health care in America.* Rockville, MD: DHHS.

OIG (Office of the Inspector General, Department of Health and Human Services). 2007. *Medicare hospice care: A comparison of beneficiaries in nursing facilities and beneficiaries in other settings.* Washington, DC: DHHS.

Olshansky, S. J. 2005. Projecting the future of U.S. health and longevity. *Health Affairs (Project Hope)* 24(Suppl 2):W5-R86-W5-R89.

Olshansky, S. J., D. J. Passaro, R. C. Hershow, J. Layden, B. A. Carnes, J. Brody, L. Hayflick, R. N. Butler, D. B. Allison, and D. S. Ludwig. 2005. A potential decline in life expectancy in the United States in the 21st century. *New England Journal of Medicine* 352(11):1138-1145.

Ormel, J., F. V. Rijsdijk, M. Sullivan, E. van Sonderen, and G. I. J. M. Kempen. 2002. Temporal and reciprocal relationship between IADL/ADL disability and depressive symptoms in late life. *Journals of Gerontology B: Psychological Sciences and Social Sciences* 57(4): P338-P347.

Parry, C., E. A. Coleman, J. D. Smith, J. Frank, and A. M. Kramer. 2003. The care transitions intervention: A patient-centered approach to ensuring effective transfers between sites of geriatric care. *Home Health Care Services Quarterly* 22(3):1-17.

Partnership for Solutions National Program Office. 2004. *Chronic conditions: Making the case for ongoing care: September 2004 update.* Baltimore, MD: Johns Hopkins University.

Plassman, B. L., K. M. Langa, G. G. Fisher, S. G. Heeringa, D. R. Weir, M. B. Ofstedal, J. R. Burke, M. D. Hurd, G. G. Potter, W. L. Rodgers, D. C. Steffens, R. J. Willis, and R. B. Wallace. 2007. Prevalence of dementia in the United States: The aging, demographics, and memory study. *Neuroepidemiology* 29(1-2):125-132.

Pleis, J. R., and M. Lethbridge-Çejku. 2007. *Summary health statistics for U.S. adults: National health interview survey, 2006.* Hyattsville, MD: National Center for Health Statistics.

Roberts, D. C., M. P. McKay, and A. Shaffer. 2008. Increasing rates of emergency department visits for elderly patients in the United States, 1993 to 2003. *Annals of Emergency Medicine* 51(6):769-774.

Robinson, K. 2007. *Trends in health status and health care use among older women.* Hyattsville, MD: National Center for Health Statistics.

Rosenheck, R. A., and A. F. Fontana. 2007. Trends: Recent trends in VA treatment of post-traumatic stress disorder and other mental disorders. *Health Affairs* 26(6):1720-1727.

Schoeni, R. F., L. G. Martin, P. M. Andreski, and V. A. Freedman. 2005. Persistent and growing socioeconomic disparities in disability among the elderly: 1982-2002. *American Journal of Public Health* 95(11):2065-2070.

Shah, M. N., J. J. Bazarian, E. B. Lerner, R. J. Fairbanks, W. H. Barker, P. Auinger, and B. Friedman. 2007. The epidemiology of emergency medical services use by older adults: An analysis of the National Hospital Ambulatory Medical Care Survey. *Academic Emergency Medicine* 14(5):441-447.

Singer, B. H., and K. G. Manton. 1998. The effects of health changes on projections of health service needs for the elderly population of the United States. *Proceedings of the National Academy of Sciences* 95:15618-15622.

Skinner, J., E. S. Fisher, and J. E. Wennberg. 2001. *The efficiency of Medicare.* Cambridge, MA: National Bureau of Economic Research.

Smith, V., R. Ramesh, K. Gifford, E. Ellis, R. Rudowitz, and M. O'Malley. 2004. *The continuing Medicaid budget challenge: State Medicaid spending growth and cost containment in fiscal years 2004 and 2005.* Washington, DC: The Henry J. Kaiser Family Foundation.

Soldo, B. J., O. S. Mitchell, R. Tfaily, and J. F. McCabe. 2006. *Cross-cohort differences in health on the verge of retirement.* Cambridge, MA: National Bureau of Economic Research.

Spillman, B. C., and K. J. Black. 2006. *The size and characteristics of the residential care population.* Washington, DC: ASPE.

Stone, R. I. 2000. *Long-term care for the elderly with disabilities: Current policy, emerging trends, and implications for the twenty-first century.* New York: Milbank Memorial Fund.

U.S. Census Bureau. 2000. *Projections of the resident population by age, sex, race, and Hispanic origin.* Washington, DC: U.S. Census Bureau.

U.S. Census Bureau. 2008. *Statistical abstract of the United States: 2008.* Washington, DC: U.S. Census Bureau.

Waidmann, T. A., and K. Liu. 2000. Disability trends among elderly persons and implications for the future. *Journals of Gerontology B: Psychological Sciences and Social Sciences* 55(5):S298-S307.

Warden, D. 2006. Military TBI during the Iraq and Afghanistan wars. *Journal of Head Trauma Rehabilitation* 21(5):398-402.

Wilber, S. T., L. W. Gerson, K. M. Terrell, C. R. Carpenter, M. N. Shah, K. Heard, and U. Hwang. 2006. Geriatric emergency medicine and the 2006 Institute of Medicine reports from the Committee on the Future of Emergency Care in the U.S. Health System. *Academic Emergency Medicine* 13(12):1345-1351.

Wolf, D. A. 2001. Population change: Friend or foe of the chronic care system? *Health Affairs* 20(6):28-42.

Wolff, J. L., B. Starfield, and G. Anderson. 2002. Prevalence, expenditures, and complications of multiple chronic conditions in the elderly. *Archives of Internal Medicine* 162(20):2269-2276.

Zabinski, D. 2007. Medicare in the 21st century: Changing beneficiary profile. Presentation at Meeting of the Committee on the Future Health Care Workforce for Older Americans, Washington, D.C. March 27, 2007.

3

New Models of Care

CHAPTER SUMMARY

This chapter presents the committee's vision for the care of older adults in the future and describes a number of new models of care delivery that show promise for achieving this vision. Widespread implementation of new models of care will require changes in traditional staffing patterns and provider roles. Despite the evidence that patient care can be improved through the implementation of new models of care, diffusion of those models has been limited, in part due to external constraints such as insufficient funding. The committee recommends improved dissemination of models that have been shown to be effective as well as increased support for research and demonstration programs that promote the development of new models of care.

The nation faces major challenges as it prepares for the growing number of older adults. There is a pressing need to develop a health care workforce that is sufficient in size and ability to meet the needs of this group. Projections indicate that there will be significant workforce shortfalls in the coming years, but simply increasing the numbers of geriatric-trained workers will not be sufficient, as it will do nothing to fix the deficiencies in the way care is delivered to older adults or to address the inefficiencies in the current system. The care that is currently provided to older adults often falls short of acceptable levels of quality. Providers' performance in the delivery of recommended care to older adults varies greatly (RAND, 2004), and there is limited coordination of care among providers. Expanding the capacity of the current system to meet the future needs of older adults would be a wasted opportunity. Instead, the current care delivery system requires significant reform in order to improve the care of this population.

This chapter begins with the committee's vision of how best to deliver health services to older adults in the future. The vision represents a major departure from the current system, and its implementation will require shifts in the way that services are organized, financed, and delivered. After this vision has been detailed, the chapter continues with a discussion of models of health care delivery that hold promise for moving closer toward the committee's vision. The chapter examines the evidence on several models as well as the challenges that will likely be encountered in disseminating these models. Although better models can lead to better care, dissemination of improved models has generally proved to be limited, in part due to financial disincentives to implementing these better models. Thus the committee offers its recommendation for how to foster dissemination of new models. Finally, the chapter discusses shifts in the workforce that may be required to support these new models, such as new roles for providers, increased delegation of responsibilities, greater use of interdisciplinary teams, and increased involvement of patients and their families.

A VISION FOR CARE IN THE FUTURE

The committee identified three key principles that need to form the basis of an improved system of care delivery for older Americans (Box 3-1). These principles are in alignment with the six aims of quality defined in *Crossing the Quality Chasm* (IOM, 2001).

First and foremost, the health needs of the older population need to be comprehensively addressed, and care needs to be patient-centered. For most older adults care needs to include preventive services (including lifestyle modification) and coordinated treatment of chronic and acute health conditions. For frail older adults social services may also be needed in order to maintain or improve health. These social services need to be integrated with health care services in their delivery and financing. Furthermore, ef-

---

BOX 3-1
Principles of Care

- The health needs of the older population need to be addressed comprehensively.
- Services need to be provided efficiently.
- Older persons need to be active partners in their own care.

forts need to be made to reduce the wide variation in practice protocols among providers, which should further enhance the quality of care for older adults.

The principle of comprehensive care also includes taking into account the increasing socio-demographic diversity of older adults. The number and percent of ethnic minorities in the older population is increasing dramatically, and even within ethnic groups there is tremendous cultural diversity. Health care providers need to be sensitive to the wide variety of languages, cultures, and health beliefs among older adults. Other segments of the older population face additional challenges. For example, older adults in rural areas often face isolation and barriers to access for some services.

The second principle underlying the vision of care in the future is that services need to be provided efficiently. Providers will need to be trained to work in interdisciplinary teams, and financing and delivery systems need to support this interdisciplinary approach. Care needs to be seamless across various care delivery sites, and all clinicians need to have access to patients' health information, as well as population data, when needed. Health information technology, such as interoperable electronic health records and remote monitoring, needs to be used to support the health care workforce by improving communication among providers and their patients, building a record of population data, promoting interdisciplinary patient care and care coordination, facilitating patient transitions, and improving quality and safety overall. Giving providers immediate access to patient information, especially for patients who are cognitively impaired and unable to provide their own clinical history, may reduce the likelihood of errors, lower costs, and increase efficiency in care delivery.

Efficiency can be further improved by ensuring that health care personnel are used in a way that makes the most of their capabilities. Expanding the scope of practice or responsibility for providers has the potential to increase the overall productivity of the workforce and at the same time promote retention by providing greater opportunities for specialization (e.g., through career lattices) and professional advancement. Specifically, this would involve a cascading of responsibilities, giving additional duties to personnel with more limited training in order to increase the amount of time that more highly trained personnel have to carry out the work that they alone are able to perform. While the necessary regulatory changes would likely be controversial in some cases, the projected shortfall in workforce supply requires an urgent response. This response will most likely have to involve expansions in the scope of practice at all levels, while at the same time ensuring that these changes are consistent with high-quality care.

The third principle is that older persons need to be active partners in their own care, except when they are too frail, mentally or physically, to do so. Such partnerships need to include the adoption of healthy lifestyles, self-management of chronic conditions, and increased participation by the patient in decision making. By becoming participants in their own care, patients can improve their health, reduce unnecessary treatments, and reduce the need for reliance on formal or informal caregivers.

Putting this vision into effect will require changes in policy and a restructuring of the health care financing and delivery systems. The purposes of this chapter are to highlight those models of care delivery that hold promise for providing high-quality and cost-effective care for older adults and for promoting the committee's vision for the future of care delivery; to discuss the dissemination of new models of care; and to explore the changes to the workforce that would best support those models.

NEW MODELS OF CARE DELIVERY

A number of new models of care have been developed with the aim of improving quality and patient outcomes, promoting cost savings, or both. The proliferation of these new models indicates not only a recognition that services for older adults need to be improved but also a willingness among providers, private foundations, and federal and state policy makers to commit resources to learning about better ways to finance and deliver care.

Nonetheless, while it is widely accepted that the current way of caring for older adults can be improved, there is little guidance available to provider organizations about which interventions are most effective. Obtaining information on the effectiveness of various models is challenging for two reasons. First, a general information gap exists. Many promising approaches have not yet generated reliable or complete findings, and some may never undergo rigorous evaluation because the resources required to systematically collect data on a program can be prohibitive. Second, evaluations often come up with conflicting results. Many models have elements in common (e.g., interdisciplinary teams, care coordination, disease management), and some evaluations of particular elements may indicate success while others find no effect. It can be difficult to explain such discrepancies because evaluations rarely provide information about key inputs, such as staffing and training, or about the effects that these inputs have on program outcomes.

In order to obtain a better understanding of the models that hold the most promise, the committee commissioned a paper to identify those approaches to comprehensive health care delivery for older adults that have the strongest evidence base. The review focused on frail older persons and was limited to models that have been shown, in high-quality controlled trials, to produce significant improvements in quality or efficiency (i.e., utilization and cost). The threshold for inclusion was the existence of one meta-analysis or at least three randomized controlled trials or quasi-experimental studies showing positive results. Undoubtedly these constraints led to the exclusion of a number of approaches that may actually show promise in the future, but a full analysis of every approach ever devised is beyond the scope of this report.

The scope of the review was limited to articles published between January 1987 and May 2007 on care models that were staffed primarily by health care professionals and that in some way involved comprehensive care (that is, were related to treatment for several chronic conditions, to treatment for several aspects of one condition, or to treatment from multiple providers).

Altogether, the authors of the commissioned paper reviewed 128 articles reporting positive results. Because the number of new models of care that have been developed is so large, it is not possible to discuss each one. The models of care described here offer a few examples of the innovative ways in which care is being provided to older adults at several points along the care continuum and in a variety of settings. Notably, many of the models strive to provide care in a manner that is consistent with the committee's vision—in a more comprehensive way (e.g., by providing services beyond those normally available), more efficiently (e.g., through the coordination of medical and social services and the shifting of traditional provider responsibilities), and with encouragement for older adults to take on more active roles in their own care.

Private-Sector Models

Improving Mood: Promoting Access to Collaborative Treatment for Late Life Depression (IMPACT)

Depression in older adults is common, particularly among individuals with chronic illness (Katon, 2003). Because of the importance of this disease to the older adult population, the John A. Hartford Foundation assembled a panel of national experts to design a program to treat depression in the primary care setting. The result was the IMPACT program, a care model that builds upon evidence-based treatment for depression and that incorporates approaches used in managing other chronic diseases, such as diabetes. Those approaches include collaboration among patients, primary care providers, and specialists (including the use of targeted consultations); development of a personalized treatment plan; proactive follow-up and monitoring; and protocols for stepped care (Unutzer et al., 2002).

Patients participating in IMPACT receive educational materials about late-life depression and visit a depression-care manager at a primary care clinic. The care managers (typically nurses, psychologists, and social workers) are trained as depression clinical specialists and work with the patient's regular primary care provider to establish a treatment plan. These care managers are supervised by a team psychiatrist and a primary care physician.

Under the IMPACT program, the care managers monitor patients in person or by telephone and have contact with each patient at least once every other week. They encourage patients to engage in social events, and they refer them for additional health or social services as necessary. If a patient recovers from depression, a relapse-prevention plan is developed, and the care manager continues to follow up with the patient. If a patient does not respond to treatment, the patient's case is discussed by the IMPACT team, the patient receives a consultation with a psychiatrist at the primary care clinic, and the patient's medications may be altered.

The IMPACT program has reported successes according to a variety of measures. Participants had higher rates of depression treatment, for example, and greater reductions in depressive symptoms compared to nonparticipants (Unutzer et al., 2002). Participants were also more satisfied with their care and reported less functional impairment and greater quality of life. They experienced an average of 107 more depression-free days over a 2-year period than did patients receiving usual care (Katon et al., 2005). Positive results also held over time. One year after IMPACT activities ended, participants maintained improvements with respect to antidepressant treatment, depressive symptoms, remission of depression, physical functioning, quality of life, self efficacy, and satisfaction with care as compared with a control group (Hunkeler et al., 2006).

Results from the model indicate that evidence-based care for major depression can be successfully delivered by specially trained nurses, psychologists, and social workers in primary care settings. Total outpatient costs were $295 higher for participants during the course of the program, or an average of $2.76 for each additional depression-free day. Another evaluation of IMPACT, limited to older adults with depression and diabetes, found that the incremental outpatient cost for each depression-free day was 25 cents (Katon et al., 2006). It is difficult to know, however, the degree of cost savings that may have been realized through the prevention of unnecessary hospitalizations or other treatments associated with unmanaged depression.

Geriatric Resources for Assessment and Care of Elders (GRACE)

Providing health care for low-income older adults is challenging for a number of reasons, including their high incidence of chronic illness, limited access to care, low health literacy, and socioeconomic stressors (Counsell et al., 2007). To improve the care provided to these patients, the GRACE model was developed by researchers from the Indiana University School of Medicine, the Indiana University Center for Aging Research, and the

Regenstrief Institute. The GRACE intervention provides home-based, integrated geriatric care by a team consisting of a nurse practitioner and a social worker that visits patients at their homes for an initial assessment and then follows up with the patients at least once a month, either by phone or face to face. The team also visits the patients at home after any emergency-department or hospital visit. This two-person team is supported by a larger interdisciplinary team which is led by a geriatrician and which also includes a pharmacist, physical therapist, mental health social worker, and community-based services liaison. This group, using input from the patient's primary care physician, establishes a care plan for the patient which incorporates protocols that have been developed for the treatment of 12 targeted geriatric conditions. The GRACE interdisciplinary team meets weekly to discuss the patient's progress with the smaller team. The team's efforts are also supported by an electronic medical record and web-based tracking system.

In a controlled clinical trial, Counsell and colleagues found that the GRACE program resulted in improved quality of care and reduced acute-care utilization among a group of high-risk, low-income seniors. However, improvements in health-related quality of life were mixed, and physical functional outcomes did not differ from the control group (Counsell et al., 2007). These somewhat mixed results may be explained by several factors, including the difficulty of quantifying the comprehensiveness, coordination, and patient-centeredness of the care. Furthermore, the study duration may have been too short to allow a complete assessment of the intervention (Reuben, 2007).

The Green House Model

Historically, residents' quality of life in nursing homes has received insufficient attention (Bowers, 2006). For example, nursing home residents often have little choice in their schedules or daily activities. Over the past decade, however, a small but growing movement has developed whose goal is to change the culture of traditional nursing-home care both to improve workers' job satisfaction and to improve the residents' quality of life through transformed environments, greater choice, and more empowerment of the direct-care staff. Several new models of nursing-home care have been developed that move away from a medical model of care toward a more patient-centered approach.

One such model is the Green House (GH), which is designed to make residents feel at home (March, 2007). The GH model emphasizes residents living their lives under normal, rather than therapeutic, circumstances. The model was based on the principles of the Eden Alternative, a movement to foster culture change within nursing homes by creating a home-like culture with plants, pets, and visits by children (Hamilton and Tesh, 2002). The Eden Alternative also decentralizes the organizational structure of nursing homes to empower certified nursing assistants (CNAs) to develop their own schedules and daily assignments and to provide companionship to the residents. GHs take the concept one step further by creating a more residential social setting.

The initial development and implementation of the GH model was supported by grants from private foundations. The model involves three key elements. First, the environment is composed of a small, technologically sophisticated house that functions as a home for eight to ten residents. Each resident has a private room and bathroom, and the residents' individual rooms are clustered around a central area with a shared kitchen, dining room, and living room. GHs serve as real homes in appearance and function and, as such, do not have nurses' stations, medication carts, or public address systems (Kane et al., 2007).

Second, the frontline caregivers have broad roles that include personal care, cooking, housekeeping, and assuring that residents spend time according to their preferences. These direct-care workers, referred to as shahbazim, receive 120 hours of training above those required to be a CNA. This level of training is significantly beyond federal and state requirements and reflects the CNAs' expanded role in a GH. In addition, there are "sages," older adults who serve as coaches or mentors to the shahbazim, and "guides," who are supervisors and serve as liaisons between the shahbazim and other staff. This system of support is the basis of the care team.

Third, professional healthcare providers (e.g., nurses, physicians, social workers, and pharmacists) form visiting clinical support teams that provide specialized assessments for residents. Licensed nurses are available and responsible for the clinical care in the GH. A nurse is available to shahbazim whenever needed, 24 hours a day, by emergency pager (NCB Capital Impact, 2007).

While information on the effectiveness of GHs is preliminary, a recent evaluation of the model showed that GH residents reported better quality of life on several measures, higher satisfaction with their place of residence, and better emotional health than a comparison group (Kane et al., 2007). No difference in self-reported health was noted. Quality of care was at least as good in the GH group as in the control group. The GH group also had a lower prevalence of residents on bed rest, fewer residents with limited activity, and a lower prevalence of depression compared with residents of traditional nursing homes.

In addition to its potential to promote patient-centered care, the GH model also holds promise for improved recruitment of direct-care workers. The first GH site received only two responses to advertisements for a CNA but received more than 70 when the ad was for a shahbaz (Angelelli, 2006).

Shahbazim are paid approximately 10 percent more than CNAs for their additional responsibilities and training hours (NCB Capital Impact, 2007). The additional pay is made possible through stabilization of the direct-care workforce (i.e., lower costs due to decreased turnover rates), operational efficiencies, and diminished need for middle-management positions. However, GHs do require providers to adapt to new roles. For example, attending physicians and medical directors provide care in disaggregated homes where shahbazim are central to the care of residents and are responsible for monitoring their status based on the direction of physicians (Kane et al., 2007). This is different from the situation in the typical nursing home setting, where physicians have traditionally had little communication with direct-care staff.

The Advanced Illness Management (AIM) Program

Numerous studies have shown deficiencies in the quality of care at the end of life. Many older adults die with inadequate palliative care (Zerzan et al., 2000), and often patient preferences are not assessed, communicated, or followed (Haidet et al., 1998; Hofmann et al., 1997). Most patients prefer to die at home, yet most deaths occur in the hospital (Brumley et al., 2007; Grande et al., 1999). And although hospice care can lead to higher patient and family satisfaction at a lower cost (Brumley et al., 2007), many individuals do not receive hospice care (NHPCO, 2005), and those who do receive it rarely use the full Medicare hospice benefits (Ciemins et al., 2006).

In an effort to bridge the gap between curative care and hospice care, Sutter Visiting Nurse Association and Hospice created the Advanced Illness Management (AIM) program, which provides both disease-modifying care and comfort care in the home setting to those with advanced illnesses who are eligible for home care but not yet eligible for hospice care (Ciemins et al., 2006). Patients are included regardless of Medicare eligibility or insurance coverage. The program coordinates hospital services, home health care, and, when needed, hospice services. The goals of the program are to provide seriously ill patients with an array of home-based services, to ease their transition from home health care to hospice care, and to avoid unnecessary hospitalizations.

The program uses a combination of home care and hospice staff. Nurse case managers (known as AIM nurses) are the primary providers for AIM patients. They educate patients on disease process and prognosis, treatment alternatives, advance care planning, avoidance of unnecessary hospitalization, management of pain and symptoms, and hospice enrollment. Additionally, AIM nurses receive training classes that cover such topics as palliative care definition and philosophy, insurance coverage, home care and hospice regulations, and facilitating difficult conversations. They also attend biweekly patient-centered conferences.

An early evaluation of the program found that AIM program patients had higher rates of hospice utilization (Ciemins et al., 2006). Notably, the program was successful in increasing hospice utilization by African Americans, a group that has traditionally had very low rates of hospice use.

Medicare Research and Demonstration Projects

In addition to private-sector initiatives, a number of models have been tested by the Centers for Medicare and Medicaid Services (CMS). These demonstration projects have examined mechanisms to restructure the Medicare and Medicaid programs in ways that support more efficient and more effective care delivery for older adults. For example, older adults with long-term health care needs often face fragmentation in their care because the Medicare program finances acute care at the national level while state-administered Medicaid programs are the predominant payers for long-term care services (Kaiser Family Foundation, 2006). Discontinuities between the two programs can translate into discontinuities in care as well as into higher costs, as the two programs often seek to shift costs to each other (National Commission for Quality Long Term Care, 2006). CMS demonstration projects have tested a number of ways to improve quality in Medicare (and often Medicaid as well). Several of these projects are described below.

Programs of All-Inclusive Care for the Elderly (PACE)

PACE is a managed-care program that was developed to address the spectrum of needs for adults aged 55 and older with disability levels that make them eligible for nursing-home care (Tritz, 2005). The program is based on the belief that the well-being of older adults can be improved by serving them in the community (Mukamel et al., 2007). PACE was modeled after an innovative initiative in San Francisco, On Lok, that was designed to help the Asian American community care for older adults in their homes (Greenwood, 2001).

Start-up funds for PACE were provided by private foundations, and its implementation was supported by congressional authorization of Medicare and Medicaid waivers (Gross et al., 2004). The PACE model funds a comprehensive set of services by combining federal Medicare dollars, state and federal Medicaid funds, and the individuals' own contributions (National PACE Association, 2007). The PACE service package includes all Medicare and Medicaid covered services plus additional services, including adult day care, nutritional counseling, recreational therapy, transportation, and personal-care services, such as meals at home (CMS, 2005). PACE also pays for nursing-home care, if appropriate.

PACE services are provided by an interdisciplinary team composed of at least the following members: a primary care physician, a registered nurse, a social worker, a physical therapist, a pharmacist, an occupational therapist, a recreational therapist, a dietician, a PACE center manager, a home-care coordinator, personal-care attendants, and drivers (Mukamel et al., 2007). The team approach in PACE is innovative in its inclusion of both professionals and direct-care workers as part of the care team. Each member of the team performs an initial assessment of each patient, and then the group works together to create a single care plan that takes the different assessments into account. The team holds weekly care-planning meetings during which the care plans are reassessed.

The services, which are provided primarily at an adult day-care center, are also highly coordinated (Cooper and Fishman, 2003; Mukamel et al., 2006). The center includes a health clinic and at least one common room for social and recreational activities. PACE enrollees attend the day center approximately three days per week, enabling team members to identify subtle changes in health status or mood and to address them quickly. Team members regularly reassess the medical, functional and psychosocial conditions of patients and document any changes in the medical record.

An evaluation of the PACE demonstration program found that enrollment was associated with higher patient satisfaction, improved health status and physical functioning, an increased number of days in the community, improved quality of life, and lower mortality (Chatterji et al., 1998). The benefits of PACE were even greater for the frailest older adults, whose enrollment was associated with lower rates of service utilization in hospitals and nursing homes and higher rates of ambulatory care services.

An analysis showed that capitated payments under PACE were about 10 percent higher than the payments that would have been likely under the fee-for-service (FFS) program. The analysis found savings for Medicare but higher costs for Medicaid. Capitated Medicare payments were 42 percent lower than projected Medicare FFS expenditures, but capitated Medicaid payments were 86 percent higher than projected FFS expenditures (Grabowski, 2006; White et al., 2000).

It is also notable that PACE programs have achieved some success in the recruitment of direct-care workers (Hansen, 2007). The program has a 12 percent annual turnover rate among aides, well below rates reported nationally. Aides at PACE sites are given opportunities for career advancement, and PACE provides financial support to direct-care workers seeking additional training.

Evercare

The Evercare program, originally developed by United Health Care Corporation, assigns nursing-home residents to a risk-bearing health maintenance organization (HMO) (Inglis et al., 2004) that coordinates Medicare acute-care services and nursing-home services under Medicaid (Hansen, 2007). Under the program, nurse practitioners provide more intensive primary care services than is typical for nursing-homes residents, and they coordinate enrollees' care with the nursing-home staff (Stone, 2000). The nurse practitioners have relatively small caseloads and visit each of the nursing homes every second or third day. They are engaged in clinical work, spending about one-third of their days on direct patient care, and they also serve in a coordinating role, communicating information to various parties, including nursing-home staff, families, and patients' physicians. The nurse practitioners work with nursing-home staff to monitor treatment and to identify changes in patient status. The Evercare program also educates nursing-home staff through formal in-service training as well as through less formal on-the-job training.

An evaluation of the Evercare program showed that it succeeded in reducing hospital admissions and in providing high-quality coordinated care to patients, with a number of caveats (Kane et al., 2002). The analysis showed that, on average, the use of nurse practitioners saved approximately $88,000 per year per nurse practitioner in reduced hospital usage. In large part this reduction in hospital usage resulted from Evercare's use of intensive service days, through which nursing homes were paid an extra fee to take on cases that might otherwise be handled in the hospital. The evaluation concluded that providing more intensive primary care to nursing-home residents produced more efficient crisis care, but it typically did not prevent the crises themselves. In addition, the capitated payments resulted in overpayment to the plan and no Medicare cost savings (Kane et al., 2002). Nonetheless, the Medicare Modernization Act (MMA) of 2003[1] made the Evercare program a permanent option.

Social HMO Demonstrations

The Social HMO (SHMO) demonstrations focused on new approaches for providing care on a capitated basis to patients with complex medical needs, specifically frail patients at risk for nursing-home placement (Vladeck, 1996). The Deficit Reduction Act of 1984[2] called for a demonstration of the SHMO concept (SHMO I), which sought to integrate health care services and long-term care services. A second demonstration model (SHMO II) was authorized in the Omnibus Budget Reconciliation Act of

---

[1] *Medicare Modernization Act of 2003*. Public Law 108-173. 108th Congress. (2003).
[2] *Deficit Reduction Act of 1984*. Public Law 98-369. 98th Congress. (1984).

1990.[3] Four sites became operational under SHMO I, and only one plan participated in SHMO II (Thompson, 2002).

Enrollees of the SHMOs received coordinated acute-care and community-care benefits, including personal care, homemaking services, adult day care, personal emergency response service, transportation, respite, durable medical equipment, and short-term institutional care for convalescent and respite stays (Leutz and Capitman, 2005). Integration of acute care and long-term care involved operational linkages, including referral systems, as well as sharing of assessments and clinical data, management of transitions across settings, and benefit coordination. The project did not generally involve such strategies as changing the practice patterns of primary care physicians to include geriatric principles or the hiring of a variety of geriatric practitioners. The SHMO II model incorporated a more team-oriented geriatric approach to care than did the first demonstration, and it brought together primary care physicians, geriatricians, specialists, pharmacists, dieticians, and nurse case managers (Thompson, 2002).

Project evaluations for SHMO I generally found the effects of the program to be limited in terms of cost and enrollee outcomes, although the methodologies employed by these analyses have been criticized (Atkinson, 2001; Manton et al., 1993). A study by Manton and colleagues found that SHMOs produced better outcomes for healthy and acutely ill enrollees than for impaired persons or for acutely ill persons with chronic impairments (Manton et al., 1993). The same report found that neither the long-term care services provided by the SHMOs nor their integration with acute care appeared to be effective. An evaluation conducted for CMS in 2002 found that payments to SHMOs were 15 percent to 30 percent higher than standard HMOs would have received for the same enrollees (Thompson, 2002). Another study, however, found that the termination of the Minneapolis SHMO project in 1994 was associated with a 40 percent increase in long-term institutional placement, indicating that the program had been effective in its primary objective of keeping older adults in community-based settings (Fischer et al., 2003).

Other Medicare Demonstrations

In addition to the demonstration projects described above, the Medicare program has developed and implemented a number of other demonstration projects that have tested new ways of delivering care to older adults. CMS's demonstration authority allows the agency to waive certain rules concerning which services are covered and how they are reimbursed in

---

[3]*Omnibus Budget Reconciliation Act of 1990.* Public Law 101-508. 101st Congress. (1990).

order for the agency to be able to test and measure the effects of potential program changes (Thompson, 2002).

Table 3-1 offers details on several of the demonstration projects. These demonstrations were designed to encourage coordinated care for chronically ill beneficiaries and to address some of the structural impediments to providing appropriate care for these beneficiaries. The designs of many of the projects were based on disease-management programs developed in the private sector (CMS, 2007b). The hope was that the demonstration projects would point to ways to improve treatment plans, reduce avoidable admissions, and promote improved patient outcomes without increasing cost. Unfortunately, the majority of these demonstration projects had little effect on patient outcomes and produced no cost savings. In fact, in a number of cases Medicare expenditures increased as a result of the project, in part because of expansion of services and in part because the specific savings that had been projected were not realized. As discussed previously, the mixture of results makes it difficult to pinpoint which elements of these models are most likely to lead to successful improvements in patient care.

The evaluations revealed that the demonstration projects encountered a number of difficulties, including problems enrolling patients in the demonstrations, low levels of enthusiasm for the program by patients and physicians, inexperienced or inadequately trained staff, and hardware and software problems with patient-monitoring equipment (Guterman, 2007). Still, considering the evidence that the Medicare program often falls short on various dimensions of quality and efficiency, the need to research and develop alternative approaches to care delivery remains paramount.

Despite this need, however, relatively little investment has been made in the research and development of innovative models of care that could improve outcomes or lower costs, particularly as compared with how much is spent each year on the health care of older adults. In fiscal year 2007, for example, the total budget for Medicare operations was more than $2 billion; less than 2 percent of this was spent on research, demonstration, and evaluation (Table 3-2). In fact, in recent years Medicare has spent a decreasing proportion of its operations budget on research, demonstration, and evaluation. This low investment is even more startling when compared to the hundreds of billions of dollars spent on Medicare benefits. In order to improve the way that care is delivered, more investments will be needed to explore newer and more efficient models of care.

Medicaid Demonstration Projects

Many state Medicaid programs have developed innovative models of care to integrate services, to improve care coordination, and most notably, to allow individuals a larger role in shaping the services that they receive. In

TABLE 3-1 Findings from Select Medicare Demonstration Projects

Project (Start Year)	Purpose	Outcomes
Care Management for High Cost Beneficiaries (2005)	To study various care-management models for high-cost beneficiaries in the traditional Medicare fee-for-service program who have one or more chronic diseases (e.g., Texas Senior Trails; Health Buddy).	Ongoing. Will review 3-year pilot programs implemented by six Care Management Organizations (CMOs).
Community Nursing Organization Demonstration (2003)	Tested the use of nurse case managers to coordinate care and provide enrollees with a more flexible array of services, such as prevention and health promotion, under a capitated arrangement.	Enrollment did not affect health status or utilization of services covered under the traditional Medicare benefit package. Total expenditures for treatment groups were significantly greater than the control group.
Medicare Disease Management Demonstration (2003)	To evaluate the effect of disease-management services, coupled with a prescription drug benefit, for those with advanced-stage congestive heart failure, diabetes, or coronary disease.	The three demonstration sites encountered difficulties identifying and enrolling beneficiaries, and, given the magnitude of the risk they faced, the project was discontinued prior to the intended conclusion date.
Medicare Coordinated Care Demonstration (2001)	To test whether providing coordinated-care services to Medicare beneficiaries with complex chronic conditions can yield better patient outcomes without increasing program costs.	Interim evaluation found increases in beneficiary education but no effect on satisfaction, patient adherence, self care, or Medicare expenditures. There was a small but statistically significant reduction in the proportion of patients hospitalized during the year after enrollment.
Informatics for Diabetes Education and Telemedicine (IDEAtel) (2000)	To test the use of telemedicine networks to improve primary and preventive care for Medicare beneficiaries with diabetes who live in underserved inner-city and rural areas of New York.	Interim evaluation shows the project had favorable effects on diabetes control and care, use of recommended medications, and communication with health care providers about diet and care. The demonstration did not generate savings to the Medicare program and was costly to implement ($8,200 to $8,900 per enrollee per year).
Medicare Case Management (Early Coordinated Care) Demonstrations (1995)	To provide case-management services to beneficiaries with catastrophic illnesses and high medical costs.	Despite high levels of satisfaction among the beneficiaries who participated, there was no improvement in self care or health. Medicare spending was not reduced.

SOURCE: CMS, 2008a.

TABLE 3-2 Appropriations History of Medicare Research, Demonstration, and Evaluation as Compared to Medicare Operations

Fiscal Year	Research, Demonstration, and Evaluation (in Millions)	Total Medicare Operations (in Millions)	Research, Demonstration, and Evaluation as Percent of Medicare Operations
2003	$73.7	$1,666.7	4.42%
2004	$77.8	$1,701.0	4.57%
2005	$77.5	$1,730.9	4.48%
2006	$69.4[a]	$2,200.8[b]	3.15%
2007	$41.5	$2,210.6[c]	1.88%
2008[d]	$33.7	$2,303.6	1.46%

[a]Includes Deficit Reduction Act funding.
[b]Includes Deficit Reduction Act and the Secretary's Section 202 Transfer Authority funding.
[c]Includes Tax Relief and Health Care Act of 2006 funding.
[d]2008 reflects the President's FY 2008 budget.
SOURCE: DHHS, 2007.

Maine, for example, Medicaid beneficiaries are referred to a consumer-run independent living center, which assesses their preferences and their ability to self-direct care, trains them with regard to hiring and managing their own services, and provides a list of available workers (Benjamin, 2001). Oregon's Medicaid program allows individuals, with guidance from case managers, to hire and fire workers as they choose. An evaluation of these models found that patients had greater satisfaction with services, increased feelings of empowerment, and better perceived quality of life (Stone, 2000). There is limited evidence, however, that focuses specifically on older adults and the effect that these programs have on them. Four of these programs are described below.

Arizona Long-Term Care System (Arizona)

The Arizona Long-Term Care System (ALTCS) was developed in 1989 to provide care to Medicaid-eligible individuals who are at risk of institutionalization in a long-term care setting, typically older adults and disabled persons. ALTCS is a capitated, mandatory long-term care system in which services are integrated by a managed care organization into a single delivery package. For those beneficiaries also eligible for Medicare, providers must bill those services to Medicare and are paid through the FFS system. Services offered under ALTCS include acute medical care, behavioral health services, and case management. Services are also covered for care delivered in nursing homes, in the home setting, and in assisted-living facilities.

ALTCS pays for part of the costs for room and board, medical and hospital care, and prescription drugs.

An evaluation of ALTCS showed that, compared to New Mexico Medicaid (a traditional Medicaid program), ALTCS provided quality care at lower costs (McCall, 1997). Program savings averaged 18 percent annually, totaling $290 million in savings for medical services alone. ALTCS beneficiaries had more medical visits but fewer hospital days than beneficiaries of New Mexico Medicaid. During the first 13 years of the program, however, the quality of care was found to be higher in the traditional Medicaid program. This program is still active in Arizona.

Senior Health Options (Minnesota)

The Minnesota Senior Health Options (SHO) program was adopted with support from the Robert Wood Johnson Foundation. SHO offers enrollees a package of acute and long-term care services through a choice of managed care plans. The state is essentially treated like a health plan that contracts with CMS to provide services; the state then subcontracts with health plans that combine services from Medicare and Medicaid into one integrated benefit package for enrollees (CMS, 2004; Malone et al., 2004). At the center of the initiative is coordination of care for dually eligible beneficiaries who live in institutions or who live in the community but meet institutional placement criteria. Evaluations indicate that enrollees in the program had fewer hospitalizations and emergency room visits (Kane et al., 2004) and were more likely to receive preventive services (Kane and Homyak, 2003); however, capitation rates were higher than they would be under fee-for-service. The program, which began in 1997, continues to operate and became a statewide option in 2005 (Tritz, 2006).

Family Care (Wisconsin)

The goals of Wisconsin's Family Care program are to improve patient choices regarding type of residence and service supports that enrollees receive, improve access to services and quality of care, and achieve cost efficiencies (Justice, 2003). The program has two significant design features: a single entry point for patients (an Aging and Disability Resource Center) and patient-centered services. The center provides patients with advice and access to long-term support options, screening to determine eligibility for publicly financed services, and pre-admission consultations for those entering nursing homes or residential care facilities. The centers are staffed by social workers and nurses who are supported by direct-care workers and volunteers. Together these workers conduct a comprehensive assessment of patients' needs, preferences, and values.

Care-management organizations (CMOs) manage the Family Care benefits, providing services in community, residential, and institutional settings (Justice, 2003). Funding from multiple programs (e.g., home- and community-based waiver services, state general-revenue-funded programs, and Medicare long-term care services) are consolidated into the single Family Care program, and CMOs are paid a capitated rate. This creates an incentive for the CMOs to provide support to enrollees in their homes rather than in institutions. The program also allows enrollees to have a high level of self-direction, organizing services around enrollees' unique needs and preferences rather than strictly by allowable services or designated providers.

Through its focus on social outcomes, the program has succeeded in increasing choice and access and improving quality, but early results found no effect on claims-based measures, such as utilization, and it was not possible to determine the cost-effectiveness of the program (Alecxih et al., 2003). Regardless, enrollees did not experience a decline in service levels at the start of the program, and the demand for services from the centers has been much stronger than anticipated (Medstat, 2003).

Cash and Counseling

Under the national cash and counseling demonstration project conducted in three states, individuals received a monthly allowance (in the form of direct cash payments) to purchase disability-related goods and services. Enrollees were provided with counseling and financial assistance to help them plan and manage their choices. An evaluation found that the program improved satisfaction and the quality of life for enrollees and caregivers, reduced most unmet needs among enrollees without adversely affecting health or safety, and resulted in a reduction in nursing-home and other long-term care costs (Foster et al., 2003; RWJF, 2006). Costs were somewhat higher for enrollees because they were receiving more of the care that they were authorized to receive. Similar programs are now being adopted in 12 more states, and federal waiver authority is no longer required for states to implement cash and counseling programs.

One unusual aspect of these efforts is that they often allow patients to hire informal caregivers as their workers. Critics suggest that this allowance presents an opportunity for fraud and abuse and worry that costs will soar if informal caregivers currently providing unpaid care start to demand payment for their services (Stone, 2000). Others contend that the allowance will expand the pool of available caregivers and that the services provided may be more in line with patients' preferences (Benjamin, 2001). Evidence of the effect of hiring relatives is not clear. One study found that about one in five paid informal caregivers had not been providing care prior to the formal hiring. The study also found that beneficiaries had a greater sense of security and choice in hiring a family member. Overall, the results of the cash and counseling demonstration, which allowed enrollees to hire family, indicate that the project did not result in misuse of Medicaid funding.

Features of Innovative Models

The committee did not attempt to rank the models described above or to recommend one model of care over another. In fact, little evidence exists that one might use to rate the relative effectiveness of these different approaches. Typically, evaluations focus on whether a single model proved to be successful rather than identifying which of several models produced the strongest results. The committee concluded that no single one of the models described above would be sufficient to meet the needs of all older adults. Instead, a variety of models will need to be employed to meet the targeted needs of older adults. For example, preventive home visits may be too costly to expand to all older persons, the majority of whom may not even require that level of care. Similarly, caregiver-support programs may not be sufficient for older adults with more intensive needs. The health care needs of the older population are diverse, and addressing those needs will require varying models of care. Fortunately, the models described above have generally been successful in enrolling mainly those older adults who would best benefit from the expanded services.

After reviewing the evidence on a number of different models of care, the committee concluded that some of the models with the strongest evidence of success in improving care quality, health-related outcomes, or efficiency have common features which may contribute to their success (Table 3-3).

The model components described in Table 3-3 have shown positive outcomes, at least in some circumstances, but these findings need to be interpreted with caution. First, the list is derived from an examination of only those interventions that have been rigorously evaluated and published in the peer-reviewed literature; many others have not yet been thoroughly evaluated. Furthermore, because the models have proved successful in only certain settings, one cannot be certain that they will experience the same success if they are adopted more widely. Adoption of a model in rural areas or at community hospitals, for instance, may not yield the same results as when the initiatives were undertaken at urban academic medical centers. Similarly, there is limited information on the scalability of the models, that is, on whether they could be successfully applied to a much larger population of patients. Finally, the literature review commissioned by the committee focused on identifying interventions that have produced successful results. In some cases, alternative evaluations of the same model may show

TABLE 3-3 Features of New Models (Select Research Findings Showing Positive Results)

Description	Findings in Support of the Intervention
Interdisciplinary team care. Providers from different disciplines collaboratively manage the care of a patient. These providers may include primary care physicians, registered nurses, social workers, physical therapists, pharmacists, occupational therapists, recreational therapists, dieticians, home-care providers, personal-care attendants, and drivers. The members of the team communicate regularly with each other about their patients.	Some studies demonstrated improved survival and quality of life (QOL) (improved well-being, less anxiety, and dyspnea), quality of care, health outcome scores, and patient satisfaction. Some also showed lower total costs, fewer hospital admissions, physician visits, emergency department visits, and x-rays.
Care management. In most forms a nurse or social worker provides patients (and sometimes families) a combination of health assessment, planning, education, behavioral counseling, and coordination. Their communication with primary care providers varies from frequent to rare, depending on the care-management program.	Studies examining care management for patients with heart failure demonstrated improved satisfaction, use of appropriate medications, QOL, and survival, as well as fewer hospital admissions and days.
Chronic disease self-management programs. Self-management programs are structured, time-limited interventions designed to provide health information and to empower patients to assume an active role in managing their chronic conditions. Some are led by health professionals and focus on the management of specific conditions, such as stroke, while others are led by trained laypersons and address chronic conditions more generally.	Improved QOL (psychosocial function, control of symptoms, pain, stiffness), functional autonomy (e.g., mobility, fewer bed days, walking capacity), and satisfaction. Fewer hospital admissions and days, lower coronary artery disease inpatient costs.
Pharmaceutical management. Advice about medications is provided by pharmacists to patients, either directly or through the actions of interdisciplinary teams. Recommendations are intended to encourage the safe, effective use of prescribed and over-the-counter medications.	Improved quality of care (adherence to medication guidelines), QOL (fewer symptoms), control of blood pressure, and survival. Insufficient evidence to indicate efficiency improvements.
Preventive home visits. Home visits are provided to older persons by nurses or other visitors to monitor health and functional status and to encourage self-care and appropriate use of health care services. These visitors usually visit their clients quarterly and communicate regularly with their patients' primary care providers.	Improved QOL, survival, functional autonomy. Fewer nursing-home and hospital admissions.

TABLE 3-3 Continued

Description	Findings in Support of the Intervention
Proactive rehabilitation. As a supplement to primary care, rehabilitation therapists provide outpatient assessments and interventions designed to help disabled older persons to maximize their functional autonomy, home safety, and quality of life. Most of the few existing experimental programs operate in concert with patients' primary care physicians.	Improved QOL (less pain, fewer symptoms, decreased fear of falling, improved self efficacy), functional autonomy (improved activities of daily living [ADLs] and instrumental activities of daily living [IADLs], functional independence, chance of remaining at home), and survival. Insufficient evidence to indicate efficiency improvements.
Caregiver education and support. These programs are designed to help the informal caregivers of older persons with chronic conditions such as dementia and stroke. Led by psychologists, social workers, or rehabilitation therapists, these programs provide varying combinations of health information, training, access to professional and community resources, emotional support, counseling, and coping strategies. They communicate with primary care providers primarily through their clients.	Improved QOL (e.g., mood) and physical functioning of care recipients. Lower total cost of care, delayed and fewer nursing home admissions.
Transitional care. Typically a nurse or an advanced-practice nurse prepares and coaches the patient and informal caregiver for the transition from hospital to home. The nurse visits the patient at home to ensure that all needed medication, equipment, and supplies are available and that the patient and caregiver know how to use them, how to self-monitor, and whom to call if problems arise. The nurse continues to monitor the situation for several weeks until the patient has returned to pre-admission status, contacting the primary care physician as needed.	Improved QOL and survival. Lower total costs, fewer hospital readmissions.

SOURCE: Boult et al., 2007.

no improvement in quality, outcomes, or efficiency. Still, the results from these evaluations give reason to be cautiously optimistic that the diffusion of models with these features could result in improved care for older adults and perhaps introduce greater efficiencies into the Medicare and Medicaid programs.

PAYING FOR NEW MODELS OF CARE

The models of care with the strongest evidence base often expand the range of services provided to older patients, for example, with the addition of social services, caregiver education and support, and preventive home visits. Yet, Medicare typically does not cover these additional services, even if evaluations indicate that they reduce costly hospitalizations or nursing-home use in the long run. This lack of coverage contributes to the failure of many models to gain widespread traction. This section reviews the way in which Medicare services are currently paid for and presents several alternatives that could be used to foster the development and implementation of new models of care.

Fee-for-Service Medicare

One major problem is that brief visits are a poor way of managing chronic conditions even though care for chronic conditions is the most common reason that Medicare patients seek physician care (Hing et al., 2006; McGlynn et al., 2003; Scherger, 2005). Furthermore, under the FFS system, more visits lead to higher physician and hospital revenues regardless of the quality or efficacy of the services being delivered (MedPAC, 2006). Payment is directed to individual physicians and emphasizes treatment for in-person care, which serves as a barrier to care coordination. This disincentive is particularly significant since most Medicare patients seek care from multiple providers (MedPAC, 2006). Furthermore, such a payment mechanism provides no financial incentive for health care providers to deliver services that extend beyond the typical office visit, such as ongoing patient education to teach older adults how to better manage their chronic conditions between visits (Brown et al., 2007).

Medicare is required by statute to apply its rules uniformly to all providers, limiting its ability to reward exemplary performance (Berenson and Horvath, 2003). CMS cannot provide additional payment or greater flexibility to organizations that offer additional services to patients, even if they are targeting frail older adults or some other particularly needy group of older adults. Overall, the traditional FFS system limits innovation in care delivery.

Shifting the focus of care delivery away from acute care is difficult in part because of the rather complicated process that CMS must follow in order to add coverage for newer services, such as preventive home visits or care coordination. CMS must determine that the service fits into a statuto-rily established benefit category and that it is "reasonable and necessary" in order to diagnose or treat an illness, and then it must assign the service an appropriate payment code. Many services that are critical components of new models of care would have difficulty fitting into these criteria. For example, neither patient education to promote self-management nor interdisciplinary team meetings to discuss patients' health status fit easily into a statutorily established benefit category (Berenson and Horvath, 2003). Furthermore, many geriatric care models require the services of care managers, typically nurses or social workers, but these workers often do not qualify for Medicare reimbursement. Statutory changes will be needed to make it possible to pay for these services.

Medicare Advantage

Nineteen percent of Medicare beneficiaries are enrolled in Medicare Advantage (MA), Medicare's managed care program. MA's capitated payment system puts health plans at financial risk, which gives them an incentive to identify high-risk enrollees and assist them in averting medical complications and also to promote continued good health among older beneficiaries who are not chronically ill. The goal of this approach is to encourage health plans to promote appropriate, cost-effective care across settings (Berenson and Horvath, 2003).

Capitated payments allow for greater innovation in care delivery and can promote the adoption of new models of care. For example, Kaiser Permanente's Medicare HMO has been able to hire greater numbers of geriatricians and increase payments for their services. In addition, MA plans offer benefits beyond those that are available in the traditional FFS system, including preventive dental services. Care coordination, which is generally not available to beneficiaries under FFS, is routinely offered by MA plans and is administratively easier to perform under capitation because of the plans' provider networks. Plans are required to use any cost savings they realize to provide benefits beyond those required by the Medicare program.

Studies indicate that older adults who choose to enroll in MA are generally healthier and have lower medical costs than FFS beneficiaries, and at least one study suggests that the incentive for MA plans to maintain this member composition may persist despite the implementation of risk adjustment (MedPAC, 2007a). CMS began phasing in risk-adjustment payments in 2004, and by 2007 payments were based entirely on risk-adjusted rates (Berenson and Horvath, 2003). At the same time, CMS also included a hold-harmless adjustment so that plan payments would not decline due to risk adjustment. In fact, payments to MA plans are about 12 percent higher than the average FFS costs in the same area (Kaiser Family Foundation, 2007). That difference is expected to decrease as the hold-harmless adjustment is phased out through 2011 (MedPAC, 2007b).

Although capitation appears to be a reasonable means to incorporate cost-effective new models of care into practice, this promise has not been fully realized. Based on recent experience, health plans have typically contracted with all available physicians and hospitals rather than developing tighter networks, and the quality of care for individuals with chronic disease in FFS and managed care has ended up being roughly equivalent (Norwalk, 2007). However, a review of studies conducted by Miller and Luft found that enrollees in Medicare HMOs reported worse results on measures of access to care and patient satisfaction (Miller and Luft, 2002). In short, considerable debate still exists about whether the added funds provided to MA plans have been worth the investment.

New Financing Mechanisms

Given the challenges associated with traditional FFS Medicare and MA, a new model of payment is needed to support effective models of care and the integration across various settings of service that are necessary to prevent or delay declines in functional and health status for older adults (Biles et al., 2006; Guterman and Serber, 2007). Even with start-up funding from a foundation, insurer, or provider organization, the long-term sustainability of such services is limited in the absence of appropriate reimbursement from Medicare and other payers.

It is beyond the scope of this report to recommend a specific method of reimbursement to support new models of care, but the committee did identify several promising methods. In general, it is important to note that during the research and demonstration phase of a new model CMS typically sets up financial arrangements that differ significantly from the traditional FFS arrangement. In order to move from the demonstration stage to widespread adoption, the general financing system will also need to be altered, likely requiring that some sort of capitated arrangement be put in place.

Special Needs Plans

As a result of the Medicare Modernization Act (MMA) of 2003,[4] special needs plans (SNPs) were created within the MA program. SNPs can target their enrollment to high-needs patients such as institutionalized beneficiaries, dually eligible beneficiaries, or beneficiaries with severe or disabling conditions (CMS, 2007c). Targeted enrollment allows plans to design clinical programs that can accommodate those with distinct health needs, which can potentially result in reduced hospitalization and institutionalization (CMS, 2007a). SNPs are paid under the same system (risk-adjusted capitation) and regulated in the same manner as other MA plans.

The number of SNPs has been growing rapidly, increasing from 276

---

[4]*Medicare Modernization Act of 2003.* Public Law 108-173. 108th Congress. (2003).

in 2006 to 775 in 2008. As of November 2007, SNPs had enrolled more than 1 million Medicare beneficiaries (Harrison and Podulka, 2007). SNPs were reauthorized through the end of 2009,[5] including a 1-year moratorium for new SNPs. To evaluate the effect of using SNPs, CMS contracted with the National Committee for Quality Assurance (NCQA) to develop SNP-specific measures based on those used for the Healthcare Effectiveness Data and Information Set (HEDIS). Measures specific to the care of older adults include glaucoma screening, osteoporosis management, and use of high-risk medication (NCQA, 2008). SNPs were required to report on these measures by June 30, 2008; data regarding the results of this evaluation were not available at the time this report was prepared.

MedPAC Approaches

A number of additional proposals to support new models of care have been developed. MedPAC proposed two approaches for enhancing care coordination in Medicare FFS (Stone, 2000). Under the first approach, group practices or integrated delivery systems would furnish care-coordination services to high-risk patients (e.g., a nurse care manager would share space with the physicians). These group practices would be responsible for investing in information technology and in a nurse-manager infrastructure in order to better manage care. Under the second approach, solo or small group practices would refer high-risk patients to an affiliated care-management organization that would employ the care-manager nurses and have information systems to assess patient severity levels and target interventions. Medicare would pay the care-coordination entity (either the group practice or the care-management organization) for services, and that payment would be tied to cost savings and quality goals. Payment would be either shared savings or an at-risk care managed fee. Medicare would also provide an incentive payment to physicians to encourage them to collaborate with the care managers.

Addition of Medicare Benefits

Another way to support new models of care would be for Congress to create additional Medicare benefits. For example, one proposal calls for the creation of a modified home visit benefit for beneficiaries in need of extended home-nursing and personal-care services (Berenson and Horvath, 2003). The new, lower-level home health benefit would not be as intensive as the current home health benefit, but it could allow instead for physicians

---

[5]*Medicare, Medicaid, and SCHIP Extension Act of 2007.* Public Law 110-173. 110th Congress. (2007).

to authorize their nurses or physician assistants to periodically conduct home visits for patients unable to come into the office. It would cover such services as medical assessment, medical monitoring, and medication management. Delivery of such services would allow the physician to receive more direct knowledge than could be obtained if similar services were provided through a separate home health agency. This approach of legislating additional benefits could potentially be applied to other types of services, such as chronic-disease self-management training and caregiver education and support.

Advanced Medical Homes

Finally, a more radical departure from the current FFS system is a proposal that calls for the creation of advanced medical homes through comprehensive payment for primary care (Goroll et al., 2007). In this system physicians would be paid a risk-adjusted, per-member, per-month fee that would cover care coordination and medical services provided to the patient (Berenson, 2007). Payment would be considerably higher than current FFS or MA payments, allowing practices a greater opportunity to support different models of care. Participating practices would be required to undergo structural and organizational changes (e.g., the adoption of interoperable electronic health records with decision support and the use of interdisciplinary teams) that follow established standards. A portion of the payment would then be based on performance.

Risk adjustment would make it less likely that physicians would avoid high-risk or psychosocially disadvantaged patients and would also influence the pay-for-performance goals (Goroll et al., 2007). Several validated diagnosis-based models of risk adjustment exist and have been modified for payments to health plans (Ash et al., 2000; Kronick et al., 2000; Newhouse et al., 1997). Those models would need to be further modified for the practice level and need to include the spectrum of risk determinants, including patient behaviors. Although costs would initially be high, proponents of this revised payment system believe that long-term costs would be tempered by reductions in administrative costs, inefficiencies, and overutilization.

This proposal differs from some capitated payment systems in that physicians would not be at risk for hospital, specialist, and ancillary service costs. Appropriate utilization of services would be achieved through the use of evidence-based guidelines and decision-support systems, and the pay-for-performance bonuses would be based both on outcomes and efficiency. If responsibility for a patient is transferred to a specialist—for example, in the case of a patient with cancer—the specialist may receive some or all of the per-member, per-month payment.

Additional payments to practices under this proposal provide the means to offer new services or deliver care in a new manner (e.g., preventive home visits and use of interdisciplinary teams).

It should be noted that CMS is implementing a new Medical Home demonstration program in 2008 that is similar in many ways to the advanced medical home concept. According to the statutory language, physicians will be required to (1) provide ongoing support, oversight, and guidance to implement an integrated, coherent, cross-discipline plan for ongoing medical care, which will be developed in partnership with the patient and all other physicians, medical personnel, and agencies (e.g., home health agencies) providing care to the patient; (2) use evidence-based medicine and clinical decision support tools to guide decision making; (3) use health information technology (e.g., remote monitoring and patient registries) to monitor and track the health status of patients and to provide them with enhanced and convenient access to services; and (4) encourage patients to engage in the management of their own health through education and support systems (CMS, 2008b). Participating physicians will be reimbursed under the traditional Medicare Physician Fee Schedule but will also be eligible for a care-management fee for each participating beneficiary under their care and a bonus based on the achievement of savings and quality goals (ACP, 2006). However, while the concept of an advanced medical home was intended to be applicable to all individuals, the demonstration project will be limited to those with multiple chronic illnesses.

DISSEMINATION OF NEW MODELS OF CARE

Identifying successful models of care is just the first challenge in improving the delivery of services to older adults. Successful models need to be replicated and incorporated widely into practice in order to reach a large patient population, and, in general, the adoption of best practices has occurred very slowly in the health care sector as well as other industries (Berwick, 2003). Indeed, evidence shows that innovations that have been demonstrated to improve the quality of patient care can take more than 17 years to become common practice (Balas and Boren, 2000). Little is known about the best way to promote the exchange of information concerning how to improve the quality of care (IOM, 2006a). Rogers' diffusion of innovations theory defined five categories related to the adopters of new practices:

- Innovators, who embrace new ideas
- Early adopters, who are the opinion leaders of a community
- Early majority, who are convinced by the early adopters to adopt the innovation

- Late majority, who adopt the innovation mostly due to peer pressure
- Laggards, who are skeptical and resistant to change

This theory suggests that the adoption of new ideas by a select few will lead to a process of natural diffusion through which ideas spread throughout a community. Rogers also described how perceptions of the innovations can contribute to the adoption of a new practice. These perceptions include

- relative advantage (comparison of the innovation to current practice);
- compatibility (how the innovation fits with the adopter's values, needs, etc.);
- complexity (difficulty of adopting the innovation);
- triability (if the innovation can be tested before full investment); and
- observability (whether others have successfully adopted the innovation) (Rogers, 2003).

Aside from these characteristics, a variety of other factors affect the adoption of new ideas, including both external factors (e.g., financial incentives and politics) and internal factors (e.g., competing priorities and resources) (IOM, 2006a). Finally, successful adoption of innovations demands commitment and a readiness for change as well as the support of organizational leadership in the adopting institution.

In the case of new models of care, dissemination has traditionally been slow and many models have been proved to be unsustainable (Leipzig et al., 2002; Reuben, 2002; Wolff and Boult, 2005). According to Rogers's theory, a number of factors, if present, can be expected to improve the perception and potential appeal of new models of care for older patients. They include

- the model having an intuitive appeal;
- the existence of a strong evidence base demonstrating benefits for patients;
- potential cost savings;
- patient dissatisfaction with existing care; and
- secular trends, such as the aging of the population, recognition of the importance of managing chronic disease, and the move toward community-based care (Leff, 2007; Rogers, 2003).

A number of factors can also diminish the potential appeal of new models. They include

- information gaps in the literature that leave potential adopters with insufficient detail about the model, including a lack of information about such things as the optimal target population, staffing requirements, and the training and supervision necessary for staff;
- an evidence base that focuses on patient-related outcomes but not on other outcomes relevant to adopting organizations;
- the existence of few or no financial incentives or even of significant short-term financial disincentives, such as substantial startup costs;
- lack of awareness by patients and families of the potential personal value of these models;
- reliance on teams of providers, which makes the models complex and difficult to implement;
- riskiness caused by the model having been implemented and observed in only a few other locations; and
- poor alignment with the circumstances of a potential adopter's local health system (Frank et al., 2003).

Experiences with Individual Models of Care

While the published literature on the dissemination challenges associated with the adoption of specific models of care for older adults is generally limited, some information is available on the dissemination experiences of the IMPACT and PACE models (described above) as well as on the Hospital Elder Life Program (HELP), a model of care designed to prevent delirium and functional decline in hospitalized older adults (Inouye et al., 2006).

Experience from the IMPACT Model

The IMPACT model for depression treatment was originally implemented between 1999 and 2001 in 18 clinics nationwide; by 2007, 67 individuals or organizations had implemented or were pursuing IMPACT or key components of the program (IMPACT Implementation Center, 2007). The spread of the IMPACT model, though somewhat limited, has been aided by the IMPACT Implementation Center, which is funded by private foundations and provides resources and technical assistance to organizations seeking to adopt the IMPACT model.

Although it has not been widely adopted, IMPACT has served as a foundation for the creation of other models, such as the Prevention of Suicide in Primary Care Elderly: Collaborative Trial (PROSPECT), sponsored by the National Institute of Mental Health (Bruce et al., 2004). Like IMPACT, PROSPECT provides depression-care management to older patients in primary-care settings in an effort to reduce the burden of depressive symptoms, remove suicidal ideation, and improve health-related quality of life. Twenty practices in New York, Philadelphia, and Pittsburgh provided a total of 598 participants with either treatment as usual or depression care management similar to that employed in IMPACT. An evaluation of PROSPECT in a 53-month follow up found that the program resulted in significantly better response and remission rates for major depression, faster resolution of suicidal ideation, and reduced mortality.

Despite the effectiveness of models that provide depression treatment in primary care settings, financial and organizational barriers have made the interventions difficult to sustain in clinical practice (Barry and Frank, 2006; Frank et al., 2003; Pincus et al., 2003). The cost of providing IMPACT care for one individual is approximately $580 per year (Bachman et al., 2006), but capitated payment creates an incentive for primary care physicians to deliver fewer services, not more. Further, additional payment (under FFS or capitation) is not available for the use of depression-care managers in the primary care setting. Behavioral health carve-outs also serve to reinforce the disincentives to treat depression in the primary care setting. Carve-outs allow primary care physicians to refer patients for specialized care without penalty, and they preclude the physician from billing for mental health procedures. The higher co-payments charged to patients receiving mental health care services also discourage utilization. These factors all serve as barriers to the adoption of models such as IMPACT or PROSPECT, even if care in the primary care setting is cost-effective or most appropriate for patients.

Furthermore, physician education and training does not always promote or encourage depression care in the primary care setting (Pincus et al., 2003). Behavioral health training is limited and highly variable in both family medicine and general internal medicine, and it is not made clear during physician training whether primary care providers are responsible for providing behavioral health services. Primary care providers may view diagnostic systems as too complex to implement (Pincus et al., 2003) and may feel little pressure to implement depression care models in the absence of demand from patients or payers. Eliminating the current disparities in mental health copayments would be one way to increase patient demand.

Experience of the PACE Model

The initial success of the PACE approach led Congress in 1997 to designate PACE as a permanent Medicare provider and to give state Medicaid agencies the option to include PACE as a Medicaid benefit (Degruy,

1996). By 2004 Congress had authorized 180 PACE programs, but while approximately 3 million older adults were eligible for PACE in that year, only about 10,000 were being served by a PACE program. Currently 42 PACE programs are operating in 22 states (National PACE Association, 2007). Overall, the growth of PACE has not met expectations.

The initial PACE programs received significant start-up funding from private foundations, allowing the development of many independent, freestanding programs (Gross et al., 2004). But once grant funds became unavailable, only large health care organizations, such as hospitals, health care systems, and long-term care systems, had the funds to make the initial investment. Securing facilities and staffing for the programs requires significant capital expenditures (Gross et al., 2004). Organizations attempting to set up a PACE program may also have difficulty in collecting an adequate patient base because of geography (i.e., sparse populations in rural areas) or because of an insufficient number of adults in a community who qualify for the program.

A further hurdle has been local labor shortages, particularly in nursing and therapies, which have made it difficult to fill open positions even when funding is available. On the other hand, the environment and regular hours offered by PACE programs have generally made it easier than it otherwise would have been to attract and retain staff. Marketing the programs has also been difficult in some cases. Many PACE programs operate in competitive, service-rich environments which offer a number of other service options for older adults. Moreover, PACE centers receive a combined capitated rate of approximately $4,900 per member per month from Medicare and Medicaid. For older adults who are not eligible for Medicaid, this cost is often prohibitively high (Hansen, 2007).

The National PACE Association, largely funded by private foundations, offers a number of resources and technical assistance to organizations that wish to establish PACE programs. The association also awards grants to states to expand their capacity to administer PACE programs. In addition, Congress has appropriated funding to the Health Resources and Services Administration (HRSA) to support technical assistance and assess the staffing and training needs of rural providers in developing PACE programs.

Experience of the Hospital Elder Life Program (HELP)

As noted above, the HELP is a model of care designed to prevent delirium in hospitalized older adults. Delirium is defined as an acute decline in cognitive functioning and attention, and it is the most frequent complication of hospitalization in older persons, being estimated to occur in 14 percent to 56 percent of older hospitalized adults (Leslie et al., 2005). Delirium is also associated with increased morbidity, mortality, and health care costs.

The HELP interdisciplinary team consists of a geriatric nurse-specialist, a specially trained "Elder Life Nurse Specialist," a geriatrician, and trained volunteers. The Elder Life Nurse Specialist is the program and volunteer coordinator and is responsible for screening and enrolling patients, and keeping track of the program's adherence to the HELP guidelines. The Elder Life Nurse Specialist has specialized training in geriatrics and carries out nursing-related assessments and intervention protocols targeted toward six delirium risk factors (cognitive impairment, sleep deprivation, immobility, visual impairment, hearing impairment, and dehydration) (Inouye et al., 2006). Evaluations of HELP indicate that it is effective in preventing delirium and functional decline, and that it is cost effective in hospitals and long-term care settings (Inouye et al., 2006).

In 2000, a HELP Dissemination Program was established with funding from private foundations. A dissemination team (a full-time nurse practitioner, 10 percent time for the geriatrician who developed the program, and 25 percent time for a dissemination project director) provided training materials, offered ongoing support for HELP hospital staff implementing HELP, and held an annual conference for HELP sites. Additionally, a HELP website was created to make resources on HELP readily available to interested organizations.

Like IMPACT and PACE, dissemination of HELP has been modest. The dissemination team assisted 17 sites with the implementation of HELP, and several more sites have since adopted HELP. Through interviews with HELP staff at nine sites, researchers identified six challenges associated with implementation of the program: (1) gaining internal support for the program despite differing requirements and goals of administration and clinical staff, (2) ensuring effective clinician leadership, (3) integrating with existing geriatric programs, (4) balancing program fidelity with hospital-specific circumstances, (5) documenting positive outcomes of the program despite limited resources for data collection and analysis, and (6) maintaining the momentum of implementation in the face of unrealistic time frames and limited resources (Bradley et al., 2004a). A second study was conducted to identify key elements that make it easier to sustain the program. The researchers identified three factors: the presence of clinical leadership, the ability and willingness to adapt the original HELP protocols to local hospital circumstances and constraints, and the ability to obtain longer-term resources and funding for HELP (Bradley et al., 2005).

Like many other models, HELP requires the delivery of additional clinical services that are not typically reimbursed under Medicare, and the diffusion of HELP has largely depended upon staff funded specifically to disseminate the program (Bradley et al., 2004b).

Fostering the Dissemination of New Models of Care

One of the major challenges to the adoption of a new model is that it can require collaboration among a variety of stakeholders, including public and private insurers, health systems and hospitals, health care regulators, and practicing professionals. Much of the research on the dissemination of innovations has focused on physicians, with little consideration for the role of other workers. The Medicare payment system itself presents many barriers, including the focus on provider-specific reimbursement, the limitations on who can bill for services, and the complex regulatory environment that makes legislative changes difficult. Additionally, the health care workforce may lack sufficient numbers of providers to fully staff these models.

Contextual factors, such as the challenges in changing the cultures of health care organizations and gaining internal support for adoption from the organization's leadership, are also critical to dissemination, but such factors are not well understood. Creating culture change in health care settings requires that organizations and individuals consider better ways to deliver care, including changing the ways that health care personnel function (Shields, 2005). Additionally, when implementing new models, health care organizations need to become effective learning organizations. That is, they need to be able to learn from their experiences and change course as a result of that learning. In 1990 Senge defined the characteristics of successful learning organizations (Senge, 1990). They include

- systems thinking (determination of how individual parts of the system interact);
- personal mastery (recognition by the individual of his or her role in the system);
- mental models (examination of individual perceptions and willingness to change);
- shared vision (development of a common goal); and
- team learning (enhancement of individual capabilities to achieve the shared vision).

These learning organizations need strong leaders who are committed to changing the system, ongoing dialogue among all members of the system, and a commitment to continuous quality improvement, including the ability to learn from mistakes (IOM, 2007). In addition to dealing with institutional resistance to culture change, health care organizations that are attempting to change their vision of how care is delivered needs to take into account public perceptions of the use of alternative models and also the types of workers they need to carry out that vision.

While some models are difficult to diffuse because of their inherent design, others may be hard to diffuse because of administrative or financial barriers.

The committee concluded that innovative models of care for older patients generally fall into the latter category—models that are difficult to diffuse because of administrative or financial barriers—and that these administrative and financial barriers should be addressed.

Recommendation 3-1: Payers should promote and reward the dissemination of those models of care for older adults that have been shown to be effective and efficient.

Incentives to adopt new models of care should include enhanced payments for services under these models; provision of capital for infrastructure, such as health information technology; the streamlining of administrative and regulatory requirements; and the elimination of existing impediments to the use of innovative models by older patients, such as Medicare's copayment disparity for mental health and other services.

DEVELOPMENT OF FUTURE MODELS AND FURTHER RESEARCH

The committee's commissioned review of models of care revealed several types of models that hold promise for providing high-quality and cost-effective care for older adults at several points along the care continuum. The committee supports the continued development of models in these areas. Still, as discussed previously, the evidence base on models of care for older adults remains somewhat limited, and the information regarding which models are most suitable for dissemination needs to be improved. Considering the current relative lack of investment in research and demonstration programs for new models of care, especially in comparison to annual spending on health care services, much more funding is needed to develop this evidence base. In particular, efforts should target those areas of care that demonstration programs have traditionally overlooked and should look for the most efficient ways to use the workforce in staffing new models of care.

Recommendation 3-2: Congress and foundations should significantly increase support for research and demonstration programs that

- **promote the development of new models of care for older adults in areas where few models are currently being tested, such as prevention, long-term care, and palliative care; and**
- **promote the effective use of the workforce to care for older adults.**

Relatively few models of care focus on improving the rates of utilization of preventive clinical services among older adults or address behavioral health risks, such as exercise, smoking, and weight management. This may be due in part to a misconception that older adults are too old to benefit from prevention efforts (Hansen, 2007; The John A. Hartford Foundation, 2000). In reality, however, about one-fifth of older adults have no chronic illness and are generally in very good health; models should be explored that can promote the continuation of good health for this group.

Models of long-term care appropriate for middle-class older adults should also be explored further. Many of the models tested to date have focused on dually eligible older adults and have relied upon the integration of Medicare and Medicaid financing. The median household income of older adults is approximately $28,000 per year, however, which is well above the eligibility threshold for Medicaid (Fleming, 2002).

Models of palliative care offer another example of where more research is needed. About half of families report concerns about the care provided at the end of life, particularly about the patient not receiving enough emotional support (DeNavas-Walt et al., 2007). End-of-life care varies considerably by race and ethnicity and by where a patient receives the care (Teno et al., 2004). More information is needed on the best way to improve the access to and the quality of palliative and end-of-life care.

It is important to note, however, that these three areas—preventive services, long-term care for middle-class older adults, and palliative care—are meant only as examples of the types of models that warrant development and are not meant as an exhaustive list. There are other areas where few models are currently being tested that also deserve attention.

Any such new models of care need to be tested for their appropriateness and effectiveness for special populations, such as low-income groups, racial and ethnic minorities, rural populations, and gay, lesbian, bisexual, and transgender groups. Older adults are a diverse group, with differences in language proficiencies, risks for diseases, education, acculturation, income, and family systems (e.g., dependency on adult children), all of which may affect their health and access to appropriate care. Models need to be developed that benefit diverse groups of patients.

Not only is more information needed on efficient and effective models of care, but more research is needed to determine how best to create an effective workforce. Best practices need to be developed for increasing the size of the health care workforce (e.g., through improved recruitment and retention) and expanding its capabilities (e.g., through advanced education and training). More information is needed on how the size and capabilities of the health care workforce affect patient care in terms of quality and outcomes. If care continues to be provided in the same way, there will simply not be enough providers in the coming years to deliver the care that is needed. Therefore, new research and demonstration projects should be developed to test alternative approaches that advance the use of the health care workforce, including

- programs to retain direct-care workers in nursing-home and home-care settings;
- models of recruiting older volunteers to help care for older persons; and
- financial incentives to increase the availability of informal caregivers.

The challenges associated with caring for an aging society are not unique to the United States. Most other countries around the world are also experiencing increased demand for health care and social services due to increases in elderly and disabled populations (WHO, 2003). Many have been struggling with same issues of how to improve quality, organization, and resources for such care (Kodner, 2004). While some have successfully managed to address these issues, it is difficult to draw from the experiences of other countries given the very different nature of each health system's organizational and financial structures.

As the United States goes forward in developing new models of care, however, some lessons may be drawn from international efforts. Countries that have successfully addressed these challenges have several common attributes associated with their efforts. Among them are administrative consolidation (the reorganization of key functions, such as client assessment, care planning, service coordination, quality management and financial oversight, into a single agency at the level closest to the target population), co-location of services (reducing service fragmentation by locating multiple elder care agencies in single service centers), and service-enriched housing (providing housing situations or physical environments that accommodate each patient's individual health needs or preferences, allowing greater freedom in choice of care settings).

One specific lesson, for example, is the value of job delegation, which has been used successfully around the globe in various professions or populations, although not necessarily in situations related to the care of older adults. For instance, countries in Africa expanded their traditional workforce models in response to the HIV epidemic (Samb et al., 2007). In countries such as Malawi, where persons living with HIV/AIDS outnumber doctors 7,435 to 1 and nurses 286 to 1, the delegation of tasks has been essential to meeting care needs. Another example of job delegation is the way that countries such as Canada, New Zealand, Finland, and the United Kingdom developed auxiliary dental professions (e.g., an advanced dental hygienist or dental aide therapist) to solve overwhelming oral-health work-force shortages (Kravitz and Treasure, 2007).

IMPLICATIONS FOR THE WORKFORCE

As discussed previously, changing the way that health care services are delivered to older Americans will require an overall culture change by all segments of the workforce and delivery organizations, including changes in ideas about who needs to provide specific services and how those individuals need to interact with each other. Adopting new models of care will require the care teams to be flexible so that the workforce will be sufficient in both size and skill to meet the needs of older adults. While it is not possible to discuss in detail the implications of each individual model for the health care workforce for older adults, the committee determined that the models have certain common themes that demonstrate the need for the different segments of the health care workforce to adapt to changes in the way that care is delivered to older adults.

The models that have the strongest bases of evidence typically require providers of different disciplines to work together to improve the coordination of care. In addition, several of the models require providers to take on new roles and assume greater levels of responsibility. As more models depend on patients and informal caregivers being part of the health care team, these individuals will need to be given more education and training so that they can be more effective members of the team. Finally, as is true for the health care workforce as a whole, the development and use of new technologies will have implications for the health care workforce for older adults; the implications will arise not only from the need to train individuals in the use of these new technologies but also from their potential ability to assist existing health care workers in performing tasks and their potential for reducing the number of workers needed. These types of adaptations are discussed in general terms below and then in greater detail in subsequent chapters where their implications for different parts of the health care workforce are considered.

New Roles and Responsibilities

Many of the new models of care require the workforce to change its practices in various ways. For example, as discussed previously, the shah-bazim from the Green House model take on far more responsibility and are more involved in residents' lives than are traditional CNAs. They interact regularly with the residents' health care providers and alert them to changes in residents' status. Under the IMPACT program, depression-care managers are responsible for the majority of patient care and monitoring (Sibbald and Roland, 1998).

Many of these new roles and responsibilities require additional training, although the training in some cases can be provided by the hiring organization and may not require a higher educational degree. IMPACT's depression-care managers, for example, underwent a 2-day orientation session and 2-day training meetings (Wagner et al., 2001). Some models of care also require the professional providers to serve as the instructors to patients or informal caregivers.

Overall, new models of care often require all members of the care team—whether they are health care professionals, formal direct-care workers, informal caregivers, or patients—to take on added responsibilities. Cascading various patient-care responsibilities—shifting them from one type of worker to another—will be an essential tool in efforts to alleviate the projected shortages in the numbers of providers available to meet the care needs of an aging society. In some cases, the assumption of these new responsibilities will require regulatory changes, most often through the expansion of state-based definitions of scopes of work.

> Recommendation 3-3: Health care disciplines, state regulators, and employers should look to expand the roles of individuals who care for older adults with complex clinical needs at different levels of the health care system beyond the traditional scope of practice. Critical elements of this include
>
> - development of an evidence base that informs the establishment of new provider designations reflecting rising levels of responsibility and improved efficiency;
> - measurement of additional competence to attain these designations; and
> - greater professional recognition and salary commensurate with these responsibilities.

These new roles and responsibilities have implications for the workforce beyond the need for more training. First, as new and expanded roles are delineated, more will need to be done to assure the competence of those providing increased levels of care. Second, as more responsibilities are delegated by professionals to other members of the health care workforce, these professionals will have increased responsibility for management and supervision but will need to be taught the skills required for these roles. Finally, the assumption of increased responsibility, especially for direct-care workers, has been associated with greater job satisfaction, and ultimately, higher retention and potential improvement in patient outcomes. Specific examples of changing roles, delegation of responsibilities, and expanded scopes of work are discussed later in this report as they relate to each segment of the workforce.

Patients and Informal Caregivers

Some models of care introduce new and expanded roles for patients and informal caregivers and integrate those individuals into the care team. An important element of the chronic-care model is engaging patients in their health and providing them with the education and tools to make decisions about their own care and to manage it (Arehart-Treichel, 2006; Unutzer et al., 2001). As more services are delivered in home- and community-based settings, patients and informal caregivers will become even more important to the delivery of care. And, as models of care recognize the contributions needed by these individuals to improve care, more will need to be done to educate and train them in principles of self-management, proper methods of service provision (e.g., wound care and medication administration), and use of new technologies. (See Chapter 6 for more on patients and informal caregivers.)

Interdisciplinary Care

The introduction of interdisciplinary teams into care delivery will pose a number of challenges. Although in the long run the use of such teams has the potential to reduce the use of intensive health services such as hospitalization, these teams are not adequately reimbursed at this time. Furthermore, since team care requires greater effort with respect to primary care and patient monitoring, the introduction of interdisciplinary teams to manage patients may strain the existing capacity of primary care providers even further. An additional challenge is that team training is not a focus of the curriculum for many providers, so that they may be unfamiliar with this practice style (see Chapter 4). Finally, effective teams also require a certain level of respect, comfort, and trust among members, which in some cases may not be present (Boult et al., 2001; Sommers et al., 2000).

Care Coordination

As discussed in Chapter 2, the coordination of care among providers and across settings, especially during transitions, can greatly influence patient outcomes. Older adults often see multiple providers—on average, Medicare beneficiaries are treated by five physicians annually, and beneficiaries with chronic conditions (e.g., heart failure, coronary artery disease, or diabetes) see an average of 13 physicians annually (IOM, 2007). As a result, the care that these beneficiaries receive from physicians and other health care providers is often fragmented and not well coordinated. The lack of coordination stems from a variety of factors, including poor definitions of accountability, misaligned financial incentives (including the inability to reimburse for care coordination under FFS), lack of connection among information systems, and minimal training of providers in cross-site collaboration (Coleman, 2003; Coleman and Berenson, 2004; IOM, 2006b). In the 2007 IOM report *Rewarding Provider Performance*, the committee recommended that Medicare, in order to reduce fragmentation of services, encourage beneficiaries to identify a primary accountable source of care to act as that patient's care coordinator and guide the patient through the health care (IOM, 2007).

Many new models of care strive to improve care coordination, and these efforts can affect the use and development of the health care workforce. Some models, for example, require a geriatric care manager who helps patients navigate the health care system (see Chapter 4). Additionally, many efforts to improve care coordination call for enhancing communication among providers; this enhancement of communication among providers—and also between caregivers and patients—will require providers to change their practice patterns in a variety of ways. Furthermore, as patients and their families assume more responsibility in care delivery, it will be essential to involve these individuals in the coordination of care, which in turn will make it necessary to recognize the barriers to effective communication that some older adults experience, including hearing and vision deficiencies. (See next section for more on self-management.) Finally, one of the easiest ways to improve the coordination of care will be to enhance the use of those information technologies that help to share important patient information.

Health Technology

Many models of care require an increased use of health information technology (HIT), such as electronic health records and personal health records, to facilitate the sharing of information among providers and to improve their ability to coordinate the complex care of older patients. Health information technologies may also be used to build databases on the health of older populations which may be very useful to practitioners and researchers in aging. Other technologies used in new models may reduce the need for certain types of workers. For example, remote-monitoring technologies can extend the reach of health care professionals into the home.

As a result, many members of the health care workforce will need to be trained in the proper use of all of these technologies.

Technologies that assist in performing activities of daily living may reduce the demands placed on direct-care workers and informal caregivers, effectively shifting these responsibilities back to the patient's level. The interaction between developing technologies and the health care workforce is discussed further in later chapters, and recommendations are offered for encouraging the development and use of health technologies.

CONCLUSION

Simply expanding the size of the workforce qualified to provide the needed health care services to older adults will not be sufficient to address the challenge that will face this country over the next two decades. It will be necessary to develop new models of financing and care delivery in order to promote greater efficiencies in the use of the existing workforce while at the same time promoting improvements in care quality. Although a number of innovative models have already been developed, few have been widely adopted, and in large part this is because no adequate financing mechanism is in place to encourage the promotion of these models. Given that no single model of care will be sufficient to meet the needs of all older adults in all settings of care across the health care continuum, the committee recommends both an improved dissemination of models that have been shown to be effective and the development of new models of care that address specific settings or populations that have largely been overlooked and that encourage more effective use of the health care workforce.

The adaptation of these new models of care will have important implications for the development of a better health care workforce for older adults. Common features of new models include expanding the roles of workers (including expansion of the involvement of patients and their families), creating new provider roles, using interdisciplinary care teams, and improving the coordination of care through improvements in communication. Today's health care workforce is not properly prepared to perform its work in the ways that these new models demand, so all segments of the health care workforce will need to be educated and trained in the new care principles that underlie these models. The remainder of this report discusses the education, training, recruitment, and retention of the various segments of the health care workforce, with a particular emphasis on how the roles of health care providers will need to change in order to provide high-quality and cost-effective care to older Americans.

REFERENCES

ACP (American College of Physicians). 2006. *Tax Relief and Health Care Act of 2006 and other changes affecting 2007 Medicare payments.* http://www.acponline.org/advocacy/where_we_stand/medicare/sgr2007faq.pdf (accessed March 11, 2008).

Alexcih, L., B. Olearczyk, C. Neill, and S. Zeruld. 2003. *Wisconsin Family Care final evaluation report.* http://www.legis.state.wi.us/lab/reports/03-0FamilyCare.pdf (accessed March 11, 2008).

Angelelli, J. 2006. Promising models for transforming long-term care. *Gerontologist* 46(4): 428-430.

Arehart-Treichel, J. 2006. Using care managers improves depression outcome in seniors. *Psychiatric News* 41(7):31.

Ash, A. S., R. P. Ellis, G. C. Pope, J. Z. Ayanian, D. W. Bates, H. Burstin, L. I. Iezzoni, E. MacKay, and W. Yu. 2000. Using diagnoses to describe populations and predict costs. *Health Care Financing Review* 21(3):7-28.

Atkinson, J. G. 2001. *Social health maintenance organizations: Transition into Medicare+Choice.* Washington, DC: The Health Care Financing Organization.

Bachman, J., H. A. Pincus, J. K. Houtsinger, and J. Unutzer. 2006. Funding mechanisms for depression care management: Opportunities and challenges. *General Hospital Psychiatry* 28(4):278-288.

Balas, E. A., and S. A. Boren. 2000. Managing clinical knowledge for health care improvement. *Yearbook of medical informatics 2000: Patient-centered systems.* Stuttgart, Germany: Schattaver Verlasgesellschaft. Pp. 65-70.

Barry, C. L., and R. G. Frank. 2006. Commentary: An economic perspective on implementing evidence-based depression care. *Administration and Policy in Mental Health and Mental Health Services Research* 33(1):41-45.

Benjamin, A. E. 2001. Consumer-directed services at home: A new model for persons with disabilities. *Health Affairs* 20(6):80-95.

Berenson, R. A. 2007. *Statement of Robert A. Berenson, M.D.* Testimony before the House Committee on Ways and Means, Subcommittee on Health, Washington, DC. May 10, 2007.

Berenson, R. A., and J. Horvath. 2003. Confronting the barriers to chronic care management in Medicare. *Health Affairs Web Exclusive* W3:37-53. http://www.dmaa.org/members/downloads/ConfrontingtheBarrierstoChronicCareManagement.pdf (accessed January 12, 2008).

Berwick, D. M. 2003. Disseminating innovations in health care. *Journal of the American Medical Association* 289(15):1969-1975.

Biles, B., L. H. Hersch, and S. Guterman. 2006. *Medicare beneficiary out-of-pocket costs: Are Medicare Advantage plans a better deal?* Washington, DC: The Commonwealth Fund.

Boult, C., L. Boult, L. Morishita, B. Dowd, R. Kane, and C. F. Urdangarin. 2001. A randomized clinical trial of outpatient geriatric evaluation and management. *Journal of the American Geriatrics Society* 49(4):351-359.

Boult, C., A. Green, L. B. Boult, J. T. Pacala, C. Snyder, and B. Leff. 2007 (unpublished). *Successful Models of Comprehensive Health Care for Multi-Morbid Older Persons: A Review of Effects on Health and Health Care.* Paper commissioned by the IOM Committee on the Future Health Care Workforce for Older Americans.

Bowers, B. 2006. *Innovative models in long-term care.* Paper read at Littlefield Lecture Series, University of Wisconsin. September 22, 2006.

Bradley, E. H., M. Schlesinger, T. R. Webster, D. Baker, and S. K. Inouye. 2004a. Translating research into clinical practice: Making change happen. *Journal of the American Geriatrics Society* 52(11):1875-1882.

Bradley, E. H., T. R. Webster, D. Baker, M. Schlesinger, S. K. Inouye, M. C. Barth, K. L. Lapane, D. Lipson, R. Stone, and M. J. Koren. 2004b. *Translating research into practice: Speeding the adoption of innovative health care programs.* http://www.futureofaging.org/publications/pub_documents/bradley_translating_research.pdf?pubid=13 (accessed March 11, 2008).

Bradley, E. H., T. R. Webster, D. Baker, M. Schlesinger, and S. K. Inouye. 2005. After adoption: Sustaining the innovation. A case study of disseminating the hospital elder life program. *Journal of the American Geriatrics Society* 53(9):1455-1461.

Brown, R., D. Peikes, A. Chen, J. Ng, J. Schore, and C. Soh. 2007. *The evaluation of the Medicare coordinated care demonstration: Findings for the first two years.* Washington, DC: Mathematica Policy Research, Inc.

Bruce, M. L., T. R. Ten Have, C. F. Reynolds III, I. I. Katz, H. C. Schulberg, B. H. Mulsant, G. K. Brown, G. J. McAvay, J. L. Pearson, and G. S. Alexopoulos. 2004. Reducing suicidal ideation and depressive symptoms in depressed older primary care patients: A randomized controlled trial. *Journal of the American Medical Association* 291(9):1081-1091.

Brumley, R., S. Enguidanos, P. Jamison, R. Seitz, N. Morgenstern, S. Saito, J. McIlwane, K. Hillary, and J. Gonzalez. 2007. Increased satisfaction with care and lower costs: Results of a randomized trial of in-home palliative care. *Journal of the American Geriatrics Society* 55(7):993-1000.

Chatterji, P., N. R. Burstein, D. Kidder, and A. White. 1998. *The PACE demonstration: The impact of PACE on participant outcomes.* Cambridge, MA: Abt Associates, Inc.

Ciemins, E. L., B. Stuart, R. Gerber, J. Newman, and M. Bauman. 2006. An evaluation of the advanced illness management (AIM) program: Increasing hospice utilization in the San Francisco Bay area. *Journal of Palliative Medicine* 9(6):1401-1411.

CMS (Centers for Medicare and Medicaid Services). 2004. *Minnesota senior health options/Minnesota disability health options: Medicare payment/Medicaid waiver demonstration fact sheet.* Baltimore, MD: CMS.

CMS. 2005. *PACE overview.* http://www.cms.hhs.gov/pace/ (accessed July 25, 2007).

CMS. 2007a. *Improving access to integrated care for beneficiaries who are dually eligible for Medicare and Medicaid.* http://www.cms.hhs.gov/apps/media/press/release.asp?Counter=1912 (accessed July 27, 2007).

CMS. 2007b. *Overview: Demonstration projects and evaluation reports.* http://www.cms.hhs.gov/DemoProjectsEvalRpts/01_Overview.asp#TopOfPage (accessed July 19, 2007).

CMS. 2007c. *Special needs plan—fact sheet & data summary.* http://www.cms.hhs.gov/SpecialNeedsPlans/Downloads/FSNPFACT.pdf (accessed July 27, 2007).

CMS. 2008a. *Medicare demonstrations.* http://www.cms.hhs.gov/DemoProjectsEvalRpts/MD/list.asp (accessed March 11, 2008).

CMS. 2008b. *Medicare demonstrations: Details for Medicare medical home demonstration.* http://www.cms.hhs.gov/DemoProjectsEvalRpts/MD/ItemDetail.asp?ItemID=CMS1199247 (accessed March 11, 2008).

Coleman, E. A. 2003. Falling through the cracks: Challenges and opportunities for improving transitional care for persons with continuous complex care needs. *Journal of the American Geriatric Society* 51:549-555.

Coleman, E. A., and R. A. Berenson. 2004. Lost in transition: Challenges and opportunities for improving the quality of transitional care. *Annals of Internal Medicine* 141:533-536.

Cooper, B. S., and E. Fishman. 2003. *The interdisciplinary team in the management of chronic conditions: Has its time come?* Baltimore, MD: Partnership for Solutions.

Counsell, S. R., C. M. Callahan, D. O. Clark, W. Tu, A. B. Buttar, T. E. Stump, and G. D. Ricketts. 2007. Geriatric care management for low-income seniors: A randomized controlled trial. *Journal of the American Medical Association* 298(22):2623-2633.

Degruy, F. V., III. 1996. The DSM-IV-PC: A manual for diagnosing mental disorders in the primary care setting. *Journal of the American Board of Family Practice* 9(4):274-281.

DeNavas-Walt, C., B. D. Proctor, J. Smith, and U.S. Census Bureau. 2007. *Income, poverty, and health insurance coverage in the United States: 2006.* Washington, DC: U.S. Government Printing Office.

DHHS (Department of Health and Human Services). 2007. *Centers for Medicare and Medicaid Services justification of estimates for the Appropriations Committee.* Washington, DC: DHHS

Fischer, L. R., C. A. Green, M. J. Goodman, K. K. Brody, M. Aickin, F. Wei, L. W. Phelps, and W. Leutz. 2003. Community-based care and risk of nursing home placement. *Medical Care* 41(12):1407-1416.

Fleming, D. 2002. *CDC's role in improving the health of older Americans.* Paper presented at Subcommittee on Oversight and Investigations, Committee on Energy and Commerce, Washington, DC. May 23, 2002.

Foster, L., R. Brown, B. Phillips, J. Schore, and B. L. Carlson. 2003. Improving the quality of Medicaid personal assistance through consumer direction. *Health Affairs* 22(2003): w162-w175.

Frank, R. G., H. A. Huskamp, and H. A. Pincus. 2003. Aligning incentives in the treatment of depression in primary care with evidence-based practice. *Psychiatric Services* 54(5):682-687.

Goroll, A. H., R. A. Berenson, S. C. Schoenbaum, and L. B. Gardner. 2007. Fundamental reform of payment for adult primary care: Comprehensive payment for comprehensive care. *Journal of General Internal Medicine* 22(3):410-415.

Grabowski, D. C. 2006. The cost-effectiveness of noninstitutional long-term care services: Review and synthesis of the most recent evidence. *Medical Care Research and Review* 63(1):3-28.

Grande, G. E., C. J. Todd, S. I. G. Barclay, and M. C. Farquhar. 1999. Does hospital at home for palliative care facilitate death at home? Randomised controlled trial. *British Medical Journal (Clinical research edition)* 319(7223):1472-1475.

Greenwood, R. 2001. *The PACE model.* Washington, DC: Center for Medicare Education.

Gross, D. L., H. Temkin-Greener, S. Kunitz, and D. B. Mukamel. 2004. The growing pains of integrated health care for the elderly: Lessons from the expansion of PACE. *Milbank Quarterly* 82(2):257-282.

Guterman, S. 2007. *Enhancing value in Medicare: Chronic care initiatives to improve the program.* Testimony before the U.S. Senate Special Committee on Aging. May 9, 2007.

Guterman, S., and M. P. Serber. 2007. *Enhancing value in Medicare: Demonstrations and other initiatives to improve the program.* Washington, DC: The Commonwealth Fund.

Haidet, P., M. B. Hamel, R. B. Davis, N. Wenger, D. Reding, P. S. Kussin, A. F. Connors, Jr., J. Lynn, J. C. Weeks, and R. S. Phillips. 1998. Outcomes, preferences for resuscitation, and physician-patient communication among patients with metastatic colorectal cancer. *American Journal of Medicine* 105(3):222-229.

Hamilton, N., and A. S. Tesh. 2002. The North Carolina EDEN coalition: Facilitating environmental transformation. *Journal of Gerontological Nursing* 28(3):35-40.

Hansen, J. C. 2007. *The PACE model: An overview.* Presentation at Meeting of the Committee on the Future Health Care Workforce for Older Americans, San Francisco, CA. June 28, 2007.

Harrison, S., and J. Podulka. 2007. *Special needs plans and an update on the Medicare advantage program.* Washington, DC: MedPAC.

Hing, E., D. K. Cherry, and B. A. Woodwell. 2006. *National ambulatory medical care survey: 2004 summary. Advance data from vital and health statistics; no 374.* Hyattsville, MD: National Center for Health Statistics.

Hofmann, J. C., N. S. Wenger, R. B. Davis, J. Teno, A. F. Connors, Jr., N. Desbiens, J. Lynn, and R. S. Phillips. 1997. Patient preferences for communication with physicians about end-of-life decisions. *Annals of Internal Medicine* 127(1):1-12.

Hunkeler, E. M., W. Katon, L. Tang, J. W. Williams, Jr., K. Kroenke, E. H. B. Lin, L. H. Harpole, P. Arean, S. Levine, L. M. Grypma, W. A. Hargreaves, and J. Unutzer. 2006. Long term outcomes from the impact randomised trial for depressed elderly patients in primary care. *British Medical Journal* 332(7536):259-262.

IMPACT Implementation Center. 2007. *Participating organizations.* http://impact-uw.org/implementation/planning.html (accessed October 9, 2007).

Inglis, S., S. McLennan, A. Dawson, L. Birchmore, J. D. Horowitz, D. Wilkinson, and S. Stewart. 2004. A new solution for an old problem? Effects of a nurse-led, multidisciplinary, home-based intervention on readmission and mortality in patients with chronic atrial fibrillation. *Journal of Cardiovascular Nursing* 19(2):118.

Inouye, S. K., D. I. Baker, P. Fugal, and E. H. Bradley. 2006. Dissemination of the Hospital Elder Life Program: Implementation, adaptation, and successes. *Journal of the American Geriatrics Society* 54(10):1492-1999.

IOM (Institute of Medicine). 2001. *Crossing the quality chasm: A new health system for the 21st century.* Washington, DC: National Academy Press.

IOM. 2006a. *Medicare's quality improvement organization program.* Washington, DC: The National Academies Press.

IOM. 2006b. *Performance measurement.* Washington, DC: The National Academies Press.

IOM. 2007. *Rewarding provider performance.* Washington, DC: The National Academies Press.

The John A. Hartford Foundation. 2000. *Annual report.* New York: The John A. Hartford Foundation.

Justice, Diane. 2003. *Promising practices in long term care system reform: Wisconsin Family Care.* Washington, DC: Medstat.

Kaiser Family Foundation. 2006. *Medicaid and long-term care services.* Washington, DC: Kaiser Family Foundation.

Kaiser Family Foundation. 2007. *Medicare advantage.* Washington, DC: Kaiser Family Foundation.

Kane, R. L., and P. Homyak. 2003. *Minnesota senior health options evaluation focusing on utilization, cost, and quality of care.* http://www.cms.hhs.gov/reports/downloads/kane2003_1.pdf (accessed March 11, 2008).

Kane, R. L., G. Keckhafer, and J. Robst. 2002. *Evaluation of the Evercare demonstration program final report.* http://www.cms.hhs.gov/DemoProjectsEvalRpts/downloads/Evercare_Final_Report.pdf (accessed February 12, 2008).

Kane, R. L., P. Homyak, B. Bershadsky, S. Flood, and H. Zhang. 2004. Patterns of utilization for the Minnesota Senior Health Options program. *Journal of the American Geriatrics Society* 52(12):2039-2044.

Kane, R. A., T. Y. Lum, L. J. Cutler, H. B. Degenholtz, and T.-C. Yu. 2007. Resident outcomes in small-house nursing homes: A longitudinal evaluation of the initial Green House program. *Journal of the American Geriatrics Society* 55(6):832-839.

Katon, W. J. 2003. Clinical and health services relationships between major depression, depressive symptoms, and general medical illness. *Biological Psychiatry* 54(3):216-226.

Katon, W. J., M. Schoenbaum, M. Y. Fan, C. M. Callahan, J. Williams, Jr., E. Hunkeler, L. Harpole, X. H. A. Zhou, C. Langston, and J. Unutzer. 2005. Cost-effectiveness of improving primary care treatment of late-life depression. *Archives of General Psychiatry* 62(12):1313-1320.

Katon, W., J. Unutzer, M. Y. Fan, J. W. Williams, Jr., M. Schoenbaum, E. H. B. Lin, and E. M. Hunkeler. 2006. Cost-effectiveness and net benefit of enhanced treatment of depression for older adults with diabetes and depression. *Diabetes Care* 29(2):265-270.

Kodner, D. L. 2004. Whole-system approaches to health and social care partnerships for the frail eldery: An exploration of North American models and lessons. *Health and Social Care in the Community* 14(5):384-390.

Kravitz, A. S., and E. T. Treasure. 2007. Utilisation of dental auxiliaries—attitudinal review from six developed countries. *International Dental Journal* 57(4):267-273.

Kronick, R., T. Gilmer, T. Dreyfus, and L. Lee. 2000. Improving health-based payment for Medicaid beneficiaries: CDPS. *Health Care Financing Review* 21(3):29-63.

Leff, B. 2007. *Dissemination of models of geriatric care: Facilitators and barriers.* Presentation at Meeting of the Committee on the Future Health Care Workforce for Older Americans, San Francisco, CA. June 28, 2007.

Leipzig, R. M., K. Hyer, K. Ek, S. Wallenstein, M. L. Vezina, S. Fairchild, C. K. Cassel, and J. L. Howe. 2002. Attitudes toward working on interdisciplinary healthcare teams: A comparison by discipline. *Journal of the American Geriatrics Society* 50(6):1141-1148.

Leslie, D. L., Y. Zhang, S. T. Bogardus, T. R. Holford, L. S. Leo-Summers, and S. K. Inouye. 2005. Consequences of preventing delirium in hospitalized older adults on nursing home costs. *Journal of the American Geriatrics Society* 53(3):405-409.

Leutz, W. N., and J. Capitman. 2005. Met needs, unmet needs, and satisfaction among social HMO members. *Journal of Aging and Social Policy* 19(1):1-19.

Malone, J., L. Morishita, D. Paone, and C. Schraeder. 2004. *Minnesota Senior Health Options (MSHO) care coordination study.* http://www.dhs.state.mn.us/main/groups/healthcare/documents/pub/dhs_id_028242.pdf (accessed March 11, 2008).

Manton, K. G., R. Newcomer, G. R. Lowrimore, J. C. Vertrees, and C. Harrington. 1993. Social/health maintenance organization and fee-for-service health outcomes over time. *Health Care Financing Review* 15(2):173-202.

March, A. 2007. *Case study: Elder homes replace nursing homes in Tupelo, MS.* Washington, DC: The Commonwealth Fund.

McCall, N. 1997. Lessons from Arizona's Medicaid managed care program. *Health Affairs* 16(4):194-199.

McGlynn, E. A., S. M. Asch, J. Adams, J. Keesey, J. Hicks, A. DeCristofaro, and E. A. Kerr. 2003. The quality of health care delivered to adults in the United States. *New England Journal of Medicine* 348(26):2635-2645.

MedPAC (Medicare Payment Advisory Commission). 2006. *Report to the Congress: Increasing the value of Medicare.* Washington, DC: MedPAC.

MedPAC. 2007a. *Medicare advantage benchmarks and payments compared with average Medicare fee-for-service spending.* Washington, DC: MedPAC.

MedPAC. 2007b. *Report to the Congress: Promoting greater efficiency in Medicare.* Washington, DC: MedPAC.

Medstat. 2003. *Wisconsin—resource centers offering access to services and comprehensive information.* http://www.cms.hhs.gov/PromisingPractices/Downloads/wioss.pdf (accessed March 11, 2008).

Miller, R. H., and H. S. Luft. 2002. HMO plan performance update: An analysis of the literature, 1997-2001. *Health Affairs* 21(4):63-86.

Mukamel, D. B., H. Temkin-Greener, R. Delavan, D. R. Peterson, D. Gross, S. Kunitz, and T. F. Williams. 2006. Team performance and risk-adjusted health outcomes in the program of all-inclusive care for the elderly (PACE). *Gerontologist* 46(2):227-237.

Mukamel, D. B., D. R. Peterson, H. Temkin-Greener, R. Delavan, D. Gross, S. J. Kunitz, and T. F. Williams. 2007. Program characteristics and enrollees' outcomes in the program of all-inclusive care for the elderly (PACE). *Milbank Quarterly* 85(3):499-531.

National Commission for Quality Long Term Care. 2006. *Out of isolation: A vision for long-term care in America.* http://www.qualitylongtermcarecommission.org/pdf/out_of_isolation.pdf (accessed February 11, 2008).

National PACE Association. 2007. *What is PACE?* http://www.npaonline.org/website/article.asp?id=12. (accessed October 1, 2007).

NCB Capital Impact. 2007. *The green house projects.* http://www.ncbcapitalimpact.org/default.aspx?id=150 (accessed October 10, 2007).

NCQA (National Committee for Quality Assurance). 2008. http://www.ncqa.org/tabid/620/Default.aspx (accessed March 11, 2008).

Newhouse, J. P., M. B. Buntin, and J. D. Chapman. 1997. Risk adjustment and Medicare: Taking a closer look. *Health Affairs* 16(5):26-43.

Norwalk, L. V. 2007. *Statement on the Medicare advantage program.* Paper read at House Ways & Means, Subcommittee on Health, Washington, DC. February 13, 2007.

Pincus, H. A., L. Hough, J. K. Houtsinger, B. L. Rollman, and R. G. Frank. 2003. Emerging models of depression care: Multi-level ('6 p') strategies. *International Journal of Methods in Psychiatric Research* 12(1):54-63.

RAND. 2004. The quality of health care received by older adults. Santa Monica, CA: RAND.

Reuben, D. B. 2002. Organizational interventions to improve health outcomes of older persons. *Medical Care* 40(5):416.

Reuben, D. B. 2007. Better care for older people with chronic diseases: An emerging vision. *Journal of the American Medical Association* 298(22):2673-2674.

Rogers, E. M. 2003. *Diffusion of innovations (5th Edition).* New York: Free Press.

RWJF (Robert Wood Johnson Foundation). 2006. *Choosing independence.* Princeton, NJ: RWJF.

Samb, B., F. Celletti, J. Holloway, W. Van Damme, K. M. De Cock, and M. Dybul. 2007. Rapid expansion of the health workforce in response to the HIV epidemic. *New England Journal of Medicine* 357(24):2510-2514.

Scherger, J. E. 2005. The end of the beginning: The redesign imperative in family medicine. *Family Medicine* 37(6):513-516.

Senge, P. 1990. *The fifth discipline: The art and practice of the learning organization.* New York: Doubleday.

Shields, S. 2005. *Culture change in nursing homes.* http://www.commonwealthfund.org/spotlights/spotlights_show.htm?doc_id=265189 (accessed March 11, 2008).

Sibbald, B., and M. Roland. 1998. Understanding controlled trials: Why are randomised controlled trials important? *British Medical Journal (Clinical research edition)* 316(7126):201.

Sommers, L. S., K. I. Marton, J. C. Barbaccia, and J. Randolph. 2000. Physician, nurse, and social worker collaboration in primary care for chronically ill seniors. *Archives of Internal Medicine* 160(12):1825-1833.

Stone, R. I. 2000. *Long-term care for the elderly with disabilities: Current policy, emerging trends, and implications for the twenty-first century.* New York: Milbank Memorial Fund.

Teno, J. M., B. R. Clarridge, V. Casey, L. C. Welch, T. Wetle, R. Shield, and V. Mor. 2004. Family perspectives on end-of-life care at the last place of care. *Journal of the American Medical Association* 291(1):88-93.

Thompson, T. G. 2002. *Evaluation results for the social/health maintenance organization II demonstration.* Washington, DC: Department of Health and Human Services.

Tritz, K. 2005. *A CRS series on Medicaid: Dual eligibles.* Washington, DC: Congressional Research Service.

Tritz, K. 2006. *Integrating Medicare and Medicaid Services through managed care*. Washington, DC: Congressional Research Service.
Unutzer, J., W. Katon, J. W. Williams, Jr., C. M. Callahan, L. Harpole, E. M. Hunkeler, M. Hoffing, P. Arean, M. T. Hegel, M. Schoenbaum, S. M. Oishi, and C. A. Langston. 2001. Improving primary care for depression in late life: The design of a multicenter randomized trial. *Medical Care* 39(8):785-799.
Unutzer, J., W. Katon, C. M. Callahan, J. W. Williams, Jr., E. Hunkeler, L. Harpole, M. Hoffing, R. D. Della Penna, P. H. Noel, E. H. B. Lin, P. A. Arean, M. T. Hegel, L. Tang, T. R. Belin, S. Oishi, and C. Langston. 2002. Collaborative care management of late-life depression in the primary care setting: A randomized controlled trial. *Journal of the American Medical Association* 288(22):2836-2845.
Vladeck, B. C. 1996. *Testimony on long-term care options: PACE and S/HMOs*. Paper presented at Testimony before the House Ways and Means, Subcommittee on Health, Washington, DC. April 18, 1996.
Wagner, E. H., B. T. Austin, C. Davis, M. Hindmarsh, J. Schaefer, and A. Bonomi. 2001. Improving chronic illness care: Translating evidence into action. *Health Affairs* 20(6):64-78.
White, A., Y. Abel, and D. Kidder. 2000. *Evaluation of the program of all-inclusive care for the elderly demonstration: A comparison of the PACE capitation rates to projected costs in the first year of enrollment*. Cambridge, MA: ABT Associates Inc.
WHO (World Health Organization). 2003. *Collection on long-term care: Key policy issues in long-term care*. http://whqlibdoc.who.int/publications/2003/9241562250.pdf (accessed March 11, 2008).
Wolff, J. L., and C. Boult. 2005. Moving beyond round pegs and square holes: Restructuring Medicare to improve chronic care. *Annals of Internal Medicine* 143(6):439-445.
Zerzan, J., S. Stearns, and L. Hanson. 2000. Access to palliative care and hospice in nursing homes. *Journal of the American Medical Association* 284(19):2489-2494.

4

The Professional Health Care Workforce

CHAPTER SUMMARY

The need for health care professionals trained in geriatric principles is escalating, but even though opportunities for geriatric specialization exist, few providers choose this career path. The education and training of professionals in the area of geriatrics is hampered by a scarcity of faculty, inadequate and variable academic curricula and clinical experiences, and a lack of opportunities for advanced training. Furthermore, the education and training of geriatric health care professionals is often limited in scope and needs to be expanded both to take into account the diversity of health care needs among older populations and to prepare professionals for the coming new models of care, many of which will require changed or expanded roles. The committee recommends that more be done to ensure that all professionals have competence in geriatric principles. Finally, the recruitment and retention of geriatric professionals are hampered by several factors, including the persistent stereotypes of older populations, the aging of the workforce itself, and significant financial disincentives. The committee recommends that several types of financial incentives be offered to promote the recruitment and retention of clinical and academic geriatric specialists.

In the coming decades demand is expected to increase markedly for all types of health care professionals in all settings of care for the elderly population. This chapter examines issues related to the education, training, recruitment, and retention of health care professionals in the care of older adults. This chapter begins with a brief overview of the supply of and demand for professionals who care for older patients. The overall pattern here is that older Americans account for a disproportionate share of professional health care services but, in spite of this demand, the number of geriatric specialists remains low. Next the chapter focuses on a few individual professions essential to the care of older adults. It goes on to examine overarching themes in geriatric education and training. While improvements in the education and training of the health care workforce in geriatrics are evident, these efforts have failed to ensure that all providers who treat older adults have the necessary knowledge and skills to provide competent care. The chapter then considers future trends in education and training. Not only will there be a need for many more professionals working with older adults, but health care workers of the future will need to take on new and expanded roles. As discussed in Chapter 3, these changing responsibilities will affect the entire workforce, including the direct-care workforce, informal caregivers, and patients themselves. (These populations are examined in more detail in Chapters 5 and 6.) Finally, the chapter concludes with strategies for recruiting and retaining professionals in geriatric specialties. These strategies largely depend on overcoming financial disincentives, such as relatively low salaries and the high cost of training.

SUPPLY AND DISTRIBUTION

The number of professional workers directly involved in the care of older adults is difficult to quantify, for a number of reasons: changes in employment status, differing measures (e.g., licensed vs. active professionals), and the presence of ill-defined and overlapping titles for many occupations. Furthermore, many professionals treat older patients without being identified as geriatric providers either by title or certification. Health care-related careers, including medical assistants, physician assistants, physical therapists, mental health counselors, pharmacy technicians, and dental hygienists, account for about half of the country's 30 fastest-growing occupations (BLS, 2007a). Despite the rapid growth, however, the supply of health care workers does not satisfy current demands and will certainly fall short of the increased demands expected in the future. In fact, the United States will need an additional 3.5 million health care providers by 2030 just to maintain the current ratio of health care workers to population (Table 4-1).

While the general need for professionals who care for older patients is high, the particular need for geriatric specialists is even greater. For example, geriatricians[1] are the physicians who are specially trained in care

---

[1]While a physician who has extensive experience with elderly patients may specialize in geriatrics, the term "geriatrician" refers to a physician who has been certified in the subspecialty of geriatric medicine, or received a certificate of added qualifications in geriatric medicine.

TABLE 4-1 Number of Providers in 2005 and Projected Number Needed in 2030 to Maintain Current Provider-to-Population Ratios (in Thousands)

	2005	2030	Difference
Total health providers	9,994	13,522	3,528
Registered nurses	2,458	3,326	868
Nursing aides	2,009	2,719	709
Physicians	804	1,088	284
Licensed practical and vocational nurses	654	885	231
Pharmacists	236	319	83
Dentists	163	220	57
Other providers	3,670	4,965	1,295

NOTE: Numbers are for overall health care workforce and not limited to geriatric population.
SOURCE: Mather, 2007.

of the elderly population as a subspecialty of internal or family medicine. These specialists account for only a very small portion of the total physician workforce—just 7,128 physicians are certified geriatricians, or one geriatrician for every 2,546 older Americans (ADGAP, 2007b). By 2030, assuming current rates of growth and attrition, one estimate shows that this number will increase to only 7,750 (one for every 4,254 older Americans), far short of the total predicted need of 36,000 (ADGAP, 2007b; Alliance for Aging Research, 2002). In fact, some argue that there could be a net decrease in geriatricians because of the decreasing number of physicians entering training programs as well as the decreasing number of geriatricians who choose to recertify (Gawande, 2007). Geriatric psychiatry faces a similar shortage. Only 1,596 physicians are currently certified in geriatric psychiatry, or one for every 11,372 older Americans, and by 2030 that total is predicted to rise to only 1,659, which would then be only one for every 20,195 older Americans (ADGAP, 2007b).

Other professions have similarly low numbers of geriatric specialists. For example, just 4 percent of social workers and less than 1 percent of physician assistants identify themselves as specializing in geriatrics (AAPA, 2007; Center for Health Workforce Studies, 2006). Less than 1 percent of registered nurses (Kovner et al., 2002) and pharmacists[2] are certified in geriatrics. In short, dramatic increases in the number of geriatric specialists are needed in all health professions. Even with tremendous effort, it is

---

[2]Personal communication, T. Scott, American Society of Consultant Pharmacists, November 6, 2007.

unlikely that we can completely fulfill the projected needs, but, still, much can be done to begin to close the gaps.

Aside from concerns about the total numbers of health care workers with geriatric competencies, the composition and distribution of the health care workforce for older Americans should also be considered. This includes racial and ethnic diversity as well as the geographic distribution of professionals trained to provide care to older adults.

Racial and Ethnic Diversity

The committee commissioned a paper on the increasing diversity of older populations (Yeo, 2007) and found that the diversity of the workforce is important for several reasons. First, minority patients often prefer to be treated by health care professionals of the same ethnic background (Acosta and Olsen, 2006; IOM, 2004; Mitchell and Lassiter, 2006; Tarn et al., 2005). Second, a provider from a patient's own background may have better understanding of culturally appropriate demonstrations of respect for older populations and may also be more likely to speak the same language (in the case of bilingual providers). Finally, providers from minority populations often account for most of the services provided to underserved populations (HRSA, 2006a). For example, while only 3.4 percent of dentists are black, they treat almost two-thirds (62 percent) of black patients (Mitchell and Lassiter, 2006).

While older adults are more diverse than ever before, the younger generations training to care for them are even more diverse (see Chapter 2). The pattern of this diversity, however, will not necessarily match up with the pattern of diversity among older Americans. Table 4-2 demonstrates, for example, that there is significant diversity among resident physicians in geriatrics, but the percentage of white residents (39 percent) is much lower than the percentage of whites in the elderly population, and the percentage of Asian residents (42 percent) is much higher that the percentage of Asians in the elderly population.

Geographic Distribution

The distribution of both professionals and older adults varies widely across the country. Since both of these populations may be unevenly distributed across regions, states, and local communities, different areas may have different workforce needs. The committee commissioned a paper on state profiles of the U.S. health care workforce (Mather, 2007). This report showed there is an average of 443 dentists per 100,000 population aged 65 and older in the United States, but this ratio varies widely among the states. There are 759 dentists per 100,000 older adults in New Hampshire, but

TABLE 4-2 Race and Ethnic Origin of Residents in Geriatric Medicine and Psychiatry, 2006

	Black	American Indian/ Alaskan Native	White	Asian	Native Hawaiian/ Pacific Islander	Other/ Unknown	Hispanic Origin[a]	Total
Geriatrics (Family Medicine)	4	0	22	15	1	2	5	44
Geriatrics (Internal Medicine)	23	0	92	103	5	20	23	243
Geriatric Psychiatry	7	0	25	32	1	7	8	72
Total	34	0	139	150	7	29	36	359

[a]Hispanic origin was determined separately from race, and so the categories are not mutually exclusive.
SOURCE: Brotherton and Etzel, 2007.

only 104 dentists per 100,000 older adults in Kansas. This variance must be caused by a variety of factors, since these states do not have similar distributions in the numbers of other types of professionals. New Hampshire has a lower-than-average number of pharmacists per population of older adults, for example, while Kansas has a higher-than-average number of registered nurses. The need for health care workers with geriatric skills can also vary according to the distribution of older adults. For example, as discussed in Chapter 2, older adults make up 16.8 percent of Florida's total population, while they account for only 6.8 percent of Alaska's population (U.S. Census Bureau, 2008). Differences by community are likely to also vary widely. Therefore, the needed distribution of the health care workforce for older American can vary by both the state and the individual profession.

The recruitment and retention of health care professionals in rural areas is especially challenging (IOM, 2005), and this is an important factor when discussing the health care needs of the geriatric population, since older adults are disproportionately over-represented in rural areas (Hawes et al., 2005). Older adults that live in rural areas tend to be less healthy than those in urban areas and to have a higher rate of difficulty with activities of daily living (ADLs) (Brand, 2007; Magilvy and Congdon, 2000), while their access to health services is limited by the relatively small number of providers (especially specialists) that choose to work in rural areas. Because of the relatively small number of specialists, physician assistants and nurse practitioners play significant roles in providing health services to the rural aging population (Henry and Hooker, 2007). Among the challenges in recruiting any type of professional to rural areas are professional isolation, heavy call schedules, and few job opportunities for the spouses of the health care professionals. The best strategies for recruitment and retention may be those that focus on the training of existing rural providers in geriatric skills via distance education in conjunction with the use of remote technologies to increase the availability of outside geriatric experts for rural elderly populations.

THE CURRENT STATE OF GERIATRIC EDUCATION AND TRAINING

For more than 30 years the IOM (IOM, 1978, 1993) and others (LaMascus et al., 2005; Olson et al., 2003) have called for improvements in the geriatric education and training of virtually all types of health care providers. While progress is evident, many formal training programs still do not include robust coursework in geriatrics (Berman et al., 2005; Eleazer et al., 2005; Linnebur et al., 2005; Scharlach et al., 2000). Among the barriers to increased education and training in geriatrics for all professions are the lack of faculty, lack of funding, lack of time in already-busy curricula, and the lack of recognition of the importance of geriatric training (Bragg et al., 2006; Hash et al., 2007; Hazzard, 2003; Rubin et al., 2003; Simon et al., 2003; Thomas et al., 2003; Warshaw et al., 2006). Furthermore, very little is known about the best methods to improve the knowledge and skills of professionals in caring for older adults (Gill, 2005).

It is not possible to discuss every profession in detail, as virtually every professional cares for older patients to some degree. In the following section, several professions instrumental to the care of older adults are examined. (See Table 4-3 for an overview.) Specifically, the status of geriatric education and training within each profession is discussed. While some professions are discussed more extensively than others, the committee does not intend for this to imply any conclusion about their importance to the care of older adults. Rather, this is a reflection of the amount of data available and the extensiveness of the existing education and training programs in geriatrics. Overall, the breadth and depth of geriatric education and training remains inadequate to prepare all professionals for the health care needs of the future elderly population.

Physicians

Older Americans account for a disproportionate share of physician services, but a 2002 survey of primary care physicians showed that only half of these physicians believed that their colleagues could adequately treat geriatric conditions (Moore et al., 2004). This section examines the education and training of all physicians in the care of older adults, with a focus on the path for geriatricians.

Geriatric Content

The geriatric curricula in medical schools has had notable improvements. The percent of medical schools with requirements for "geriatric exposure" has increased from 82 percent in 1985-1986 to 98 percent in 1996-1997 (Eleazer et al., 2005). Still, much of this exposure is inadequate or occurs too late in the educational process to influence which specialities the students select. As noted above, several major public and private initiatives support improvement in the geriatric education of physicians. In May 2001 the Donald W. Reynolds Foundation awarded $19.8 million in grants to 10 institutions in order to develop comprehensive training programs in geriatrics (Donald W. Reynolds Foundation, 2007). Because of the success of this effort, the Donald W. Reynolds Foundation repeated the grants in 2003 and 2005, distributing almost $20 million in each round, and in October 2007 the Donald W. Reynolds Foundation issued a request for proposals for a fourth series of grants. In addition to this effort, the Donald W. Reynolds Foundation has established two departments of geriatric medicine.

The Health Resources and Services Administration (HRSA) distributes grants to support Geriatric Education Centers (GECs), which educate and train individuals in the care of older patients. These centers are often collaborative efforts among several health-profession schools or health care facilities and have a special focus on interdisciplinary training.

In July 2007 the John A. Hartford Foundation and the Association of American Medical Colleges (AAMC) hosted the National Consensus Conference on Geriatric Education. There the participants developed a set of minimum standards for the knowledge, skills, and attitudes of graduating medical students with respect to the care of older patients (Leipzig, 2007). The standards covered a number of domains, including

- cognitive and behavioral disorders;
- medication management;
- self-care capacity;
- falls, balance, gait disorders;
- atypical presentation of disease;
- palliative care;
- hospital care for older adults; and
- health care planning and promotion.

TABLE 4-3 Overview of the Education and Training of Professionals in Geriatrics

	Nurses	Oral-Health Workers	Pharmacists
Total jobs held (2006)[a,1]	RNs: 2.5 million[b,2] LPNs: 749,000	Dentists: 161,000; (General dentists: 136,000) Dental hygienists: 167,000	243,000
Geriatric specialization or certification	Less than 1% of RNs and about 2.6% of APRNs certified[3,28]	Unknown	1,297 certified (less than 1%)[4]
Academic leadership	76% of baccalaureate programs have at least one full-time "expert," 29% have a certified faculty member[8]	63% of dental schools have a geriatric director or chairman[9]	43% have two full-time faculty; most rely on part-time faculty[10]
Exposure to geriatrics in schools	One-third of baccalaureate programs require exposure; 94% of fundamental courses integrate geriatric content[8]	100% of dental and dental hygiene schools have identifiable content; 18.8% of dental hygiene schools have a discrete course[14]	43% have a discrete course; all schools provide opportunity for advanced training in geriatrics or long-term care[10]
Advanced geriatric training programs	Less than 100 master's and post-master's programs; five programs in geropsychiatric nursing[3]	13 programs for geriatric dental academic training; no residencies specific to geriatric dentistry[18]	10 residency programs; one fellowship program[19]
Number of advanced geriatric trainees	Approximately 300 geriatric APRNs produced annually[3]	Unknown	13 resident slots; one fellowship slot[19]
Explicit testing on non-geriatric board certification exams?[c]	Yes[21]	No[22]	No general certification; national licensure exam organized by approaches[23]

Physician Assistants	Physicians	Social Workers
66,000	633,000	595,000
Less than 1% specialize[5]	7,128 certified in geriatric medicine; 1,596 certified in geriatric psychiatry[6]	About 4% of social workers specialize[7]
27% of program directors surveyed had some form of geriatric training[11]	Less than 1% of faculty specialize; all programs have an identifiable leader in geriatrics[12]	40% of schools have no faculty knowledgeable in aging[13]
Accreditation requires geriatric exposure, including clinical experience in long-term care[15]	98% of schools require some form of exposure[16]	80% of BSW students have no coursework in aging[17]
None	Medicine: 139 fellowship programs (468 1st-year positions)[6] Psychiatry: 58 fellowship programs (142 1st-year positions)[6]	29% of MSW programs offer aging certificate, specialization, or concentration[20] DSW: unknown
Not Applicable	Medicine: 253 in 1st year; 34 in 2nd year[6] Psychiatry: 72[6]	Unknown
Yes[24]	Internal Medicine: 10% of exam[25] Family Medicine: optional module[26] Psychiatry: yes[27]	No general certification; national licensure exam organized by approaches[28]

continued

TABLE 4-3 Continued

	Nurses	Oral-Health Workers	Pharmacists
Geriatric certification body	American Nurse Credentialing Center (ANCC)	None Fellowship status offered by American Society for Geriatric Dentistry (ASGD) and diplomate status offered by American Board of Special Care Dentistry (ABSCD)	Commission for Certification in Geriatric Pharmacy (CCGP)

ABBREVIATIONS: Advanced Practice Registered Nurse (APRN); Bachelor of Social Work (BSW); Doctor of Social Work (DSW); Licensed Practical Nurse (LPN); Master of Social Work (MSW); Registered Nurse (RN).

[a]Number of jobs may be greater than number of practicing professionals, since some professionals work in more than one position.

[b]As of 2004, there were 240,260 jobs held by APRNs.

[c]Relies on description of exam content.

The group then developed a total of 36 competencies based on these domains (AAMC/The John A. Hartford Foundation, 2007). The competencies included

- identification of medications to be avoided or used with caution in older adults;
- ability to define and distinguish delirium, depression, and dementia;
- assessment of ADLs and IADLs;
- identification of physiological changes due to aging;
- identification of psychological, social, and spiritual needs of patients; and
- performance of examination to assess skin pressure ulcer status.

While the coverage of geriatric issues at medical schools is increasing, students still express significant reservations about their abilities to treat older patients. The AAMC's 2002 Medical School Graduate Questionnaire found 55 percent of graduates perceived inadequate coverage of geriatric issues in medical school; only 68 percent felt adequately prepared to care

Physician Assistants	Physicians	Social Workers
None	American Board of Internal Medicine (ABIM), American Board of Family Medicine (ABFM), American Board of Psychiatry and Neurology (ABPN), American Osteopathic Board of Family Practice (AOBFP), American Osteopathic Board of Internal Medicine (AOBIM)	National Association of Social Workers (NASW)

SOURCES: [1]BLS, 2008; [2]HRSA, 2006; [3]Kovner et al., 2002; [4]Personal communication, T. Scott, American Society of Consultant Pharmacists, November 6, 2007; [5]AAPA, 2007; [6]ADGAP, 2007b; [7]Center for Health Workforce Studies, 2006; [8]Berman et al., 2005; [9]Mohammad et al., 2003; [10]Odegard et al., 2007; [11]Olson et al., 2003; [12]LaMascus et al., 2005; Warshaw et al., 2002; [13]Scharlach et al., 2000; [14]Mohammad et al., 2003; Tilliss et al., 1998; [15]Brugna et al., 2007; [16]Eleazer et al., 2005; [17]Lubben et al., 1992; [18]HRSA, 2005; [19]ACCP, 2007; ASHP, 2007; [20]Cummings and DeCoster, 2003; [21]NCSBN, 2007; [22]ABGD, 2007; [23]NABP, 2008; [24]NCCPA, 2008; [25]ABIM, 2007; [26]ABFM, 2007; [27]ABPN, 2007c; ASWB, 2007; [28]HRSA, 2006b.

for older persons in acute-care settings, and only half felt prepared to care for them in long-term care settings (Eleazer et al., 2005). In spite of this, less than 3 percent of medical students take geriatric electives (Moore et al., 2004).

Advanced Training

Postdoctoral training of physicians occurs during both residency and fellowship programs. As of 2003, 27 types of medical residency programs (accounting for 70 percent of trainees) included Accreditation Council for Graduate Medical Education (ACGME) requirements for some form of geriatrics training, but the extent of such training is highly variable (Bragg and Warshaw, 2005; Bragg et al., 2006; Simon et al., 2003). One survey showed that only about half of graduating family-practice and internal-medicine residents (48 percent and 52 percent, respectively) felt very prepared to care for elderly patients (Blumenthal et al., 2001). Although a large majority of graduating psychiatry residents felt very prepared to diagnose and treat delirium (71 percent) and major depression (96 percent), only 56 percent felt very prepared to diagnose and treat dementia.

Several specialties that treat large numbers of older patients, including ophthalmology, general surgery, and dermatology, do not include any requirements for geriatric training (Bragg and Warshaw, 2005). Since 1994 the John A. Hartford Foundation has funded the Geriatrics-for-Specialists Initiative, which aims to improve geriatric knowledge of surgical specialists and related medical specialists. Their Geriatrics Education for Specialty Residents Program encourages interaction between directors of specialty residencies and the geriatricians within their facilities.

After completion of a residency in internal medicine, family medicine, or general psychiatry, a physician can pursue a fellowship in geriatric medicine or geriatric psychiatry, which may last one or more years. Fellows may be graduates of allopathic or osteopathic schools of medicine, or they may be international medical graduates (IMGs). This finding is notable in that IMGs have become increasingly relied upon to provide primary care services and care to underserved populations in the United States (Hart et al., 2007).

About half of geriatric-medicine and geriatric-psychiatry fellows (58.2 percent and 44.4 percent, respectively) are female, and about two-thirds of the two types of fellows (64.1 percent and 61.1 percent, respectively) are IMGs (Brotherton and Etzel, 2007). By comparison, across all specialties IMGs make up only 26.9 percent of the entire resident-physician population. As seen in Figures 4-1 and 4-2, while the number of positions available in geriatric-medicine and geriatric-psychiatry fellowship programs has been increasing, the percentage of positions filled has been decreasing. Very few fellows continue past the first year, possibly because of the decrease in the requirement for the length of training that is needed to pursue certification (discussed later in this section).

The Veterans Administration (VA) plays an important role in the development of geriatric fellowships. In the 1970s, in anticipation of the wave of aging World War II veterans, the VA established Geriatric Research, Education and Clinical Care Centers (GRECCs) to improve geriatric knowledge (Goodwin and Morley, 1994; Warshaw and Bragg, 2003). These centers are still in operation and often educate and train multiple disciplines in geriatric care. At around the same time the VA first established fellowship programs in geriatric medicine and geriatric psychiatry, often in conjunction with a GRECC. Today, about 25 percent of geriatric-medicine fellowship positions and almost 50 percent of geriatric-psychiatry fellowship positions are supported by the VA, and many other geriatric fellows will receive part of their training in VA facilities (VA, 2007a). The VA also funds four fellowships in geriatric neurology (VA, 2007b).

Other branches of the federal government also support the geriatric education and training of physicians. HRSA administers the Title VII Geriatrics Health Professions Program. Although funding was eliminated for

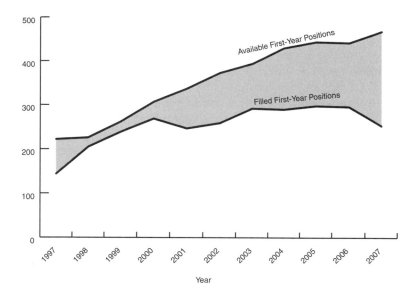

FIGURE 4-1 First-year geriatric medicine fellowship positions, available and filled.
SOURCE: ADGAP, 2007b.

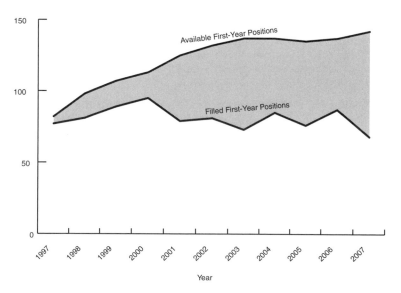

FIGURE 4-2 First-year geriatric psychiatry fellowship positions, available and filled.
SOURCE: ADGAP, 2007b.

fiscal year 2006, it was restored for fiscal year 2007, with $31.5 million for the support of 48 GECs, 88 Geriatric Academic Career Awards (GACAs) for individuals, and 11 Geriatric Training for Physicians, Dentists, and Behavioral/Mental Health Professions Program awards given to institutions to prepare faculty for these professions (ADGAP, 2007c). In 2007 Congress approved a fiscal year 2008 Labor-Education-HHS appropriations bill[3] that included continuation of the Title VII geriatrics programs at the same funding level as for fiscal year 2007, but President Bush vetoed the bill on November 13, 2007, and the House of Representatives failed to override the veto on November 15, 2007.

Finally, CMS is the major financial supporter of the residency training of all physicians. In fiscal year 2004 it paid $7.9 billion for graduate medical education (GME) (GAO, 2006). Medicare pays for a portion of the cost of GME for physician residents and fellows through direct and indirect medical-education payments. Direct medical education (DME) payments support hospitals' direct cost of operating a GME program, especially salary support for residents; indirect medical education (IME) payments cover a portion of the added patient care costs associated with teaching hospital settings (MedPAC, 2003). Through GME, Medicare has specifically supported advanced training in geriatrics by counting geriatric fellows as full-time equivalent (FTE) residents, while all other subspecialty fellows count only as one-half of a full-time equivalent. Thus hospitals that train geriatricians receive more GME funding than hospitals that train other types of subspecialists (MedPAC, 2003). Furthermore, when GME updates were frozen in the 1990s, geriatric programs were exempt.

Sites of Training

The training of medical students and residents tends to occur in discrete episodes of care, within single disciplines, and usually only in the hospital or ambulatory setting, which means that residents generally do not have the opportunity to follow patients longitudinally over time and across settings of care. Thus many students and residents lack exposure to alternative sites of care of importance to the geriatric patient—namely, home-care settings, nursing homes, and assisted-living facilities. Deterrents to increasing student clinical experiences in these sites include the need for an on-site supervisor of the same discipline, the need for collaboration with site staff, a lack of student interest, and a lack of time in already crowded programs (Leipzig et al., 2002; Warshaw et al., 2006).

In one national survey, only 27 percent of graduating family-practice

---

[3]*Departments of Labor, Health and Human Services, and Education, and Related Agencies Appropriations Act, 2008.* HR 3043. 110th Congress. July 13, 2007.

residents and only 13 percent of graduating internal-medicine residents felt very prepared to care for nursing-home patients (Blumenthal et al., 2001). Still, clinical experiences in alternative sites of care have increased somewhat from past years (Cheeti and Schor, 2002; Matter et al., 2003). For example, Weill Cornell Medical College implemented a clerkship in which third- and fourth-year medical students accompanied a geriatrics team on home visits to patients living with chronic illness; when interviewed about the experience, 84 percent of recent graduates felt that it had had a positive effect on their delivery of care (Yuen et al., 2006).

Among the obstacles to expanding training sites is a lack of funding to cover the expenses of residents while in non-hospital settings. As described above, Medicare distributes GME funds, primarily to hospitals, to support the training of residents. However, the Balanced Budget Amendment of 1997 allows for other providers, including federally qualified health centers, rural health clinics, and managed care organizations to receive GME funds directly (AAMC, 2007c). Furthermore, since 1987 hospitals have been allowed to count the time that residents spend in settings outside the hospital, such as nursing homes and physician offices, subject to certain agreed-upon conditions between the hospital and the outside entity. Still, this does not happen often enough. Since most care of older patients occurs in non-hospital settings, more needs to be done to ensure that professionals are fully trained in how to care for patients in these settings.

The committee concluded that comprehensive care of older patients should include training in non-hospital settings.

Recommendation 4-1: The committee recommends that hospitals should encourage the training of residents in all settings where older adults receive care, including nursing homes, assisted-living facilities, and patients' homes.

Residency program directors need to ensure that their residents' schedules include adequate time rotating through these alternative settings, and the directors and hospital administrators need to be willing to collaborate with the outside entities to reach mutually agreeable conditions for partnership.

Board Certification

Physicians may pursue voluntary national board certification in many major specialties and then become certified in the subspecialties of geriatric medicine or geriatric psychiatry. It was in 1988 that the American Board of Family Medicine (ABFM) and the American Board of Internal Medicine

(ABIM) first offered a 10-year certificate of added qualifications (CAQ) in the subspecialty of geriatric medicine.[4] Originally CAQs were available only to physicians with at least 2 years of specialty geriatric training or to those who had substantial clinical experience (the "practice pathway"). In 1994 the ABIM and ABFM phased out the practice-pathway option, and in 1998 they lowered the training requirement to only 1 year, resulting in a slight upward trend in the recruitment of geriatric fellows. As seen in Figure 4-3, the number of physicians certified annually surged and then sharply decreased when the practice-pathway option was eliminated; only 13.4 percent of all new certifications occurred after the practice-pathway option ended.

Osteopathic physicians may pursue CAQs from the ABIM or ABFM and also from the American Osteopathic Board of Family Physicians (AOBFP) or the American Osteopathic Board of Internal Medicine (AOBIM), which have offered certification since 1991. The AOBIM ended the practice-pathway option in 1994, and the AOBFP ended it in 2002.

The American Board of Psychiatry and Neurology (ABPN) recognized geriatric psychiatry as a subspecialty in 1989 and first awarded 10-year CAQs in 1991 (ABPN, 2007a). In 1996 the ABPN phased out the practice-pathway option and subsequently reduced post-graduate training requirements from 2 years to 1 year. Figure 4-4 shows a similar surge and then a drop in certification related to these events.[5] Only 13 percent of all geriatric psychiatrists ever certified became certified after the practice pathway was phased out.

As the geriatric certifications expire, many physicians do not pursue recertification; most of these physicians were certified via the practice pathway. Reasons for not recertifying are multifactorial, including retirement, the burden of the process, and the lack of perceived benefit. Table 4-4 shows that only about half of all physicians certified in geriatric medicine or geriatric psychiatry before 1994 have been recertified (ADGAP, 2005). By comparison, 89 percent of physicians who received specialty certificates in other disciplines[6] from the ABIM between 1990 and 1995 enrolled in the maintenance of certification process; of those, 81 percent completed the process (ABIM, 2005). The comparable rate of recertification in geriatrics among other health professions is unknown.

---

[4]In 2006, the ABIM recognized geriatric medicine as a subspecialty of internal medicine instead of as a CAQ (ABIM, 2006).

[5]The ABPN dropped the term "of added qualifications" in 1997 (ABPN, 2007b).

[6]Excluding clinical cardiac electrophysiology, critical care medicine, and geriatric medicine.

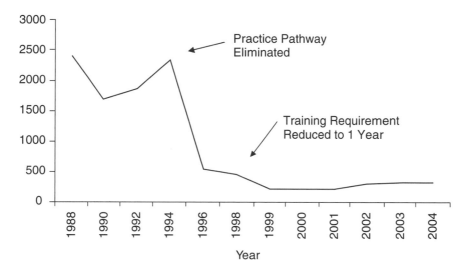

FIGURE 4-3 Numbers of physicians newly certified in geriatric medicine, 1988-2004.
SOURCE: ADGAP, 2005.

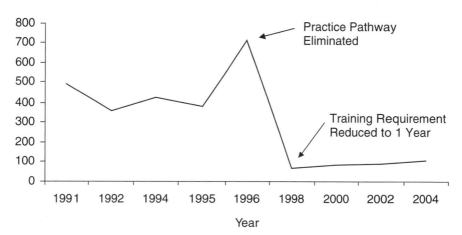

FIGURE 4-4 Numbers of physicians newly certified in geriatric psychiatry, 1991-2004.
SOURCE: ADGAP, 2005.

TABLE 4-4 Number of Physicians Certified and Recertified in Geriatrics

Year[a]	Family Medicine		Internal Medicine		Psychiatry	
	Certified	Recertified	Certified	Recertified	Certified	Recertified
1988	752	477	1,654	801	NA	NA
1990	473	313	1,204	524	NA	NA
1991	NA	NA	NA	NA	490	323
1992	597	359	1,254	605	359	236
1994	771	371	1,568	585	422	154
TOTAL	2,593	1,520	5,679	2,515	1,271	713
		(58.6%)		(44.3%)		(56.1%)

NOTE: NA = not applicable.
[a]Certification examinations by each body were not available in every calendar year.
SOURCE: ADGAP, 2005.

Nurses

Professional nurses[7] represent the largest sector of the health care workforce responsible for patient care in most health care settings. The professional nurse workforce consists of registered nurses (RNs) and advanced practice registered nurses (APRNs), who are RNs prepared in master's degree programs. With few exceptions, almost all professional nurses are involved in the care of older adults. In addition to direct care, professional nurses supervise licensed practical nurses (LPNs)[8] and certified nurse aides (CNAs) (discussed in Chapter 5). While the current and impending nursing shortage has received much attention, there have been some improvements; enrollment in baccalaureate programs increased by 5 percent from 2005 to 2006, and the number of graduates increased by 18 percent (AACN, 2006). However, this upswing is tempered by the fact that more than 32,000 qualified applicants to nursing programs (baccalaureate level or higher) were not accepted; about half the schools identified lack of faculty as the main barrier to admitting more students (AACN, 2006; Anderson, 2007). Additionally, men remain underrepresented in the nursing profession and need to be considered for recruitment efforts to allay workforce shortages (see Chapter 5).

Licensed Practical Nurses

LPNs have a more limited scope of practice than RNs, but this scope can vary widely among states, especially in light of the nursing shortage.

---

[7]In this report, "professional nurses" refers to nurses who have graduated from an approved baccalaureate, associate degree, or diploma nursing program and who have passed a national licensing examination, the NCLEX-RNs.

[8]In some states, this level of nurse is referred to as a licensed vocational nurse (LVN).

With about 26 percent of all LPNs working in nursing homes, LPNs are especially important to the care of older adults in long-term care settings (BLS, 2007b). LPNs often provide more hours of care per nursing home resident per day than do RNs (Harrington et al., 2006). LPNs receive about 1 year of training through technical or vocational schools or through junior or community colleges. With experience and training, LPNs may supervise nurse aides. For example, the Institute for the Future of Aging Services is developing a leadership training program to teach LVNs the necessary skills and competencies to be more effective supervisors (IFAS, 2008). Some of the elements of this training include communication, critical thinking, conflict resolution, and cultural competency. Little is known about the geriatric training of LPNs.

Registered Nurses

As with other professions, nurses generally receive little or no preparation in the principles that underlie geriatric nursing in their basic nursing education. In 2005, 31 percent of new RNs received baccalaureate degrees, but only one-third of the baccalaureate programs required a course focused on geriatrics. Almost all baccalaureate programs include some geriatric content, but the extent of this content is unknown (Berman et al., 2005). While 42 percent of RNs receive their initial education through associate degree nursing programs (HRSA, 2006b), the degree of integration of geriatrics into these programs is also unknown. Given the paucity of geriatric content in programs preparing nurses, it is appropriate to assume that most practicing RNs have little formal preparation in geriatrics.

There exist a number of efforts aimed at ensuring nursing competency in geriatric care. In 2000, for example, the American Association of Colleges of Nursing (AACN) developed guidelines for geriatric competencies in baccalaureate programs. The National Council of State Boards of Nursing (NCSBN) mapped those guidelines against the National Council Licensure Examination (NCLEX), which is required for licensure of all nurses, to ensure adequate testing on geriatric issues (Wendt, 2003). Still, more needs to be done to analyze the depth of this content (Bednash et al., 2003).

As with other professions, there exist various public and private efforts aimed at increasing the geriatric content of nursing programs and developing geriatric nursing leaders. Since 1996 the John A. Hartford Foundation has invested $60 million in the Hartford Geriatric Nursing Initiative, which includes the Institute for Geriatric Nursing and the Centers of Geriatric Nursing Excellence. These programs foster the development of academic leaders and increase geriatric content in the education and training of nurses. In 2002 the Atlantic Philanthropies funded a 5-year initiative to improve nursing competence in treating older adults (Box 4-1). Under the

---

BOX 4-1
Nurse Competence in Aging Initiative

"Nurse Competence in Aging (NCA) is an initiative to improve the quality of health care older adults receive by enhancing the geriatric competence—the knowledge, skills and attitudes—of the 400,000 nurses who are professionally identified as members of approximately 57 specialty nursing associations. Nurse Competence in Aging is committed to:

"*Enhancing Geriatric Activities of National Specialty Nursing Associations* Associations apply for grant funding and receive technical assistance to move forward with geriatric best practice initiatives. Funded associations are designated ANA-SNAPGs, or American Nurses Association-Specialty Nursing Association Partners in Geriatrics.

"*Promoting Gerontological Nursing Certification* to encourage specialty nurses to obtain dual certification and validate their geriatric competence along with their specialty expertise. Scholarships available!

"*Providing a Web-based Comprehensive Geriatric Nursing Resource Center* GeroNurseOnline is a comprehensive website providing current best practice information on care of older adults. We invite you to explore GeroNurseOnline and become a Gero Smart Nurse!

"Nurse Competence in Aging was a 5-year initiative funded by The Atlantic Philanthropies (USA) Inc., awarded to the American Nurses Association (ANA) through the American Nurses Foundation (ANF), and represented a strategic alliance among ANA, the American Nurses Credentialing Center (ANCC) and the John A. Hartford Foundation Institute for Geriatric Nursing, New York University."

SOURCE: ANA, 2007.

Nurse Reinvestment Act,[9] the Comprehensive Geriatric Education Program provides funds for clinical training of nurses in geriatrics, the development and dissemination of geriatric nursing curricula, and the preparation of nursing faculty to teach geriatrics. Funding for this program has remained at around $3.4 million annually since fiscal year 2004 (HRSA, 2007b). The Nurse Education, Expansion, and Development Act of 2007[10] proposes to

---

[9]*Nurse Reinvestment Act.* Public Law 107-205. 107th Congress. August 1, 2002.

[10]*Nurse Education, Expansion, and Development Act of 2007.* S 446. 110th Congress, 1st session. January 31, 2007.

offer grants to nursing schools to increase the integration of geriatrics into their core curricula.

Similar initiatives have also been developed to support education and training in geropsychiatric nursing. For example, in 2007 the John A. Hartford Foundation awarded $1.2 million to establish the Geropsychiatric Nursing Collaborative. This group will establish a core set of geropsychiatric competencies in order to develop basic curricula for all levels of nurse training (The John A. Hartford Foundation, 2007).

Advanced Practice Registered Nurses

An RN may become an APRN by obtaining a master's degree and may become certified either through a national certifying examination or through state certification mechanisms. An APRN functions as an independent health care provider, addressing the full range of a patient's health problems and needs within an area of specialization. There are a number of different types of APRNs, including: nurse practitioners (NPs), who provide primary care; clinical nurse specialists, who typically specialize in a medical or surgical specialty; certified nurse anesthetists; and certified nurse midwives. The pipeline for producing APRNs with a specialization in geriatrics is inadequate to meet the need. As with other types of nurses, the John A. Hartford Foundation has been a key supporter in the development of the geriatric APRN workforce. In particular, the Building Academic Geriatric Nursing Capacity Scholars and Fellows Awards Program targets doctoral and post-doctoral nurses and APRNs who want to redirect their careers toward geriatrics (Fagin et al., 2006).

NPs represent a particularly important component of the workforce caring for older adults because of their ability to provide primary care as well as care for patients prior to, during, and following an acute care hospitalization and also to care for residents in institutional long-term care settings. NPs treat a disproportionate number of older adults—23 percent of office visits and 47 percent of hospital outpatient visits with NPs are made by people 65 and older (Center for Health Workforce Studies, 2005). Furthermore, NPs care for a higher proportion of elderly poor adults than do physicians or physician assistants (Cipher et al., 2006). Finally, NPs have been shown to provide high-quality care and be cost-effective (Hooker et al., 2005; Melin and Bygren, 1992; Mezey et al., 2005).

While APRNs care for large numbers of older adults in ambulatory care, hospitals, and institutional long-term care settings, APRN education programs lack specific geriatric requirements. The AACN publishes a set of competencies called Nurse Practitioner and Clinical Nurse Specialist Competencies for Older Adult Care (AACN, 2004), but it does not require that these competencies be incorporated into educational programs. Some of these competencies include

- ability to distinguish between illness and normal aging;
- assessment of geriatric syndromes;
- identification of changes in mental status;
- education of patients and their families about prevention and end-of-life care;
- assessment of cultural and spiritual concerns; and
- collaboration with other health care professionals.

Little is known about on-the-job opportunities for APRNs to gain knowledge and skill in geriatric nursing care.

Oral-Health Care Workers

The oral health needs of older adults are significantly different from the needs of younger people, and older adults face a variety of challenges in meeting these needs. One of the barriers facing older adults who need oral-health services is lack of access to care. This lack of access is often due to the lack of coverage under Medicare for routine services, but it is also the case that many oral-health professionals are reluctant to travel to alternative sites of care (such as community-based settings) or to manage the complicated social and medical challenges associated with older patients. Even though the delivery of basic oral-health services to nursing home patients is supported by government regulation, less than 20 percent of residents of government-certified institutions received dental services in 1997 (MacEntee et al., 2005). In 1987 the National Institute on Aging (NIA) predicted a need for 1,500 geriatric dental academicians and 7,500 dental practitioners with training in geriatric dentistry by the year 2000 (NIA, 1987). By the mid-1990s, however, only about 100 dentists in total had completed advanced training in geriatrics (HRSA, 1995), and little has changed since then.

The availability of geriatric training for dentists has improved over the past few decades. In 1976, only 5 percent of dental schools offered courses in geriatric dentistry and, at that time, more than half of the programs (52 percent) did not foresee geriatric dentistry as part of their future curricula (Mohammad et al., 2003). However, by 1981 about half of all schools had developed geriatric dentistry programs, and an additional 25 percent planned to add geriatric curricula in the near future. As of 2001, all dental schools reported having some curricula related to geriatric dentistry, and almost one-third operated a geriatric clinic (Mohammad et al., 2003). The geriatric content varies greatly among schools. A school may offer only a single elective course, for example, or material information may be imparted via guest lecturers. Additionally, exposure to clinical experiences is lagging behind the didactic requirements. Of the students graduating in 2001, almost 20 percent did not feel prepared to care for the elderly population, and 25 percent felt the geriatric dental curriculum was inadequate (Mohammad et al., 2003).

The American Dental Association currently does not recognize geriatric dentistry as a separate specialty, and none of the 509 residencies recognized by the American Dental Education Association are specifically devoted to the care of geriatric patients; in contrast, specialty recognition and 71 residencies exist for pediatric dentistry. In fiscal year 2005, HRSA supported seven residency programs in pediatric or general dentistry; one program specifically requested funds to improve clinical and didactic curriculum in geriatric dentistry, but the residency is not focused on geriatrics (HRSA, 2005b). The VA's Advanced Fellowship in Geriatrics program allows dentists (and other health care professionals) to pursue advanced research in geriatrics at one of 16 GRECCs (VA, 2007a). Previous VA fellowships in geriatric dentistry are no longer available. As mentioned previously, HRSA administers the Title VII Geriatrics Health Professions Program, which includes awards to institutions to prepare geriatrics faculty in dentistry, medicine, and behavioral/mental health.

The American Board of General Dentistry (ABGD) offers board certification in general dentistry following completion of a post-graduate residency; exam content does not explicitly require questions on geriatric care or on special-care dentistry, but it does explicitly require knowledge of pediatric dentistry (ABGD, 2007). Also, while the ABGD's general dentistry certification process has minimum requirements for continuing dental education in several areas (e.g., periodontics, orthodontics, and pediatric dentistry), it has no minimum requirements for "special patient care," although it is a listed category. The American Society for Geriatric Dentistry (ASGD), part of the Special Care Dentistry Association, offers fellowship status to ASGD members who meet requirements for post-graduate and continuing education and who pass an oral examination. The American Board of Special Care Dentistry further offers diplomate status to ASGD fellows based on time in practice and membership in the SCDA. The American Dental Association, however, does not recognize this specialty board.

Less is known about the geriatric education and training of dental hygienists, although dental hygienists are increasingly important in providing care to special populations, especially those in rural areas and long-term care settings. Dental hygienists usually earn associate degrees, but some programs grant up to a master's level degree. Dental hygienists are licensed by individual states, must pass written and clinical examinations, and have variable requirements for continuing education. While all schools have integrated geriatric content, about half (49.5 percent) consider their geriatric curricula to be inadequate (Tilliss et al., 1998).

Pharmacists

There is currently a significant national shortage of pharmacists in the United States, which is due to a number of factors, including increased use of prescription medications, increased workloads, changing sites of service, demographic changes in the workforce, and expanding scopes of work (HRSA, 2000). While the absolute number of pharmacists has grown, supply has not kept up with demand, and wide variations in the numbers of pharmacists per capita exist from state to state (Walton et al., 2007). The current shortage causes problems for older adults, who tend to be heavy users of prescription drugs and to rely on pharmacists for counseling on the proper use of medications and on the monitoring of medication-related problems, such as interactions, duplications, adverse events, and adherence irregularities (Cooksey et al., 2002).

The role of pharmacists in the interdisciplinary care of older patients was reinforced in 1974 when Medicare first mandated drug regimen reviews (now called a Medication Regimen Review) in nursing homes by consultant pharmacists (Levenson and Saffel, 2007). In this setting, the role of the consultant pharmacist includes the provision information and recommendations to physicians regarding medications, identification of improper use of medications or the prescription of incompatible medications, and collaboration with the medical director and other staff to develop proper protocols for response to adverse events. This role has increased importance with the escalation of the number of medications given to the most frail and chronically ill patients. Additionally, with the advent of Medicare Part D, pharmacists potentially have a role in the education of older adults on their plan options and associated implications.

The doctor of pharmacy (PharmD) degree requires 4 years of pharmacy education. The Accreditation Standards and Guidelines for the Professional Program in Pharmacy Leading to the Doctor of Pharmacy Degree, adopted in 2006, implies that geriatrics should be a part of the pharmacy curriculum but does not explicitly require its inclusion. However, the science foundation of programs must consider populations that have altered pharmacological needs because of physiology or other reasons; this may include geriatric patients. Some of the competencies needed for the care of older patients include knowledge of the influence of aging on drug therapy, provision of medication and wellness counseling, and knowledge of geriatric syndromes (Odegard et al., 2007).

The American Society of Health-System Pharmacists (ASHP) accredits 1-year residencies in pharmacy, community pharmacy, or managed care pharmacy, which are referred to as PGY-1, for Post Graduate Year 1. Pharmacists may pursue a second year of residency training (PGY-2) in a focused area, including geriatric pharmacy. The ASHP currently accredits (or pre-accredits) 351 PGY-2 programs (ASHP, 2007). There are eight accredited programs in geriatric pharmacy, and two other programs are pre-candidates for accreditation. The American College of Clinical Pharmacy offers one fellowship position in geriatrics to prepare pharmacists for academia and independent research; this 2-year fellowship focuses on Alzheimer's Disease (ACCP, 2007). Viability of these programs has been hindered by inconsistent funding; with the exception of GECs, there are few federal or private-foundation-funded programs or initiatives that support pharmacist education and research training in geriatrics.

Pharmacist licensure, which is performed by individual states and jurisdictions, depends on passing a national examination, and 46 jurisdictions require an additional examination on federal law and state-specific regulations (CCP, 2006). Some states also require laboratory and oral examinations. Re-licensure requires a minimum of continuing education credits. Currently, neither continuing education in geriatrics nor demonstrated geriatric competency is required for pharmacist re-licensure in any state. However, a 2005 survey of state pharmacy laws found that one state requires all pharmacists to participate in 2 hours of continuing education in end-of-life care every 2 years, and two states require all pharmacists working as long-term care consultants to have at least a portion of their continuing education activities focused on the care of older adults (Linnebur et al., 2005).

Physician Assistants

Physician assistants (PAs) represent an important part of the workforce for the elderly population (Olshansky et al., 2005). PAs work under the supervision of a physician, but they can often work apart from the physician's direct presence and can prescribe medications and bill for health care services. Unlike some of the other professions described above, the PA workforce tends to be younger and is growing rapidly. About half of PAs work in family medicine or general medicine (Brugna et al., 2007; Hooker and Berlin, 2002). The 65-and-older population accounts for about 32 percent of office visits to PAs (Hachmuth and Hootman, 2001), and 78 percent of PAs report treating at least some patients over the age of 85 (Center for Health Workforce Studies, 2005).

PAs are an especially important source of care in underserved areas, where they often act as the principal care provider in clinics, with physicians attending on an intermittent basis. In this vein, they are a potential source of care to meet the increased need that is projected for long-term care settings. Their use may be a particularly attractive strategy since, as with NPs, the use of PAs has been shown to be cost-effective (Ackermann and Kemle, 1998; Brugna et al., 2007). On the other hand, according to a survey of more than 23,000 PAs, only 5 percent of respondents reported spending any time in a nursing home or other long-term care facility, and less than 1 percent identified their primary practice as geriatrics (AAPA, 2007). Of those respondents who specialize in geriatrics, 67 percent reported working primarily in a nursing home or long-term care facility, and 75 percent reported spending at least some time in those settings. Almost 18 percent of PAs who specialize in geriatrics spend some time caring for patients at home, compared to 1.3 percent of all other types of PAs. And almost 22 percent of PAs specializing in geriatrics are employed by the government, primarily by the VA, while only 9 percent of all other types of PAs work for the government.

The overwhelming majority of the 136 accredited PA programs are located within universities and colleges, but a few exist within hospitals, community colleges, and military institutions (BLS, 2007c). Most of these programs offer a master's level degree, while others offer bachelor's and associate-level degrees. Virtually all students in these programs—99 percent—pursue primary-care tracks. Most programs follow traditional curricula of medical schools (Hooker and Berlin, 2002), and while some PAs receive advanced training, the bulk of the advanced programs focus on surgical and emergency care (APPAP, 2008). Accreditation standards require training in geriatrics but do not specify a minimum workload (BLS, 2007c). As is the case with other professions, there have been many calls for increased education and training of PAs in geriatrics (Brugna et al., 2007; Olson et al., 2003; Segal-Gidan, 2002; Woolsey, 2005). Unfortunately, very little has been done to examine the quality and quantity of current geriatric education and training among PA programs. In one survey, PA program administrators who were asked which areas of the curricula needed increased emphasis said that geriatric issues related to pharmacology and mental health deserved the highest priority (Olson et al., 2003).

Social Workers

The need for geriatric social workers has been recognized for decades (NIA, 1987; Saltz, 1997). In 1987 the NIA estimated that there would be a need for 70,000 social workers prepared in geriatrics by 2020, or a 43 percent increase over the needs at that point in time. In spite of this urgency, the number of social workers trained in geriatrics has not kept pace with the need. While 73 percent of social workers report that they work with adults aged 55 and over, and between 7.6 and 9.4 percent of social workers are employed in long-term care settings, only about 4 percent actually specialize in geriatrics (ASPE, 2006; Center for Health Workforce Studies, 2006). Between 1996 and 2001 the number of students specializing in aging decreased by 15.8 percent (ASPE, 2006). On the other hand, many social workers begin to specialize in the care of older persons after graduation and do so without formal training in geriatrics (Cummings and DeCoster, 2003).

Social workers receive training through either bachelors-level (BSW) or masters-level (MSW) programs, which may be accredited by the Council on Social Work Education. As of 2006, the Council accredited 458 BSW programs and 181 MSW programs; there were also 74 doctoral programs in social work (DSW or PhD) at the time (BLS, 2007d). Combined, BSW and MSW programs graduate about 31,000 students annually (ASPE, 2006). Social workers with BSW degrees are more likely to work in long-term care settings than those with MSW degrees. A 1995 survey showed that 11.5 percent of BSW social workers worked in nursing homes or hospices, compared to 1 percent of MSW holders, and 16.5 percent identified aging services as their primary practice, compared to 3.7 percent of MSW holders (ASPE, 2006).

In spite of the long-recognized need for social workers trained in aging issues, most social work programs contain little or no geriatric content in their curricula. In fact, the proportion of programs offering specialization in aging is decreasing. In the early 1980s almost half of MSW programs offered an aging specialization; by the early 1990s this had dropped to about one-third of programs, and as of 2003 only about 29 percent of MSW programs offered an aging concentration, specialization, or certificate program (Cummings and DeCoster, 2003; Scharlach et al., 2000). Existing aging curricula often have limited content, rarely offering more than one or two elective courses. In 1988 the vast majority of BSW programs—about 80 percent—did not offer specific instruction on aging issues (Lubben et al., 1992). The inadequacy of curricula is compounded by the fact that social-work students show low levels of interest in taking courses on aging and have persistent negative attitudes about working with older people (Hash et al., 2007; Lubben et al., 1992).

In 2000 the Council on Social Work Education, in conjunction with Strengthening Aging and Gerontology Education for Social Work (SAGE-SW), surveyed social workers about the competencies that geriatric social workers and other types of social workers need in order to care for older patients effectively (Rosen et al., 2000). Sixty-five competencies were identified, of which 35 were described by the respondents as being needed by all types of social workers. These competencies included

- knowledge of the physical, social, and psychological changes of aging;
- knowledge of the diversity of attitudes about aging;
- use of case management skills to get access to needed resources;
- collaboration with other health professionals;
- identification of one's own biases toward aging; and
- respect of diverse cultural and ethnic needs.

Several initiatives aim to promote education and training in geriatric social work:

- The Social Work Leadership Institute at the New York Academy of Medicine, funded by the Atlantic Philanthropies and the John A. Hartford Foundation, coordinates the Practicum Partnership Program, an innovative educational model to train masters level social workers in their field work (Box 4-2).
- The Atlantic Philanthropies established the Institute for Geriatric Social Work, which, in partnership with the American Society on Aging and other groups, promotes the training of practicing social workers in issues related to the elderly population (IGSW, 2007).
- In 2000-2004 the John A. Hartford Foundation supported the Geriatric Enrichment Program (GeroRich) to increase geriatric content in basic social work courses at both the BSW and MSW levels (Hash et al., 2007).
- The John A. Hartford Foundation also supports the Council on Social Work Education Gero-Ed Center, which serves as a resource for both faculty and students to become competent in geriatric issues.

Very few social-work trainees do advanced training or field work in aging, and of those who do, most are students in MSW programs. This lack of training is primarily due to a lack of funding for program support or stipends (ASPE, 2006; Scharlach et al., 2000). In partnership with the Social Work Leadership Institute, the John A. Hartford Foundation supports 60 MSW programs in an effort to increase the quality and content of field experiences in aging. The effort aims to increase the numbers of MSW students who go on to specialize in geriatrics.

In 1998 the National Association of Social Workers (NASW), the voluntary professional organization of social workers, created a new specialty section on aging. Recently the NASW has developed three specialty certifications in gerontology available to its members (NASW, 2007).

BOX 4-2
The Practicum Partnership Program

"The Practicum Partnership Program sponsored by the New York Academy of Medicine and the Hartford Foundation is in its eighth year. It has trained more than 1,000 social workers to work with older adults using a specialized field education model for students at masters-level social work programs. PPPs across the country form a strong educational foundation to grow the ranks of leaders with aging specializations.

"The PPP differs from traditional MSW field education models. Based on innovative partnerships between universities and community-based agencies, the PPP provides students with wide-ranging, hands-on experience in older adult care. Over the course of either one or two years, students rotate through multiple field settings, gaining exposure to different care systems and a broad spectrum of life phases.

"Evaluations of the program have already demonstrated promising results: in our pilot study, 80 percent of PPP graduates have gone on to pursue careers in the field of aging. Since 1999, with support from the John A. Hartford Foundation, 45 PPPs have been established at colleges and universities nationwide."

SOURCE: SWLI, 2007.

Allied Health and Other Professions and Occupations

Many other professionals also provide essential health services to older Americans. These professionals are pressed to meet the needs of the growing older population because of shortages of supply, increases in demand, and deficiencies in geriatric education and training that are similar to those already discussed. For example,

- HRSA's 1995 report on the status of geriatric education showed only 17 percent to 19 percent of physical therapy programs had at least 75 percent of their students complete a geriatric internship even though 39 percent of the physical therapy patients were over 65 (HRSA, 1995).
- The Emergency Medical Technician—Basic: National Standard Curriculum, developed by the National Highway Traffic Safety Administration, includes modules dedicated to the care of obstetrics and pediatric patients, but none are dedicated to the older adult patient (NHTSA, 1994).

- While 84 percent of optometry schools and colleges reported a required geriatrics course, the content of these courses was variable.
- Only one of the eight schools of podiatric medicine has a discrete course devoted to the care of geriatric patients, while six list courses specific to the care of pediatric patients (AACPM, 2007).
- In a 2004 survey of dietetics and nutrition programs, 22 percent of the undergraduate programs and 44 percent of the graduate programs offered courses in aging (Rhee et al., 2004). In comparison, maternal and child health courses were offered in 31 and 51 percent of the programs, respectively. Thirty-seven percent of graduate programs had no faculty in geriatrics.
- None of the following specialties with high volumes of older patients has a subspecialty certificate available in geriatrics: dermatology, emergency medicine, physical medicine and rehabilitation, or surgery. By contrast, all have certification in pediatrics (ABMS, 2007).

Of particular importance are the many occupations that fall under the broad category of "allied health care workers." This term is ill-defined, and the many definitions that have been developed are often contradictory (Lecca et al., 2003). In general, allied health care workers represent nearly 200 different occupations, including various types of technologists, technicians, therapists, and health-information professionals. Many of the allied health occupations are currently experiencing shortages and are projected to be among the fastest-growing occupations in the United States (BLS, 2007a). These groups face significant increases in need for their services in all care settings (Chapman et al., 2004). The geriatric education and training of the allied health care workforce is highly variable and is usually structured according to the standards of the appropriate accrediting body.

Other Issues in Geriatric Education and Training

In addition to the particular professional concerns discussed in the previous section, there are a number of other overarching issues that all professions face in the geriatric education and training of their practitioners. First, the education and training of all types of professionals depends on the availability of qualified faculty. Second, practitioners should be aware of the unique health care needs of several special elderly populations; these populations include various racial and ethnic groups as well as the growing number of lesbian, gay, and bisexual older adults.[11] Third, all practitioners

---

[11] There are insufficient data on transgendered older adults to include in this section.

who care for older adults should be educated and trained in the full spectrum of health care needs, from health promotion to palliative care. Finally, as discussed in Chapter 3, interdisciplinary care of older adults shows promise, so students in all professions should be trained on how to be an effective member of an interdisciplinary team.

Leadership

A well-recognized barrier to geriatric education and training of all health care providers is the inadequate number of available and qualified academic faculty (Berkman et al., 2000; Berman et al., 2005; Cavalieri et al., 1999; Graber et al., 1999; Hazzard, 2003; Kovner et al., 2002; Rhee et al., 2004; Rubin et al., 2003; Simon et al., 2003; Warshaw et al., 2006). Any effort to increase geriatric education will find itself limited by the availability of trained faculty. Furthermore, beyond the need for a greater number of geriatric faculty, all geriatric fields need strong expert leaders to develop new knowledge and recruit new students.

It is a controversial question whether advanced geriatric training programs should be designed to train geriatric specialists for clinical practice or to train them for academic research and leadership. Some argue that, for the sake of the efficient use of scarce resources, geriatric specialists should concentrate on their roles of performing research and training the future health care workforce and should act as clinical consultants in only the most complex cases.

Beyond academics and clinical care, geriatric leaders need to learn the skills to manage staff, promote quality, and create a healthy work environment. For example, the relationship between nursing supervisors and nurse aides plays a significant role in the development of a hospitable work environment that leads to increased job satisfaction (see Chapter 5 for more on job satisfaction and turnover among direct-care workers) (Tellis-Nayak, 2007). In addition, certain management principles, such as providing rewards to nurse aide staff, have been associated with improved patient outcomes (Barry et al., 2005). This relationship will also have increased importance as direct-care workers assume more patient responsibility in the cascading mechanism of job delegation (discussed more later in this chapter).

To increase the number of geriatric leaders, a number of public and private entities have developed programs to promote research and teaching capacities in geriatrics. Examples include the following:

- The Hartford Geriatric Social Work Faculty Scholars Program, funded by the John A. Hartford Foundation, aims to develop leaders in geriatric social work through research support, mentoring, skills-based workshops, and nurturing of professional relationships (GSWI, 2007; Maramaldi et al., 2004).

- HRSA's Geriatric Training for Physicians, Dentists, and Behavioral/ Mental Health Professions Program is the country's sole source of postgraduate training for preparing dentists to teach geriatrics (HRSA, 2005a). In fiscal year 2005 HRSA funded 13 programs with a total of $6.3 million in grants. It is unknown, however, whether all of these programs filled their available dental positions.

- The Atlantic Philanthropies and the John A. Hartford Foundation support the Dennis W. Jahnigen Career Development Scholars Awards to develop geriatric academic leaders in surgical and related specialties, such as anesthesiology, ophthalmology, and emergency medicine. The two foundations are also responsible for the establishment and continuation of the T. Frank Williams Research Scholars Award, which supports research by medical subspecialists in geriatrics or aging.

- In July 2004 the Donald W. Reynolds Foundation awarded a total of $12 million in grants to four academic health centers for them to train their medical faculty in geriatrics (Donald W. Reynolds Foundation, 2007).

- HRSA grants GACAs (Geriatric Academic Career Awards) directly to junior faculty at allopathic and osteopathic medical schools to support teaching (HRSA, 2005a).

- The John A. Hartford Foundation's Centers of Excellence in geriatric medicine, psychiatry, and nursing help to train larger numbers of competent geriatric academicians and also allow specialists to devote time to geriatric research in addition to their work training future clinicians.

Recognizing the scarcity of geriatric leaders, several institutions have developed innovative approaches to spread knowledge of geriatric principles. For example,

- In 1997 the Practicing Physician Education Project used geriatric experts to train non-geriatrician physician leaders to educate their peers on various geriatric syndromes (Levine et al., 2007).

- Since 1992, the Nurses Improving Care for Health System Elders (NICHE) program has worked with nurses in hospital settings to implement models and protocols that improve the care of geriatric patients. In the Geriatric Resource Nurse (GRN) model, a geriatric APRN trains a staff nurse to be the clinical resource on geriatric issues for other nurses (NICHE, 2008).

- The Boston University Medical Center developed the Chief Resident Immersion Training (CRIT) Program in the Care of Older Adults to improve understanding and teaching of geriatric principles among residents in non-geriatric fields (ADGAP, 2007a). The program is being disseminated nationally.
- In 2003-2004 the Society of General Internal Medicine and the John A. Hartford Foundation worked in Collaborative Centers for Research and Education in the Care of Older Adults to enhance the ability of general internists to teach geriatrics (Williams et al., 2007).
- HRSA administers the National Advisory Council on Nurse Education and Practice, which, in response to the Nursing Reinvestment Act, provided grants for the geriatric education and training of registered nurses so that they can act as leaders and trainers for CNAs and LPNs (HRSA, 2003).
- Geriatric experts have tried to infuse geriatrics into training programs for personnel who might not normally gain exposure to geriatric principles. Faculty at Northern Michigan University developed a training program for correctional workers that focused on the needs of the aging prison population (Cianciolo and Zupan, 2004).

Special Populations

Ethnogeriatrics   As discussed in Chapter 2, the elderly population of the future will be more diverse than today's older adults. Thus increased knowledge of different cultural belief systems will be important to the development of comprehensive and effective plans of action. For example, older Asian adults may not disclose their non-Western health beliefs, including the use of herbal medications or alternative health procedures, unless directly asked (McBride et al., 1996). These concerns are especially important considering the potential mismatch between the diversity of the health care workforce and the diversity of the older adult population. For example, the high proportion of IMGs among fellows in geriatric medicine and geriatric psychiatry was demonstrated earlier in this chapter. However, concerns exist for issues of communication and cultural competency in particular when IMGs care for older adults (Howard et al., 2006; Kales et al., 2006).

Several efforts have been started to improve upon the ethnogeriatric education and training of the health care workforce in settings where providers are responsible for taking care of diverse populations. For example, the Collaborative for Ethnogeriatric Education produced a five-module Core Curriculum in Ethnogeriatrics and 11 Ethnic Specific Modules which can be

---

BOX 4-3
Knowledge and Skills Needed in Ethnogeriatrics

Knowledge:

- Differential health risks
- Diverse cultural health beliefs and practice systems
- Historic experiences that cohorts of older adults are likely to have experienced
- Palliative care

Skills:

- Showing culturally appropriate respect to older adults
- Performing culturally appropriate assessments
- Eliciting elders' explanatory models of their conditions
- Working with older adults' families from different cultures
- Identifying cultural guides[a]

---

[a]Cultural guides are often individuals from the local community who help patients navigate the health care system, keeping cultural preferences in mind.
SOURCE: Yeo, 2007.

---

used as resources in different geographic areas to provide content on local populations (www.stanford.edu/group/ethnoger). Box 4-3 lists some of the knowledge and skills needed to properly care for diverse populations.

Lesbian, gay, and bisexual persons   Approximately 1 million to 3 million adults ages 65 and older are gay, lesbian, or bisexual (GLB), and by 2030 that number is expected to rise to 4 million (Cahill et al., 2000). The few existing studies on the health care needs of older GLB patients report similarities to the health care needs of heterosexual older adults, with a few important differences. Many GLB patients do not feel comfortable disclosing their sexual orientation to their health care providers. Surveys reveal that discrimination based on sexual orientation is widespread in health care and other social-service settings, and it often causes GLB persons to avoid seeking health care (Cahill et al., 2000; Ryan and Futterman, 1998; Schatz and O'Hanlan, 1994). The discomfort of revealing sexual orientation to health care providers is heightened for older adults who came of age at a time when society was even less accepting of homosexuality (Brotman et al., 2003).

Knowledge of a patient's sexuality can be critical to high-quality patient care. A recent study estimated that approximately 100,000 adults ages 50 and older are HIV positive (ASA, 2007). Older adults with HIV/AIDS may be misdiagnosed because health care providers do not perceive HIV/AIDS to be a risk among older adults and because older adults often do not disclose the nature of their sexual activity to health care providers (AIDS InfoNet, 2007; NAHOF, 2007). Additionally, GLB older adults often do not have the same family support systems as heterosexual older adults, particularly since GLB older adults are less likely to have children and are more likely to live alone (Cahill et al., 2000).

The Continuum of Care

Geriatric education is highly variable in its level of comprehensiveness, and it often fails to address the health care needs of older adults across the continuum of care, ranging from preventive to palliative care. Health care professionals should be aware that older adults have a vast range of health care needs. Many students still are not taught about or exposed to older populations at either end of the continuum of care.

Health promotion/disease prevention   Health promotion is beneficial for people of all ages and all health conditions, but it may be especially important to the growing cohort of healthy older adults—that is, the 20 percent of older Americans who have no chronic disease and who require only preventive and episodic care. Traditionally, the training of professionals in the care of older adults has focused only on the treatment of disease and has given little attention to the promotion of health. For example, poor nutrition is prevalent among seniors (IOM, 2000), but most professionals are still not trained in the nutritional needs of older adults (Bonnel, 2003; Rhee et al., 2004). Government agencies and professional societies have developed guidelines for health promotion and disease prevention in elderly populations which include goals typically promoted for other populations, including increased physical activity, smoking cessation, and weight management (Fields and Nicastri, 2004). These guidelines are based on research that shows the benefits of health promotion and disease prevention in elderly populations. For example, studies have shown that older persons who practice tai chi experience fewer falls (Li et al., 2002, 2005; Wolf et al., 1996).

Screening guidelines are important in nursing homes for the early detection of depression and pressure ulcers (McElhone et al., 2005). Unfortunately, prevention and screening guidelines often lump all elderly persons into one group (65 years and older), and recommendations are often based on studies performed in younger age groups (Nicastri and Fields, 2004). More research is needed on preventive services for older adults, especially for the "oldest old," and health care professionals need to be aware of the value of these services for all of their older patients.

The activities of professional groups today reflect a growing awareness of the importance of health promotion and disease prevention for older patients. For example, the Geriatrics Section of the American Physical Therapy Association has an interest group on "Health Promotion & Wellness" that aims to improve the education, clinical practice, and research of physical therapists in health and wellness among older adults (APTA, 2007). The American Geriatrics Society lists "health promotion and disease prevention strategies" among the areas of knowledge needed for the successful preparation of internal medicine physicians who care for older adults (AGS, 2004). The American Dietetic Association includes the provision of nutrition care across the lifespan, "infants through geriatrics," as one of the core competencies for entry-level dietitians and dietetic technicians (ADA, 2008).

Palliative care   Within geriatric education and training programs, palliative care skills are especially important since 80 percent of American deaths occur among those over age 65 (Ersek and Ferrell, 2005). Skills that are particularly important include identification and relief of physical and emotional stress, effective communication, interdisciplinary team work, recognition of the signs and symptoms of imminent death, and support of the bereavement process (National Consensus Project for Quality Palliative Care, 2004). The opportunities for exposure to these topics has improved greatly in recent years; almost all medical schools offer some form of end-of-life care education, and 62 percent of pharmacy schools surveyed reported didactic training in end-of-life care (Billings and Block, 1997; Herndon et al., 2003).

Despite such improvements, however, the overall education and training of the health care workforce in palliative care is deficient (Billings and Block, 1997; Ersek and Ferrell, 2005; Holley et al., 2003; IOM, 1997; Paice et al., 2006; Walsh-Burke and Csikai, 2005). In one survey of medical students, residents, and faculty, less than 20 percent reported that they received formal education in end-of-life care, 39 percent felt unprepared to address patient fears, and almost half felt unprepared to deal with their own feelings about death (Sullivan et al., 2003). Another survey showed that less than half of graduating family medicine and internal medicine residents (41 percent and 43 percent, respectively) felt very prepared to counsel patients on end-of-life issues (Blumenthal et al., 2001). In contrast, a 2005 study showed 70 percent of geriatric medicine fellows reported completing rotations in palliative care, end-of-life care, or hospice, and only 2.7 percent felt unprepared to care for dying patients (Pan et al., 2005).

In October 2006 the American Board of Medical Specialties (ABMS) announced Hospice and Palliative Medicine as a new subspecialty for ten different specialty boards (ABMS, 2006). The first certifying exams will be administered in October 2008.

Interdisciplinary Team Training

One element common to many models described in Chapter 3 is the use of interdisciplinary teams. The value of interdisciplinary teams for the care of older adults with complex care needs has been increasingly acknowledged in recent years (Dyer et al., 2003; Howe and Sherman, 2006; Inouye et al., 2000; Maurer et al., 2006; Wheeler et al., 2007; Williams et al., 2006). The term "interdisciplinary team" implies an interaction and an interdependence among practitioners with different areas of expertise who are working together to treat a single patient. Still, health care professionals are typically trained separately by discipline, which fosters ideas of hierarchy and responsibility for individual decision making (Hall and Weaver, 2001). As a result, providers may gain little understanding of or appreciation for the expertise of other providers or the skills needed to effectively participate in an interdisciplinary team. However, most health care professions identify interdisciplinary team practice as a necessary competency in the care of older adults.

The field of geriatrics led the movement toward team training in health services. In the 1970s the VA developed the Interdisciplinary Team Training in Geriatrics (ITTG) Program, and in the 1980s HRSA began awarding grants for GECs to teach collaboration and teamwork to health care professionals working in geriatrics (Heinemann and Zeiss, 2002).

In 1997 the John A. Hartford Foundation funded eight national programs to develop geriatric interdisciplinary team training (GITT) programs for students in nursing, social work, and medicine in order to foster the skills needed for effective team care. These programs often included other professionals, such as pharmacists, dentists, and rehabilitation therapists. GITT seeks to train health professionals to work more effectively on geriatric care teams. The announced goals included the creation of a national model to forge partnerships between geriatric care providers and institutions of education, the development of educational curricula for interdisciplinary team training, training health care professionals in team skills, and the testing of new models of training for practicing professionals (Flaherty et al., 2003).

To evaluate this training, several measures have been developed to assess trainees' knowledge of interdisciplinary geriatric-care planning, their knowledge of team dynamics, their attitudes toward geriatrics and teams, and their skills in team care (Flaherty et al., 2003). One evaluation showed that the most improvement came on measures of attitudes, especially self-reported measures of team skills; no changes were seen in care planning, and few changes were seen in team dynamics, depending on the question and the discipline (Fulmer et al., 2005). Obstacles identified for interdisciplinary training within the GITT programs included differing lengths of rotation among the disciplines, differing levels of experience among the participants, and the inability of clinicians to supervise students from other disciplines (Reuben et al., 2003, 2004). Physicians were the least experienced with and the most averse to sharing responsibilities of patient care. Similar results have been documented in studies of other similar models (Fitzgerald et al., 2006; Leipzig et al., 2002; Williams et al., 2006).

HRSA has been a strong supporter of interdisciplinary training in geriatrics and has stated that interdisciplinary geriatric education should be a core requirement for every health profession (HRSA, 1995). As mentioned above, GECs provide interdisciplinary training of faculty, students, and practitioners in the diagnosis, treatment, and prevention of disease, disability, and other health problems of older adults (HRSA, 2007c). While more and more professionals are gaining experience in interdisciplinary training, little evidence exists to determine which methods are best for imparting the knowledge and skills necessary to work as a team member or to show how such training affects patterns of practice (Cooper et al., 2001; Hall and Weaver, 2001; Remington et al., 2006).

Conclusions

The education and training of professionals in geriatrics has improved because of the expansion of school-based opportunities, increased efforts in interdisciplinary training, and the development of alternative pathways to gaining geriatric knowledge and skills (discussed in more detail later in this chapter). Professional groups, private foundations, and public agencies all support and promote multiple efforts.

Even so, the committee concludes that in the education and training of the health care workforce, geriatric principles are still too often insufficiently represented in the curricula, and clinical experiences are not robust.

This is true in general for all the relevant professions. Very few professions have robust advanced training programs in geriatrics; of those professionals that do have options for advanced training, few individuals take advantage of these opportunities. One barrier to the development of more opportunities for advanced training in geriatrics is a lack of funding (discussed later in this chapter).

Professionals may also learn about the care of older adults through continuing-education activities. Most licensed professionals have state-based requirements that they must complete a specific number of continuing-education approved hours in order to maintain their licenses. Requirements vary widely among states, both in the number of hours required and regarding the content of those activities. Continuing-education requirements may also depend on requirements for board certification or for membership in professional societies. The content of the continuing education required of professionals is usually not specified. Many professionals fail to receive adequate education and training in geriatric issues while in school, and of those who do receive such education and training, some fail to keep up to date with this knowledge.

Since almost all professionals find themselves caring for older adults to some degree, they need to have a minimum level of competence in geriatrics. The general competence of health care professionals is ensured via mechanisms of state- or jurisdiction-based licensure and national board certification, both of which may require completion of a verbal examination, a written examination, or minimum amounts of annual education and training. Professional licensure provides the primary and most comprehensive route to ensure that practitioners are competent in the principles of geriatric care, since virtually all health care professionals must be licensed in order to provide care. Board certification, a voluntary process, is a secondary mechanism to ensure geriatric competency of professionals. Often neither licensure nor certification examinations have explicit geriatric content, or, if they do, the content is inadequate to ensure competency. By comparison, many of these examinations have explicit content concerning other patient populations, most notably pediatric populations.

The committee considered many mechanisms for facilitating the improvement of competence in geriatrics, including requiring schools to improve curricula as a basis of accreditation or requiring a certain percentage of continuing education hours to be spent on geriatric issues. Ultimately, the committee concluded that the most comprehensive way to facilitate this change would be through the explicit inclusion of geriatrics content on examinations for licensure and certification.

> **Recommendation 4-2: All licensure, certification, and maintenance of certification for health care professionals should include demonstration of competence in the care of older adults as a criterion.**

For many professionals, education and training programs are devised to prepare students for licensure and certification examinations, and so the inclusion of geriatrics in standardized examinations may encourage schools to increase the levels of geriatric education in their curricula. Exceptions may be made where appropriate (i.e., certain pediatric specialists and obstetricians). More will need to be done to improve the tools that evaluate this competence, such as ensuring the breadth and depth of questions on examinations are adequate to prove competence. In addition, educators, professional organizations, board examiners, and state licensing boards will need to work together to determine the best methods for assuring that the educational and training curricula for each discipline are devised to impart the competencies (i.e., knowledge, skills, and abilities) that these examinations will assess.

TRENDS AFFECTING THE FUTURE OF
EDUCATION AND TRAINING

Developing an effective health care workforce for older Americans will require taking a number of factors into account, including the demands of the future elderly population and changes that may affect the education and training of professionals. Furthermore, needs may develop for new types of workers and new skill sets, especially in light of new models of care and the emergence of new technologies. This section describes alternatives to traditional education, including the greater use of distance education and community colleges. Distance education is an efficient way to spread geriatric knowledge held by a small number of experts to large numbers of professionals, while community colleges can train certain types of new and existing workers, providing a source of education for some professionals who might have previously received only on-the-job training and also offering a way to standardize training. Finally, the section examines how emerging technologies and models of care may create needs for new types of workers or skill sets. This includes the possibility of having current workers take on different jobs so as to create a more flexible workforce that uses all individuals efficiently (to their maximum levels of competence).

Internet-Based Education

In recent years there has been a significant increase in the use of Internet-based education for the initial and continuing education and training of professionals in geriatrics (Gainor et al., 2004; Supiano et al., 2002; Swagerty et al., 2000). This is one way to achieve wider dissemination of geriatric knowledge, especially to those—such as health care providers in rural areas—who are unable to attend courses because of geographic, financial, and time-based constraints (Murphy-Southwick and McBride, 2006).

Internet-based education is also a useful tool for dealing with the lack of available leaders to teach the various courses.

Educators recognize that distance education has a number of valuable attributes, such as improved access to geriatric materials for non-traditional students, increased access to experts, and an increased ability to share information among disciplines. A survey of members of the Association for Gerontology in Higher Education found that 35 percent of the member institutions used distance education, with most of them (79 percent) having been using the modality for less than 5 years (Johnson, 2004). A survey of various medical education programs found that 79 percent used the Internet for geriatric education, and 56 percent reported that they were currently developing Internet-based products (Hajjar et al., 2007). There is also evidence, however, that some Internet-based geriatric information is of poor or inadequate quality (Hajjar et al., 2005).

Community Colleges

Innovative community college programs have great potential for playing a role in both the initial and the continuing geriatric education of certain professionals. Indeed, community colleges have already been instrumental in the education and training of large parts of the health care workforce for older patients. For example, community colleges educate a large number of the nurses who receive associate degrees (Mahaffey, 2002), and they provide refresher courses to those nurses already in the workforce (Sussman, 2006). Community colleges may provide career ladder programs for entry-level workers and partner with nursing homes and home health agencies to develop programs for continuing education.

Community colleges have also been essential in the development of many new certificate programs and education courses. Community colleges have the advantage of being able to tailor programs to local needs and state-based requirements and to use approaches that will be most acceptable to workers in that community. Recognizing this, the Allied and Auxiliary Health Care Workforce Project, sponsored by the California HealthCare Foundation and the California Endowment, funded seven model programs at community colleges to create new courses and credentialing processes for health care workers (Chapman et al., 2004). Mt. San Antonio College, one recipient of the funding created a new certificate program for entry-level mental health workers. City College of San Francisco and Jewish Vocational Services created a "Gateway to Health Careers Program" to introduce local residents to health care careers and to provide basic skills training for college readiness. Community college programs offer one approach to standardizing curricula for new types of workers who care for older patients and to ensuring the competency of those workers.

The federal government supports the use of community colleges to train new health workers. For example, the Employment and Training Administration within the U.S. Department of Labor supports Community-Based Job Training Grants that increase the capacity of community colleges to provide training in high-demand industries. Examples include a $2 million grant to Polk Community College in Florida to address the shortage of cardiovascular technologists and technicians to meet the demand from older patients and a $2.1 million grant to Manchester Community College in Connecticut to produce a larger number of graduates in nursing and allied health (DOL, 2006).

Technology

New technologies will affect how health care is delivered. These technologies may require providers to acquire new skills, such as how to operate new devices or to monitor patients from a distance via telemedicine, and that may change which types of providers are used to perform certain functions (Mullan, 2002). For example, imaging clinicians may need to expand their skill sets by learning how to operate and interpret a number of different imaging modalities, or new sub-specialty jobs may be created for people with expertise in a single specific imaging modality. The technologies most likely to affect the health care workforce in terms of types of workers and the necessary skill sets include

- technologies that may alter clinical practice, such as new forms of imaging and minimally invasive surgery;
- technologies that may use the workforce more efficiently, such as remote monitoring;
- technologies that may improve access to information, such as electronic health records; and
- technologies that may improve ergonomics, such as assistive devices for patient mobility and transport, and that may help prevent injury to workers (Health Technology Center, 2007).

As new technologies emerge, current workers will have to adapt to their use by acquiring new skills, or new types of workers may appear. While some technologies may impose new responsibilities on the health care workforce, others may relieve workers of their current duties or replace them altogether. One class of technologies that will be of particular importance to the health care workforce in light of current and future shortages are those technologies that will help older adults in the performance of activities of daily living (ADLs) and thus reduce the need for health care workers in this area. These technologies are discussed in more depth in Chapter 6.

New Professions

The health care workforce has a history of creating new professions in response to need, often as a result of the emergence of new technologies or the development of new models of care. At other times, new professions arise because of a serious shortage of providers. The profession of physician assistants, for example, was created in the 1960s to meet the urgent need for providers of primary care. In the same way, new professions may arise in response to the demand for services from older populations.

One type of new worker that has recently emerged in the care of older adults is the geriatric care manager. This new role stems from the development of a formal title for a care coordinator, a job which currently is often undertaken by a variety of providers without formal recognition. In most states, anyone can use this title without any requirement of training or certification (Stone et al., 2002), although many geriatric care managers are certified in other professions, most often in either social work or nursing. Recently, however, the number of certification programs for care managers has surged; one survey found more than 40 different certification designations that might be appropriate for care managers, such as "certified family life educator" and "certified case manager" (Reinhardt, 2003). As more people become aware of the importance of care coordination, especially for the older, frail elderly population, it can be expected that there will be increased need for health care workers who can fill this role. At the same time, the competencies needed to be an effective care manager will need to be developed, a task that will be made more difficult by the fact that no one profession "owns" this position.

Expanding Roles

To compensate for the serious shortages of providers that will characterize the coming decades, workers will need to be used more efficiently. More specifically, health care providers of all levels of education and training will need to assume additional responsibilities—or relinquish some responsibilities that they already have—to help ensure that all members of the health care workforce are used at their highest level of competence. Some professionals will likely need to increase their skills in order to be competent in more areas of care, while higher-level professionals may need to delegate some duties in order to be able to devote more of their time to providing the complex services that only they can provide. (See Chapters 3 and 5 for more on job delegation.) However, professionals are often not prepared for the role of delegator. For example, while RNs are increasingly responsible for supervision and delegation of care tasks to assistive personnel, they often are not taught the necessary decision-making skills associated with this role (Parsons, 1999). One survey of newly graduated baccalaureate nurses pointed to lack of education as the single most important barrier to effective delegation and that skills were generally learned through trial and error (Thomas and Hume, 1998). Formal efforts to help nurses learn these skills are increasing, often through continuing education (Kleinman and Saccomano, 2006).

States can play a role in changing the structure of the health care workforce by passing laws that recognize scopes of practice for new types of providers and that expand the legal scope of work for existing providers, although this may be controversial among professional groups (Carson-Smith and Minarik, 2007; RCHWS, 2003; Rossi, 2003; Wing et al., 2004). For example, there has been a great deal of debate in the United States over the use of advanced dental hygienists—known as dental therapists in other countries—to provide some basic dental services to underserved patients (Mertz and O'Neil, 2002; Ryan, 2003). And, as has been seen with team-based training, physicians are often reluctant to delegate responsibilities for care to other workers (Reuben et al., 2004). Among nurses, the delegation of medication administration duties from RNs to CNAs or unlicensed personnel has received much attention (Reinhard et al., 2003). First, there is extreme variation and ambiguity in state laws regarding which tasks may be delegated, ranging from the ability to merely remind patients to take their medications to physical administration of the medication. Confusion about these tasks has led to concern for liability among nursing supervisors. Second, there have been some concerns for patient safety. However, little research has been performed to examine the impact of using CNAs or unlicensed personnel for medication administration on patient care, such as comparison of medication error rates between RNs and unlicensed staff. But, some RNs argue that these workers have fewer distractions, leading to more accurate delivery of medications (Reinhard et al., 2003).

There is good deal of precedent for the idea of expanding scopes of work or delegating responsibilities in response to workforce needs. Both the physician assistant and the advanced nurse practitioner professions, for instance, have undergone expansions of their legal scopes of practice, most notably in the state-based regulations regarding prescription authority. There has also been an expansion of work roles among many types of allied workers. For example, some physicians have trained their medical assistants to teach self-management skills to patients (Bodenheimer, 2007). And pharmacy technicians have assumed increased responsibility for tasks not requiring professional clinical judgment (Muenzen et al., 2005). While pharmacy technicians most often dispense medications and maintain inventory, they have increasingly become involved in more skilled areas, such as in supervising processes of quality assurance (e.g., medication order entry and separating similar-looking or similar-sounding medications). In response, many state boards of pharmacy have allowed a broadening of pharmacy technician responsibilities.

As new or enhanced scopes of practice are developed, effort will be needed to avoid policies that impede the flexible and effective use of these personnel. While a detailed discussion of state scope-of-practice laws is beyond the scope of this report, the issue is central to improving the capacity of the health care workforce for older Americans.

RECRUITMENT AND RETENTION

Health care providers who care for older patients serve a complex, challenging population, and evidence shows that working with geriatric patients is highly satisfying. One study showed, for example, that geriatric medicine has the highest percentage of "very satisfied" specialists among physicians surveyed in the 1996-1997 Community Tracking Physician Survey (Leigh et al., 2002). Another study found that 79 percent of geriatricians surveyed felt their geriatric fellowship had a positive effect on their career satisfaction level, and almost 90 percent said they would recommend a geriatric fellowship to others (Shah et al., 2006). In spite of this, many geriatric fellowship positions remain unfilled. Among professionals who have a choice, most do not choose geriatric specialties or choose to work in long-term care settings. Among high school students considering a nursing career almost half have no interest in specializing in geriatrics, whereas 87 percent report having an interest in pediatric nursing (Evercare, 2007). In 2002, 15 percent of the RN positions and 13 percent of the LPN positions at nursing homes were vacant (National Commission on Nursing Workforce for Long-Term Care, 2005).

This section describes the barriers to recruitment and retention of professionals in geriatric fields, with a particular emphasis on the recruitment technique of offering financial support in exchange for service commitments. Many of these barriers are not unique to the health care professionals who care for older patients, but this section will focus specifically on these issues as they relate to the health care professionals who care for older patients or who work primarily in long-term care settings.

Barriers

The barriers to recruiting and retaining health care professionals in the geriatric field include negative stereotypes of working with older patients, the complexity of geriatric cases, a lack of mentors, the availability of more attractive opportunities in non-health care professions, and also various financial disincentives. It is particularly difficult to retain and recruit care providers into institutional long-term care because of the stressful and physically demanding working conditions, relatively low salaries, and low job satisfaction. Turnover of health care professionals in these settings contributes to poorer patient outcomes and increased turnover of other workers. For example, increased turnover of RNs has been associated with decreased quality of care (Castle and Engberg, 2005); high rates of turnover among nursing home administrators and managers has been associated with both poorer patient outcomes and increased turnover of RNs and LPNs (Castle, 2001, 2005).

This section highlights some of the challenges to the recruitment and retention of health care providers to care for older patients. The first challenge discussed is that the workforce itself is aging. Large groups of workers are expected to retire in the coming decades, and they will have to be replaced, which will only heighten the need for health care providers. The second challenge is that stereotypes persist about caring for older patients; many assume that the work is depressing and that most older patients are extremely sick, frail, or demented. Next is the lack of opportunity for providers to receive advanced training in geriatrics; if no training opportunities exist, health care professionals will be unable or unwilling to specialize in geriatric care. The last challenges discussed are the financial ones. Because of the costs of extra training and the failure of payment systems to compensate geriatric specialists properly, financial disincentives are probably the greatest obstacles to the recruitment and retention of more geriatric-specific health care professionals. The section concludes with an examination of the use of programs that offer financial support in exchange for service commitments.

Aging of the Health Care Workforce

One challenge to the health care workforce in general is the aging of its members. As of January 2007, 23.3 percent of all active physicians were 60 or older (AAMC, 2007a). In 2001, 81 percent of all dentists were over age 45, and the number of dentists expected to retire by 2020 is larger than the number of new dentists expected to enter the workforce by that time (Center for Health Workforce Studies, 2005). By 2020 almost half of all registered nurses will be over age 50 (AHA, 2007; Buerhaus et al., 2000), and about one-third of all currently practicing social workers will soon be of retirement age (National Commission for Quality Long-Term Care, 2007).

More needs to be done to retain some of these older workers, recognizing their importance as on-the-job mentors, most likely by the development of less physically demanding roles or more flexible work schedules (Rosenfeld, 2007). Their roles could be made less physically demanding, for instance, by the development of technologies that perform the more labor-intensive of their duties. Another retention strategy would be to recruit older workers into leadership roles (Rosenfeld, 2007). Retired geriatric-health professionals have invaluable knowledge and expertise, and they could become academic leaders in the training of future generations. This would be of great value, especially considering the scarcity of faculty described above. Retired generalists, with additional training, could also re-enter their fields as geriatric experts. The social work profession has embraced this concept with the development of the Retired Social Workers Project, which uses both distance and in-person education to train retired social workers in geriatric concepts so that they might return to the work-force to assist older patients (IGSW, 2007).

Negative Stereotypes

While the current elderly population is healthier and more educated and has higher rates of volunteerism than previous generations of the same age, negative stereotypes of older adults persist, including that they are typically physically disabled, senile, and disconnected from social activities (Krout and McKernan, 2007; Wood and Mulligan, 2000). In spite of the job satisfaction that has been documented among geriatric providers, students still see working with these populations as depressing, which may be one of the reasons that when students are asked about their specialization preferences, they continue to rank geriatrics near the bottom (Anderson and Wiscott, 2004; Cummings and Galambos, 2002).

Early exposures to a broad range of geriatric patients—and especially to healthier older adults—has a positive effect on interest in geriatric fields (Bernard et al., 2003; Cummings et al., 2003, 2005; Linn and Zeppa, 1987; Medina-Walpole et al., 2002; Reuben et al., 1995; Woolsey, 2007). One particularly effective strategy for providing students with this sort of positive experience is pairing them with older patients who act as mentors (Corwin et al., 2006; Stewart and Alford, 2006; Waldrop et al., 2006). In such a mentoring program a student will typically meet regularly with a healthy older adult over a certain period of time, often to complete specific assignments; the older patient acts to sensitize the student to the positive aspects of aging, to dispel myths, and to create empathy for the frustra-tions faced by seniors. A second strategy whose effectiveness is supported by evidence is to expose students to professional role models or mentors who reinforce the positive aspects of geriatric care and, by doing so, inspire students to enter geriatric fields themselves (Hazzard, 1999; Johnson and Valle, 1996; Maas et al., 2006; Mackin et al., 2006; Medina-Walpole et al., 2002).

Lack of Opportunity

The recruitment of health care professionals to become geriatric specialists is often hindered by a simple lack of opportunity. As discussed previously, many professionals have neither adequate introduction to geriatrics nor opportunities for advanced training in the field. While GME supports the general training of physicians in geriatrics, workers in other professions often lack the opportunity for advanced training in geriatrics, usually because there is not enough funding for the programs or not enough funding for salary support.

Indeed, this is part of a pattern that extends far beyond geriatrics. Generally speaking, with the exception of physicians, few professionals have significant support for advanced training. In response, some efforts have arisen in recent years to increase the training opportunities for these professionals. The Medicare program, for example, not only supports the training of residents but has made some payments to hospitals for its share of the direct costs of nursing and allied health training programs. In 2001 Congress introduced the All Payer Graduate Medical Education Act,[12] which would collect additional GME funds through a 1 percent tax on private health plans. Part of this revenue was directed toward the graduate education of "non-physician health professionals" (AAMC, 2007b). The Nurse Education, Expansion, and Development Act[13] proposes to provide grants to nursing schools, in part, to develop "post-baccalaureate residency programs to prepare nurses for practice in specialty areas where nursing shortages are more severe." These measures are for the training of professionals in general, however, and do not necessarily support advanced geriatric training.

In the area of geriatrics, advanced training programs for professionals other than physicians often must look to private foundations for support, or else it falls to the individual students to pay for the programs without any source of subsidy. For example, in 2007 the John A. Hartford Foundation awarded a $5 million renewal grant to the Gerontological Society of America for the purpose of preparing doctoral students in geriatric social work (The John A. Hartford Foundation, 2007).

Financial Concerns

Financial burdens create great challenges in the recruitment and retention of all types of professionals.

---

[12]*All Payer Graduate Medical Education Act of 2001.* HR 2178. 107th Congress. June 14, 2001.

[13]*Nurse Education, Expansion, and Development Act of 2007.* S 446. 110th Congress, 1st session. January 31, 2007.

Recommendation 4-3: Public and private payers should provide financial incentives to increase the number of geriatric specialists in all health professions.

Specific types of financial incentives will be recommended throughout the rest of this chapter. Medicare and Medicaid policies will be especially important in the implementation of financial incentives due both to their role in the financing of health care services for older adults as well as the influence of their policies on other payers.

The costs associated with extra years of geriatric training do not translate into additional income, and geriatric specialists tend to earn significantly less income than specialists in other areas and often less than the generalists within their own fields. In fact, the additional training needed to become a geriatric specialist has been shown to have a negative effect on future earnings. In 1999 a physician who pursued a 1-year geriatric medicine fellowship stood to lose $7,016 annually, and the completion of a 2-year fellowship translated into a net annual loss of $8,592 (Weeks and Wallace, 2004). In 2005 a geriatrician's median salary was only 93 percent of the median salary for a general internist (ADGAP, 2007b). Similar disparities exist for other professions. For instance, compared with nurses in hospital settings, full-time RNs who work in nursing homes or other extended-care facilities receive lower annual earnings on average, even though they work more hours per week, incur more hours of overtime, and have a larger percentage of overtime hours that are mandatory (HRSA, 2006b). PAs who specialize in geriatrics have lower salaries than other types of PAs (AAPA, 2007). One survey of recent MSW graduates showed that while 70 percent strongly agreed that geriatric care is an important part of social work, only 36 percent strongly agreed that geriatric social work offered good career opportunities (Cummings et al., 2003).

In part this income disparity is due to the fact that a larger proportion of a geriatric specialist's reimbursement tends to come from Medicare and Medicaid. Additionally, as the population ages, many non-geriatric specialists will experience similar difficulties. Rates of reimbursement are low for primary care codes in general, especially as compared with the procedural codes typically used by other specialists. Medicare and Medicaid reimbursements do not take into account the fact that the care of frail older adults with complex care needs is very time-consuming, a situation that causes geriatric specialists to have fewer patient encounters and fewer billings (MedPAC, 2003).

Recommendation 4-3a: All payers should include a specific enhancement of reimbursement for clinical services delivered to older adults by practitioners with a certification of special expertise in geriatrics.

This enhancement should apply to all types of professionals certified in geriatric care. Several mechanisms can and should be used to facilitate this enhancement due to the variety of providers and mechanisms for delivery of compensation. Whatever the mechanism, this enhancement should raise salaries enough to create greater appeal to entering geriatric fields.

As one example, in 2005, the net clinical compensation of a geriatrician was about $163,000, while that of a general internal medicine physician was about $175,000 (ADGAP, 2007d). However, the disparities between geriatric medicine and other subspecialties of internal or family medicine are even greater. Table 4-5 shows that other non-procedure driven subspecialties of internal medicine have markedly higher fill rates for advanced training programs, as well as substantially higher salaries.

In this example, to raise salaries for the existing geriatricians from $163,000 to $200,000 (to be in accordance with other similar subspecialties) for each of the existing 7,128 geriatricians would cost about $263 million. However, the committee supports creating incentives to markedly increase the number of providers. The committee presents two hypothetical examples of estimates for extra annual costs (due to payment enhancements) under assumptions associated with two different goals for the growth in number of certified geriatricians. Under the first scenario (Table 4-6), the goal is to double the number of geriatricians over 10 years; this goal requires a 20 percent increase in the number of geriatric fellows graduating annually. Under the second scenario (Table 4-7), the goal is to triple the number of geriatricians over 20 years; this goal requires a 10 percent annual increase in the number of fellows graduating annually. The committee recognizes both of these goals are ambitious and beyond the capacity of the current system to produce these numbers of graduates unless significant changes are made. These differing scenarios, however, serve to provide two different

TABLE 4-5 Fill Rate for Subspecialty Training in Internal Medicine Programs and Median Compensation

Subspecialty	Number of Program Year 1 Positions Filled (as of 12/31/2006)	Total Number of Program Year 1 Positions Available (as of 12/31/2006)	Fill Rate (%)	Median Compensation (in Thousands) (2005)
Geriatric medicine[a]	253	468	54%	$163
Endocrinology	232	252	92%	$189
Hematology and oncology	410	432	95%	$358
Infectious disease	324	348	93%	$205
Rheumatology	176	184	96%	$207

[a]Includes fellowships as a subspecialty of either internal medicine or family medicine.

TABLE 4-6 Timeline for Extra Costs Associated with Geriatrician Salary Increase Assuming Doubling of Numbers Over 10 Years

Year	Annual Number of Graduates (Assuming 20% Annual Increase)	Total Number of Geriatricians	Extra Annual Costs (in Millions, 2008 Dollars)
2008	253[a]	7,381	$273.1
2009	304	7,685	$284.3
2010	365	8,050	$297.8
2011	438	8,488	$314.1
2012	526	9,014	$333.5
2013	631	9,645	$356.9
2014	757	10,402	$384.9
2015	908	11,310	$418.5
2016	1,090	12,400	$458.8
2017	1,308	13,708	$507.2
2018	1,570	15,278	$565.3

NOTE: These estimations calculate growth in the number of geriatricians based on an assumption of growth in the number of fellows and do not include estimations of attrition. Costs were estimated assuming $37,000 in extra annual costs for each of the geriatricians practicing in that year, and have not been adjusted for cost-of-living increases or inflation.

[a]The initial number of graduates is based on the current number of first-year fellows in geriatrics.

strategies that highlight the amount of effort that will be needed to close the gap between the numbers of current supply and the numbers needed in the future. Ultimately, the chosen strategy will depend on the ability of the current system to increase its capacity, the development of an increased interest in geriatrics among providers, and the availability of immediate and future funding sources. While the committee recognizes the current high level of attrition among these providers, it also contends that attrition will likely decrease if greater financial incentives exist. Estimates do not take attrition into account.

One mechanism to increase salaries would be to develop a special fee schedule for services provided by geriatric specialists that increased the relative value of the provider. Another option would be to create a new modifier that allows for increased payment. Modifiers are added to billing codes to indicate special circumstances surrounding the delivery of a service. For example, the "22" modifier recognizes that "For any given procedure code, there could typically be a range of work effort or practice expense required to provide the service. Thus, carriers may increase or decrease the payment for a service only under very unusual circumstances based upon review of medical records and other documentation" (CMS, 2007). This modifier is currently only available for surgical procedures and involves much documentation to justify its use, but it serves as an example of how a modifier could be developed for use by geriatric specialists for billing purposes.

TABLE 4-7 Timeline for Extra Costs Associated with Geriatrician Salary Increase Assuming Tripling of Numbers Over 20 Years

Year	Annual Number of Graduates (Assuming 10% Annual Increase)	Total Number of Geriatricians	Extra Annual Costs (in Millions, 2008 Dollars)
2008	253[a]	7,381	$273.1
2009	278	7,659	$283.4
2010	306	7,965	$294.7
2011	337	8,302	$307.2
2012	371	8,673	$320.9
2013	408	9,081	$336.0
2014	449	9,530	$352.6
2015	494	10,024	$370.9
2016	543	10,567	$391.0
2017	597	11,164	$413.1
2018	657	11,821	$437.4
2019	723	12,544	$464.1
2020	795	13,339	$493.5
2021	875	14,214	$525.9
2022	963	15,177	$561.5
2023	1,059	16,236	$600.7
2024	1,165	17,401	$643.8
2025	1,281	18,682	$691.2
2026	1,409	20,091	$743.4
2027	1,550	21,641	$800.7
2028	1,705	23,346	$863.8

NOTE: These estimations calculate growth in the number of geriatricians based on an assumption of growth in the number of fellows and do not include estimations of attrition. Costs were estimated assuming $37,000 in extra annual costs for each of the geriatricians practicing in that year, and have not been adjusted for cost-of-living increases or inflation.

[a]The initial number of graduates is based on the current number of first-year fellows in geriatrics.

Other aspects of reimbursement policies can create financial disincentives to geriatric specialization. For instance, Medicare and Medicaid often lack codes for care coordination and other advance services; by supporting these types of advanced services through the development of "medical homes," Medicare could realize savings of as much as $194 billion over 10 years (Commonwealth Fund, 2007). And insurers often allow only for a pharmacist dispensing fee, failing to reimburse for advanced pharmacist services, including those activities shown to improve patient outcomes or lower health care costs. In response to these concerns, the 2006 implementation of the Medicare Modernization Act of 2003 established a mechanism by which pharmacists are eligible to receive payment for providing medication-therapy management services as a benefit of the Part D program (CMS, 2005). Psychiatrists thinking of specializing in geriatrics may be pushed toward other areas since Medicare requires a 50 percent copayment for outpatient mental health services, compared to 20 percent for most other medical services (ADGAP, 2007a). Furthermore, Medicare does not cover any routine oral-health services.

Financial burdens affect the recruitment and retention of clinical and academic geriatric experts. A 2004 survey of second-year MSW students found that over 60 percent expressed interest in an aging-related internship—if a stipend were available for this activity (Cummings et al., 2005). Junior faculty in geriatrics have lower compensation than those in family or internal medicine (ADGAP, 2004). At higher faculty positions the median dollars paid to those in geriatrics become similar to those paid for other specialties, but the pay of geriatrics specialists still lags behind that of the higher-paid procedural specialties. Between 2002 and 2003 salaries for geriatric physician faculty decreased by 3 percent; during this time period, family medicine salaries increased by 1.5 percent, and general internal medicine salaries remained the same.

GACAs have been instrumental in the development of academic geriatricians. These awards are especially appealing since the grants directly support teaching services during the life of the award.

Recommendation 4-3b: Congress should authorize and fund an enhancement of the Geriatric Academic Career Award (GACA) program to support junior geriatrics faculty in other health professions in addition to allopathic and osteopathic medicine.

The committee supports the extension of GACAs to all doctorate-level health care professionals. As has been discussed, many of the geriatric specialties are limited by the availability of faculty and mentors. The creation of GACAs for other doctoral-level health care professions would help to promote not only the geriatric professions, but would enable educational programs to better educate all professionals in the care of older adults. Recognizing the lag time between the initial training of professionals until the time they are available to become faculty, these training opportunities should begin now.

In June 2007, Senator Bingaman introduced a bill[14] that would provide GACAs to doctorate level nurses certified in geriatrics or geropsychiatry. This bill proposed a funding level of $1.875 million per fiscal year (plus administrative costs) to allow for a total of 125 5-year awards for $75,000 in total between 2008 and 2015. A loftier goal could be to have one GACA at every institution that prepares advanced practice professionals. For ex-

---

[14]*Nurse faculty and physical therapist education act of 2007.* S 1628. 110th Congress, 1st session. June 14, 2007.

ample, about 81 programs exist to prepare geriatric nurse practitioners. The availability of a $75,000 GACA for each of these 81 faculty positions would amount to about $6.1 million annually (plus administrative costs) for the nursing profession alone. (Similar efforts should be made for other professions.) The committee recognizes that geriatric educators are also needed at institutions that do not have specific programs in geriatrics, as all professionals need to be trained in geriatric principles. However, the availability of these awards at advanced programs is an achievable first step.

To avoid some of the pitfalls experienced by the GACA program for physicians, the committee supports making the GACA an institutional award (instead of an individual award). Additionally, as the number of professionals entering the different disciplines increases, the number of GACAs needs to proportionately increase.

Linking Financial Support to Service

Most efforts to recruit and retain professionals for in-need populations seek to relieve professionals of at least part of the financial burden associated with their education and training. These recruitment efforts usually consist of offering some type of financial support—generally scholarships or loan forgiveness, or both—in exchange for the professional promising to serve a certain number of years with a population in need. Programs exist at both the state and national levels, and many programs entail a collaboration between the two. Five general types of programs link financial support and service (Table 4-8).

Scholarships and loan repayments are by far the most common types of programs. However, very few studies have assessed the effect of these programs on completion of service or retention of practitioners (Pathman et al., 2000). These programs also change frequently without any evidence of immediate or lasting effectiveness. Since they are the most common, the rest of this section will focus on scholarship and loan-repayment programs.

State Efforts

Many states attempt to recruit needed members to the health care workforce with programs that offer financial support in exchange for future service. Such programs date back to the 1940s. In 1987 HRSA created the State Loan Repayment Program (SLRP), which authorizes the National Health Service Corps (discussed below) to provide matching funds to states that develop educational loan-repayment programs. These funds are specifically designated for primary care physicians in exchange for service in a so-called health-professions shortage area, or HPSA.

Some state-level programs operate with federal support, while others

TABLE 4-8 Classification of Support-for-Service Programs

Program Type	Eligibility	Service[a]	Use of Funds	Typical Design	Impact in State-Based Programs[b]
Scholarship	Students	Required	Up-front training costs	Funds to students for tuition, fees, books, and living expenses, with service expected after training	On average, 66.5% complete service obligations; 27.2% repay loans instead of providing service Second shortest retention; least likely to repeat the process
Loan	Students	Optional	Up-front training costs	Loans to students for tuition, fees, books, and living expenses; loan is repaid after training either financially or by providing service	On average, 44.7% complete service obligations; 49.2% repay loan rather than provide service
Resident support	Junior residents	Required	Variable	Unrestricted funds for junior and, occasionally, senior residents, with service expected after training	On average, 93% complete service obligations (combined with next two groups) Combined with next 2 groups, only 2.3% repay loans instead of providing service Shortest retention
Loan repayment	Senior residents and practitioners	Required	Repayment of educational loans	Funds to repay outstanding educational loans of graduating residents and practitioners in exchange for service	See "Resident Support Programs" Longest retention
Direct financial incentive	Senior residents and practitioners	Required	Unrestricted	Unrestricted funds for graduating residents and practitioners in exchange for service	See "Resident Support Programs"

[a]While service is "required" for some types of programs, many have buyout options (with associated penalties).
[b]Based on one study (Pathman et al., 2004).
SOURCE: Pathman et al., 2000, 2004. Copyright 2000, American Medical Association. All rights reserved.

operate without. A 1996 survey found that 82 programs in 41 states supported almost 1,700 professionals (Pathman et al., 2000). Most of these programs (84 percent) supported medical students, residents, and practicing physicians; about half (44 percent) were available to PAs and APRNs, and about 20 percent were available to other professionals, such as dentists and podiatrists. The programs offered support amounts that ranged from $3,000 to $38,000 annually, and they had service commitments ranging from 1 to 60 months.

When Pathman and colleagues sought to evaluate the effectiveness of state-level support-for-service programs, they found that participants in such programs practiced in needier areas and cared for more Medicaid and uninsured patients than non-participants (Pathman et al., 2004). Retention was also slightly higher for participants in the program than it was for non-participants. Overall, loan repayment and direct financial incentives proved to be the most successful methods. Scholarships and other student-focused programs were challenged by the administrative burden of keeping track of these students over the course of their educational paths.

Some state-level loan-repayment programs focus specifically on geriatricians. For example, in May 2005 South Carolina introduced the Geriatric Loan Forgiveness Program, which forgives $35,000 of medical school debt for each year of fellowship training in geriatric medicine or geriatric psychiatry; loan forgiveness is dependent on the physician practicing in the state of South Carolina for at least 5 years (Lt. Governor's Office on Aging, 2005).

Indian Health Service

The Indian Health Service (IHS) Loan Repayment Program repays up to $20,000 in education loans per year (plus additional tax benefits) for practitioners in certain health professions who commit to practicing for at least 2 years in an IHS facility or other approved program (IHS, 2007). While all professionals are eligible for this program, physicians and nurses usually get highest priority.

National Institutes of Health Loan Repayment Program

The National Institutes of Health (NIH) offers loan repayment to doctoral-level researchers in exchange for commitments to perform research. For a 2-year commitment the NIH pays off up to $35,000 per year of educational debt, plus additional tax benefits. Individuals may perform the research at any nonprofit organization, university, or government organization. Loan repayment is currently available for researchers in

- clinical research;
- pediatric research;
- health-disparities research;
- clinical research for individuals from disadvantaged backgrounds; and
- contraception and infertility research (NIH, 2007g).

Repayment for researchers in clinical research comprises more than half of the NIH repayment program's contracts and funds. For fiscal year 2006, 38 percent of the 1,044 new applications and 71 percent of the 777 renewal applications for clinical research were accepted (NIH, 2007a). More than half of the contracts for clinical research were made with medical doctors; other clinicians given contracts included optometrists, dentists, psychologists, pharmacists, doctors of naturopathic medicine, and doctors of osteopathic medicine (NIH, 2007d). Contracts for clinical research totaled almost $40 million (for 945 contracts), and contracts for pediatric research totaled $18.8 million (for 403 contracts). Contracts for all five areas of research together added up to approximately $70 million (for 1,651 contracts) (NIH, 2007b,c,d,e,f).

National Health Service Corps

Perhaps the best known program offering health professionals financial support for educational and training expenses in exchange for service is the National Health Service Corps (NHSC). The NHSC, which was established in 1972 in an amendment to the Emergency Health Personnel Act, operates as part of the Public Health Service and places health care practitioners in HPSAs. Under the loan-forgiveness program, practitioners receive up to $25,000 per year of service for the first 2 years of service. After completing that 2-year minimum, commitments may be extended annually, and practitioners who extend their service in the HPSA beyond the first 2 years can receive as much as $35,000 in loan forgiveness per year in the succeeding years. Reviews of the effectiveness of the NHSC have been mixed, mostly because of questions about its ability to retain practitioners over the long term (Mullan, 1999; Pathman et al., 2006). The fiscal year 2006 budget for the NHSC was about $125.4 million, of which $85.2 million was used for the loan-repayment and scholarship programs (HRSA, 2007a). Over its entire history, more than 27,000 professionals have served with the NHSC, and currently about 4,000 are in service (HRSA, 2007d). The NHSC recruits the following types of professionals:

- Primary care physicians
- Nurse practitioners

- Dentists
- Mental and behavioral health professionals
- Physician assistants
- Certified nurse-midwives
- Dental hygienists

In addition to loan forgiveness for the various types of professionals, the NHSC offers scholarships for students in

- allopathic medical schools;
- osteopathic medical schools;
- family nurse practitioner and nurse-midwifery programs;
- physician assistant programs; and
- dental schools.

These scholarships pay for up to 4 years of education, including tuition and related educational expenses plus a stipend. Students commit to 1 year of service in a shortage area for each year of financial support (with a 2-year minimum).

Little has been done to evaluate the impact and effectiveness of the NHSC. However, a 1995 report found that, as is the case with in-state programs, NHSC scholarship programs have worse outcomes (in terms of service completion, satisfaction, and retention) and higher administrative costs than loan-repayment programs (GAO, 1995). Indeed, the report showed that loan-repayment participants end up costing the government one-half to one-third less than scholarship recipients.

Recently, members of Congress proposed the use of NHSC to improve the recruitment and retention of geriatricians. The most recent attempt was the Geriatricians Loan Forgiveness Act of 2007,[15] which called for fellowship years in either geriatric medicine or geriatric psychiatry to be recognized as a period of service to an underserved population. Similar bills have been introduced in both the House and Senate multiple times, so far without success.

The committee concluded that programs that link financial support to service have been effective in increasing the numbers of health care professionals that serve in underserved areas of the country and that they serve as good models for the development of similar programs to address shortages of geriatric providers.

---

[15]*Geriatricians Loan Forgiveness Act of 2007*. HR 2502. 110th Congress, 1st session. May 24, 2007.

For example, as discussed above, some geriatric professions have existing opportunities for advanced training, but practitioners do not pursue the positions (e.g., only 54 percent of available first-year positions in geriatric medicine were filled in 2006-2007). If financial support was available, it might encourage professionals to pursue such advanced training. The availability of scholarships could also get students interested in geriatrics earlier in their careers, which in turn would create a need for the development of more robust geriatric curricula and more advanced training options.

Recommendation 4-3c: States and the federal government should institute programs for loan forgiveness, scholarships, and direct financial incentives for professionals who become geriatric specialists. One such mechanism should include the development of a National Geriatric Service Corps, modeled after the National Health Service Corps.

One mechanism to create incentives for students to enter geriatric specialties is a National Geriatric Health Service Corps which would offer loan repayment for newly graduating professionals in geriatrics. There are many mechanisms for achieving this increased recruitment and retention; loan repayment is one example. For example, the committee estimated the costs required to institute loan repayment for graduating fellows of geriatric medicine. As in Tables 4-6 and 4-7, the committee presents costs for a loan repayment program associated with two hypothetical goals: to either double the number of geriatricians over 10 years, or to triple their numbers over 20 years. Under these scenarios, the costs for loan repayment for physicians is estimated at $35,000 per year for 4 years (or $140,000 per physician). Tables 4-9 and 4-10 demonstrate rough estimates for loan repayment to graduating fellows of geriatric medicine based on 2008 dollars assuming, as in Tables 4-6 and 4-7, either a 20 percent or 10 percent annual increase in the number of geriatric fellows.

CONCLUSION

This chapter addressed the education, training, recruitment, and retention of the professional health care workforce. Overall, there is an inadequate supply of professionals in general for meeting the health care needs of the future older adults and also an inadequate number of geriatric specialists both to care for these patients and to teach other professionals about geriatric care. Although the situation is improving, most professional education programs still do not have sufficient geriatric content in their curricula or adequate experiences in clinical settings. When the opportunity exists, most professionals are not choosing to receive specialized training in geriatrics, and some professions lack the opportunity for advanced geriatric

TABLE 4-9 Timeline for Costs Associated with Geriatrician Loan
Repayment Assuming Doubling of Numbers Over 10 Years

Year	Annual Number of Graduates (Assuming 20% Annual Increase)	Total Number of Geriatricians	Annual Costs for Loan Repayment (in Millions, 2008 Dollars)
2008	253[a]	7,381	$35.4
2009	304	7,685	$42.6
2010	365	8,050	$51.1
2011	438	8,488	$61.3
2012	526	9,014	$73.6
2013	631	9,645	$88.3
2014	757	10,402	$106.0
2015	908	11,310	$127.1
2016	1,090	12,400	$152.6
2017	1,308	13,708	$183.1
2018	1,570	15,278	$219.8

NOTE: These estimations calculate growth in the number of geriatricians based on an assumption of growth in the number of fellows and do not include estimations of attrition. Annual costs were estimated assuming $140,000 in loan repayments for each of the fellows graduating in that year, and have not been adjusted for cost-of-living increases or inflation. Administrative costs have also not been included in these estimates.

[a]The initial number of graduates is based on the current number of first-year fellows in geriatrics.

training. Distance-education programs and community colleges are providing viable alternatives for the education and training of many professionals in geriatric principles. The future workforce will likely need to fulfill new roles, be more flexible, and possess new skills. The committee recommends that more be done to increase the breadth of geriatric experiences among health care professionals and to ensure the geriatric competence of all providers.

Barriers to recruitment and retention include the aging of the workforce itself and negative stereotypes about working with older adults. Financial disincentives include disparities in the reimbursement system, such as lack of payment for care coordination, and the high costs associated with advanced training. The committee recommends that financial incentives be implemented in order to encourage more professionals to become geriatric specialists; such incentives should include the enhancement of payments to geriatric specialists, an expansion of the GACA program, and the institution of loan forgiveness, scholarships, or direct financial incentives to assist with the high costs of tuition among all types of health care professionals who care for older adults. While all of these areas have shown improvement, much more needs to be done to educate, train, recruit, and retain a competent and ample professional workforce to care for the older population in 2030.

TABLE 4-10 Timeline for Costs Associated with Geriatrician Loan Repayment Assuming Tripling of Numbers Over 20 Years

Year	Annual Number of Graduates (Assuming 10% Annual Increase)	Total Number of Geriatricians	Annual Costs for Loan Repayment (in Millions, 2008 Dollars)
2008	253[a]	7,381	$35.4
2009	278	7,659	$42.1
2010	306	7,965	$42.8
2011	337	8,302	$47.2
2012	371	8,673	$51.9
2013	408	9,081	$57.1
2014	449	9,530	$62.9
2015	494	10,024	$69.2
2016	543	10,567	$76.0
2017	597	11,164	$83.6
2018	657	11,821	$92.0
2019	723	12,544	$101.2
2020	795	13,339	$111.3
2021	875	14,214	$122.5
2022	963	15,177	$134.8
2023	1,059	16,236	$148.3
2024	1,165	17,401	$163.1
2025	1,281	18,682	$179.3
2026	1,409	20,091	$197.3
2027	1,550	21,641	$217.0
2028	1,705	23,346	$238.7

NOTE: These estimations calculate growth in the number of geriatricians based on an assumption of growth in the number of fellows and do not include estimations of attrition. Annual costs were estimated assuming $140,000 in loan repayments for each of the fellows graduating in that year, and have not been adjusted for cost-of-living increases or inflation. Administrative costs have also not been included in these estimates.

[a]The initial number of graduates is based on the current number of first-year fellows in geriatrics.

REFERENCES

AACN (American Association of Colleges of Nursing). 2004. *Nurse practitioner and clinical nurse specialist competencies for older adult care.* http://www.hartfordign.org/case_study/Geriatric%20Competencies%20for%20non-GNPs.pdf (accessed February 1, 2008).

AACN. 2006. *Student enrollment rises in U.S. nursing colleges and universities for the 6th consecutive year.* http://www.aacn.nche.edu/06Survey.htm (accessed July 9, 2007).

AACPM (American Association of Colleges of Podiatric Medicine). 2007. *American Association of Colleges of Podiatric Medicine: School links.* http://www.aacpm.org/html/collegelinks/cl_schools.asp (accessed August 22, 2007).

AAMC (Association of American Medical Colleges). 2007a. *2007 state physician workforce data book.* http://med.ucmerced.edu/docs/AAMC2007StateDataWorkbook.pdf (accessed January 29, 2008).

AAMC. 2007b. *"All-payer" GME trust fund legislation.* http://www.aamc.org/advocacy/library/gme/gme0011.htm (accessed December 7, 2007).

AAMC. 2007c. *Medicare direct graduate medical education (DGME) payments.* http://www.aamc.org/advocacy/library/gme/gme0001.htm (accessed December 7, 2007).

AAMC/The John A. Hartford Foundation. 2007. *Minimum geriatric competencies for medical students.* http://www.pogoe.org/frames.aspx (accessed January 8, 2008).

AAPA (American Academy of Physician Assistants). 2007. *2007 AAPA physician assistant census report.* Alexandria, VA: AAPA.

ABFM (American Board of Family Medicine). 2007. *Certification/recertification examination content.* https://www.theabfm.org/cert/CertRecertExaminationOutline.pdf (accessed December 5, 2007).

ABGD (American Board of General Dentistry). 2007. *American Board of General Dentistry: Rules and procedures.* http://www.abgd.org/docs/rules_web2.htm#1 (accessed October 24, 2007).

ABIM (American Board of Internal Medicine). 2005. *Maintenance of certification enrollment.* http://www.abim.org/resources/mocenroll.shtm (accessed October 23, 2007).

ABIM. 2006. *ABIM recognizes added qualifications as subspecialties of internal medicine.* http://www.abim.org/news/news/06_07_14_added_q.aspx (accessed December 28, 2007).

ABIM. 2007. *Internal medicine certification examination blueprint.* http://www.abim.org/pdf/blueprint/im_cert.pdf (accessed December 5, 2007).

ABMS (American Board of Medical Specialties). 2006. *ABMS establishes new subspecialty certificate in hospice and palliative medicine.* http://www.abms.org/News_and_Events/downloads/NewSubcertPalliativeMed.pdf (accessed December 26, 2007).

ABMS. 2007. *Recognized physician specialty and subspecialty certificates.* http://www.abms.org/Who_We_Help/Physicians/specialties.aspx (accessed December 28, 2007).

ABPN (American Board of Psychiatry and Neurology). 2007a. *Certification statistics.* http://www.abpn.com/cert_statistics.htm (accessed March 9, 2007).

ABPN. 2007b. *Initial certification in the subspecialty of geriatric psychiatry.* http://www.abpn.com/gp.htm (accessed December 28, 2007).

ABPN. 2007c. *Part I examination in psychiatry A: 2008 content outline.* http://www.abpn.com/downloads/content_outlines/Initial%20Cert/2008_PartI_Psych_AandB.pdf (accessed January 4, 2008).

ACCP (American College of Clinical Pharmacy). 2007. *Directory of residencies, fellowships, and graduate programs.* http://www.accp.com/resandfel/ (accessed December 4, 2007).

Ackermann, R. J., and K. A. Kemle. 1998. The effect of a physician assistant on the hospitalization of nursing home residents. *Journal of the American Geriatrics Society* 46(5): 610-614.

Acosta, D., and P. Olsen. 2006. Meeting the needs of regional minority groups: The University of Washington's programs to increase the American Indian and Alaskan Native physician workforce. *Academic Medicine* 81(10):863-870.

ADA (American Dietetic Association). 2008. *Dietetics education curriculum requirements.* http://www.eatright.org/cps/rde/xchg/ada/hs.xsl/CADE_813_ENU_HTML.htm (accessed February 9, 2008).

ADGAP (Association of Directors of Geriatric Academic Programs). 2004. Financial compensation for geriatricians in academic and private practice. *Training & Practice Update* 2(2):1-7.

ADGAP. 2005. Geriatricians and geriatric psychiatrists. *Training & Practice Update* 3(1): 1-7.

ADGAP. 2007a. *Chief resident immersion training in the care of older adults: A national dissemination of the successful Boston University Medical Center program.* http://www. Americangeriatrics.org/adgap/crit/default.asp (accessed August 20, 2007).

ADGAP. 2007b. Fellows in geriatric medicine and geriatric psychiatry programs. *Training & Practice Update* 5(2):1-7.

ADGAP. 2007c. *Fiscal year 2007 awardees.* http://www.Americangeriatrics.org/adgap/2007 ghp_awards.asp (accessed December 4, 2007).

ADGAP. 2007d. *Table 1.7: Total annual compensation for private practice physicians, 2001-2005.* http://www.adgapstudy.uc.edu/Files/Table_1_7.pdf (accessed January 29, 2008).

AGS (American Geriatrics Society). 2004. *Curriculum guidelines for geriatrics training in internal medicine residency programs.* http://www.Americangeriatrics.org/education/resident. shtml (accessed October 25, 2007).

AHA (American Hospital Assocation). 2007. *Trends affecting hospitals and health systems, April 2007.* http://www.aha.org/aha/research-and-trends/chartbook/2007chartbook.html (accessed January 29, 2008).

AIDS InfoNet. 2007. *Fact Sheet 616: Older people and HIV.* http://www.thebody.com/content/ whatis/art6036.html?ts=pf (accessed January 29, 2008).

Alliance for Aging Research. 2002. *Medical never-never land: Ten reasons why America is not ready for the coming age boom.* Washington, DC: Alliance for Aging Research.

ANA (American Nurses Association). 2007. *Nurse competence in aging.* http:// www.nursingworld.org/MainMenuCategories/ThePracticeofProfessionalNursing/ NursingKnowledge/NurseCompetenceinAging.aspx (accessed December 26, 2007).

Anderson, D., and R. Wiscott. 2004. Comparing social work and non-social work students' attitudes about aging: Implications to promote work with elders. *Journal of Gerontological Social Work* 42(2):21-36.

Anderson, S. 2007. *Deadly consequences: The hidden impact of America's nursing shortage.* Arlington, VA: National Foundation for American Policy.

APPAP (Association of Postgraduate AP Programs). 2008. *APPAP programs by specialty.* http://www.appap.org/prog_specialty.html (accessed January 2, 2008).

APTA (American Physical Therapy Association). 2007. *Section on geriatrics: Health promotion & wellness SIG.* http://www.geriatricspt.org/members/sig-health.cfm (accessed October 28, 2007).

ASA (American Society on Aging). 2007. HIV hits 100,000 older adults—and climbing. *Aging Today,* 28(2):7-8.

ASHP (American Society of Health-System Pharmacists). 2007. *Online residence directory.* http://www.ashp.org/s_ashp/residency_index.asp?CID=1212&DID=1254 (accessed December 4, 2007).

ASPE (Assistant Secretary for Planning and Evaluation, U.S. Department of Health and Human Services). 2006. *The supply and demand of professional social workers providing long-term care services.* Washington, DC: ASPE Office of Disability, Aging and Long-Term Care Policy.

ASWB (Association of Social Work Boards). 2007. *ASWB exam information: Examination content outlines.* http://www.aswb.org/exam_info_NEW_content_outlines.shtml (accessed December 28, 2007).

Barry, T., D. Brannon, and V. Mor. 2005. Nurse aide empowerment strategies and staff stability: Effects on nursing home resident outcomes. *Gerontologist* 45(3):309-317.

Bednash, G., C. Fagin, and M. Mezey. 2003. Geriatric content in nursing programs: A wake-up call. *Nursing Outlook* 51(4):149-150.

Berkman, B., B. Silverstone, W. J. Simmons, P. J. Volland, and J. L. Howe. 2000. Social work gerontological practice: The need for faculty development in the new millennium. *Journal of Gerontological Social Work* 34(1):5-23.

Berman, A., M. Mezey, M. Kobayashi, T. Fulmer, J. Stanley, D. Thornlow, and P. Rosenfeld. 2005. Gerontological nursing content in baccalaureate nursing programs: Comparison of findings from 1997 and 2003. *Journal of Professional Nursing* 21(5):268-275.

Bernard, M. A., W. J. McAuley, J. A. Belzer, and K. S. Neal. 2003. An evaluation of a low-intensity intervention to introduce medical students to healthy older people. *Journal of the American Geriatrics Society* 51(3):419-423.

Billings, J. A., and S. Block. 1997. Palliative care in undergraduate medical education: Status report and future directions. *Journal of the American Medical Association* 278(9): 733-738.

BLS (Bureau of Labor Statistics). 2007a. *Fastest growing occupations, 2006-2016* (November 2007 Monthly Employment Review). http://www.bls.gov/emp/emptab21.htm (accessed December 17, 2007).

BLS. 2007b. *Occupational outlook handbook, 2008-09 edition: Licensed practical and licensed vocational nurses.* http://www.bls.gov/oco/ocos102.htm (accessed December 28, 2007).

BLS. 2007c. *Occupational outlook handbook, 2008-09 edition: Physician assistants.* http://www.bls.gov/oco/ocos081.htm (accessed December 28, 2007).

BLS. 2007d. *Occupational outlook handbook, 2008-09 edition: Social workers.* http://www.bls.gov/oco/ocos060.htm (accessed December 28, 2007).

BLS. 2008. Occupational outlook handbook (OOH), 2008-09 edition. http://www.bls.gov/oco/home.htm (accessed January 3, 2008).

Blumenthal, D., M. Gokhale, E. G. Campbell, and J. S. Weissman. 2001. Preparedness for clinical practice: Reports of graduating residents at academic health centers. *Journal of the American Medical Association* 286(9):1027-1034.

Bodenheimer, T. 2007. A 63-year-old man with multiple cardiovascular risk factors and poor adherence to treatment plans. *Journal of the American Medical Association* 298(17): 2048-2055.

Bonnel, W. 2003. Nutritional health promotion for older adults: Where is the content? *Journal of the American Academy of Nurse Practitioners* 15(5):224-229.

Bragg, E. J., and G. A. Warshaw. 2005. ACGME requirements for geriatrics medicine curricula in medical specialties: Progress made and progress needed. *Academic Medicine* 80(3):279-285.

Bragg, E. J., G. A. Warshaw, C. Arenson, M. L. Ho, and D. E. Brewer. 2006. A national survey of family medicine residency education in geriatric medicine: Comparing findings in 2004 to 2001. *Family Medicine* 38(4):258-264.

Brand, M. 2007. *The future healthcare workforce for older Americans: Rural recruitment and retention.* Presentation at Meeting of the Committee on the Future Health Care Workforce for Older Americans, San Francisco, CA. June 28, 2007.

Brotherton, S. E., and S. I. Etzel. 2006. Graduate medical education, 2005-2006. *Journal of the American Medical Association* 296(9):1154-1169.

Brotherton, S. E., and S. I. Etzel. 2007. Graduate medical education, 2006-2007. *Journal of the American Medical Association* 298(9):1081-1096.

Brotman, S., B. Ryan, and R. Cormier. 2003. The health and social service needs of gay and lesbian elders and their families in Canada. *Gerontologist* 43(2):192-202.

Brugna, R. A., J. F. Cawley, and M. D. Baker. 2007. Physician assistants in geriatric medicine. *Clinical Geriatrics* 15(10):22-29.

Buerhaus, P. I., D. O. Staiger, and D. I. Auerbach. 2000. Implications of an aging registered nurse workforce. *Journal of the American Medical Association* 283(22):2948-2954.

Cahill, S., K. South, and J. Spade. 2000. *Outing age: Public policy issues affecting gay, lesbian, bisexual and transgender elders.* New York: National Gay and Lesbian Task Force Policy Institute.

Carson-Smith, W. Y., and P. A. Minarik. 2007. Advanced practice nurses: A new skirmish in the continuing battle over scope of practice. *Clinical Nurse Specialist* 21(1):52-54.

Castle, N. G. 2001. Administrator turnover and quality of care in nursing homes. *Gerontologist* 41(6):757-767.

Castle, N. G. 2005. Turnover begets turnover. *Gerontologist* 45(2):186-195.

Castle, N. G., and J. Engberg. 2005. Staff turnover and quality of care in nursing homes. *Medical Care* 43(6):616-626.

Cavalieri, T. A., P. Basehore, E. Perweiler, and A. Chopra. 1999. Training osteopathic geriatric academicians: Impact of a model geriatric residency program. *Journal of the American Osteopathic Association* 99(7):371-376.

CCP (Council on Credentialing in Pharmacy). 2006. *Credentialing in pharmacy.* Washington, DC: CCP.

Center for Health Workforce Studies. 2005. *The impact of the aging population on the health workforce in the United States.* Rensselaer, NY: School of Public Health, University at Albany.

Center for Health Workforce Studies. 2006. *Licensed social workers serving older adults, 2004.* Rensselaer, NY: School of Public Health, University at Albany.

Chapman, S. A., J. A. Showstack, E. M. Morrison, P. E. Franks, L. Y. Woo, and E. H. O'Neil. 2004. *Allied health workforce: Innovations for the 21st century.* San Francisco, CA: Center for the Health Professions, University of California, San Francisco.

Cheeti, K., and J. D. Schor. 2002. Long-term care experience in an internal medicine residency program. *Journal of the American Medical Directors Association* 3(3):125-129.

Cianciolo, P. K., and L. L. Zupan. 2004. Developing a training program on issues in aging for correctional workers. *Gerontology & Geriatrics Education* 24(3):23-38.

Cipher, D. J., R. S. Hooker, and E. Sekscenski. 2006. Are older patients satisfied with physician assistants and nurse practitioners? *Journal of the American Academy of Physician Assistants* 19(1):36, 39-40, 42-44.

CMS (Centers for Medicare and Medicaid Services). 2005. Medicare prescription drug benefit; final rule. *Federal Register* 70:4279-4283.

CMS. 2007. *Medicare claims processing manual: Chapter 12—Physicians/nonphysician practitioners.* http://www.cms.hhs.gov/manuals/downloads/clm104c12.pdf (accessed January 29, 2008).

Commonwealth Fund. 2007. *Bending the curve: Options for achieving savings and improving value in U.S. health spending.* New York: The Commonwealth Fund Commission on a High Performance Health System.

Cooksey, J. A., K. K. Knapp, S. M. Walton, and J. M. Cultice. 2002. Challenges to the pharmacist profession from escalating pharmaceutical demand. *Health Affairs* 21(5):182-188.

Cooper, H., C. Carlisle, T. Gibbs, and C. Watkins. 2001. Developing an evidence base for interdisciplinary learning: A systematic review. *Journal of Advanced Nursing* 35(2):228-237.

Corwin, S. J., K. Frahm, L. A. Ochs, C. E. Rheaume, E. Roberts, and G. P. Eleazer. 2006. Medical student and senior participants' perceptions of a mentoring program designed to enhance geriatric medical education. *Gerontology & Geriatrics Education* 26(3):47-65.

Cummings, S. M., and V. A. DeCoster. 2003. The status of specialized gerontological training in graduate social work education. *Educational Gerontology* 29(3):235-250.

Cummings, S. M., and C. Galambos. 2002. Predictors of graduate social work students' interest in aging-related work. *Journal of Gerontological Social Work* 39(3):77-94.

Cummings, S. M., C. Galambos, and V. A. DeCoster. 2003. Predictors of MSW employment in gerontological practice. *Educational Gerontology* 29(4):295-312.

Cummings, S. M., G. Adler, and V. A. DeCoster. 2005. Factors influencing graduate-social-work students' interest in working with elders. *Educational Gerontology* 31(8):643-655.

DOL (Department of Labor). 2006. *The president's community-based job training grants.* http://www.doleta.gov/business/Community-BasedJobTrainingGrants.cfm (accessed February 6, 2007).

Donald W. Reynolds Foundation. 2007. *Aging & quality of life.* http://www.dwreynolds.org/Programs/National/Aging/AboutAging.htm (accessed December 5, 2007).

Dyer, C. B., K. Hyer, K. S. Feldt, D. A. Lindemann, J. Busby-Whitehead, S. Greenberg, R. D. Kennedy, and E. Flaherty. 2003. Frail older patient care by interdisciplinary teams: A primer for generalists. *Gerontology & Geriatrics Education* 24(2):51-62.

Eleazer, G. P., R. Doshi, D. Wieland, R. Boland, and V. A. Hirth. 2005. Geriatric content in medical school curricula: Results of a national survey. *Journal of the American Geriatrics Society* 53(1):136-140.

Ersek, M., and B. R. Ferrell. 2005. Palliative care nursing education: Opportunities for gerontological nurses. *Journal of Gerontological Nursing* 31(7):45-51.

Evercare. 2007. *Evercare survey of graduating high school seniors finds prospective nurses lack interest in geriatrics despite growing senior population.* http://home.businesswire.com/portal/site/google/index.jsp?ndmViewId=news_view&newsId=20070801005845&newsLang=en (accessed August 27, 2007).

Fagin, C. M., P. D. Franklin, D. I. Regenstreif, and G. J. Huba. 2006. Overview of the John A. Hartford Foundation Building Academic Geriatric Nursing Capacity Initiative. *Nursing Outlook* 54(4):173-182.

Fields, S., and C. Nicastri. 2004. Health promotion/disease prevention in older adults—an evidence-based update: Part II: Counseling, chemoprophylaxis, and immunizations. *Clinical Geriatrics* 12(12):18-26.

Fitzgerald, J. T., B. C. Williams, J. B. Halter, T. L. Remington, M. A. Foulk, N. W. Persky, and B. R. Shay. 2006. Effects of a geriatrics interdisciplinary experience on learners' knowledge and attitudes. *Gerontology & Geriatrics Education* 26(3):17-28.

Flaherty, E., K. Hyer, R. Kane, N. Wilson, N. Whitelaw, and T. Fulmer. 2003. Using case studies to evaluate students' ability to develop a geriatric interdisciplinary care plan. *Gerontology & Geriatrics Education* 24(2):63-74.

Fulmer, T., K. Hyer, E. Flaherty, M. Mezey, N. Whitelaw, M. Orry Jacobs, R. Luchi, J. C. Hansen, D. A. Evans, C. Cassel, E. Kotthoff-Burrell, R. Kane, and E. Pfeiffer. 2005. Geriatric interdisciplinary team training program: Evaluation results. *Journal of Aging and Health* 17(4):443-470.

Gainor, S. J., R. T. Goins, and L. A. Miller. 2004. Using online modules is a multi-modality teaching system: A high-touch high-tech approach to geriatric education. *Gerontology & Geriatrics Education* 24(4):45-59.

GAO (Government Accountability Office). 1995. *National Health Service Corps: Opportunities to stretch scarce dollars and improve provider placement.* Washington, DC: GAO.

GAO. 2006. *Health professions education programs: Action still needed to measure impact.* Washington, DC: GAO.

Gawande, A. 2007. The way we age now: Medicine has increased the ranks of the elderly. Can it make old age any easier? *New Yorker* April 30:50-59.

Gill, T. M. 2005. Education, prevention, and the translation of research into practice. *Journal of the American Geriatrics Society* 53(4):724-726.

Goodwin, M., and J. E. Morley. 1994. Geriatric research, education and clinical centers: Their impact in the development of American geriatrics. *Journal of the American Geriatrics Society* 42(9):1012-1019.

Graber, D. R., J. P. Bellack, C. Lancaster, C. Musham, J. Nappi, and E. H. O'Neil. 1999. Curriculum topics in pharmacy education: Current and ideal emphasis. *American Journal of Pharmaceutical Education* 63(2):145-151.

GSWI (Geriatric Social Work Initiative). 2007. *Hartford faculty scholars.* http://www.gswi. org/programs/hfs.html (accessed August 1, 2007).

Hachmuth, F. A., and J. M. Hootman. 2001. What impact on PA education? A snapshot of ambulatory care visits involving PAs. *Journal of the American Academy of Physician Assistants* 14(12):22-24, 27.

Hajjar, I., S. A. Gable, V. P. Jenkinson, L. T. Kane, and R. A. Riley. 2005. Quality of Internet geriatric health information: The GeriatricWeb project. *Journal of the American Geriatrics Society* 53(5):885-890.

Hajjar, I. M., J. G. Ruiz, T. A. Teasdale, and M. J. Mintzer. 2007. The use of the Internet in geriatrics education: Results of a national survey of medical geriatrics academic programs. *Gerontology & Geriatrics Education* 27(4):85-95.

Hall, P., and L. Weaver. 2001. Interdisciplinary education and teamwork: A long and winding road. *Medical Education* 35(9):867-875.

Harrington, C., H. Carrillo, and C. LaCava. 2006. *Nursing facilities, staffing, residents and facility deficiencies, 1999 through 2005.* http://www.pascenter.org/documents/OSCAR 2005.pdf (accessed January 29, 2008).

Hart, L. G., S. M. Skillman, M. Fordyce, M. Thompson, A. Hagopian, and T. R. Konrad. 2007. International medical graduate physicians in the United States: Changes since 1981. *Health Affairs* 26(4):1159-1169.

Hash, K. M., J. Gottlieb, K. V. Harper-Dorton, G. Crawley-Woods, K. Shelck-Furbee, J. D. Smith, and R. Brown. 2007. Infusing and sustaining aging content in social work education: Findings from gerorich projects. *Gerontology & Geriatrics Education* 28(1): 1-18.

Hawes, C., C. D. Phillips, S. Holan, M. Sherman, and L. L. Hutchison. 2005. Assisted living in rural America: Results from a national survey. *Journal of Rural Health* 21(2):131-139.

Hazzard, W. R. 1999. Mentoring across the professional lifespan in academic geriatrics. *Journal of the American Geriatrics Society* 47(12):1466-1470.

Hazzard, W. R. 2003. General internal medicine and geriatrics: Collaboration to address the aging imperative can't wait. *Annals of Internal Medicine* 139(7):597-598.

Health Technology Center. 2007 (unpublished). *Health care workforce and future technologies.* Paper commissioned by the IOM Committee on the Future Health Care Workforce for Older Americans.

Heinemann, G. D., and A. M. Zeiss, eds. 2002. *Team performance in health care.* New York: Kluwer Academic/Plenum Publishers.

Henry, L. R., and R. S. Hooker. 2007. Retention of physician assistants in rural health clinics. *Journal of Rural Health* 23(3):207-214.

Herndon, C. M., K. Jackson Ii, D. S. Fike, and T. Woods. 2003. End-of-life care education in United States pharmacy schools. *American Journal of Hospice and Palliative Medicine* 20(5):340-344.

Holley, J. L., S. S. Carmody, A. H. Moss, A. M. Sullivan, L. M. Cohen, S. D. Block, and R. M. Arnold. 2003. The need for end-of-life care training in nephrology: National survey results of nephrology fellows. *American Journal of Kidney Diseases* 42(4):813-820.

Hooker, R. S., and L. E. Berlin. 2002. Trends in the supply of physician assistants and nurse practitioners in the United States. *Health Affairs* 21(5):174-181.

Hooker, R. S., D. J. Cipher, and E. Seksenski. 2005. Patient satisfaction with physician assistant, nurse practitioner, and physician care: A national survey of Medicare beneficiaries. *Journal of Clinical Outcomes Management* 12(2):88-92.

Howard, D. L., C. D. Bunch, W. O. Mundia, T. R. Konrad, L. J. Edwards, M. Ahinee Amamoo, and Y. Jallah. 2006. Comparing United States versus international medical school graduate physicians who serve African-American and white elderly. *Health Services Research* 41(6):2155-2181.

Howe, J. L., and D. W. Sherman. 2006. Interdisciplinary educational approaches to promote team-based geriatrics and palliative care. *Gerontology & Geriatrics Education* 26(3):1-16.

HRSA (Health Resources and Services Administration). 1995. *A national agenda for geriatric education: White papers*. Washington, DC: HRSA.

HRSA. 2000. *The pharmacist workforce: A study of the supply and demand for pharmacists*. Washington, DC: HRSA.

HRSA. 2003. *National Advisory Council on Nurse Education and Practice: Third report to the Secretary of Health and Human Services and the Congress*. Washington, DC: HRSA.

HRSA. 2005a. *Geriatric training for physicians, dentists, and behavioral and mental health professions: FY 2005 grantee contracts and abstracts*. http://bhpr.hrsa.gov/interdisciplinary/gtpd05.htm (accessed August 8, 2007).

HRSA. 2005b. *Residency training in general and pediatric dentistry—FY 2005 grant summaries*. http://bhpr.hrsa.gov/medicine-dentistry/05summaries/dental.htm#la (accessed January 4, 2008).

HRSA. 2006a. *The rationale for diversity in the health professions: A review of the evidence*. http://bhpr.hrsa.gov/healthworkforce/reports/diversity/default.htm (accessed December 26, 2007).

HRSA. 2006b. *The registered nurse population: Findings from the March 2004 National Sample Survey of Registered Nurses*. Washington, DC: HRSA.

HRSA. 2007a. *Fiscal year 2008 justification of estimates for appropriations committees: Clinician recruitment and service*. http://www.hrsa.gov/about/budgetjustification08/Clinicianrecruitment.htm (accessed December 4, 2007).

HRSA. 2007b. *Fiscal year 2008 justification of estimates for appropriations committees: Health professions*. http://www.hrsa.gov/about/budgetjustification08/Comprehensive GeriatricEducation.htm (accessed December 7, 2007).

HRSA. 2007c. *Geriatric education centers*. http://bhpr.hrsa.gov/interdisciplinary/gec.html (accessed February 12, 2007).

HRSA. 2007d. *National health service corps: About NHSC: Our achievements*. http://nhsc.bhpr.hrsa.gov/about/our/where.asp (accessed October 29, 2007).

IFAS (Institute for the Future of Aging Services). 2008. *LVN leadership enrichment and development (LVN LEAD)*. http://www.futureofaging.org/developing_workforce/current_projects/workforce_projects/lvn_project.asp (accessed February 9, 2008).

IGSW (Institute for Geriatric Social Work). 2007. *Institute for geriatric social work: Education & training*. http://www.bu.edu/igsw/education/index.html (accessed March 13, 2007).

IHS (Indian Health Service, U.S. Department of Health and Human Services). 2007. *Loan repayment program*. http://www.ihs.gov/JobsCareerDevelop/DHPS/LRP/Intropro.asp (accessed October 29, 2007).

Inouye, S. K., S. T. Bogardus, Jr., D. I. Baker, L. Leo-Summers, and L. M. Cooney, Jr. 2000. The hospital elder life program: A model of care to prevent cognitive and functional decline in older hospitalized patients. *Journal of the American Geriatrics Society* 48(12): 1697-1706.

IOM (Institute of Medicine). 1978. *Aging and medical education*. Washington, DC: National Academy Press.

IOM. 1993. *Strengthening training in geriatrics for physicians*. Washington, DC: National Academy Press.

IOM. 1997. *Approaching death: Improving care at the end of life*. Washington, DC: National Academy Press.

IOM. 2000. *The role of nutrition in maintaining health in the nation's elderly: Evaluating coverage of nutrition services for the Medicare population*. Washington, DC: National Academy Press.

IOM. 2004. *In the nation's compelling interest: Ensuring diversity in the health care workforce.* Washington, DC: The National Academies Press.

IOM. 2005. *Quality through collaboration: The future of rural health.* Washington, DC: The National Academies Press.

The John A. Hartford Foundation. 2007. *Recent grants.* http://www.jhartfound.org/recent_grants.htm (accessed February 9, 2008).

Johnson, H. A. 2004. Overview of geriatric distance education for academic courses and continuing education. *Gerontology & Geriatrics Education* 24(4):9-22.

Johnson, T. M., 2nd, and G. Valle. 1996. Mentoring in the growth and development of the geriatric fellow. *Journal of the American Geriatrics Society* 44(12):1486-1487.

Kales, H. C., A. R. DiNardo, F. C. Blow, J. F. McCarthy, R. V. Ignacio, and M. B. Riba. 2006. International medical graduates and the diagnosis and treatment of late-life depression. *Academic Medicine* 81(2):171-175.

Kleinman, C. S., and S. J. Saccomano. 2006. Registered nurses and unlicensed assistive personnel: An uneasy alliance. *Journal of Continuing Education in Nursing* 37(4):162-170.

Kovner, C. T., M. Mezey, and C. Harrington. 2002. Who cares for older adults? Workforce implications of an aging society. *Health Affairs* 21(5):78-89.

Krout, J. A., and P. McKernan. 2007. The impact of gerontology inclusion on 12th grade student perceptions of aging, older adults and working with elders. *Gerontology & Geriatrics Education* 27(4):23-40.

LaMascus, A. M., M. A. Bernard, P. Barry, J. Salerno, and J. Weiss. 2005. Bridging the workforce gap for our aging society: How to increase and improve knowledge and training. Report of an expert panel. *Journal of the American Geriatrics Society* 53(2):343-347.

Lecca, P. J., P. A. Valentine, and K. J. Lyons. 2003. *Allied health: Practice issues and trends in the new millennium.* Binghamton, NY: The Hawthorn Press, Inc.

Leigh, J. P., R. L. Kravitz, M. Schembri, S. J. Samuels, and S. Mobley. 2002. Physician career satisfaction across specialties. *Archives of Internal Medicine* 162(14):1577-1584.

Leipzig, R. M. 2007. *Medical student competencies in geriatric medicine.* http://www.americangeriatrics.org/newsletter/FIT/fall_2007_story01.asp (accessed January 29, 2008).

Leipzig, R. M., K. Hyer, K. Ek, S. Wallenstein, M. L. Vezina, S. Fairchild, C. K. Cassel, and J. L. Howe. 2002. Attitudes toward working on interdisciplinary healthcare teams: A comparison by discipline. *Journal of the American Geriatrics Society* 50(6):1141-1148.

Levenson, S. A., and D. Saffel. 2007. The consultant pharmacist and the physician in the nursing home: Roles, relationships, and a recipe for success. *The Consultant Pharmacist* 22(1):71-82.

Levine, S. A., B. Brett, B. E. Robinson, G. A. Stratos, S. M. Lascher, L. Granville, C. Goodwin, K. Dunn, and P. P. Barry. 2007. Practicing physician education in geriatrics: Lessons learned from a train-the-trainer model. *Journal of the American Geriatrics Society* 55(8):1281-1286.

Li, F., K. J. Fisher, P. Harmer, and E. McAuley. 2002. Delineating the impact of Tai Chi training on physical function among the elderly. *American Journal of Preventive Medicine* 23(2 Suppl 1):92-97.

Li, F., P. Harmer, K. J. Fisher, E. McAuley, N. Chaumeton, E. Eckstrom, and N. L. Wilson. 2005. Tai chi and fall reductions in older adults: A randomized controlled trial. *Journals of Gerontology—Series A Biological Sciences and Medical Sciences* 60(2):187-194.

Linn, B. S., and R. Zeppa. 1987. Predicting third year medical students' attitudes toward the elderly and treating the old. *Gerontology & Geriatrics Education* 7(3-4):167-175.

Linnebur, S. A., M. B. O'Connell, A. M. Wessell, A. D. McCord, D. H. Kennedy, G. DeMaagd, L. A. Dent, M. Y. Splinter, J. C. Biery, Jr., F. Chang, R. C. Jackson, S. L. Miller, and T. Sterling. 2005. Pharmacy practice, research, education, and advocacy for older adults. *Pharmacotherapy* 25(10):1396-1430.

Lt. Governor's Office on Aging. 2005. *Lt. Governor André Bauer ratifies model legislation to boost number of geriatric practitioners in South Carolina.* http://www.state.sc.us/ltgov/aging/docs/PressReleases/GeriatricLoanBillRatification06102005.pdf (accessed December 5, 2007).

Lubben, J. E., J. Damron-Rodriguez, and J. C. Beck. 1992. A national survey of aging curriculums in schools of social work. *Journal of Gerontological Social Work* 18(3-4): 157-171.

Maas, M. L., N. E. Strumpf, C. Beck, D. Jennings, D. Messecar, and E. Swanson. 2006. Mentoring geriatric nurse scientists, educators, clinicians, and leaders in the John A. Hartford Foundation centers for geriatric nursing excellence. *Nursing Outlook* 54(4):183-188.

MacEntee, M. I., M. Pruksapong, and C. C. Wyatt. 2005. Insights from students following an educational rotation through dental geriatrics. *Journal of Dental Education* 69(12):1368-1376.

Mackin, L. A., J. Kayser-Jones, P. D. Franklin, L. K. Evans, E. M. Sullivan-Marx, K. A. Herr, E. A. Swanson, S. A. Lubin, and D. C. Messecar. 2006. Successful recruiting into geriatric nursing: The experience of the John A. Hartford Foundation centers of geriatric nursing excellence. *Nursing Outlook* 54(4):197-203.

Magilvy, J. K., and J. G. Congdon. 2000. The crisis nature of health care transitions for rural older adults. *Public Health Nursing* 17(5):336-345.

Mahaffey, E. H. 2002. The relevance of associate degree nursing education: Past, present, future. *Online Journal of Issues in Nursing* 7(2):24-36.

Maramaldi, P., D. Gardner, B. Berkman, K. Ireland, S. D'Ambruoso, and J. L. Howe. 2004. Mentoring new social work faculty: A gerontological perspective. *Gerontology & Geriatrics Education* 25(1):89-106.

Mather, M. 2007 (unpublished). *State profiles of the U.S. health care workforce.* Paper commissioned by the Committee on the Future Health Care Workforce for Older Americans.

Matter, C. A., J. A. Speice, R. McCann, D. A. Mendelson, K. McCormick, S. Friedman, A. Medina-Walpole, and N. S. Clark. 2003. Hospital to home: Improving internal medicine residents' understanding of the needs of older persons after a hospital stay. *Academic Medicine* 78(8):793-797.

Maurer, M. S., A. W. Costley, P. A. Miller, S. McCabe, S. Dubin, H. Cheng, E. Varela-Burstein, B. Lam, C. Irvine, K. P. Page, G. Ridge, and B. Gurland. 2006. The Columbia Cooperative Aging Program: An interdisciplinary and interdepartmental approach to geriatric education for medical interns. *Journal of the American Geriatrics Society* 54(3):520-526.

McBride, M. R., N. Morioka-Douglas, and G. Yeo. 1996. *Aging and health: Asian and Pacific Island American elders, 2nd ed.* Stanford, CA: Stanford Geriatric Education Center.

McElhone, A. L., Y. Limb, and S. R. Gambert. 2005. Health promotion/disease prevention in older adults—an evidence-based update. Part III: Nursing home population. *Clinical Geriatrics* 13(9):24-31.

Medina-Walpole, A., W. H. Barker, P. R. Katz, J. Karuza, T. Franklin Williams, and W. J. Hall. 2002. The current state of geriatric medicine: A national survey of fellowship-trained geriatricians, 1990 to 1998. *Journal of the American Geriatrics Society* 50(5):949-955.

MedPAC (Medicare Payment Advisory Commission). 2003. *Impact of the resident caps on the supply of geriatricians.* Washington, DC: MedPAC.

Melin, A. L., and L. O. Bygren. 1992. Efficacy of the rehabilitation of elderly primary health care patients after short-stay hospital treatment. *Medical Care* 30(11):1004.

Mertz, E., and E. O'Neil. 2002. The growing challenge of providing oral health care services to all Americans. *Health Affairs* 21(5):65-77.

Mezey, M., S. G. Burger, H. G. Bloom, A. Bonner, M. Bourbonniere, B. Bowers, J. B. Burl, E. Capezuti, D. Carter, J. Dimant, S. A. Jerro, S. C. Reinhard, and M. Ter Maat. 2005. Experts recommend strategies for strengthening the use of advanced practice nurses in nursing homes. *Journal of the American Geriatrics Society* 53(10):1790-1797.

MGMA (Medical Group Management Association). 2006. *MGMA Physician Compensation and Production Survey: 2006 report based on 2005 data*. Englewood, CO: MGMA.

Mitchell, D. A., and S. L. Lassiter. 2006. Addressing health care disparities and increasing workforce diversity: The next step for the dental, medical, and public health professions. *American Journal of Public Health* 96(12):2093-2097.

Mohammad, A. R., P. M. Preshaw, and R. L. Ettinger. 2003. Current status of predoctoral geriatric education in U.S. dental schools. *Journal of Dental Education* 67(5):509-514.

Moore, M. J., P. Moir, and M. M. Patrick. 2004. *The state of aging and health in America: 2004*. Washington, DC: The Merck Institute of Aging and Health.

Muenzen, P. M., M. M. Corrigan, M. A. Mobley Smith, and P. G. Rodrigue. 2005. Updating the pharmacy technician certification examination: A practice analysis study. *American Journal of Health-System Pharmacy* 62(23):2542-2546.

Mullan, F. 1999. The muscular samaritan: The National Health Service Corps in the new century. *Health Affairs* 18(2):168-175.

Mullan, F. 2002. Time-capsule thinking: The health care workforce, past and future. *Health Affairs* 21(5):112-122.

Murphy-Southwick, C., and M. McBride. 2006. Geriatric education across 94 million acres: Adapting conference programming in a rural state. *Gerontology & Geriatrics Education* 26(4):25-36.

NABP (National Association of Boards of Pharmacy). 2008. *NAPLEX blueprint*. http://www.nabp.net/ftpfiles/NABP01/updatednaplexblueprint.pdf (accessed January 4, 2008).

NAHOF (National Association on HIV Over Fifty). 2007. *Educational tip sheet: HIV/AIDS and older adults*. http://hivoverfifty.org/tip.html (accessed October 10, 2007).

NASW (National Association of Social Workers). 2007. *New aging specialty credentials*. http://www.naswdc.org/credentials/specialty/aging.asp (accessed August 23, 2007).

National Commission for Quality Long-Term Care. 2007. *From isolation to integration: Recommendations to improve quality in long-term care*. http://www.qualitylongtermcare commission.org/pdf/Final_Report_NCQLTC_20071203.pdf (accessed January 17, 2008).

National Commission on Nursing Workforce for Long-Term Care. 2005. *Act now: For your tomorrow*. http://cowl.org/documents/The%20National%20Commission%20on%20 Nursing%20Workforce%20for%20Long%20Term%20Care2.pdf (accessed January 17, 2008).

National Consensus Project for Quality Palliative Care. 2004. *Clinical practice guidelines for quality palliative care*. http://www.nationalconsensusproject.org/Guideline.pdf (accessed January 17, 2008).

NCCPA (National Commission on Certification of Physician Assistants). 2008. *Exams: Content blueprint*. http://www.nccpa.net/EX_knowledge.aspx?r (accessed January 3, 2008).

NCSBN (National Council of State Boards of Nursing). 2007. *NCLEX-RNÆ examination*. https://www.ncsbn.org/RN_Test_Plan_2007_Web.pdf (accessed January 2, 2008).

NHTSA (National Highway Traffic Safety Administration). 1994. *Emergency medical technician-basic: National Standard Curriculum*. http://www.nhtsa.dot.gov/people/injury/ems/pub/emtbnsc.pdf (accessed February 7, 2008).

NIA (National Institute on Aging). 1987. *Personnel for health needs of the elderly through the year 2020*. Bethesda, MD: Department of Health and Human Services.

Nicastri, C., and S. Fields. 2004. Health promotion/disease prevention in older adults—an evidence-based update: Part I: Introduction and screening. *Clinical Geriatrics* 12(11): 17-25.

NICHE (Nurses Improving Care for Health System Elders). 2008. *NICHE models*. http://www.nicheprogram.org/about/models/ (accessed February 9, 2008).

NIH (National Institutes of Health). 2007a. *Clinical research loan repayment program*. http://lrp.info.nih.gov/about/lrp-clinical.htm (accessed December 28, 2007).

NIH. 2007b. *National Institutes of Health loan repayment program: Contraception and infertility research.* http://lrp.info.nih.gov/about/extramural/images/ICdegree_CIR06.htm (accessed December 28, 2007).

NIH. 2007c. *National Institutes of Health loan repayment program: Extramural clinical research for individuals from disadvantaged backgrounds.* http://lrp.info.nih.gov/about/extramural/images/ICdegree_DB06.htm (accessed December 28, 2007).

NIH. 2007d. *National Institutes of Health loan repayment program: Extramural clinical research LRP.* http://lrp.info.nih.gov/about/extramural/images/ICdegree_EC06.htm (accessed December 28, 2007).

NIH. 2007e. *National Institutes of Health loan repayment program: Extramural pediatric research LRP.* http://lrp.info.nih.gov/about/extramural/images/ICdegree_EP06.htm (accessed December 28, 2007).

NIH. 2007f. *National Institutes of Health loan repayment program: Health disparities research LRP.* http://lrp.info.nih.gov/about/extramural/images/ICdegree_HD06.htm (accessed December 28, 2007).

NIH. 2007g. *NIH loan repayment programs.* http://www.lrp.nih.gov/brochure.pdf (accessed December 28, 2007).

Odegard, P. S., R. M. Breslow, M. J. Koronkowski, B. R. Williams, and G. A. Hudgins. 2007. Geriatric pharmacy education: A strategic plan for the future. *American Journal of Pharmaceutical Education* 71(3).

Olshansky, S. J., D. J. Passaro, R. C. Hershow, J. Layden, B. A. Carnes, J. Brody, L. Hayflick, R. N. Butler, D. B. Allison, and D. S. Ludwig. 2005. A potential decline in life expectancy in the United States in the 21st century. *New England Journal of Medicine* 352(11):1138-1145.

Olson, T. H., J. Stoehr, A. Shukla, and T. Moreau. 2003. A needs assessment of geriatric curriculum in physician assistant education. *Perspective on Physician Assistant Education* 14(4):208-213.

Paice, J. A., B. R. Ferrell, R. Virani, M. Grant, P. Malloy, and A. Rhome. 2006. Graduate nursing education regarding end-of-life care. *Nursing Outlook* 54(1):46-52.

Pan, C. X., S. Carmody, R. M. Leipzig, E. Granieri, A. Sullivan, S. D. Block, and R. M. Arnold. 2005. There is hope for the future: National survey results reveal that geriatric medicine fellows are well-educated in end-of-life care. *Journal of the American Geriatrics Society* 53(4):705-710.

Parsons, L. 1999. Building RN confidence for delegation decision-making skills in practice. *Journal for Nurses in Staff Development* 15(6):263-269.

Pathman, D. E., D. H. Taylor, Jr., T. R. Konrad, T. S. King, T. Harris, T. M. Henderson, J. D. Bernstein, T. Tucker, K. D. Crook, C. Spaulding, and G. G. Koch. 2000. State scholarship, loan forgiveness, and related programs: The unheralded safety net. *Journal of the American Medical Association* 284(16):2084-2092.

Pathman, D. E., T. R. Konrad, T. S. King, D. H. Taylor, Jr., and G. G. Koch. 2004. Outcomes of states' scholarship, loan repayment, and related programs for physicians. *Medical Care* 42(6):560-568.

Pathman, D. E., G. E. Fryer, Jr., R. L. Phillips, J. Smucny, T. Miyoshi, and L. A. Green. 2006. National Health Service Corps staffing and the growth of the local rural non-NHSC primary care physician workforce. *Journal of Rural Health* 22(4):285-293.

RCHWS (Regional Center for Health Workforce Studies, Center for Health Economics and Policy, The University of Texas Health Science Center at San Antonio). 2003. *Changes in the scope of practice and the supply of non-physician clinicians in Texas.* San Antonio, TX: Regional Center for Health Workforce Studies.

Reinhard, S. C., H. Young, R. A. Kane, and W. V. Quinn. 2003. *Nurse delegation of medication administration of elders.* Rutgers, NJ: Rutgers Center for State Health Policy.

Reinhardt, U. E. 2003. Does the aging of the population really drive the demand for health care? *Health Affairs* 22(6):27-39.

Remington, T. L., M. A. Foulk, and B. C. Williams. 2006. Evaluation of evidence for interprofessional education. *American Journal of Pharmaceutical Education* 70(3).

Reuben, D. B., J. T. Fullerton, J. M. Tschann, and M. Crougban-Minihane. 1995. Attitudes of beginning medical students toward older persons: A five-campus study. *Journal of the American Geriatrics Society* 43(12):1430-1436.

Reuben, D. B., M. N. Yee, K. D. Cole, M. S. Waite, L. O. Nichols, B. A. Benjamin, G. Zellman, and J. C. Frank. 2003. Organizational issues in establishing geriatrics interdisciplinary team training. *Gerontology & Geriatrics Education* 24(2):13-34.

Reuben, D. B., L. Levy-Storms, M. N. Yee, M. Lee, K. Cole, M. Waite, L. Nichols, and J. C. Frank. 2004. Disciplinary split: A threat to geriatrics interdisciplinary team training. *Journal of the American Geriatrics Society* 52(6):1000-1006.

Rhee, L. Q., N. S. Wellman, V. H. Castellanos, and S. P. Himburg. 2004. Continued need for increased emphasis on aging in dietetics education. *Journal of the American Dietetic Association* 104(4):645-649.

Rosen, A. L., J. L. Zlotnick, A. L. Curl, and R. G. Green. 2000. *CSWE/SAGE-SW national competencies survey and report.* Alexandria, VA: Council on Social Work Education.

Rosenfeld, P. 2007. Workplace practices for retaining older hospital nurses: Implications from a study of nurses with eldercare responsibilities. *Policy, Politics, and Nursing Practice* 8(2):120-129.

Rossi, M. S. 2003. Law enhances hygienists' duties, frees dentists for complex cases. *The New York State Dental Journal* 69(9):8-9.

Rubin, C. D., H. Stieglitz, B. Vicioso, and L. Kirk. 2003. Development of geriatrics-oriented faculty in general internal medicine. *Annals of Internal Medicine* 139(7):615-620.

Ryan, C., and D. Futterman. 1998. *Lesbian & gay youth: Care & counseling.* New York: Columbia University Press.

Ryan, J. 2003. *Improving oral health: Promise and prospects.* Washington, DC: National Health Policy Forum.

Saltz, C. C. 1997. From issues to actions. *Journal of Gerontological Social Work* 27(3):89-95.

Scharlach, A., J. Damron-Rodriguez, B. Robinson, and R. Feldman. 2000. Educating social workers for an aging society: A vision for the 21st century. *Journal of Social Work Education* 36(3):521-538.

Schatz, B., and K. O'Hanlan. 1994. *Anti-gay discrimination in medicine: Results of a national survey of lesbian, gay and bisexual physicians.* San Francisco, CA: American Association of Physicians for Human Rights.

Segal-Gidan, F. 2002. Who will care for the aging American population? *Journal of the American Academy of Physician Assistants* 15(12).

Shah, U., M. Aung, S. Chan, and G. P. Wolf-Klein. 2006. Do geriatricians stay in geriatrics? *Gerontology & Geriatrics Education* 27(1):57-65.

Simon, S. R., A. R. Fabiny, and J. Kotch. 2003. Geriatrics training in general internal medicine fellowship programs: Current practice, barriers, and strategies for improvement. *Annals of Internal Medicine* 139(7):621-627.

Stewart, T., and C. Alford. 2006. Introduction: Older adults in medical education—Senior mentor programs in U.S. medical schools. *Gerontology & Geriatrics Education* 27(2):3-10.

Stone, R., S. C. Reinhard, J. Machemer, and D. Rudin. 2002. *Geriatric care manager: A profile of an emerging profession.* Washington, DC: AARP Public Policy Institute.

Sullivan, A. M., M. D. Lakoma, and S. D. Block. 2003. The status of medical education in end-of-life care: A national report. *Journal of General Internal Medicine* 18(9):685-695.

Supiano, M. A., J. C. Fantone, and C. Grum. 2002. A web-based geriatrics portfolio to document medical students' learning outcomes. *Academic Medicine* 77(9):937-938.

Sussman, D. 2006. Refresher training helps nurses reenter workforce. *T and D* 60(9):65-67.

Swagerty, D., Jr., S. Studenski, R. Laird, and S. Rigler. 2000. A case-oriented web-based curriculum in geriatrics for third-year medical students. *Journal of the American Geriatrics Society* 48(11):1507-1512.

SWLI (Social Work Leadership Institute). 2007. *Practicum partnership program*. http://social work.nyam.org/nsw/ppp/about.php (accessed October 28, 2007).

Tarn, D. M., L. S. Meredith, M. Kagawa-Singer, S. Matsumura, S. Bito, R. K. Oye, H. Liu, K. L. Kahn, S. Fukuhara, and N. S. Wenger. 2005. Trust in one's physician: The role of ethnic match, autonomy, acculturation, and religiosity among Japanese and Japanese Americans. *Annals of Family Medicine* 3(4):339-347.

Tellis-Nayak, V. 2007. A person-centered workplace: The foundation for person-centered caregiving in long-term care. *Journal of the American Medical Directors Association* 8(1):46-54.

Thomas, D. C., R. M. Leipzig, L. G. Smith, K. Dunn, G. Sullivan, and E. Callahan. 2003. Improving geriatrics training in internal medicine residency programs: Best practices and sustainable solutions. *Annals of Internal Medicine* 139(7):628-634.

Thomas, S., and G. Hume. 1998. Delegation competencies: Beginning practitioners' reflections. *Nurse Educator* 23(1):38-41.

Tilliss, T. S., S. E. Lavigne, and K. Williams. 1998. Geriatric education in dental hygiene programs. *Journal of Dental Education* 62(4):319-324.

U.S. Census Bureau. 2008. *Statistical abstract of the United States: 2008*. Washington, DC: U.S. Census Bureau.

VA (Veterans Adminstration). 2007a. *VA advanced fellowship in geriatrics*. http://www.va.gov/oaa/specialfellows/programs/SF_AdvGeriatric.asp (accessed December 5, 2007).

VA. 2007b. *VA geriatric neurology*. http://www.va.gov/oaa/specialfellows/programs/SF_GeriatricNeuro.asp (accessed December 5, 2007).

Waldrop, D. P., J. A. Fabiano, T. H. Nochajski, K. M. Zittel-Palamara, E. L. Davis, and L. J. Goldberg. 2006. More than a set of teeth: Assessing and enhancing dental students' perceptions of older adults. *Gerontology & Geriatrics Education* 27(1):37-56.

Walsh-Burke, K., and E. L. Csikai. 2005. Professional social work education in end-of-life care: Contributions of the project on death in America's social work leadership development program. *Journal of Social Work in End-of-Life & Palliative Care* 1(2):11-26.

Walton, S. M., K. K. Knapp, L. Miller, and G. T. Schumock. 2007. Examination of state-level changes in the pharmacist labor market using census data. *Journal of the American Pharmacists Association* 47(3):348-357.

Warshaw, G. A., and E. J. Bragg. 2003. The training of geriatricians in the United States: Three decades of progress. *Journal of the American Geriatrics Society* 51(7s):S338-S345.

Warshaw, G. A., E. J. Bragg, R. W. Shaull, and C. J. Lindsell. 2002. Academic geriatric programs in U.S. allopathic and osteopathic medical schools. *Journal of the American Medical Association* 288(18):2313-2319.

Warshaw, G. A., E. J. Bragg, D. C. Thomas, M. L. Ho, and D. E. Brewer. 2006. Are internal medicine residency programs adequately preparing physicians to care for the baby boomers? A national survey from the Association of Directors of Geriatric Academic Programs Status of Geriatrics Workforce Study. *Journal of the American Geriatrics Society* 54(10):1603-1609.

Weeks, W. B., and A. E. Wallace. 2004. Return on educational investment in geriatrics training. *Journal of the American Geriatrics Society* 52(11):1940-1945.

Wendt, A. 2003. Mapping geriatric nursing competencies to the 2001 NCLEX-RN test plan. *Nursing Outlook* 51(4):152-157.

Wheeler, B. K., S. Powelson, and J. H. Kim. 2007. Interdisciplinary clinical education: Implementing a gerontological home visiting program. *Nurse Educator* 32(3):136-140.

Williams, B. C., T. L. Remington, M. A. Foulk, and A. L. Whall. 2006. Teaching interdisciplinary geriatrics ambulatory care: A case study. *Gerontology & Geriatrics Education* 26(3):29-45.

Williams, B. C., V. Weber, S. F. Babbott, L. M. Kirk, M. T. Heflin, E. O'Toole, M. M. Schapira, E. Eckstrom, A. Tulsky, A. M. Wolf, and S. Landefeld. 2007. Faculty development for the 21st century: Lessons from the Society of General Internal Medicine-Hartford Collaborative Centers for the care of older adults. *Journal of the American Geriatrics Society* 55(6):941-947.

Wing, P., M. H. Langelier, E. S. Salsberg, and R. S. Hooker. 2004. The changing professional practice of physician assistants: 1992 to 2000. *Journal of the American Academy of Physician Assistants* 17(1):37-40, 42, 45.

Wolf, S. L., H. X. Barnhart, N. G. Kutner, E. McNeely, C. Coogler, and T. Xu. 1996. Reducing frailty and falls in older persons: An investigation of Tai Chi and computerized balance training. *Journal of the American Geriatrics Society* 44(5):489-497.

Wood, G. J., and R. Mulligan. 2000. Cross-sectional comparison of dental students' knowledge and attitudes before geriatric training: 1984-1999. *Journal of Dental Education* 64(11):763-771.

Woolsey, L. J. 2005. Geriatric medicine and the future of the physician assistant profession. *Perspective on Physician Assistant Education* 16(1):24-28.

Woolsey, L. J. 2007. Physician assistant attitude and expressed intent to work with geriatric patients. *Gerontology & Geriatrics Education* 28(1):61-78.

Yeo, G. 2007 (unpublished). *How will the U.S. health care system meet the challenge of the ethnogeriatric imperative?* Paper commissioned by the IOM Committee on the Future Health Care Workforce for Older Americans.

Yuen, J. K., R. Breckman, R. D. Adelman, C. F. Capello, V. Lofaso, and M. Carrington Reid. 2006. Reflections of medical students on visiting chronically ill older patients in the home. *Journal of the American Geriatrics Society* 54(11):1778-1783.

5

The Direct-Care Workforce

CHAPTER SUMMARY

This chapter describes the direct-care workforce—nurse aides, home health aides, and personal- and home-care aides—which is in many respects the linchpin of the formal health care delivery system for older adults. This collection of workers supplies a major portion of the direct care provided to older adults, including the provision of some clinical services plus assistance with bathing, dressing, housekeeping, and food preparation. Direct-care workers have rewarding but difficult jobs, and they are typically very poorly paid and receive little or no training for their duties. As a result, turnover rates are high, and recruitment and retention of these workers is a persistent challenge. In the context of rapidly increasing demand for direct-care services, the need for these workers is beginning to reach a crisis stage. This chapter discusses a range of approaches to improve the quality of direct-care occupations, including needed increases in pay and benefits. In addition, improvements in the education and training of these workers are needed to ensure that they have the knowledge and skills required to meet the care needs of older patients.

Direct-care workers, also referred to as paraprofessionals, are the primary providers of paid hands-on care, supervision, and emotional support for older adults in the United States. While not all direct-care workers care for older patients, they work primarily in settings important in the care of older adults, such as nursing homes, assisted living facilities, and home-care settings. According to the Bureau of Labor Statistics (BLS), about three

199

million workers were employed in direct-care occupations in 2006[1] (BLS, 2008c,d). Still, the current number of direct-care workers is insufficient to meet demand (GAO, 2001a,b; Stone, 2004). The need for direct-care workers is expected to increase in the coming decades, mainly because of the aging of the population but also because the number of females aged 25 to 54—the typical direct-care worker demographic—is projected to remain flat (PHI, 2001).

A further trend that may exacerbate this unfulfilled need, especially for personal- and home-care aides, is a shift away from institutional care to home- and community-based care. Policy makers and payers are increasingly implementing home- and community-based care programs in response to consumer preferences and legal mandates and with the hope that costs will be lower for at least some types of services. However, caring for older adults in these settings may require proportionately more direct care-level staff than in institutional facilities (National Center for Health Workforce Analysis, 2004). The workforce providing non-institutional personal assistance and home health services tripled between 1989 and 2004, and Medicaid spending for these services also increased significantly during that time (Kaye et al., 2006). Over that same time period, the workforce providing similar services in institutional settings remained relatively stable. In fact, the BLS predicts that personal- and home-care aides and home health aides will represent the second- and third-fastest growing occupations between 2006 and 2016 (BLS, 2007b). This trend will not only lead to an increase in demand for services in non-institutional settings but will also require home-based workers to deliver more skilled care to patients with more complex needs (Seavey, 2007b). In home- and community-based care settings, carers work more independently and rely on personal skill and judgment; however, many direct-care workers do not receive the education or training they need in order to be prepared for the care of older patients with complex care needs.

A major factor in the deficit of direct-care workers is the poor quality of these types of jobs. Direct-care workers typically receive very low salaries, garner few benefits, and work under high levels of physical and emotional stress. In 2005 the median hourly wage for all direct-care workers was $9.56, about one-third less than the median wage for all U.S. workers (Dawson, 2007). Direct-care workers are more likely to live in poverty, to lack health insurance, and to rely on food stamps than other workers (GAO, 2001b). Additionally, these workers have high rates of job-related injury, most often due to overexertion in the care of a patient (BLS, 2007a). All of these factors contribute to the unacceptably high rates of vacancies

---

[1]It is important to note that this figure does not include the many workers who are hired privately by patients and their families.

and turnover among these occupations, which can, in turn, lead to poor quality of care for patients.

Much of this chapter focuses on issues concerning direct-care workers in general because there is relatively little data on the group of direct-care workers solely involved in the care of older adults; whenever possible, however, issues related specifically to the care of older adults will be highlighted. The chapter begins with descriptions of direct-care occupations and the basic demographics of the current workforce, followed by an overview of the current state of education and training of these workers. The chapter then discusses challenges to the recruitment and retention of direct-care workers, including financial disincentives and difficulties in work environment. The chapter concludes with an examination of strategies to improve the recruitment and retention of direct-care workers, including enhancing the quality and quantity of basic education and training, increasing overall job satisfaction (including expanding roles and responsibilities), improving economic incentives, and broadening the labor pool. Overall, in order to create a more effective and efficient direct-care workforce, much more needs to be done to educate and train these workers to care for older adults, and much more needs to be done to enhance the quality of these jobs.

DIRECT-CARE OCCUPATIONS

Direct-care workers are often grouped into three categories: nurse aides (also known as nursing assistants); home health aides; and personal- and home-care aides (Harmuth and Dyson, 2005). Forty-two percent of direct-care workers care for patients in the home setting, 41 percent work in nursing homes, and the remaining 17 percent are employed in hospitals (Smith and Baughman, 2007). Table 5-1 provides details about the various types of direct-care workers, including their most common employers, the types of services they provide, and typical supervision requirements.

Nurse Aides and Home Health Aides

The occupation of nurse aide goes by a number of job titles which vary by state, setting, and situation; these titles include certified nursing assistant (CNA), geriatric aide, orderly, and hospital attendant (BLS, 2008c). Nurse aides are employed primarily in nursing homes but also work in other institutional settings, such as hospitals and assisted living facilities. They assist residents with activities of daily living (ADLs), including bathing, dressing, eating, and toileting, and they can perform such clinical tasks as taking blood-pressure readings and, in some states, administering oral medications (Reinhard et al., 2003). These workers have a major role in institutional

TABLE 5-1 Comparison of Direct-Care Occupations

	Nurse Aides (Assistants), Orderlies, and Attendants	Home-Health Aides	Personal- and Home-Care Aides
Common employers	Nursing and residential-care facilities; hospitals	Home health care agencies; social assistance agencies; nursing and residential-care facilities	Home-care agencies; individual and family services; private households
Examples of typical services provided	Answer patients' call lights; deliver messages; serve meals; make beds; help patients eat, dress, and bathe; escort patients to medical appointments; take vital signs; observe patients' physical and mental conditions	Administer oral medications; take vital signs; help patients bathe, groom, and dress; assist with prescribed exercises	Help clients get out of bed, bathe, dress, and groom; assist with housekeeping, grocery shopping, and cooking; accompany clients to doctors' appointments or on other errands
Supervision	On-site nursing and medical staff	Periodic check-ins/visits by supervisors (e.g., nurses, physical therapists, social workers, case managers)	Periodic check-ins/visits by supervisors (e.g., case managers, patients' families, nurses)

SOURCE: BLS, 2008c,d; Fishman et al., 2004.

settings, providing 70 percent to 80 percent of direct-care hours to those older Americans who receive long-term care (Harmuth and Dyson, 2005).

Home health aides (HHAs) are generally hired through a home health agency and assist individuals with ADLs in their homes. They may also assist with food preparation and housekeeping. Both nurse aides and home health aides provide a degree of clinical services (e.g., wound care) and work under the supervision of a registered nurse (RN).

Personal- and Home-Care Aides

Personal- and home-care aides may work in group or individual home settings and are somewhat more difficult to classify. These aides may be referred to as personal-care attendants, personal assistants, or direct support professionals, and they may be employed through an agency or hired directly by an individual (BLS, 2008d; Harmuth and Dyson, 2005). They help older adults maintain their independence and remain in their homes and communities by providing assistance with both ADLs and instrumental activities of daily living (IADLs), such as meal preparation and transportation. Personal-care services have been growing and all states now have waiver programs through Medicaid that provide these services to seniors and people with disabilities (Kitchener et al., 2007; Seavey and Salter, 2006).

Whereas home health aides who provide Medicare-certified home care perform their jobs under the supervision of a registered nurse (RN), personal- and home-care workers frequently have no supervision, even though they may perform many of the same services. Furthermore, many personal- and home-care workers may be hired privately by patients, without the involvement of an agency. Because of these hiring practices, little can be done to track the workers in this "grey market," which makes it difficult to create a demographic profile of the workers or to regulate their work practices (Seavey, 2007b).

As patients move rapidly away from institutional long-term care and toward home- and community-based settings, they are increasingly relying on direct-care workers to provide needed care, including more complex services than previously provided in these settings. Assisted-living facilities, which are community-based facilities that provide more services than a typical home setting but less than a nursing home, are a rapidly growing option for the residential care of older adults (Lyketsos et al., 2007), and the workers serving patients in these settings (including the patients with more complex needs) are typically personal- and home-care aides rather than home health or nurse aides. There is little to no federal regulation regarding the training or staffing requirements for assisted-living facilities; instead, each state regulates workers in these settings.

WORKFORCE DEMOGRAPHICS

Direct-care workers are overwhelmingly female (89 percent) and are typically between the ages of 25 and 55, unmarried (including those who are widowed, divorced, or separated), without college degrees, and citizens of the United States (Montgomery et al., 2005; Smith and Baughman, 2007; Yamada, 2002). Approximately 30 percent of direct-care workers are African American and 15 percent are of Hispanic or Latino origin (BLS, 2008a), although this can vary by setting and job title.

In 2005 Montgomery and colleagues examined data from the 2000 Census to create a profile of home-care aides who provide direct long-term care services, including those who are hired privately (Montgomery et al., 2005). The study revealed that as compared to hospital aides and nursing home aides, home-care aides are on average older, more likely to be of Hispanic or Latino origin, more likely to be self-employed, and less likely to have steady year-round employment (Table 5-2).

TABLE 5-2 Characteristics of Direct-Care Workers, 1999

Characteristic	Hospital Aides	Nursing Home Aides	Home-Care Aides
Demographic Characteristics			
Gender (% female)	81.2	91.3	91.8
Average age (years)	40.5	38.0	46.2
White, non-Hispanic (%)	48.4	55.6	50.3
Hispanic or Latino (%)	10.7	7.8	15.9
U.S., native-born (%)	81.5	85.5	75.1
Marital status (% married)	46.2	42.7	44.2
Education—less than high school (%)	17.6	26.3	30.9
Employment Characteristics			
Year-round, full-time employment (%)	52.4	48.3	34.3
Part-year, part-time employment (%)	13.0	14.8	24.3
Self-employed (%)	0.0	0.3	16.8

SOURCE: Montgomery et al., 2005.

A recent study found notable differences between female direct-care workers and the female workforce overall (Table 5-3) (Smith and Baughman, 2007). Black women, for example, make up a disproportionately large percentage of the female direct-care workforce relative to their presence in the female workforce overall (29 percent versus 13 percent). A second difference is that female direct-care workers are more likely to be single mothers than are female workers in general (24 percent versus 14 percent); of those who are single parents, 35 percent to 40 percent are below the poverty line (GAO, 2001b).

EDUCATION AND TRAINING REQUIREMENTS

The education and training of the direct-care workforce is insufficient to prepare these workers to provide quality care to older adults. Although there are a number of state and federal requirements for the education and training of nurse aides, home health aides, and personal- and home-care aides, these requirements are minimal (Table 5-4). Many direct-care workers have no more than a high school education, and some have even less (Montgomery et al., 2005; Smith and Baugham, 2007). Minimum training requirements for these workers are often inadequate or non-existent, and they vary across occupational categories and settings of care as well as among states. A number of other training-program characteristics vary among states as well, including the specific qualifications that instructors are expected to have, maximum student/instructor ratios, and the required program approval and oversight processes (AARP, 2006).

TABLE 5-3 Demographic Characteristics of Female Direct-Care Workers Versus All Female Workers, 2006

Characteristic	All Female Workers	All Female Direct-Care Workers	Female Hospital Aides	Female Nursing Home Aides	Female Home Health Aides
Average age (years)	42	41	40	38	45
Race and Ethnicity (%)					
White, non-Hispanic	70	51	55	51	49
Black, non-Hispanic	13	29	30	35	24
Other, non-Hispanic	6	5	5	4	7
Hispanic	11	15	11	10	21
Foreign-born	13	20	19	17	22
Marital Status (%)					
Married	54	38	35	38	39
Previously married	21	31	27	27	37
Never married	25	31	38	36	24
Children under 18 years	41	43	32	50	40
Single mothers	14	24	17	28	22

NOTE: The direct-care worker category consists of the three types listed in the last three columns (hospital aides, nursing home aides, and home health aides). The table excludes the 11 percent of the direct-care workforce that is men. Percentages listed are based on weighted data for female workers aged 19 years and older. Percentages may not sum to 100 because of rounding.
SOURCE: Smith and Baughman, 2007.

This section describes the current requirements for education and training of direct-care workers. Where possible, direct-care education and training issues that are particularly relevant to the older patient population are highlighted.

TABLE 5-4 Education and Training Requirements for Direct-Care Occupations

Nurse Aides, Orderlies, and Attendants	Home Health Aides	Personal- and Home-Care Aides
Federal requirements of 75 hours of training (for nurse aides); competency evaluation results in state certification; high school diploma and previous work experience not always required	Per federal rules, if employer receives Medicare/Medicaid reimbursement, workers must pass competency test (75 hours of classroom and practical training suggested); high school diploma and previous work experience not always required	Dependent on state, with some requiring no formal training; high school diploma and previous work experience not always required

SOURCES: BLS, 2008c,d; Fishman et al., 2004.

Nurse Aides

The Omnibus Budget Reconciliation Act of 1987[2] established the Nurse Aide Training and Competency Evaluation Program, which created minimum federal requirements for the education and training of nurse aides (OIG, 2002). Nurse aides working in Medicare- or Medicaid-certified nursing homes or home health agencies are required to successfully complete the following:

- At least 75 hours of state-approved training by, or under the general supervision of, an RN with at least 2 years of experience in nursing and at least 1 year of experience in a long-term care environment (or in home health care for training of home health aides)
- A competency evaluation (state certificate exam to become a certified nursing assistant)
- At least 12 hours per year of continuing education; for nursing homes, this must include training on providing services to individuals with cognitive impairments and on aide-specific areas of weakness identified in performance reviews

Many states have established additional requirements beyond the federally mandated minimums. For example, 27 states and the District of Colombia require more than 75 hours of initial training and 12 states plus the District require 120 hours or more (Seavey, 2007a). Under federal rules the initial 75 hours of nurse aide training must cover a number of specific subject areas (Box 5-1). That time must include 16 hours of supervised practical, or "hands on," training in a clinical setting, and the trainee must demonstrate the ability to perform specific tasks, such as taking vital signs. The 75-hour training requirement is low compared to other service professions. For example, California requires significantly more hours of training for manicurists (350 hours), skin-care specialists (600 hours), and hair stylists (1,500 hours) (Harrington, 2007a).

States are responsible for ensuring compliance with educational requirements and administering (or contracting with someone who administers) competency exams. Subject to the 75-hour minimum, states have flexibility in developing training programs. These training programs can be offered by vocational schools, nursing homes, or home health agencies as long as the institution maintains its certification requirements. Instructional facilities that are judged to be providing substandard care can lose their right to

---

[2]*Omnibus Budget Reconciliation Act of 1987*. Public Law 100-203. 100th Congress. December 22, 1987.

BOX 5-1
Federal Requirements for Nurse Aide Training,
by Subject Area

- Basic nursing skills, such as monitoring vital signs and height/weight; reporting abnormal changes in body functioning; and caring for the dying resident.
- Personal-care skills, including activities of daily living such as bathing, grooming, dressing, toileting, and skin care; feeding and hydration; and transferring, positioning, and turning.
- Mental health and social service skills, such as responding to a resident's behavior; allowing the resident to make personal choices; and drawing upon the resident's family to be a source of emotional support.
- Caring for cognitively impaired residents, such as addressing the behaviors of dementia patients and responding to residents with other cognitive impairments.
- Basic restorative skills, such as training the resident in self-care; use of assistive devices; maintaining range of motion; eating, dressing, and ambulation; and bowel and bladder training.
- Residents' rights, such as maintenance of privacy and confidentiality; promoting residents' rights to make personal choices; helping to resolve grievances and disputes; reporting any instances of abuse, mistreatment, and neglect.

SOURCE: OIG, 2002.

---

offer a nurse-aide training program, which generally makes it more difficult and more costly to recruit new aides.

Home Health Aides

Home health aides must meet federal requirements only if their employer receives Medicare or Medicaid reimbursement. Specifically, home health aides in such institutions must pass a competency test that covers 12 subject areas (Box 5-2). Federal law suggests that home health aides be provided at least 75 hours of classroom and practical training that is supervised by an RN. These training programs vary by state.

Personal- and Home-Care Aides

Since residential-care services, such as those provided in assisted-living facilities, are not paid for under the Medicare and Medicaid programs (except under some state Medicaid waivers), there are no federal requirements for residential-care personnel, and states have the primary responsibility

---

**BOX 5-2
Subject Areas Covered in
Home Health Aide Competency Tests**

- Communication skills
- Observation, reporting, and documentation of patient status and the care or services furnished
- Reading and recording vital signs
- Basic infection-control procedures
- Basic elements of body function and changes
- Maintenance of a clean, safe, and healthy environment
- Recognition of, and procedures for, emergencies
- The physical, emotional, and developmental characteristics of the patients served
- Personal hygiene and grooming
- Safe transfer techniques
- Normal range of motion and positioning
- Basic nutrition

SOURCE: *Home Health Aide Training.* 2006. 42 C.F.R. § 484.36.

---

for regulating residential-care facilities (IOM, 2001). When aides are hired directly by individuals (i.e., through consumer-directed programs), the patient or the patient's family member assumes responsibility for deciding what the worker needs to know and for providing training for those tasks, most often through direct observation (PHI and Medstat, 2004). In turn, patients may need to learn training and supervisory skills (as was discussed in Chapter 4 for the case of professionals), including effective communication and problem-solving.

While no federal requirements exist for personal-care attendants who work outside a nursing home or home health agency, states may conduct checks on the background, training, supervision, age, health, and literacy of these service providers if they receive Medicaid reimbursements (OIG, 2006). Training checks may include verification of instruction in topics such as first aid, assistance with ADLs, and basic health and hygiene. In 2006 the Office of Inspector General (OIG) found that the median number of training hours required of personal-care attendants was 28 hours, but state requirements ranged from 2 hours to 120 hours. As more personal-care attendants are hired privately by patients, making sure that these workers have the appropriate abilities will become an even more complex task.

RECRUITMENT AND RETENTION CHALLENGES

Health care workers serving older patients have high rates of turnover, and maintaining adequate levels of staffing within the industry overall is a persistent challenge. This challenge is especially pronounced among direct-care workers, who have a number of immediate, less stressful job alternatives, such as those offered by the food and hospitality industries. In 2006, for example, personal- and home-care aides had median wages of $8.54 per hour while counter attendants in cafeterias, food concessions, and coffee shops had median wage-and-salary earnings of $7.76 per hour (including tips) (BLS, 2008b).

One study found that 40 percent to 60 percent of home health aides leave after less than 1 year on a job, and 80 percent to 90 percent leave within the first 2 years (PHI, 2005). Staff turnover in assisted-living settings ranges from 21 percent to 135 percent, with an average of 42 percent (Maas and Buckwalter, 2006). In nursing homes CNA turnover averages 71 percent per year, and the turnover rate in many states is much higher (Decker et al., 2003). Turnover may have negative effects on the quality of patient care and may also increase employer costs because of the need for continuous recruitment and training. A study of direct-care workers in Pennsylvania estimated annual recurring training costs due to turnover to be almost $24 million for nursing homes and almost $5 million for home health and home-care agencies (Leon et al., 2001). It has been estimated that turnover among direct-care workers in the United States costs providers a total of $4.1 billion per year (Seavey, 2004).

While many direct-care workers find the work of caring for frail older individuals to be rewarding, the appeal of these professions is weakened by a number of other factors including low wages, few (if any) benefits, high physical and emotional demands, and a significant potential for on-the-job injury (Newcomer and Scherzer, 2006; Pennington et al., 2003). Job dissatisfaction among these workers can also result from factors related to the work environment including poor relationships with supervisors, a lack of respect from other health professionals, and few opportunities for advancement (Fleming et al., 2003; Stone, 2000). Not surprisingly, high job dissatisfaction has been associated with increased turnover (Castle et al., 2007). Conversely, improved job satisfaction can result in a greater intent to stay.

Researchers examining the predictors of high turnover in nursing homes have identified a number of key variables, including low staffing ratios, for-profit ownership, and higher numbers of beds (Castle and Engberg, 2006); low reimbursement rates, a high Medicaid census, low wages, and low administrative expenses (Kash et al., 2006); and inadequate benefits and not having a good social environment at work (Grau et al., 1991). One study examining predictors of turnover in a residential-care setting found that the physical condition of the neighborhood[3] in which the facility was located was by far the strongest predictor of turnover, outweighing other factors such as starting wages, availability of health insurance, Medicaid census, and average case mix (Konetzka et al., 2005).

In the following sections, several of these challenges are discussed in more detail, along with the effect that these factors have on patient outcomes. Initiatives to overcome these barriers are also discussed later in this chapter. It is important to note that the chapter provides only a general discussion of challenges to the recruitment and retention of direct-care workers and that, depending on the type of direct-care worker, the setting, and the source of dissatisfaction, these various factors may weigh more or less heavily in a particular situation.

Financial Disincentives

Direct-care workers receive low hourly wages, which contributes to the lower appeal of these jobs. In fact, in 2007 *Forbes* magazine profiled personal- and home-care aides as one of the top 25 worst-paying jobs in America (Maidment, 2007). Table 5-5 shows the median wages for direct-care occupations in a variety of settings that are important in the care of older adults.

The average annual earnings of female direct-care workers are significantly lower than the average annual earnings of female workers in general ($17,228 versus $30,441), and 19 percent of female direct-care workers have incomes below the poverty level versus 8 percent of female workers in general (Smith and Baughman, 2007). The low incomes of direct-care workers are due in part to the fact that many direct-care workers do not have predictable hours or the opportunity to work more hours if desired (Dawson, 2007).

Direct-care workers have limited access to employee benefits, including health insurance coverage, sick leave, and retirement benefits (Brady et al., 2002; Dawson, 2007; GAO, 2001b; Smith and Baughman, 2007). Approximately one-quarter of direct-care workers lack health insurance coverage (Hams et al., 2002; Lipson and Regan, 2004). Often these workers are unable to afford their share of the health insurance premiums or they are ineligible for coverage because they work part time or they work independently of an agency. As can be seen in Table 5-6, female direct-care workers are considerably less likely to have health insurance coverage than are female workers in general. This situation can vary dramatically by occupation and region, however. A study of home-care workers in Los

---

[3]The condition of the neighborhood was likely a proxy for many of the resource issues that cannot be measured well and typically cannot be included in these studies.

TABLE 5-5 Median Hourly Wages for Direct-Care Occupations by Setting, 2006

	Nurse Aides	Home Health Aides	Personal- and Home-Care Aides
All settings	$10.67	$9.34	$8.54
Community care facilities for older persons	$10.07	$8.87	NA
Services for older or disabled persons	NA	$9.26	$9.18
Home health care	NA	$9.14	$7.19
Nursing care facilities	$10.37	$9.76	NA

NOTE: NA = not available.
SOURCE: BLS, 2008c,d.

Angeles, for instance, found that about 45 percent of them were uninsured (Cousineau, 2000). And health insurance is not the only benefit that direct-care workers are less likely to receive. For example, approximately three-fourths of nurse aides in nursing homes and home health settings have no pension benefits (GAO, 2001b).

Non-Financial Factors

While concerns about poor wages and lack of benefits are significant, non-financial job characteristics also play a major role in the job satisfaction of direct-care workers (Bowers et al., 2003). Factors that influence job satisfaction include professional growth opportunities, adequate training, rewards for performance, and manageable workloads (Castle et al., 2007; Parsons et al., 2003). Direct-care workers often report that they do not receive enough respect for their knowledge and skills, that they have little discretion or input into care planning (despite being responsible for most of the patient care hours), and that they sense a lack of trust by manage-

TABLE 5-6 Health Insurance Coverage of Female Workers and Direct-Care Workers, 2005 (percentage)

Type of Coverage	All Female Workers	All Female Direct-Care Workers	Female Hospital Aides	Female Nursing-Home Aides	Female Home Health Aides
All private	78	60	84	63	49
Employer-based	51	38	63	44	23
Public	12	22	10	19	29
None	16	25	13	24	30

NOTE: Percentages are based on weighted data for female workers aged 19 years and older. Columns may sum to more than 100 percent because some workers are covered by more than one type of health insurance.
SOURCE: Smith and Baughman, 2007.

ment (Bowers et al., 2003). Other factors contributing to worker dissatisfaction include excessive paperwork, frequent patient deaths, combative and uncooperative patients, and inadequate staffing (Cherry et al., 2007). Aides who work in understaffed facilities feel extra time pressure, which contributes to burnout and absenteeism (Bowers et al., 2000). Research has shown that job satisfaction and organizational culture are strong predictors of worker commitment to an organization (Sikorska-Simmons, 2005), and, as discussed in Chapter 4, poor supervisory relationships are a key driver of turnover (Tellis-Nayak, 2007).

Caring for older patients can be emotionally draining, especially when patients are at the end of life (Haley et al., 2003; Holland and Neimeyer, 2005; Jezuit, 2000; Viles, 2000). Moreover, the work can be physically taxing. Direct-care staff in nursing homes have one of the highest rates of workplace injury among all occupations. In 2006, according to the BLS, the rate of non-fatal occupational injury and illness involving days away from work was 526 incidents per 10,000 workers among nursing aides, orderlies, and attendants (BLS, 2007a). This was four times the average rate among all occupations and was a higher rate than found among either construction workers (488) or truck drivers (411). Fifty-six percent of injuries and illnesses among direct-care workers were directly related to patient interaction, and 86 percent of these injuries and illnesses were due to overexertion. Nursing aides, orderlies, and attendants also had the highest rate of musculoskeletal disorders among all occupations examined.

Among personal-care aides, the documentation and treatment of on-the-job injuries is impeded when aides change employers, which can affect an individual worker's ability to access worker's compensation benefits (Scherzer, 2005, 2006b). In addition, the rate of injury to personal-care aides may be severely underestimated, largely because independent providers are generally ignored by current surveillance mechanisms.

In 1996 the IOM recommended that all personnel who provide direct care (especially in nursing homes) should receive annual training in lifting and transferring patients. The committee also concluded that hospitals and nursing homes should develop effective programs to reduce work-related injuries (IOM, 1996). Chapter 6 of this report identifies a number of technologies that have been developed to assist both direct-care workers and informal caregivers in performing some of the physically demanding tasks that are involved in caring for older adults.

Finally, trends in the care of older adults, such as the movement toward more home-based care, can affect the job environment for these home- and community-based workers. For example, as more workers are hired directly by patients under consumer-directed models of care, home-care workers may have to contend with a more ambiguous situation in terms of their lack of supervisory management. This in turn can make it less likely that these workers will have someone to deal with regarding such concerns as on-the-job injury and access to workers' compensation. One study of injured home-care workers found that individually hired workers faced greater obstacles (e.g., barriers to creating a safe working environment, receiving appropriate care for injuries, or receiving compensation benefits) than did agency-hired workers (Scherzer, 2006a).

Impact on the Quality of Patient Care

Several issues related to the difficulties of recruiting and retaining direct-care workers may have direct effects on the quality of care provided to older patients. Studies have shown, for example, that a significant relationship exists between staffing levels and the quality of patient care (Harrington, 2007b; Harrington and Swan, 2003; IOM, 1996, 2001). Research has also linked turnover rates with quality of care, although the details of that relationship remain equivocal (Bostick et al., 2006; Castle and Engberg, 2005, 2006; Cohen-Mansfield, 1997). Most of the studies simply demonstrate associations, for instance, so it is not possible to estimate the magnitude of a potential causal effect. Furthermore, most studies of turnover to date have suffered from inconsistencies in the way that turnover is calculated, both in terms of its definition and its use as a linear measure.

Although historically it has been difficult for researchers to prove direct causal links between recruitment and retention challenges and the quality of care delivered to patients, there is some evidence that the two are related. In a series of research publications, Castle and Engberg concluded that, in general, high turnover is associated with poor quality and that staff characteristics such as turnover, staffing levels, and worker stability all affect the quality of care of nursing homes (Castle and Engberg, 2007). The researchers also found that increases in nurse aide turnover, especially those from moderate to high levels, result in decreases in quality as measured by rates of physical restraint use, catheter use, contractures, pressure ulcers, psychoactive drug use, and quality of care deficiencies reported on certification surveys (Castle and Engberg, 2005). Castle and Engberg found evidence of a nonlinear relationship between turnover and quality in their examination of 1-year turnover rates among nurse aides and licensed practical nurses (LPNs) in nursing homes (Castle and Engberg, 2006). While there was no significant relationship between turnover and the quality of care at lower levels of turnover, they found that when turnover rates were greater than 50 percent, there was a significant negative relationship between turnover rates and quality.

In nursing homes, nurse aides often have to manage heavy patient loads, which not only increases the burden placed on them but can also decrease the quality of care that they provide (Schnelle et al., 2004). A report released in 2001 by the Centers for Medicare and Medicaid Services (CMS), which investigated the appropriateness of minimum nurse staffing ratios in nursing homes, noted the following:

> [W]ith one nursing assistant commonly responsible for nine or more residents on the day shift and twice as many at night, time management often degenerates into triage. Baths and meals are given on a tight schedule and at the convenience of the home's routine rather than the residents, leading to things like waking residents in the middle of the night for showers. Call lights are left unanswered, nonessential tasks such as nail care are neglected, and practices are often adopted that endanger either residents or staff. (CMS, 2001)

Conversely, improving some aspects of job quality (e.g., reducing turnover) may lead to improvements in the quality of patient care. For example, allowing nurse aides to have greater responsibility in care decisions is associated with higher social-engagement scores among patients, and lower rates of turnover and higher rates of retention have been associated with lower incidence of pressure ulcers (Barry et al., 2005). One study of residents and staff at assisted-living facilities found that a high-quality work environment, including an organizational culture that emphasizes teamwork and participatory decision-making, is associated with greater satisfaction among the residents (Sikorska-Simmons, 2006). Another study examined a skilled nursing facility that had created a staffing program that emphasized consistent scheduling, with staff permanently assigned to specific residents. The facility reported that the program had positive effects both on worker satisfaction (including a 10 percent decrease in turnover and a 50 percent decrease in injuries) and on patient outcomes (including a 40 percent decrease in pressure ulcers and an 83 percent decrease in complaints) (ASA, 2008). Again, however, it is difficult to prove a causal relationship between job satisfaction and turnover and the consequent effects on patient care. Strategies to improve the quality of direct-care jobs and the effects of these strategies on reducing turnover and increasing intent to stay are discussed in the next section.

IMPROVING RECRUITMENT AND RETENTION

In order to overcome the challenges to recruitment and retention of direct-care workers, more needs to be done to improve the overall quality and, therefore, desirability of these jobs. Strategies to do this can be grouped into three broad categories:

- Enhancing the quality and quantity of basic education and training

- Increasing economic incentives (i.e., increased wages and benefits)
- Improving the work environment (e.g., empowerment strategies and culture change)

These strategies not only are important for developing a robust health care workforce but also have direct implications for the quality of care provided to older adults. In addition to improving the quality of these jobs, the sheer number of workers needed to care for the future population of older adults makes it imperative that new sources of workers be considered. The following sections outline strategies both to improve job quality and to broaden the potential labor pool, and they include examinations of several large-scale efforts to improve the recruitment and retention of direct-care workers.

Enhancing Basic Education and Training

There are a number of indications that the current training requirements for direct-care workers are insufficient, both in terms of quality of content and quantity of training hours. Most nurse aide educators, as well as nurse aides themselves, agree that current levels of education and training for initial certification is inadequate (CMS, 2001). Moreover, 58 percent of ombudsmen identified inadequate training as a major impediment to quality care in nursing homes, and CNAs rank inadequate training among the top three problems that they face (Hawes, 2002). Poor training has also been identified as one of the factors that contributes to occurrences of neglect and abuse in nursing homes, especially for patients with behavioral difficulties associated with dementia (Hawes, 2002; IOM, 2002).

Very little is known about the quality of training for home health aides or personal- and home-care aides. Moreover, little is known about how training translates into practice. Some have suggested that these home- and community-based workers need to receive more training than workers in nursing-home settings because of the breadth of their responsibilities and their relative lack of supervision (Benjamin and Matthias, 2004; PHI and Medstat, 2004). Others have criticized attempts to standardize the training of these workers. As consumer-directed care has become more important, for example, some patients have expressed fears that personal- and home-care aides hired directly by patients or their families may not respond to the consumers' personal preferences if training standards are made too rigid. (See Chapter 6 for a fuller discussion of issues related to the trend of consumer-directed care.) However, most agree that certain basic skills and aptitudes are needed for the delivery of personal assistance.

Both the initial training and the continuing education of direct-care workers appear to be inadequate. In a survey of direct-care workers across multiple settings, only a little more than half said that their initial training was adequate, while 40 percent to 50 percent said that they could benefit from further training; 45 percent said continuing education was only somewhat useful (Menne et al., 2007). These workers identified a number of areas where their knowledge and skills needed further development, including dementia, end-of-life care, teamwork, and problem solving.

Much more research is needed to determine the competencies that direct-care workers need in order to provide high-quality care to older patients. Unfortunately, as is also the case with the professional health care workforce, expansion of training opportunities for direct-care workers is limited both by the availability of qualified trainers and by the funding available to pay for additional training.

While there is limited research on how different levels and types of training affect the quality of care provided, there is some evidence that a relationship does exist (IOM, 2001). For example, studies have shown that dementia, a common geriatric syndrome, is inadequately diagnosed and treated in assisted-living facilities, which can contribute to a quicker discharge to a nursing home (Lyketsos et al., 2007; Rosenblatt et al., 2004). In fact, in residential settings such as assisted-living facilities, the level of staff training is a key factor in determining whether residents will need to be relocated to nursing homes as their needs become more acute (Maas and Buckwalter, 2006).

Adequate training also has an effect on recruitment and retention. High levels of training have been positively associated with recruitment of home health workers (Leon et al., 2001). Increasing the skills of personal-care aides through a geriatric case-management program has shown strong influence on the workers' intent to stay and also some effect on job satisfaction (Coogle et al., 2007). Similarly, nurse aides who have received adequate training have been found to provide higher-quality patient care (Goldman et al., 2004) and to be less likely to want to leave their jobs (Castle et al., 2007).

In 2001 the IOM recommended that "all long-term care settings, federal and state governments, and providers, in consultation with consumers, develop training, education, and competency standards and training programs for staff based on better knowledge of the time, skills, education, and competency levels needed to provide acceptable consumer-centered long-term care" (IOM, 2001). This still holds true.

Content of Training

One area in which the content of direct-care worker training does not reflect the current environment is its relative lack of geriatric-specific educational content. A 2002 OIG study found that more than half (63 percent) of nursing-home supervisors interviewed believed that training had not kept pace with the care demands imposed by the increasing complexity of resident diagnoses, including Alzheimer's disease and other behavioral and cognitive disorders. Some of the specific skills for which additional training was found to be needed were related to catheter and colostomy care, lifting, skin care, feeding, hydration, and infusion therapies (OIG, 2002).

The committee concluded that direct-care workers who attend to older adults, especially frail older patients with complex health care needs, need to have specific training that will prepare them for these patients.

In addition to instruction that applies to older patients generally, staff may also need specific training in cultural competence for working with ethnically diverse patients and co-workers (Fuller, 1995; Minore and Boone, 2002). This type of training is not currently specified in federal requirements. Another area where training is inadequate is in palliative care; workers in both nursing homes and home-care settings are typically not well trained in the care of patients at the end of life (Ersek et al., 2006; Ferrell et al., 1998). Additionally, many direct-care workers need soft skills training, such as communication skills.

Quantity of Training Hours

In recent years there have been calls to increase the number of hours required for direct-care worker training. In 1998 the National Citizen's Coalition for Nursing Home Reform called for nursing assistants to be given a minimum of 160 hours of training (NCCNHR, 1998). Also in the late 1990s a panel of experts convened by the Hartford Institute for Geriatric Nursing recommended that training requirements for nursing aides be doubled, from 75 hours to 150 hours (Harrington et al., 2000). In 2002 an OIG survey of state-level directors of the Nurse Aide Training and Competency Exam Program found that 40 of the 49 respondents believed that the 75-hour federal minimum was insufficient to ensure adequate preparation for the job (OIG, 2002). In 2006 AARP examined nurse aide training programs in 10 states and found that the majority of officials interviewed believed that federal minimums need to be increased to between 100 and 120 hours (Hernandez-Medina et al., 2006).

Curricula are often overloaded, and there are challenges in covering all of the included ground in just 2 weeks (CMS, 2001). It may also be unrealistic to expect students to assimilate all of the necessary material in so little time (OIG, 2002). Moreover, the educational content for direct-care worker training has not kept pace with changes in the patient population, such as the increased prevalence of dementia and other cognitive disorders. As a result, more geriatric-specific educational content is needed. Additional hours will be required to cover this added material.

> Recommendation 5-1: States and the federal government should increase minimum training standards for all direct-care workers. Federal requirements for the minimum training of certified nursing assistants (CNAs) and home health aides should be raised to at least 120 hours and should include demonstration of competence in the care of older adults as a criterion for certification. States should also establish minimum training requirements for personal-care aides.

As described previously, more than half of states currently require more than the 75-hour federal minimum for nurse aide training, and about one-quarter require at least 120 hours (Table 5-7). This minimum should be raised in order to provide direct-care workers with the enhanced preparation they need to do their work. The committee ultimately decided to recommend 120 hours in order to raise the entire nation to the minimum standards of the top quartile of states. While data on the exact competencies needed by different types of direct-care workers when caring for older adults are minimal, the committee concluded that there is an immediate need to increase current federal minimum requirements to a higher standard. The committee recommends this new 120 hour minimum anticipating that even higher levels of required training hours may be needed to adequately cover additional knowledge and skill areas as more evidence is accumulated concerning the specific competencies that these workers need when caring for older adults. States, individual disciplines, regulators, patients, and others will need to work together to determine these competencies. This will be especially important as direct-care workers assume increasingly complex responsibilities and work more often in alternative sites of care. As data are gathered on the competencies needed for these additional and changing responsibilities, the minimum number of training hours needs to be raised accordingly.

The committee's recommendation does not offer any detail on the composition of those hours with respect to clinical training. At this time the states differ substantially in terms of how much training comes in the form of classroom instruction and how much is covered through practical training (Table 5-7). For example, North Carolina and Wyoming both require a minimum of 75 hours of nurse aide training, but North Carolina requires only 16 of those hours to be devoted to clinical training (the federal minimum), while Wyoming requires 48 hours of clinical training.

While there is already an established system for training and certifying home health aides and certified nursing assistants—a system that the com-

TABLE 5-7 Nurse Aide Training Requirements (by State), 2007

Hours	State	Minimum Training Hours/ (Minimum Clinical Hours)	
120+ hours	Missouri	175	(100)
(12 states +	California	150	(100)
DC)	Delaware	150	(75)
	Maine	150	(50)
	Oregon	150	(75)
	Alaska	140	(80)
	Arizona	120	(16)
	District of Columbia	120	(N/A)
	Florida	120	(40)
	Idaho	120	(40)
	Illinois	120	(40)
	Virginia	120	(40)
	West Virginia	120	(55)
76-119 hours	Indiana	105	(75)
(15 states)	Connecticut	100	(50)
	Hawaii	100	(70)
	Maryland	100	(40)
	New Hampshire	100	(60)
	New York	100	(30)
	Rhode Island	100	(20)
	Kansas	90	(45)
	New Jersey	90	(40)
	Georgia	85	(16)
	Washington	85	(50)
	Louisiana	80	(40)
	South Carolina	80	(40)
	Utah	80	(16)
	Nebraska	76	(N/A)
75 hours	Alabama	75	(16)
(23 states)	Arkansas	75	(16)
	Colorado	75	(16)
	Iowa	75	(30)
	Kentucky	75	(16)
	Massachusetts	75	(16)
	Michigan	75	(16)
	Minnesota	75	(37.5)
	Mississippi	75	(16)
	Montana	75	(25-30)
	North Carolina	75	(16)
	North Dakota	75	(16)
	Nevada	75	(N/A)
	New Mexico	75	(N/A)
	Ohio	75	(16)

continued

TABLE 5-7 Continued

Hours	State	Minimum Training Hours/ (Minimum Clinical Hours)	
75 hours	Oklahoma	75	(16)
(23 states)	Pennsylvania	75	(37.5)
(continued)	South Dakota	75	(16)
	Tennessee	75	(35)
	Texas	75	(24)
	Vermont	75	(16)
	Wisconsin	75	(16)
	Wyoming	75	(48)

NOTE: N/A = Not Available.
SOURCE: Seavey, 2007a.

mittee is proposing to strengthen—the methods for training and certifying personal- and home-care aides are much more inconsistent from state to state, with no formal system in existence. The committee's recommendation with regards to these workers is intended to create a basic framework for further requirements that may be implemented by states and the federal government in the future, especially as the knowledge base about the education and training of all types of direct-care workers develops.

Increasing Economic Incentives

As described previously, wages for direct-care workers are low and do not appear to adequately support the recruitment and retention of these workers. In a classic economic model of a labor shortage, wages, benefits, and other job attributes would simply improve until enough workers were willing to fill the positions, and the shortage would no longer exist. However, given that Medicaid and Medicare are responsible for about 70 percent of all long-term care dollars spent (Komisar and Thompson, 2007), there is little room for the market to adjust without the government's being willing to commit additional funds.

Evidence shows that higher wages do in fact lead to lower rates of turnover among all types of direct-care workers (Howes, 2005, 2006; Sherard, 2002). In seeking to find ways to increase wages for direct care workers in this environment, several mechanisms have been employed, including: setting a minimum service rate percentage that must to be passed through to direct-care labor costs; creating rate enhancements for providers that compensate their workers at a higher level; establishing automatic cost-of-living-adjustments to be passed through to direct-care labor costs; and establishing procurement and contracting standards that specify minimum staffing standards that providers must meet, such as worker compensation.

By far the most prevalent mechanism for stimulating increased direct-care worker pay is the wage pass-through, a state-level allocation of Medicaid funds that are added to reimbursement rates for the specific purpose of increasing direct-care staff wages. A review and evaluation of state wage pass-through laws conducted in 2003 found that 21 states had implemented such programs; nine of those programs were for skilled nursing facilities only, while the others also included home health or personal care (PHI, 2003b). Most of these programs were mandatory, but participation was voluntary in at least six of the states, and some states allowed flexibility in exactly how the funds were to be used to improve staffing.

Evaluation data for wage pass-throughs are limited and show mixed results, especially in terms of the effect on recruitment and retention. The effects on actual wages were also unclear. One reason for the lack of clarity is that Medicaid is only one payer among several and workers are not payer-specific, so facilities with different proportions of Medicaid residents received different total amounts to be spent on wage increments. A variety of other obstacles to analyzing these programs also exist, including the use of differing measures of recruitment and retention, an inability to monitor how wages are actually transferred to the employees, and difficulty in separating the effects of the wage pass-through from other interventions. The lack of data suggests the need for careful monitoring and auditing of wage pass-through programs. The evidence that is available, however, indicates that the wage increases were often too small, were unreliable year to year, lacked accountability mechanisms, and were time consuming and expensive to implement. However, some states, such as Wyoming, have implemented programs that have been deemed successful by assessors (Seavey and Salter, 2006).

Increasing wages is only one step toward improving the recruitment and retention of direct-care workers; benefits also need to be improved. This is especially true of direct-care workers in home settings, who typically have very limited benefits (Howes, 2006). According to a 2005 study, nine states had developed or were in the process of developing programs that would address the lack of health insurance among health care workers (Harmuth and Dyson, 2005). State strategies for expanding access to coverage for these workers include subsidizing employer-sponsored insurance, designing innovative employer-based insurance packages, and, in the case of Massachusetts, including the workers in a near-universal state health coverage plan (Seavey and Salter, 2006). In states such as Wisconsin, wage pass-throughs have also been considered as an option for funding the health care benefits of direct-care employees (PHI, 2006).

Recommendation 5-2: State Medicaid programs should increase pay and fringe benefits for direct-care workers through such measures as wage pass-throughs, setting wage floors, establishing minimum percentages of service rates directed to direct-care labor costs, and other means.

The committee also supports efforts to address the issue of variable hours and unstable income among direct-care workers. For example, the Guaranteed Hours Program implemented by Cooperative Home Care Associates (a home-care staffing agency in New York City) aims to reduce turnover and vacancy rates (PHI, 2007). Under this program, home health workers are considered full-time employees, are guaranteed full-time wages, and effectively serve on an "on call" basis during work hours when no client visit is scheduled. Although it has not been evaluated in isolation, it is part of a set of workforce interventions that have been documented to reduce turnover to nearly half the industry average (PHI, 2007).

Improving the Work Environment

Besides pay and benefits, a number of other factors may increase job satisfaction among direct-care workers, such as participation in decisions related to care planning and workplace improvement, the availability of career advancement opportunities, and high-quality supervision. Research has shown that job satisfaction and changes in organizational culture are strong predictors of commitment to an organization (Sikorska-Simmons, 2005) and that improved job satisfaction can result in a greater intent to stay (Castle et al., 2007). A variety of approaches, including mentoring (Hegeman, 2005), use of self-directed work teams (Yeatts et al., 2004), and career ladders (Maier, 2002), have all been closely linked to employee satisfaction.

Improving Relationships with Supervisors

As discussed in Chapter 4, the relationship between nursing supervisors and direct-care staff plays a significant role in the development of a hospitable work environment that leads to increased job satisfaction (Bishop et al., 2006; Tellis-Nayak, 2007). Positive supervision (as opposed to more punitive approaches) can greatly increase the direct-care worker's sense of value and ultimately can increase his or her level of job satisfaction and intent to stay. Evidence shows that perceived support by supervisors is also an important determinant in decreasing job-related stress (McGilton et al., 2007). A strengthening of the relationship between supervisors and staff may also enhance the practice of job delegation, as members of a workforce develop better and more interactive relationships, including improved recognition by supervisors of each worker's skills.

Increasing Recognition

Direct-care workers often feel that they do not receive adequate recognition for their work or for the contributions that they make toward quality patient care. Studies looking at the implementation of empowered CNA teams at skilled nursing facilities found that giving CNAs added decision-making responsibilities led them to become more competent and also to develop better attitudes about their jobs. This approach also takes advantage of the fact that CNAs have the most direct knowledge about the preferences of nursing home residents and as a result are often in the best position to make decisions relating to day-to-day care (Yeatts and Cready, 2007). Efforts to increase the involvement of direct-care workers in decision-making have also been linked to increased overall job satisfaction and, ultimately, decreased turnover. One study, for example, found that turnover among nursing home aides was significantly reduced when they were involved in interdisciplinary care-plan meetings (Banaszak-Holl and Hines, 1996). In a study of Pennsylvania's direct-care workforce, increased involvement of direct-care workers in care planning was associated with decreased rates of staff shortages and fewer job vacancies (Leon et al., 2001).

The Wellspring nursing home quality improvement model is one example of an effort to improve the recognition of CNAs as important members of the care team by enabling them to become leaders in continuous quality improvement. The program encourages individual staff members to acquire knowledge and skills in particular clinical areas (e.g., incontinence and pressure ulcers) so that they can lead care-resource teams in the care-planning and decision-making processes for residents (Wellspring Institute, 2005). (See the next section on career lattices for more on the development of specialty areas among direct-care workers.) These areas of training are based on best practices determined by the guidelines of both the Agency for Healthcare Research and Quality and the American Medical Directors Association as well as on other national standards of best practices (Wellspring Institute, 2005).

Evaluation of the program has shown that its training and organizational change methods have had measureable impact on retention and job satisfaction among its staff, as well as on resident satisfaction. Turnover rates were lower than at comparable facilities in the area; staff was more actively involved in assessing resident needs and providing care; and there was observational evidence of improved quality of life and interactions with staff among residents (Stone et al., 2002).

Creating Career Lattices

Another approach to increasing overall job satisfaction among direct-care workers is to expand their roles and responsibilities and to enhance their ability to develop new skills. The term "lattice" refers to how some workers move laterally in their careers (i.e., through the development of specialized skill areas) while others move linearly up the career "ladder" (e.g., advancement from CNA to LPN to RN) (CAEL, 2005). There have been many efforts to encourage the development of lattices for direct-care workers, sometimes in concert with the ability to move up a career ladder. For example, the Office of Apprenticeship in the U.S. Department of Labor (DOL) awarded grants to the Council for Adult and Experiential Learning (CAEL) and PHI with the goal of creating apprenticeship opportunities for direct-care workers to develop special skills through on-the-job training, related instruction, and mentoring (DOL, 2008c). The increased skill development associated with apprenticeships often leads to increases in wages as well (CAEL, 2005).

Council for Adult and Experiential Learning (CAEL) The CAEL has implemented the nursing career lattice program in nine sites (including both acute and long-term care settings) to develop more CNAs, LPNs, and RNs (CAEL, 2008; DOL, 2008c). As a first step, many apprentices are recruited from auxiliary areas such as housekeeping, clerical staff, and food service to be trained for CNA certification. Next, CNAs are encouraged to develop enhanced skills in specific areas including geriatrics, dementia care, and peer mentoring. CNAs are given flexible training schedules and wage increases in alignment with their increased responsibility. In this manner, the program prepares CNAs to take the required examination to become LPNs. LPNs also receive additional training based on specific competencies. For the next step on the career ladder, LPNs receive online education along with clinical training at local community colleges that prepares them to take the required examination to become RNs. This program has resulted in increased retention, reduced recruitment costs, and decreased worker shortages (CAEL, 2005, 2008).

PHI Under its grant, PHI developed the Home Health Aide Registered Apprenticeship at five sites to help home health aides gain basic skills and develop skills for specialty areas, such as hospice and palliative care, geriatrics, dementia, and peer mentoring (DOL, 2008c). As in the CAEL program, the training programs are based on specific competencies. Apprentices are required to demonstrate competence in basic skills as well as the skills needed for two specialty areas. They also receive mentoring from experienced home health aides.

Creating New Jobs and Delegating Responsibilities

As discussed in previous chapters, efficient use of the workforce will require more delegation of job duties in the coming years. This delegation has a cascading effect, with specific tasks being handed off to people in various professions and occupations, depending on the situation, which allows each worker to be used at his or her highest level of skill. The combination of the need to delegate additional duties and the desire of some direct-care workers to assume more responsibilities creates opportunities to restructure workforce assignments in ways that are potentially more satisfying for direct-care workers.

In some new models, direct-care worker roles may become much broader. For example, the Green House model described in Chapter 3 gives a more expansive role to direct-care workers. Under that model, frontline caregivers take responsibility for a broader range of tasks that include personal care, cooking, housekeeping, and making sure that residents spend time according to their preferences.

In other cases, direct-care workers take on specific tasks that require a higher level of skill than is usually expected of them. One example of this is the delegation of medication administration duties from RNs, as discussed in Chapter 4. Although there have been some concerns raised regarding patient safety, some RNs who have assessed the delegation of these responsibilities to CNAs have argued that CNAs may be able to deliver medications with greater accuracy because they face fewer distractions than RNs (Reinhard et al., 2003). If so, giving this responsibility to CNAs has the potential to increase efficiency, benefit patients, and facilitate the recruitment and retention of direct-care workers. Similarly, having home health aides assume responsibility for medication administration from RNs could help decrease the need for RN visits to homes.

If direct-care workers are to assume these increased responsibilities, they may in turn need to delegate certain of their own tasks. One example of this is the use of feeding assistants in the long-term care setting. Nurse aide training includes instruction in how to assist older adults with eating and hydration, and this is one of the primary responsibilities of CNAs. In 2003, however, CMS issued regulations allowing states to permit long-term care facilities participating in Medicare or Medicaid to use paid feeding assistants to supplement CNA services under certain conditions. Requirements for feeding assistants include the successful completion of a minimum of 8 hours of training in a state-approved course. The use of the feeding assistant has been controversial, but a preliminary analysis found that the quality of feeding done by feeding assistants was comparable to the quality of feeding by CNAs and, furthermore, that facilities did not decrease CNA hours in response (Kasprak, 2007; Simmons et al., 2007).

Using Technology

New technologies will make possible the more efficient use of the direct-care workforce in a variety of ways. As was discussed in previous chapters, the development and use of health information technologies will likely improve the coordination of patient care and enhance communication among caregivers. The development and use of assistive technologies may help patients be more independent, thereby reducing their need for assistance, especially personal-care assistance (see Chapter 6). Furthermore, the use of these technologies can reduce the physical demands of many tasks, perhaps leading to a reduction in the rate of injury among direct-care workers. One such example would be technologies that can assist with tasks that often result in muscle strain on the part of workers, such as lateral transfers, repositioning patients up or side-to-side in bed, and bed-to-chair or bed-to-wheelchair transfers (Baptiste, 2007).

Improving Safety

In addition to the use of these assistive technologies, a number of other efforts have been undertaken to prevent injuries among direct-care workers. For example, the Occupational Safety and Health Administration (OSHA) has developed ergonomic guidelines aimed at preventing musculoskeletal disorders among nursing home workers (OSHA, 2008). These guidelines offer safe methods for lifting and repositioning patients and help meet the training needs of workers in nursing home settings. Additionally, in 2002 OSHA announced a new National Emphasis Program for nursing and personal-care facilities, which aims to address ergonomics, exposures to health risks, and slip-and-fall injuries (OSHA, 2002).

OSHA also awards Safety and Health Achievement Recognition Program (SHARP) designations to small employers who exemplify high standards of safety and health management. In 1998 one such recipient, the Good Shepherd Nursing Home of Wheeling, West Virginia, analyzed its injury reports and determined that most of the injuries were the result of heavy lifting (OSHA, 2007). Subsequently, the nursing home procured a mechanical lifting device to assist with transfers and also implemented a safety program which included training, workplace analysis, and hazard prevention. In its first year the program led to a 62 percent decrease in worker injuries at the nursing home, and, thanks to the improved safety, between 2000 and 2005 the nursing home reduced its workers' compensation insurance premiums by over $800,000. The nursing home's administrator commented that "a highly efficient and highly skilled workforce makes fewer mistakes, reduces exposure to liability, and keeps insurance premiums low" (OSHA, 2007).

Broadening the Labor Pool

While improving the quality of direct-care occupations is important to the recruitment and retention of this workforce, sources for new workers also need to be considered, especially the possibility of recruiting workers from other, currently underutilized sources. A number of options exist for broadening the pool of direct-care workers (Hussein and Manthorpe, 2005; National Center for Health Workforce Analysis, 2004; Stone, 2004; Stone and Wiener, 2001). Some of the groups of people who might be recruited to enter the direct-care workforce are described below.

Men

As described previously, the population of direct-care workers is overwhelmingly female (Montgomery et al., 2005; Smith and Baughman, 2007). As a result, men represent a potential source of new workers that has so far remained essentially untapped. Given that the number of women in the United States between the ages of 25 and 54 is expected to remain level in the coming years and will not provide a labor pool sufficient to meet projected demand, more men will be needed to fill these roles. However, special consideration may be needed for male workers, including a culture change to accept male workers in an occupation that is currently dominated by females (PHI, 2003a).

Immigrants

Immigrants are already a significant part of the direct-care workforce, especially in major cities (Wilner and Wyatt, 1998), and they are frequently pointed to as a potential source of new workers in long-term care (Priester and Reinardy, 2003). However, few programs exist to train and place immigrants for careers as direct-care workers. Preparing immigrants for these roles will require instruction not only in technical skills but also in language skills and in the cultural competence needed to work with patients. Successful training models also need to help trainees to navigate immigration systems, seek housing, and prepare for higher education. Limited experience shows that with the proper training and support, immigrant workers may be an effective source of direct-care workers; without proper support, however, their presence may exacerbate existing cycles of low pay and high turnover (Leutz, 2007).

Many countries in the industrialized world have modified their immigration laws to allow an influx of low-wage workers to fill vacancies for direct-care positions (AARP, 2005). The advantage of this approach is that the number of new workers in the labor pool can potentially be increased without drawing workers away from other industries. On the other hand, this approach could have potentially serious side effects. Specifically, costs for public services and government supports could increase (National Center for Health Workforce Analysis, 2004), there may be undesirable competition for other low-wage jobs (Stone, 2004), and the difficulties that can arise when caregivers and patients are from different cultures could become more common. (See Chapter 4 for more on ethnogeriatrics.) More research is needed on the appropriate use of immigrants, including information on both the benefits and the unintended consequences.

Older Workers

As discussed in Chapter 4, as the population of older patients grows, the workforce itself will be aging. As current health care workers approach retirement age, there will be a need to recruit new health care workers as well as to find ways to retain older workers. This issue will also affect the informal workforce, particularly since spousal caregivers are becoming increasingly older themselves. From 1989 to 1999, for example, the proportion of spouse primary caregivers ages 75 or older increased from 38.2 percent to 47.4 percent (Wolff and Kasper, 2006), and by 1999, 11.1 percent of spouse caregivers (both primary and secondary) were 85 years or older (Spillman and Black, 2005). (See Chapter 6 for more on informal caregivers.)

Because of this aging of the workforce, in recent years there has been an increasing emphasis on strategies to recruit and retain older workers. These strategies include giving older workers greater access to education and training, providing them with additional tax deductions for continuing to work, and offering them opportunities for phased retirement and flexible schedules. For example, AARP has helped older workers obtain federally subsidized training through a local community college in order for them to gain needed technology skills (Taylor, 2007). Retaining older workers has a number of potential benefits aside from increasing the size of the workforce. These benefits include preventing the loss of the older workers' acquired expertise and avoiding the various costs associated with replacing these workers, such as recruitment expenses, paying for temporary replacements (per diem workers), and paying to retrain other workers.

The idea of recruiting older, non-health care professionals into new health-related careers has received increased attention. In a survey of low-income workers over the age of 55, a significant percentage (43 percent) expressed interest in direct-care work (Kosniewski and Hwalek, 2006). Additionally, more than half of employers for nursing homes and home health agencies said that older workers were more likely to be loyal employees and have desirable skills and less likely to leave the position. On the other hand, employers also thought that older workers would be more averse to using technology, and the wage expectations of the older workers who were surveyed were higher than the average for these positions. Furthermore, the older workers expressed more interest in the emotional support of patients than in hands-on tasks.

The recruitment and retention of older workers may require the creation of positions with fewer physical demands. Parsing CNA responsibilities might enable the productive use of older adults in the workforce who lack the strength to do all CNA tasks. In one example of such an approach, McKesson, a health care services company, has recruited older workers for their call centers to advise patients on medication use (Taylor, 2007). Similarly, strategies to retain existing older workers in clinical positions will likely demand the creation of health care delivery processes that are more ergonomically oriented (Buerhaus et al., 2000). Emerging technologies may assist in this regard (see Chapter 6).

Volunteers

In addition to recruiting new paid workers, workforce needs could be partially satisfied by using volunteers, both in clinical and in academic settings. Older adults themselves would seem to be a likely target group from which to recruit such volunteers, given that baby boomers have the highest volunteerism rate of any age group—they volunteer more often than past generations did at the same ages—and they constitute a very large pool of potential volunteers (Foster-Bey et al., 2007).

Members of younger generations may also be willing to provide needed services, especially community-based personal- and home-care services that would allow fellow community members to remain in their homes. Community-based models such as Beacon Hill Village in Boston have been developed to allow older adults to "age in place" (Gross, 2006). In these models older adults within a narrow community pay dues to receive support, such as accompaniment to medical appointments, delivery of meals, exercise classes, lectures on aging-related topics, and assistance with daily errands. Volunteers provide many of these services, such as transportation. Other more advanced services, such as home health aide services and home repairs, are often available for a discounted fee. These options may become more appealing as more older adults prefer to stay in their home settings and trends toward consumer-directed care continue (see Chapter 6).

Examples of Efforts to Improve Recruitment and Retention

While some efforts to improve the recruitment and retention of direct-care workers focus on a single strategy, other programs and organizations have developed a mixture of policy- and provider-based interventions. Some large-scale efforts, including those of the federal government, are detailed below. In addition, there have been several large-scale efforts to build an evidence base for the best practices in the recruitment and retention of direct-care workers. These efforts are also described below.

Better Jobs Better Care

The Better Jobs Better Care national program, which was completed in 2007, supported five state-based coalitions (in Iowa, North Carolina, Oregon, Pennsylvania, and Vermont) that designed and tested practice-based interventions and policy changes over a 4-year period. These coalitions attempted to reduce turnover and vacancy rates and improve the working environment of direct-care staff in long-term care (BJBC, 2007). Since each state used different approaches to reach these goals, no single method can be fairly highlighted over the others. All of the participating states demonstrated a range of positive results from this effort, including improvement in worker satisfaction and increased recruitment (BJBC, 2008). To accomplish this, the program improved employee pay and also pushed employers to demonstrate respect for direct-care workers in a variety of ways: by providing supervision, peer mentoring, and team building; by offering opportunities for educational advancement; and by encouraging greater communication and understanding (McDonald, 2007).

Employment and Training Administration Programs

A number of efforts to bolster the direct-care workforce have been undertaken by the Employment and Training Administration (ETA) within the DOL, which has invested hundreds of millions of dollars in grants aimed at strengthening the pipeline of needed workers. The ETA's efforts to improve career lattices through the programs of its Office of Apprenticeship were discussed above. Many of the ETA's grants focus on long-term care workers (Freking, 2007). For example, since 2004 the Community-Based Job Training Grants have funded a number of programs to prepare students for careers in high-growth industries (DOL, 2008b). In March 2008 the DOL awarded $125 million to 69 community colleges, and 24 of these grants (totaling almost $40 million) were for developing workers for the health care industry (DOL, 2008a,d).

The ETA's High Growth Job Training Initiative is aimed at giving workers the skills necessary to build a career in one of several different industries, including health care. Under this initiative, the ETA is investing more than $46 million to address health care workforce shortages, particularly among long-term care workers (DOL, 2007). The initiative will focus on such things as increasing the number of younger workers entering the market, identifying alternative labor pools, developing new educational tools and curricula, increasing faculty, and improving recruitment and retention. The initiative intends to develop approaches that can be replicated across the country.

Centers for Medicare and Medicaid Programs

CMS has also funded several initiatives to strengthen the quality of direct-care work and its services. In 2003, for instance, CMS initiated the Direct Service Workforce Demonstration, which provided grants to 10 states to test the effectiveness of various workforce interventions on the recruitment and retention of direct-care workers in the communities. According to an assessment of this program, the grants were shown to decrease worker turnover and increase retention rates. For example, over a 2-year period Kentucky reported a decrease in turnover rates from 43 percent to 29 percent and an average increase in retention rates of 5 months (University of Minnesota and The Lewin Group, 2006). Such improvements were primarily achieved by increasing the visibility of available positions and by using more accurate selection strategies to hire well-matched workers to those positions.

Later, in 2006, the National Direct Service Workforce Resource Center was created by CMS, and it continues to address the recruitment and retention challenges of direct-care workers by providing information, resources, and assistance to all relevant stakeholders (e.g., policy makers, researchers, employers, workers, and patients) involved in the provision of quality care to older adults at the state and local levels (CMS, 2008a).

Another effort by CMS to improve health services to older populations in all 50 states is its Real Choice Systems Change Grants. Since 2001 CMS has provided a total of approximately $270 million in these grants to provide support for community living (CMS, 2008b). This funding has helped build effective foundational improvements in community-integrated services and long-term care systems by allowing states to address issues regarding personal assistance services, direct-care worker shortages, and respite service for caregivers and family members, along with many other issues. Several states improved their support of the direct-care workforce by targeting the areas of recruitment, training and career development, and administrative activities (CMS, 2005). Some of the more common or effective strategies used by states to achieve better recruitment and retention of this workforce were altering training strategies, allowing for more flexibility in worker responsibilities, and broadening the definition of who can serve as a personal assistant (CMS, 2007). The funding provided to the states by this grant program has been put to use effectively, CMS reports, and "the infrastructure that has been developed enables individuals of all ages to live in the most integrated community setting suited to their medical needs, have meaningful choices about their living arrangements, and exercise more control over the services they receive" (CMS, 2008b).

The PAS Workforce Project

The 5-year PAS Workforce Project, run through the Center for Personal Assistance Services, has the goal of building and disseminating an evidence base for best practices concerning the personal assistance workforce. The information collected includes data on individual interventions as well as related legislation and policy efforts. The project pays particular attention to strategies to improve worker retention in consumer-directed programs, including issues related to wages, training, safety, and supervision, as well as to the development of infrastructures that facilitate consumer-directed programs (CPAS, 2008). To be included, a program must have documented operational experience as well as evidence of program success and replicability.

National Clearinghouse on the Direct-Care Workforce

PHI's National Clearinghouse on the Direct-Care Workforce is a national, online library of information regarding the direct-care workforce for long-term care. The clearinghouse collects government and research reports, fact sheets, briefs, and other information on issues such as career advancement, education and training, recruitment and retention, job environment, and best practices (National Clearinghouse for the Direct-Care Workforce, 2008). The clearinghouse also produces original research and analysis, including monitoring of state-based initiatives.

CONCLUSION

Because direct-care workers provide the bulk of paid direct-care services for older patients in nursing homes and other settings, it is vitally important that the capacity of this segment of the workforce be enhanced in both size and ability to meet the health care needs of older Americans. However, the recruitment and retention of sufficient numbers of these workers is challenging due to serious financial disincentives and job dissatisfaction as well as high rates of turnover and severe shortages of available workers.

As it exists today, the education and training of direct-care workers is inadequate to impart the necessary knowledge, skills, and abilities to these workers, especially as the complexity and severity of older adults' needs increase and as more adults are cared for in home- and community-based settings. The government should raise the federal minimum training requirement for nurse aides and home health aides to 120 hours and states should establish minimum standards for personal-care aides if they have not already done so. All direct-care workers should be required to demonstrate that they possess the competencies necessary to engage in this type of work. More research is needed to determine the appropriate content of training programs, which needs to be individualized for the needs of workers based on their responsibilities and the settings in which they provide care.

Improving the quality of these jobs will demand significant effort. Direct-care workers typically receive low wages and have limited access to other benefits, including health insurance. Economic incentives should be bolstered to improve the desirability of these jobs. Additionally, much more needs to be done to improve the workforce environment. Evidence shows that increased job satisfaction and decreased turnover rates may be associated with increasing worker responsibilities (including the development of new roles or career lattices), increasing the recognition of the workers' current contributions, improving safety, and improving supervisory relationships. Given all these factors, it is clear that a change in culture is needed—that both health care workers and health care organizations need to change the way they think about direct-care workers and, in particular, that direct-care workers need to be seen as a vital part of the health care team.

REFERENCES

AARP. 2005. *International forum on long-term care: Delivering quality care with a global workforce*. Washington, DC. October 20, 2005.

AARP. 2006. *Training programs for certified nursing assistants*. http://assets.aarp.org/rgcenter/il/2006_08_cna.pdf (accessed February 20, 2008).

ASA (American Society on Aging). 2008. *Innovations in recruitment, retention and promotion of nursing assistants in long-term care awards: 2001 winners*. http://www.asaging.org/awards/awards01/extendicare.html (accessed February 24, 2008).

Banaszak-Holl, J., and M. A. Hines. 1996. Factors associated with nursing home staff turnover. *Gerontologist* 36(4):512-517.

Baptiste, A. 2007. Technology solutions for high-risk tasks in critical care. *Critical Care Nursing Clinics of North America* 19(2):177-186.

Barry, T., D. Brannon, and V. Mor. 2005. Nurse aide empowerment strategies and staff stability: Effects on nursing home resident outcomes. *Gerontologist* 45(3):309-317.

Benjamin, A., and R. Matthias. 2004. Work-life differences and outcomes for agency and consumer-directed home-care workers. *Gerontologist* 44(4):479-488.

Bishop, C. E., D. B. Weinberg, L. Dodson, J. H. Gittell, W. Leutz, A. Dossa, S. Pfefferle, R. Zincavage, and M. Morley. 2006. *Nursing home workers' job commitment: Effect of organizational and individual factors and impact on resident well-being*. http://www.academyhealth.org/membership/forum/uploads/kmetter/BishopBJBCDisc2.pdf (accessed February 25, 2008).

BJBC (Better Jobs Better Care). 2007. *Who we are*. http://www.bjbc.org/Page.asp?SectionID=1 (accessed December 5, 2007).

BJBC. 2008. *The ripple effect.* http://www.bjbc.org/page.asp?pgID=233 (accessed March 11, 2008).

BLS (Bureau of Labor Statistics). 2007a. *Nonfatal occupational injuries and illnesses requiring days away from work, 2006.* http://www.bls.gov/news.release/History/osh2.txt (accessed February 23, 2008).

BLS. 2007b. *Table 6. The 30 fastest-growing occupations, 2006-2016.* http://www.bls.gov/news.release/ecopro.t06.htm (accessed December 26, 2007).

BLS. 2008a. *Household data annual averages.* http://www.bls.gov/cps/cpsa2007.pdf (accessed February 24, 2008).

BLS. 2008b. *Occupational outlook handbook, 2006-07 edition, food and beverage serving and related workers.* http://www.bls.gov/oco/ocos162.htm (accessed March 9, 2008).

BLS. 2008c. *Occupational outlook handbook, 2006-07 edition, nursing, psychiatric, and home health aides.* http://www.bls.gov/oco/ocos165.htm (accessed February 23, 2008).

BLS. 2008d. *Occupational outlook handbook, 2006-07 edition, personal and home care aides.* http://www.bls.gov/oco/ocos173.htm (accessed February 23, 2008).

Bostick, J. E., M. J. Rantz, M. K. Flesner, and C. J. Riggs. 2006. Systematic review of studies of staffing and quality in nursing homes. *Journal of the American Medical Directors Association* 7(6):366-376.

Bowers, B. J., S. Esmond, and N. Jacobson. 2000. The relationship between staffing and quality in long-term care facilities: Exploring the views of nurse aides. *Journal of Nursing Care Quality* 14(4):55-64.

Bowers, B. J., S. Esmond, and N. Jacobson. 2003. Turnover reinterpreted CNAs talk about why they leave. *Journal of Gerontological Nursing* 29(3):36-43.

Brady, G. S., A. B. Case, D. U. Himmelstein, and S. Woolhandler. 2002. No care for the caregivers: Declining health insurance coverage for health care personnel and their children, 1988-1998. *American Journal of Public Health* 92(3):404-408.

Buerhaus, P. I., D. O. Staiger, and D. I. Auerbach. 2000. Implications of an aging registered nurse workforce. *Journal of the American Medical Association* 283(22):2948-2954.

CAEL (Council for Adult and Experiential Learning). 2005. *How career lattices help solve nursing and other workforce shortages in healthcare.* http://www.cael.org/pdf/publication_pdf/Career_Lattice_guidebook.pdf (accessed March 13, 2008).

CAEL. 2008. *CAEL/DOL nursing career lattice program.* http://www.doleta.gov/oa/brochure/CAELDOL_Nursing_Career_Lattice_Program.pdf (accessed March 10, 2008).

Castle, N. G., and J. Engberg. 2005. Staff turnover and quality of care in nursing homes. *Medical Care* 43(6):616-626.

Castle, N. G., and J. Engberg. 2006. Organizational characteristics associated with staff turnover in nursing homes. *Gerontologist* 46(1):62-73.

Castle, N. G., and J. Engberg. 2007. The influence of staffing characteristics on quality of care in nursing homes. *Health Services Research* 42(5):1822-1847.

Castle, N. G., J. Engberg, R. Anderson, and A. Men. 2007. Job satisfaction of nurse aides in nursing homes: Intent to leave and turnover. *Gerontologist* 47(2):193-204.

Cherry, B., A. Ashcraft, and D. Owen. 2007. Perceptions of job satisfaction and the regulatory environment among nurse aides and charge nurses in long-term care. *Geriatric Nursing* 28(3):183-192.

CMS (Centers for Medicare and Medicaid Services). 2001. *Appropriateness of minimum nurse staffing ratios in nursing homes: Phase II report.* Baltimore, MD: CMS.

CMS. 2005. *Real choice systems change grant program: Third year report. Progress and challenges of the FY 2002 and FY 2003 grantees: October 1, 2003-September 30, 2004.* http://www.hcbs.org/files/77/3806/3rdAnnualRpt.pdf (accessed March 10, 2008).

CMS. 2007. *Real choice systems change grant program: FY 2001 community integrated personal assistance service and supports grantees and real choice grantees: Final report.* http://www.hcbs.org/files/110/5451/01CPASSFinalRpt.pdf (accessed March 11, 2008).

CMS. 2008a. *The national direct service workforce resource center.* http://www.dswresource center.org (accessed March 10, 2008).

CMS. 2008b. *Real choice: Overview.* http://www.cms.hhs.gov/RealChoice/ (accessed March 10, 2008).

Cohen-Mansfield, J. 1997. Turnover among nursing home staff: A review. *Nursing Management* 28(5):59-62, 64.

Coogle, C. L., I. A. Parham, R. Jablonski, and J. A. Rachel. 2007. Enhanced care assistant training to address the workforce crisis in home care: Changes related to job satisfaction and career commitment. *Care Management Journals* 8(2):71-81.

Cousineau, M. R. 2000. *Providing health insurance to IHSS providers (home care workers) in Los Angeles County.* http://www.directcareclearinghouse.org/download/ihss.pdf (accessed February 25, 2008).

CPAS (Center for Personal Assistance Services). 2008. *The PAS workforce project: Project abstract.* http://www.pascenter.org/pas_workforce/abstract.php (accessed March 13, 2008).

Dawson, S. 2007. *PHI: Quality care through quality jobs.* Presentation at Meeting of the Committee on the Future Health Care Workforce for Older Americans, San Francisco, CA. June 28, 2007.

Decker, F., P. Gruhn, L. Matthews-Martin, J. Dollard, A. Tucker, and L. Bizette. 2003. *Results of the 2002 AHCA survey of nursing staff vacancy and turnover in nursing homes.* http://www.samarion.com/library/nursing_shortage/Turnover.pdf (accessed March 9, 2008).

DOL (U.S. Department of Labor). 2007. *Local solutions with national applications to address health care industry labor shortages.* http://www.doleta.gov/BRG/Indprof/Health.cfm (accessed March 19, 2008).

DOL. 2008a. *2008 President's community-based job training grant awardees.* http://www.doleta.gov/whatsnew/new_releases/List_of_grantees.pdf (accessed March 13, 2008).

DOL. 2008b. *The president's community-based job training grants.* http://www.doleta.gov/business/Community-BasedJobTrainingGrants.cfm (accessed January 4, 2008).

DOL. 2008c. *Registered apprenticeship trends in health care.* http://www.doleta.gov/oa/brochure/2007%20Health%20Care.pdf (accessed March 10, 2008).

DOL. 2008d. *U.S. Department of Labor awards $125 million in third competition for President's community-based job training grants.* http://www.doleta.gov/whatsnew/new_releases/2008-03-11.cfm (accessed March 13, 2008).

Ersek, M., B. M. Kraybill, and N. R. Hansen. 2006. Evaluation of a train-the-trainer program to enhance hospice and palliative care in nursing homes. *Journal of Hospice and Palliative Nursing* 8(1):42-49.

Ferrell, B. R., R. Virani, and M. Grant. 1998. Hope: Home care outreach for palliative care education. *Cancer Practice* 6(2):79-85.

Fishman, M., B. Barnow, A. Glosser, and K. Gardiner. 2004. *Recruiting and retaining a quality paraprofessional long-term care workforce: Building collaboratives with the nation's workforce investment system.* Washington, DC: Office of Disability, Aging and Long-Term Care Policy, U.S. Department of Health and Human Services.

Fleming, K. C., J. M. Evans, and D. S. Chutka. 2003. Caregiver and clinician shortages in an aging nation. *Mayo Clinic Proceedings* 78(8):1026-1040.

Foster-Bey, J., R. J. Grimm, and N. Dietz. 2007. *Keeping baby boomers volunteering: A research brief on volunteer retention and turnover.* Washington, DC: Corporation for National and Community Service.

Freking, K. 2007. Depression reported by 7% of workforce. *The Washington Post*, October 14, A07.

Fuller, J. 1995. Challenging old notions of professionalism: How can nurses work with para-professional ethnic health workers? *Journal of Advanced Nursing* 22(3):465-472.

GAO (General Accounting Office). 2001a. *Health workforce: Ensuring adequate supply and distribution remains challenging*. Washington, DC: United States General Accounting Office.

GAO. 2001b. *Recruitment and retention of nurses and nurse aides is a growing concern*. Washington, DC: United States General Accounting Office.

Goldman, B., S. Balgobin, R. Bish, R. H. Lee, S. McCue, M. H. Morrison, and S. Nonemaker. 2004. Nurse educators are key to a best practices implementation program. *Geriatric Nursing* 25(3):171-174.

Grau, L., B. Chandler, B. Burton, and D. Kolditz. 1991. Institutional loyalty and job satisfaction among nurse aides in nursing homes. *Journal of Aging and Health* 3(1):47-65.

Gross, J. 2006. Aging at home: For a lucky few, a wish come true. *The New York Times*, February 9. http://www.nytimes.com/2006/02/09/garden/09care.html?pagewanted=1&_r =2&sq=Aging%20at%20Home:%20For%20a%20lucky%20Few,%20a%20Wish%20 Come%20True&st=nyt&scp=1 (accessed March 26, 2008).

Haley, W. E., D. G. Larson, J. Kasl-Godley, R. A. Neimeyer, and D. M. Kwilosz. 2003. Roles for psychologists in end-of-life care: Emerging models of practice. *Professional Psychology: Research and Practice* 34(6):626-633.

Hams, M., N. Herold, M. Lee, and A. Worters. 2002. *Health insurance access survey of direct care workers in nursing homes and home-based care agencies in Boston, New Bedford/ Fall River*. http://www.directcareclearinghouse.org/download/Health_Insurance_access_ survey.pdf (accessed March 12, 2008).

Harmuth, S., and S. Dyson. 2005. *Results of the 2005 national survey of state initiatives on the long-term care direct-care workforce*. The National Clearinghouse on the Direct Care Workforce and the Direct Care Workers Association of North Carolina.

Harrington, C. 2007a. *Nursing home labor market issues*. http://www.iom.edu/Object.File/ Master/43/900/Harrington%20.pdf (accessed December 14, 2007).

Harrington, C. 2007b. *Proposals for improvements in nursing home quality*. http://aging. senate.gov/events/hr172ch.pdf (accessed May 2, 2007).

Harrington, C., and J. H. Swan. 2003. Nursing home staffing, turnover, and case mix. *Medical Care Research and Review* 60(3):366-392.

Harrington, C., C. Kovner, M. Mezey, J. Kayser-Jones, S. Burger, M. Mohler, R. Burke, and D. Zimmerman. 2000. Experts recommend minimum nurse staffing standards for nursing facilities in the United States. *Gerontologist* 40(1):5-16.

Hawes, C. 2002. *Elder abuse in residential long-term care facilities: What is known about prevalence, causes, and prevention*. Testimony before the U.S. Senate Committee on Finance, Washington, DC. June 18, 2002.

Hegeman, C. R. 2005. Turnover turnaround. *Health Progress (Saint Louis, MO)* 86(6): 25-30.

Hernandez-Medina, E., S. Eaton, D. Hurd, and A. White. 2006. *Training programs for certi-fied nursing assistants*. Washington, DC: American Association of Retired Persons.

Holland, J. M., and R. A. Neimeyer. 2005. Reducing the risk of burnout in end-of-life care settings: The role of daily spiritual experiences and training. *Palliative & Supportive Care* 3(3):173-181.

Howes, C. 2005. Living wages and retention of homecare workers in San Francisco. *Industrial Relations* 44(1):139-163.

Howes, C. 2006. Building a high quality home care workforce: Wages, benefits and flexibility matter. http://www.bjbc.org/content/docs/ExecSummary_Conn_College_FINAL COLOR8-06.pdf (accessed February 24, 2008).

Hussein, S., and J. Manthorpe. 2005. An international review of the long-term care workforce: Policies and shortages. *Journal of Aging and Social Policy* 17(4):75-94.

IOM (Institute of Medicine). 1996. *Nursing staff in hospitals and nursing homes: Is it adequate?* Washington, DC: National Academy Press.

IOM. 2001. *Improving the quality of long-term care.* Washington, DC: National Academy Press.

IOM. 2002. *Elder mistreatment: Abuse, neglect, and exploitation in an aging America.* Washington, DC: The National Academies Press.

Jezuit, D. L. 2000. Suffering of critical care nurses with end-of-life decisions. *MEDSURG Nursing* 9(3):145-152.

Kash, B. A., N. G. Castle, G. S. Naufal, and C. Hawes. 2006. Effect of staff turnover on staffing: A closer look at registered nurses, licensed vocational nurses, and certified nursing assistants. *Gerontologist* 46(5):609-619.

Kasprak, J. 2007. *Regulation of feeding assistants.* http://www.cga.ct.gov/2007/rpt/2007-R-0065.htm (accessed December 4, 2007).

Kaye, H. S., S. Chapman, R. J. Newcomer, and C. Harrington. 2006. The personal assistance workforce: Trends in supply and demand. *Health Affairs* 25(4):1113-1120.

Kitchener, M., T. Ng, and C. Harrington. 2007. Medicaid state plan personal care services: Trends in programs and policies. *Journal of Aging and Social Policy* 19(3):9-26.

Komisar, H. L., and L. S. Thompson. 2007. *National spending for long-term care.* Washington, DC: Georgetown University Long-Term Care Financing Project.

Konetzka, R. T., S. C. Stearns, T. R. Konrad, J. Magaziner, and S. Zimmerman. 2005. Personal care aide turnover in residential care settings: An assessment of ownership, economic, and environmental factors. *Journal of Applied Gerontology* 24(2):87-107.

Kosniewski, K., and M. Hwalek. 2006. *Older workers in direct care: A labor force expansion study.* http://www.iowacaregivers.org/uploads/pdf/053106opableexecsummaryfinal.pdf (accessed March 12, 2008).

Leon, J., J. Marainen, and J. Marcotte. 2001. *Pennsylvania's frontline workers in long-term care: The provider perspective.* Jenkintown, PA: Polisher Research Institute at the Philadelphia Geriatric Center.

Leutz, W. N. 2007. *Immigration and the elderly: Foreign-born workers in long-term care.* http://www.ailf.org/ipc/infocus/infocus_0708.pdf (accessed March 12, 2008).

Lipson, D., and C. Regan. 2004. *Health insurance coverage for direct care workers: Riding out the storm.* http://www.bjbc.org/content/docs/BJBCIssueBriefNo3.pdf (accessed February 25, 2008).

Lyketsos, C. G., Q. M. Samus, A. Baker, M. McNabney, C. U. Onyike, L. S. Mayer, J. Brandt, P. Rabins, and A. Rosenblatt. 2007. Effect of dementia and treatment of dementia on time to discharge from assisted living facilities: The Maryland assisted living study. *Journal of the American Geriatrics Society* 55(7):1031-1037.

Maas, M., and K. C. Buckwalter. 2006. Providing quality care in assisted living facilities: Recommendations for enhanced staffing and staff training. *Journal of Gerontological Nursing* 32(11):14-22.

Maidment, P. 2007. *America's 25 worst-paying jobs.* http://www.forbes.com/2007/06/04/jobs-careers-compensation-lead-careers-cx_pm_0604worstjobs_slide_14.html?thisSpeed =15000 (accessed March 20, 2008).

Maier, G. 2002. Career ladders: An important element in CNA retention. *Geriatric Nursing* 23(4):217-219.

McDonald, I. 2007. *Respectful relationships: The heart of Better Jobs Better Care*. http://www.bjbc.org/content/docs/BJBCIssueBriefNo7.pdf (accessed March 11, 2008).

McGilton, K. S., L. McGillis Hall, W. P. Wodchis, and U. Petroz. 2007. Supervisory support, job stress, and job satisfaction among long-term care nursing staff. *Journal of Nursing Administration* 37(7):366-372.

Menne, H. L., F. K. Ejaz, L. S. Noelker, and J. A. Jones. 2007. Direct care workers' recommendations for training and continuing education. *Gerontology and Geriatrics Education* 28(2):91-108.

Minore, B., and M. Boone. 2002. Realizing potential: Improving interdisciplinary professional/paraprofessional health care teams in Canada's northern aboriginal communities through education. *Journal of Interprofessional Care* 16(2):139-147.

Montgomery, R. J. V., L. Holley, J. Deichert, and K. Kosloski. 2005. A profile of home care workers from the 2000 Census: How it changes what we know. *Gerontologist* 45(5):593-600.

National Center for Health Workforce Analysis. 2004. *Nursing aides, home health aides, and related health care occupations—national and local workforce shortages and associated data needs*. Rockville, MD: Health Resources and Services Administration.

National Clearinghouse on the Direct Care Workforce. 2008. *About us: Overview*. http://www.directcareclearinghouse.org/a_index.jsp (accessed March 13, 2008).

NCCNHR (National Citizens' Coalition for Nursing Home Reform). 1998. *Proposed minimum staffing standards for nursing homes*. http://nursinghomeaction.org/govpolicy/51_162_472.cfm (accessed December 9, 2007).

Newcomer, R., and T. Scherzer. 2006. *Who counts? On (not) counting occupational injuries in homecare*. Paper read at American Public Health Association 134th Annual Meeting and Exposition, Boston, MA. November 7.

OIG (Office of Inspector General, U.S. Department of Health and Human Services). 2002. *Nurse aide training*. Washington, DC: Office of Inspector General.

OIG. 2006. *States' requirements for Medicaid-funded personal care service attendants*. Washington, DC: Office of Inspector General.

OSHA (Occupational Safety and Health Administration). 2002. *OSHA announces National Emphasis Program for nursing and personal care facilities*. http://www.osha.gov/pls/oshaweb/owadisp.show_document?p_table=NEWS_RELEASES&p_id=1311 (accessed March 20, 2008).

OSHA. 2007. *Good Shepherd Nursing Home works with OSHA on-site consultation, reduces workers' compensation costs over $800,000*. http://www.osha.gov/dcsp/success_stories/sharp/ss_good_shepherd.html (accessed March 20, 2008).

OSHA. 2008. *Guidelines for nursing homes: Ergonomics for the prevention of musculoskeletal disorders*. http://www.osha.gov/ergonomics/guidelines/nursinghome/final_nh_guidelines.pdf (accessed March 20, 2008).

Parsons, S. K., W. P. Simmons, K. Penn, and M. Furlough. 2003. Determinants of satisfaction and turnover among nursing assistants: The results of a statewide survey. *Journal of Gerontological Nursing* 29(3):51-58.

Pennington, K., J. Scott, and K. Magilvy. 2003. The role of certified nursing assistants in nursing homes. *Journal of Nursing Administration* 33(11):578-584.

PHI (Paraprofessional Healthcare Institute). 2001. *Direct-care health workers: The unnecessary crisis in long-term care*. http://www.directcareclearinghouse.org/download/Aspen.pdf (accessed February 20, 2008).

PHI. 2003a. *Long-term care financing and the long-term care workforce crisis: Causes and solutions*. http://www.directcareclearinghouse.org/download/CLTC_doc_rev1.pdf (accessed March 12, 2008).

PHI. 2003b. *State wage pass-through legislation: An analysis.* http://www.paraprofessional. org/publications/WorkforceStrategies1.pdf (accessed February 20, 2008).

PHI. 2005. *The role of training in improving the recruitment and retention of direct-care workers in long-term care.* http://www.directcareclearinghouse.org/download/Workforce Strategies3.pdf (accessed February 21, 2008).

PHI. 2006. *Subsidizing health insurance coverage for the home care workforce in two Wisconsin counties: An analysis of options.* http://www.directcareclearinghouse.org/download/ HealthInsCovWIreport.pdf (accessed February 21, 2008).

PHI. 2007. *The guaranteed hours program: Ensuring stable, full-time, direct-care employment.* http://www.paraprofessional.org/Sections/documents/WorkforceStrategiesNo4.pdf (accessed January 17, 2008).

PHI and Medstat. 2004. *The right start: Preparing direct-care workers to provide home- and community-based care.* http://www.directcareclearinghouse.org/download/Rightstart.pdf (accessed March 13, 2008).

Priester, R., and J. R. Reinardy. 2003. Recruiting immigrants for long-term care nursing positions. *Journal of Aging and Social Policy* 15(4):1-19.

Reinhard, S. C., H. Young, R. A. Kane, and W. V. Quinn. 2003. *Nurse delegation of medication administration of elders.* http://www.theceal.org/downloads/CEAL_1177377300.pdf (accessed February 25, 2008).

Rosenblatt, A., Q. M. Samus, C. D. Steele, A. S. Baker, M. G. Harper, J. Brandt, P. V. Rabins, and C. G. Lyketsos. 2004. The Maryland assisted living study: Prevalence, recognition, and treatment of dementia and other psychiatric disorders in the assisted living population of central Maryland. *Journal of the American Geriatrics Society* 52(10):1618-1625.

Scherzer, T. 2005. Barriers to documenting occupational injuries among personal assistance services workers. *American Journal of Industrial Medicine* 50(7):536-544.

Scherzer, T. 2006a. *How do diverse homecare workers address occupational hazards and injury?* Presentation at the American Public Health Association 134th Annual Meeting and Exposition, Boston, MA. November 7, 2006.

Scherzer, T. 2006b. *Who counts? On (not) counting occupational injuries in homecare.* Presentation at the American Public Health Association 134th Annual Meeting and Exposition, Boston, MA. November 7, 2006.

Schnelle, J. F., S. F. Simmons, C. Harrington, M. Cadogan, E. Garcia, and B. M. Bates-Jensen. 2004. Relationship of nursing home staffing to quality of care. *Health Services Research* 39(2):225-250.

Seavey, D. 2004. *The cost of frontline turnover in long-term care.* http://www.bjbc.org/content/ docs/TOCostReport.pdf (accessed March 16, 2008).

Seavey, D. 2007a. *State nurse aide training requirements.* http://www.directcareclearinghouse. org/download/StateNurseAide_TrainingRequirements2007.pdf (accessed March 9, 2008).

Seavey, D. 2007b. *Written statement of Dorie Seavey, Ph.D.* Testimony before the House Committee on Education and Labor, Subcommittee on Workforce Protections, Washington, DC. October 25, 2007.

Seavey, D., and V. Salter. 2006. *Paying for quality care: State and local strategies for improving wage and benefits for personal care assistants.* Washington, DC: AARP.

Sherard, B. D. 2002. *Report to the Joint Appropriations Committee on the impact of funding for direct staff salary increases in adult developmental disabilities community-based programs.* http://www.pascenter.org/documents/WY_2002.pdf (accessed February 24, 2008).

Sikorska-Simmons, E. 2005. Predictors of organizational commitment among staff in assisted living. *Gerontologist* 45(2):196-205.

Sikorska-Simmons, E. 2006. Linking resident satisfaction to staff perceptions of the work environment in assisted living: A multilevel analysis. *Gerontologist* 46(5):590-598.

Simmons, S. F., R. Bertrand, V. Shier, R. Sweetland, T. J. Moore, D. T. Hurd, and J. F. Schnelle. 2007. A preliminary evaluation of the paid feeding assistant regulation: Impact on feeding assistance care process quality in nursing homes. *Gerontologist* 47(2):184-192.

Smith, K., and R. Baughman. 2007. Caring for America's aging population: A profile of the direct-care workforce. *Monthly Labor Review* 130(9):20-26.

Spillman, B. C., and K. J. Black. 2005. *Staying the course: Trends in family caregiving.* Washington, DC: AARP.

Stone, R. I. 2000. *Long-term care for the elderly with disabilities: Current policy, emerging trends, and implications for the twenty-first century.* New York: Milbank Memorial Fund.

Stone, R. I. 2004. The direct care worker: The third rail of home care policy. *Annual Review of Public Health* 25:521-537.

Stone, R. I., and J. M. Wiener. 2001. *Who will care for us? Addressing the long-term care workforce crisis.* Washington, DC: The Urban Institute.

Stone, R. I., S. C. Reinhard, B. Bowers, D. Zimmerman, C. D. Phillips, C. Hawes, J. A. Fielding, and N. Jacobson. 2002. *Evaluation of the Wellspring Model for improving nursing home quality.* http://www.cmwf.org/usr_doc/stone_wellspringevaluation.pdf (accessed March 11, 2008).

Taylor, E. 2007. More seniors decide to stay on the job. *East Family Tribune,* April 29.

Tellis-Nayak, V. 2007. A person-centered workplace: The foundation for person-centered caregiving in long-term care. *Journal of the American Medical Directors Association* 8(1):46-54.

University of Minnesota and The Lewin Group. 2006. *CMS direct service workforce demonstration: Promising practices in marketing, recruitment and selection interventions.* http://rtc.umn.edu/docs/DSWPromisingPracticesFINAL.pdf (accessed March 11, 2008).

Viles, L. 2000. Death and the practitioner. *Respiratory Care* 45(12):1513-1519.

Wellspring Institute. 2005. *Modules synopsis.* http://www.wellspringis.org/modules.html (accessed March 11, 2008).

Wilner, M. A., and A. Wyatt. 1998. *Paraprofessionals on the front lines: Improving their jobs improving the quality of long-term care.* http://www.directcareclearinghouse.org/download/Paraprofessionals_on_the_Front_Lines_ExecSum.pdf (accessed February 21, 2008).

Wolff, J. L. and J. D. Kasper. 2006. Caregivers of frail elders: Updating a national profile. *Gerontologist* 46(3):344-356.

Yamada, Y. 2002. Profile of home care aides, nursing home aides, and hospital aides: Historical changes and data recommendations. *Gerontologist* 42(2):199-206.

Yeatts, D. E., and C. M. Cready. 2007. Consequences of empowered CAN teams in nursing home settings: A longitudinal assessment. *Gerontologist* 47(3):323-339.

Yeatts, D. E., C. Cready, B. Ray, A. DeWitt, and C. Queen. 2004. Self-managed work teams in nursing homes: Implementing and empowering nurse aide teams. *Gerontologist* 44(2):256-261.

6

Patients and Informal Caregivers

CHAPTER SUMMARY

Patients play a sizable role in their own care, not just as recipients of care services but also as prominent actors in the delivery process. Moreover, family members, friends, and other unpaid caregivers provide the backbone for much of the care that is received by older adults in the United States. This chapter discusses the need to support patients and caregivers through a number of means, including greater opportunities for training. These training opportunities can improve the care received by older adults while also easing the strain on informal caregivers, who often feel unprepared for the tasks they are required to perform. The chapter also discusses the role that assistive technologies can play in enhancing and prolonging the independent functioning of older adults, making them less reliant on direct-care workers and informal caregivers. The committee recommends that federal agencies take steps to assist in the development and increased availability of these technologies. Taking these measures to promote the health and well-being of both patients and caregivers will help ease the strain on the workforce providing medical care for older adults.

The role of patients in the care process extends far beyond their role as recipients of services. Patients play a major part in determining treatment plans, navigating the delivery system to obtain services, and ensuring overall adherence to the selected course of treatment. For older adults, these care plans often involve multiple providers and settings, and they can find themselves functioning as coordinators of the entire process. Older adults frequently communicate relevant information from one provider to another, or may even detect ways in which the treatment plans are at odds.

As patients continue to age and experience declines in their health, they begin to require greater assistance in performing their roles in the health care process. In response, family members and friends assume increasingly greater responsibility for making treatment decisions, accompanying the patients on office visits, and providing other sources of support. In a great many cases, these family members and friends also become informal caregivers, providing many of the same services that direct-care workers provide, including assistance with the activities of daily living (ADLs), such as bathing and dressing, and the instrumental activities of daily living (IADLs), such as driving and shopping.

The number of informal caregivers in the United States far exceeds the number of paid direct-care workers. There are concerns, however, that the number of caregivers is declining—a trend that is especially worrisome in light of the fact that the direct-care workforce is already stretched thin. Any reductions in caregiver support could have serious negative implications for the adequacy of the direct-care workforce, which makes it particularly important to determine how best to support caregivers in order to maintain the availability of their services.

Both patients and informal caregivers are important parts of the health care team, yet little has been done to impart the necessary knowledge or skills to these team members. Ensuring adequate communication with this part of the workforce is especially important for the older adult population because of hearing, vision, and mental acuity deficiencies (including among some informal caregivers), thereby increasing the likelihood of adverse effects due to the miscommunication. Additionally, as the use of remote information technologies becomes more common, patients and their families will need to be educated on their proper use. Ultimately, any plan for enabling informal caregivers and patients to become more capable members of the health care team is likely to require increased training along with greater support from and integration with the formal health care system.

PATIENTS

Given the vital role that patients play in shaping and implementing their own care, they need to be viewed not just as recipients of care, but also as members of the care team. This is especially true in light of the increasing prevalence of chronic disease. The management of chronic illness is complex, and patients are required to take on greater responsibilities than they typically would for acute care. Managing conditions such as diabetes involves day-to-day decision making with respect to lifestyle, prevention, medication use, and other components of health and health care (Newman et al., 2004). Self-management extends beyond basic adherence to treatment guidelines; it includes such things as self-monitoring and the application of appropriate cognitive, behavioral, and emotional responses.

The evolution of the patient's role includes an increasing emphasis on collaborative care. Health care professionals and patients are familiar with the traditional provider-patient treatment model, in which providers assume responsibility for all decisions (Funnell, 2000). However, the role of the patient has undergone a redefinition in recent years and their role is now considerably more expansive. This has altered the environment that older adults will encounter as they enter their retirement years and, in most cases, begin to utilize the health care system more extensively.

Self-Management

In an ideal model of collaborative care, patients first work with their providers to set realistic goals; this requires skills in collaborative goal setting and in the development of an action plan (Bodenheimer et al., 2002; Hibbard, 2003). Then, once the goals and the plan are set, patients are responsible for executing the daily routines that are necessary to effectively treat or ameliorate their conditions; this part of the process is termed self-management.

Self-management interventions are designed to help patients understand how their behaviors affect their illness and their lives and to use that information to shape their decision making. They address real-world challenges, such as those encountered by patients who are both diabetic and asthmatic and have trouble maintaining their exercise regimens. Only a small percentage of the educational content of self-management programs concerns disease-specific information. The majority of the content deals with generic lifestyle issues, such as exercise, nutrition, and coping skills. This self-management education supplements—but does not replace—traditional patient education, and it emphasizes the acquisition of skills rather than just knowledge (Wagner, 2000). Studies show that teaching patients these types of self-management skills is more effective than providing information alone (Bodenheimer et al., 2002).

Self-management is predicated on the assumption that patients have both the ability to understand basic health care information ("health literacy") and the ability to use that knowledge to help manage their own care ("patient activation")[1] (Greene et al., 2005). Individuals with low health-literacy rates report having poorer health status and using fewer preventive services (Williams et al., 1998). In general, older adults tend to have lower health literacy and lower activation levels than younger adults

---

[1]These concepts would not apply to older adults with significant cognitive impairments.

(Baker et al., 1997; Scott et al., 2002), although baby boomers may prove to be an exception, as they are better educated than previous generations (Cutilli, 2007; IOM, 2004) and may be more proactive in their own health care (CBO, 1993).

While there is evidence that getting older patients engaged in their own care results in improved clinical outcomes and higher patient satisfaction (Bodenheimer et al., 2002), there are a number of barriers to educating and training patients in their own self-care. Many self-management programs, for instance, are limited to a single disease or lack information on either basic principles of self-management or the long-term benefits of actively managing chronic disease. And while there is evidence that case managers and others can successfully train frail elders in self-management skills (Chodosh et al., 2005; Ersek et al., 2003), this type of education and training is not currently reimbursable under most insurance plans, including Medicare and Medicaid (Quijano et al., 2007). Nevertheless, supporting these types of programs is important because if patients are able to manage their conditions more effectively, they are likely to use fewer health care resources and thereby reduce the strain on the health care workforce.

Assistive Technologies

As the number of older Americans with ADL or IADL limitations increases over the coming years, one likely result will be an increase in the use of assistive technologies (Tomita et al., 2004). These devices help with many of the issues that commonly lead older adults to leave their homes for care institutions, including the need for medical monitoring and medication management, decreased mobility, caregiver burnout, dementia, and problems with eating, toileting, safety, isolation, transportation, housekeeping, money management, shopping, and wandering (Haigh et al., 2006). Assistive technologies are designed to support and extend the independent functioning of older adults, which can in turn reduce the need for support from direct-care workers and family caregivers. These technologies can also help lower rates of injury among direct-care workers and caregivers by reducing their physical strain. For example, these technologies can assist with tasks such as lateral transfers, repositioning patients up or side-to-side in bed, and bed-to-chair or bed-to-wheelchair transfers (Baptiste, 2007).

The Institute of Medicine (IOM) report *The Future of Disability in America* refers to assistive technology devices as "items designed for and used by individuals with the intent of eliminating, ameliorating, or compensating for individual functional limitations" (IOM, 2007). These items include a broad range of tools and technologies that help individuals perform ADLs and IADLs and thus reduce their need for personal assistance. Several studies demonstrate, for instance, that the use of assistive devices can reduce the hours of personal assistance that older adults require in their daily activities (Agree, 1999; Freedman et al., 2006; Mann et al., 1999). One study found that people who needed assistance with ADLs and who did not use any assistive devices required an average of 4 additional hours of personal care per week compared with individuals who did employ the devices (Hoenig et al., 2003). With newer technologies on the horizon, it may be possible to make even further reductions in the amount of personal assistance required.

Examples

Assistive technologies range from the very basic to the highly complex. Examples include products such as canes, walkers, hand rails, shower seats, and bath mats, as well as durable equipment such as power wheelchairs and medical devices such as hearing aids. Recent advances in medication-related technologies include smart patches, which assist in regulating drug release, and smart caps, which are placed on medication vials and allow for remote monitoring of medication adherence.

A number of more complex technologies have also been developed, such as environmental intelligence systems that assist older adults in maintaining independent functioning, reducing the need for personal assistance and putting off the time they must leave their homes for some place where others can help take care of them (Mann et al., 1999). "Smart homes," for example, allow older adults to operate household fixtures and appliances (e.g., lights, televisions, dishwashers, window blinds, and other electrical devices) more easily. Many of these homes include motion detectors that sense movement and respond by lighting pathways; other features include remote control shelves and cupboards that can automatically adjust in height when needed for use. Smart kitchen components, such as smart microwaves and smart stoves, can help older adults in cooking their own meals.

Another group of technologies, telemonitoring and telesurveillance devices, allow health care providers to monitor older adults in their homes. For patients with medical needs and cognitive impairments, these devices provide a direct link to care without the need for visits by medical personnel to the site. This can improve patient access to care, as well as the efficiency of the care provided. Although there are privacy concerns, these technologies provide older adults with direct and immediate medical contact if they need it. In addition to increasing patient safety (Mann et al., 2001), this type of communication system has been shown in one study to reduce hospital stays, reduce demand for home-care services, and assist in relieving caregiver stress (Vincent et al., 2006).

Product Development and Availability

While many of these technologies can be produced and sold at reasonable or even inexpensive prices, others, such as robotics and smart home components, are much more costly. For patients the cost of these products can be a major impediment to their purchase and use, especially given that insurance does not always provide adequate coverage for them.

In addition to cost, another significant barrier to the broader diffusion of these technologies is a lack of product information. Older adults frequently do not have adequate information on the basic use of specific devices, or the suitability of these devices to their specific needs (Hoenig et al., 2002). Furthermore, patients often lack information about product quality and performance. More technical assessments are needed to help patients determine the effectiveness of various assistive technologies.

The IOM report *The Future of Disability in America* also noted that the financial incentives for developing better assistive technologies and bringing them to market are currently very weak (IOM, 2007). The report concluded that this was a persistent problem and recommended a number of countermeasures. Specifically, the report called upon policy makers to revise coverage criteria so that the criteria take into account the contribution of a technology to an individual's overall independence, including the individual's participation in the workforce and the community. The report also recommended that policy makers eliminate or modify Medicare's requirement of "in-home use" with respect to coverage of durable medical equipment and that they investigate new approaches for supplying covered technologies, as well as providing timely and appropriate repairs.

> **Recommendation 6-1: Federal agencies (including the Department of Labor and the Department of Health and Human Services) should provide support for the development and promulgation of technological advancements that could enhance an individual's capacity to provide care for older adults. This includes the use of activity-of-daily-living (ADL) technologies and health information technologies, including remote technologies, that increase the efficiency and safety of care and caregiving.**

In addition to testing the use of health-information technology to improve provider communication and promote interdisciplinary care (as described in Chapter 3), research and demonstrations also need to focus on the application of assistive technologies. These demonstrations need to assess the effectiveness of these technologies in promoting functional independence and in easing the physical strain on, and the need for, direct-care workers and informal caregivers.

INFORMAL CAREGIVERS

Informal caregivers[2] may be relatives, friends, or neighbors who provide assistance related to an underlying physical or mental disability but who are unpaid for those services. The motivation for providing this type of assistance is, most commonly, emotional commitment and personal relationship. Public policy has traditionally viewed informal caregivers' service as a personal, moral obligation, and not as an extension of the workforce. Partly as a result, research has not provided a systematic accounting of their numbers, qualifications, and competence.

Families and friends of disabled older adults are the predominant providers of long-term care and in general are thought to provide task assistance that is of low cost, high quality, and consistent with older adults' preferences. In addition to the home setting, many families provide support to older family members in assisted living facilities, nursing homes and low-income senior housing and are key components in helping to manage resident decline (Ball et al., 2004). The vast majority of care recipients report high levels of satisfaction with the assistance received from family and friends (Kasper et al., 2000; McCann and Evans, 2002), and family members have been characterized as being more responsive than paid helpers (Greene, 1983). However, for a number of older adults—such as those who were never married and have no children—informal caregivers are not available. Moreover, for a number of reasons, the overall availability of informal caregivers is decreasing, which has led to calls to increase the support that is provided to them.

While the average informal caregiver provides 20-25 hours of assistance per week (Johnson and Wiener, 2006; National Alliance for Caregiving and AARP, 2004), the intensity of help provided varies by disability level and population subgroup. Spouses, women, co-residents, and caregivers who support patients with dementia and end-of-life stages typically provide help with greater frequency and intensity (Bertrand et al., 2006; Donelan et al., 2002; Schulz et al., 2003b). Nearly 80 percent of adults who receive care at home rely exclusively on unpaid help from family and friends, while less than 10 percent received all of their care from paid workers (ILC-SCSHE Taskforce, 2007). In other words, informal caregivers provide at least some level of support for more than 90 percent of people receiving care at home.

The unpaid services provided by informal caregivers have a substantial economic value when compared against the payment rates that direct-care workers receive. In fact, the value of informal home care vastly exceeds the value of paid home care (AARP, 2007). Overall, the economic value

---

[2]Informal caregivers are also, at times, referred to as family caregivers. For consistency, the term "informal caregivers" is used throughout this report.

derived by informal caregivers' collective involvement and time is easily in the tens to hundreds of billions of dollars annually. Arno estimates that informal caregivers' contribution to the workforce in 2004 was $306 billion, almost twice the amount spent on home-care and nursing-home services combined ($158 billion) (Arno, 2006). Similarly, the AARP calculated that the value of caregiver services had an economic value of $350 billion in 2006 (AARP, 2007). Questions remain about these numbers, however, as there are several difficult methodological challenges involved in making the estimates (see below).

The following sections describe the size and composition of the informal caregiver population in the United States, the responsibilities they assume and the specific tasks they perform, the effect they have on patient outcomes, and possible supports that might be provided to them, such as increased training to help to promote greater competency among this group.

Size and Composition

Estimates of the number of informal caregivers in the United States vary widely depending upon the data source and methodology. The most commonly cited figures indicate that there are between 29 million and 52 million unpaid caregivers nationally, which represents as many as 31 percent of all adults in the United States. Using data derived from population estimates from two national surveys (the Survey on Income and Program Participation and the National Survey of Families and Households), Arno found that in 2004 there were 29 million Americans providing informal care services (Arno, 2006). AARP estimates that between 30 million and 38 million people above the age of 18 provide care to an adult who has an ADL or IADL limitation (AARP, 2007). An earlier study conducted by the Assistant Secretary for Planning and Evaluation (ASPE) and the Administration on Aging (AOA) using broader criteria found that each year 52 million Americans (31 percent of the adult population aged 20 to 75) provide informal care to a family member or friend who is ill or disabled (ASPE and AOA, 1998).

National surveys and observational data sets show that informal caregivers for older adults are predominantly spouses or middle-aged daughters (Johnson and Wiener, 2006; Spillman and Pezzin, 2000). Married older adults tend to depend on their spouses, while unmarried individuals most likely rely on an adult child (Barrett and Lynch, 1999; Soldo et al., 1990). Adult daughters have traditionally served as the primary caregivers of frail unmarried adults (Johnson and Lo Sasso, 2006). Despite the perception that many people actively provide care to an older adult while concurrently raising children (the "sandwich generation"), household surveys indicate that such caregivers are actually few in number because most people old enough to have very elderly parents are too old to have young children (Spillman and Pezzin, 2000; Wolff and Kasper, 2006). Individuals who actively provide assistance to an older adult while simultaneously working are substantially greater in number, representing more than half of all adult child caregivers (Johnson and Wiener, 2006).

Methodologies

Estimates for the numbers of informal caregivers for older adults in the United States depend on how these caregivers are defined and identified. In contrast to the results cited above, household surveys that use a narrower definition of caregiving examine only the care provided to a more narrowly defined group of disabled older adults, and use much shorter time-frames for providing care yield substantially smaller estimates of the number of family caregivers. For example, several iterations of the National Long-Term Care Survey (NLTCS) found 3.8 million to 4.4 million informal caregivers assisting a disabled older adult in the week prior to being interviewed (Spillman and Pezzin, 2000). However, informal caregivers who are assisting older adults because of an acute-onset illness, who assist for a brief period of time prior to death, or who assist older adults residing in institutional long-term care facilities are likely to be underrepresented in many estimates.

AARP identified five publications released between 2004 and 2006 that were based on nationally representative surveys and that included estimates of the number of caregivers in the United States. Table 6-1 describes the sources of data that were used for each publication and the way in which the term caregiver was defined. Because of the differing definitions of caregiving in the different survey instruments, the differing ages of care recipients, and the various dates of the surveys, the number of caregivers reported is not directly comparable across sources.

Recent Trends

For a variety of reasons, the overall availability of informal caregivers is decreasing (Wolff and Kasper, 2006). The factors contributing to this trend include the entry of more women into the workforce (increasing the number of other obligations they face), decreased birth rates (resulting in fewer children available to provide care), and the geographic dispersion of families (stemming from job migration and increased divorce and remarriage rates) (Fleming et al., 2003; Stone, 2000).

The demographic make-up of informal caregivers is also changing, reflecting various health and demographic trends among older adults. For

TABLE 6-1 Recent Studies Giving Estimates of Caregiving Prevalence and/or Hours

Publication	Source Data and Year	Caregiver Definition
Estimated Prevalence and Economic Value of Family Caregiving, by State (2004) (National Family Caregivers Association & Family Caregiver Alliance, 2006).	Estimates for 2004, updated from 1986 Survey of Income and Program Participation (SIPP) and 1987-1988 National Survey of Families and Households (NSFH)	SIPP: Care recipient 15+, with health condition, caregiver 15+, within last month; NSFH: Care recipient 18+, caregiver 18+, with long-term illness or disability, within last month
Many Older Americas Engage in Caregiving Activities (Johnson and Schaner, 2005).	2002 Health and Retirement Study	Care recipient any age, caregiver 55+, within last month (for care of spouse) or last 2 years (for care of parents/in-laws)
A Profile of Frail Older Americans and Their Caregivers (Johnson and Wiener, 2006).	2002 Health and Retirement Study	Care recipient 65+, ADL or IADL dependency, caregiver 18+, within last month
Caregiving: A National Profile and Assessment of Caregiver Services and Needs (McKune et al., 2006).	2000 Behavioral Risk Factor Surveillance System	Care recipient 60+, with long-term illness or disability, caregiver 18+, within last month
Caregiving in the U.S. (National Alliance for Caregiving and AARP, 2004).	Survey designed for the publication, 2003	Care recipient 18+, ADL or IADL dependency, caregiver 18+, within last year

SOURCE: AARP, 2007.

example, spousal caregivers are increasingly older themselves. The proportion of spousal primary caregivers who are aged 75 and above increased from 38 percent in 1989 to 47 percent in 1999 (Wolff and Kasper, 2006). Given the increasing ages of care recipients and their spouses, children are fulfilling the role of primary caregiver more and more often (Spillman and Black, 2005; Wolff and Kasper, 2006). This trend may at least partly explain why the data show declines in secondary caregiving, as adult children who previously filled in as secondary caregivers now find themselves assuming principal responsibility. Spillman found that the declines in aggregate numbers of informal caregivers between 1984 and 1994 were largely attributed to a drop from 1.7 million to 1.1 million individuals serving as secondary caregivers, with no evidence to suggest fewer primary caregivers

(Spillman and Pezzin, 2000). Another study found that in 1999 just 28 percent of primary caregivers received assistance from other family members and friends, a decline from 39 percent in 1989 (Wolff and Kasper, 2006). A number of studies found that during the decade ending in 1994, chronically disabled older adults increasingly relied on paid care (Liu et al., 2000). In many cases, however, primary caregivers simply "go it alone." In 1999, 53 percent of primary caregivers were the exclusive source of assistance, compared to just 35 percent of primary caregivers in 1989 (Wolff and Kasper, 2006). Primary caregivers with no secondary caregiver involvement were most likely to be caring for the least impaired recipients and least likely to be caring for the most disabled.

Tasks and Responsibilities

Informal caregivers assume many different responsibilities in providing care support for older adults (Table 6-2). In performing these functions, they in effect take on the roles of both patient and provider. On the one hand, they take responsibility for much of the patient's role with respect to logistics, care management, and medical decision-making. For example, they often schedule medical appointments for older adults, provide transportation, and handle billing questions. They assume greater responsibility in presenting the patient's history and listening to the clinicians' assessments and instructions. They frequently make, or influence, decisions regarding the appropriate course of treatment. They also take on a health status monitoring function, as envisioned under the self-management paradigm described previously. On the other hand, caregivers also take on the role of health care provider, performing many of the functions that direct-care workers perform on a paid basis, including support with ADLs and IADLs. The sections below detail several of these roles.

Activities of Daily Living and Instrumental Activities of Daily Living

Informal caregivers provide older adults with help in performing ADLs—typically bathing, dressing, eating, toileting, and transferring—and IADLs, such as shopping, meal preparation, money management, light housework, and laundry. Data from the NLTCS and its Informal Caregivers Survey indicate that caregivers commonly assist with the full range of these tasks. In one study, large percentages of primary caregivers reported helping chronically disabled older adults with shopping and/or transportation (85.3 percent), household tasks (77.7 percent), finances (49.4 percent), personal care and nursing (48.5 percent), and indoor mobility (35.1 percent) (Wolff and Kasper, 2006). A substantial portion of informal caregivers (43-53 per-

TABLE 6-2 Health-Related Responsibilities Assumed by Informal Caregivers

Role	Function	Examples
Companion	Provide emotional support	Discuss ongoing life challenges, troubleshoot problems, facilitate and participate in leisure activities
Coach	Encourage patient self-care activities	Prompt patient's engagement in health care, encourage lifestyle (diet, exercise) and treatment adherence
Homemaker	Manage household activities	Inventory, purchase food and medications, prepare meals
Scheduler	Arrange medical care	Schedule tests, procedures, and services
Driver	Facilitate transportation	Provide transportation to medical appointments and emergency hospital visits
Patient extender	Facilitate provider understanding	Attend appointments; clarify and expand on patient history, symptoms, concerns; introduce topics to provider
Technical interpreter	Facilitate patient understanding	Clarify providers' explanations, technical terms, record and remember discussions with providers
Decision maker	Make medical decisions	Select among treatment alternatives; decide among settings of care
Coordinator	Coordinate care across providers and settings	Ensure flow of information among providers
Financial manager	Handle financial issues	Resolve issues relating to insurance claims, secondary coverage, co-pays, and benefit limits
Health provider	Deliver medical care	Administer medications, operate equipment
Attendant	Provide task assistance	Hands-on personal care task assistance
Monitor	Assess health status	Ensure that changes in health status are noted and properly addressed

SOURCE: Wolff, 2007.

cent) also fulfill medically oriented tasks such as helping with wound care, injections, equipment, or medication administration (Wolff and Kasper, 2006). A study following stroke and traumatic brain injury patients and their caregivers from hospital discharge found that during the home health period, families provided three-fourths of total patient care hours (Levine et al., 2006).

Other Support Roles

Informal caregivers frequently coordinate and arrange medical appointments for older adults. In fact, the time that they spend performing this function has given rise to a new line of elder care referral services, which employers have begun to offer as a way to save lost work time among employees. Caregivers frequently accompany older patients to office visits, and they are often involved in treatment decisions (Deimling et al., 1990; Kapp, 1991), particularly those involving patients who are older and who carry a greater disease burden (Ende et al., 1989; Ishikawa et al., 2005). In the case of critically ill and hospitalized patients, families and friends are often kept apprised of the patient's health status, they advocate for needed services and attention, and they provide patients with emotional support (Hickey, 1990). Family may also assume a role in coordinating patient transitions across settings of care—for example, from hospital to home (Coleman, 2003; DesRoches et al., 2002). In addition, as providers of assistance to frail older adults with physical and cognitive disabilities, informal caregivers often help to ensure the safety of the home environment.

When older adults do not speak English, health care providers often ask family members or friends to interpret. In fact, it is estimated that 79 percent of hospitals frequently rely on family and friends to serve as interpreters (Wilson-Stronks and Galvez, 2007). This practice risks misinterpretation and the transmission of inaccurate information, especially when the translators are young children. As a result, recent state laws prevent using the family for this purpose and several organizations have developed reports and guidelines about how to implement language services in health care organizations.

Still, the knowledge that family members have about the patient and their ability to articulate this knowledge allow them to advocate on the patient's behalf and to enhance the provider's understanding of the older adult's social environment, health conditions, and care preferences. Similarly, family members' understanding of the providers' treatment recommendations and their ongoing interactions with the patient at home and in the community can influence the patient's behaviors, treatment adherence, and health.

Impact on Outcomes

There is strong evidence that informal caregivers have a profound effect on long-term care processes and outcomes. Engaging families in patient care has been shown to improve outcomes in dementia (Mittelman et al., 2006; Vickrey et al., 2006) and in schizophrenia care (Glynn et al., 2006) and also to postpone institutionalization (Miller and Weissert, 2000; Yoo et al., 2004). Yet while there is growing recognition of the relevance of family involvement to health care delivery processes (Fisher and Weihs, 2000), there is still little knowledge about which particular attributes of family involvement are efficacious in improving health outcomes.

Older adults strongly prefer independent living (Kasper et al., 2000) and are highly averse to nursing-home placement (Mattimore et al., 1997). Caregiver support may allow older people to remain in their communities in cases where it would not otherwise be possible otherwise and the importance of informal caregivers in reducing the risk of nursing home entry is well documented (Miller and Weissert, 2000). In addition, the availability of family has been linked to shorter lengths of hospital stays (McClaran et al., 1996; Picone et al., 2003). The converse is also true, that is, that an absence of adequate caregiving is associated with problematic hospital discharges (Procter et al., 2001) and readmissions (Lotus Shyu et al., 2004; Schwarz and Elman, 2003).

Living alone is associated with greater risk of nursing home entry, while, conversely, greater familial and caregiver support is associated with a lower likelihood (Miller and Weissert, 2000; Muramatsu et al., 2007). Individuals with few social supports are more likely to have unmet needs in personal care and household tasks (Kennedy, 2001; Lima and Allen, 2001) and are also more likely to miss medical appointments and to fail to fill prescriptions (Allen and Mor, 1997). One study found that unmarried individuals present to the hospital with a greater severity of illness than do their married peers, suggesting that the presence of a spouse leads to admission at an earlier stage of illness (Gordon and Rosenthal, 1995).

The availability and preparedness of informal caregivers can also influence where patients receive their post-acute care following hospitalization and also the course of their recovery (Kane et al., 2000; Weinberg et al., 2007). A meta-analysis of 122 studies found that patients who received instrumental assistance were 3.6 times more likely to adhere to medical instructions and prescriptions. This was twice as effective as emotional support, which was associated with 1.8 times greater likelihood of adherence (DiMatteo, 2004). The effect of family support varies, however; individuals with close and cohesive families are three times more likely to adhere to instructions than those from conflicted families.

Training

Along with the increasing awareness of the role that family and friends play in the provision of ongoing chronic care, there has been a growing understanding of the potential benefits of educating these informal caregivers and integrating them more fully into the health care delivery team. While it is clear that caregivers are able to provide a tremendous amount of support to older adults, the extent to which they are prepared for the role they assume remains unknown. For example, according to one national survey, nearly one in five informal caregivers who assisted with medication management had received no instruction from a health care professional regarding how to perform this task; for those who assisted with changing dressings or bandages, one in three had received no training (Donelan et al., 2002).

As home-based medical technologies have become widely diffused, they have expanded the range of services that may be provided to technology-dependent patients in the community, including at-home parenteral nutrition (i.e., intravenous feeding), intravenous medication infusion, peritoneal dialysis, mechanical ventilation, and apnea monitoring. Yet there has been little attention directed toward identifying, developing, and disseminating the education and training needed to provide patients and caregivers with the skills and knowledge they need to operate sophisticated equipment and to manage complex treatment regimens (Given et al., 2001; Thielemann, 2000). Not surprisingly, studies find that informal caregivers perceive themselves as insufficiently prepared to assist with complex home-based technologies (Silver et al., 2004; Winkler et al., 2006) and medically-oriented treatments in the post-acute period (DesRoches et al., 2002; Mackenzie et al., 2007). This is also true of more basic tasks, such as lifting, turning, feeding, and helping those with Alzheimer's disease.

To improve the care that older patients receive in private settings and to support informal caregivers who are often ill-equipped to perform the necessary medical tasks, the committee recommends that more training opportunities be made available.

Recommendation 6-2: Public, private, and community organizations should provide funding and ensure that adequate training opportunities are available in the community for informal caregivers.

These initiatives may be modeled after those provided by the AOA, which has established a program to assist caregivers in making decisions and solving problems related to their roles. Other potential models include programs developed by the Centers for Medicare and Medicaid Services (CMS), the Health Resources and Services Administration (HRSA), and Geriatric Education Centers. The committee suggests that state attorneys general recognize these types of caregiver training initiatives as an option by which non-profit hospitals can satisfy their requirements for providing benefits to their local communities in exchange for tax-exempt status.

A number of reviews and meta-analyses have synthesized findings from training initiatives aimed at caregivers for patients with various diseases, including stroke (Lee et al., 2007), cancer (Harding and Higginson, 2003), and dementia (Pinquart and Sorensen, 2006). Sorensen and colleagues identified a number of different approaches to supporting caregivers, including education about ways to reduce stress, supportive interventions, psychotherapy, patient day care, and training of the care recipient (Sorensen et al., 2002). Findings indicate that such interventions have a positive, albeit small effect for several outcomes, most notably caregiver depression, strain, and burden (Sorensen et al., 2002). There is a growing consensus that the most successful interventions are comprehensive and individually tailored, actively engage both caregivers and recipients, and provide a combination of education, skills, and coping techniques (Brodaty et al., 2003; Gallagher-Thompson and Coon, 2007).

An intervention in the United Kingdom that trained the informal caregivers of hospitalized stroke patients in basic nursing and personal-care tasks achieved decreases in caregivers' reported burden, anxiety, and depression (Kalra et al., 2004). And while patients' mortality, institutional placement, and disability outcomes remained comparable, annual health care costs for the intervention group were lower by more than £4000 (roughly $8,000), largely due to shorter hospital lengths of stay (Patel et al., 2004). A multi-component counseling and support group intervention for spouses of dementia patients was found to reduce caregivers' depressive symptoms (Mittelman et al., 2004) and to delay recipients' nursing-home entry by more than 1 year (Mittelman et al., 2006).

Lastly, the Resources for Enhancing Alzheimer's Caregiver Health (REACH) study was an ambitious program that enrolled a diverse group of 1,222 dementia caregivers at six intervention sites (Schulz et al., 2003a). Nine active interventions were tested, and a coordinating center developed standard eligibility protocols and measurement procedures. After 6 months, the study found small but statistically significant improvements for measures of caregiver burden and, in one site, caregiver depression (Gitlin et al., 2003). An extension of the study found statistically significant and clinically important improvements in measures of caregivers' quality of life (including depression) but not in institutionalization (Belle et al., 2006).

Integration with Medical Team

A more explicit recognition of informal caregivers as providers and partners in health care processes could benefit both patients and caregivers in the management of the health needs of older adults in the community. One aspect of patient-centered care described by the IOM report *Crossing the Quality Chasm* is that providers should "focus on accommodating family and friends on whom patients may rely, involving them as appropriate in decision making, supporting them as caregivers, making them welcome and comfortable in the care-delivery setting, and recognizing their needs and contributions" (IOM, 2001). Exactly when and how providers need to incorporate the family into health care processes is not yet well understood, but such incorporation is relevant across the full spectrum of institutional, ambulatory, and residential patient-care settings.

Despite the potential benefits to older patients of enhancing communication among their many care providers (formal and informal), such coordination has yet to receive adequate attention. Family members describe a "vortex" of uncertainty and frustration resulting from the medical community's poor communication and unease with their presence (Kirchhoff et al., 2002; Teno et al., 2004). The Health Insurance Portability and Accountability Act (HIPAA)[3] has further exacerbated this situation by limiting families' access to information.

In assuming specific tasks and responsibilities, informal caregivers become part of the health care delivery team and contribute directly to health outcomes, although this is not always recognized in the health care community. For example, caregivers play a role in promoting patient adherence to medications, ensuring medication safety, and reducing the likelihood of adverse drug events. One large cohort study of Medicare beneficiaries who were treated within a multi-specialty group practice found some 20 percent of serious adverse drug events in the ambulatory setting to be potentially avoidable; they were caused by such mistakes as taking the wrong dose, continuance of medication despite instructions by the physician to discontinue drug therapy, and continuance despite recognition of an adverse effect or drug interaction (Gurwitz et al., 2003). The authors noted that in the ambulatory setting, unlike the situation with institutional care, it is the patient—and often the patient's family members—who are responsible for adherence to medical instructions.

Despite this, there have been few patient safety innovations that have explicitly included the family as an ally in monitoring changes in treatment regimens or symptoms. Electronic personal health records could give informal caregivers improved access to patient information and provide a convenient method for them to communicate with the patient's health care team online (Seavey, 2005). These electronic records could also provide decision support for common problems and help older adults in managing their conditions at home. The Veterans Administration's HealtheVet record system provides an example of this type of electronic support. The system provides veterans with access to the data in their health record, advice on steps they can take improve their health condition, and a means to self-enter structured medical information (MyhealtheVet, 2008). Establishing better linkages between the medical care team and informal caregivers is

---

[3]*Health Insurance Portability and Accountability Act of 1996.* Public Law 191. 104th Congress. August 21, 1996.

potentially beneficial for both older adults and caregivers. The Rosalynn Carter Institute for Caregiving has sought to do this by bringing paid and informal caregivers together to learn about caregiving issues, share ways to work together more effectively, and gain a greater understanding of each other's perspectives. Informal caregivers place high value on both the emotional support that is provided through friendships with home-care workers and also these workers' affirmation of their caregiver efforts (Piercy and Dunkley, 2004). Medicare reimbursement changes have been proposed that would create a more integrated system in which direct-care workers would be paid to assess the caregiving needs of families, observe their caregiving skills, and teach them to perform various, duties such as ambulation and comfort care (Seavey, 2005).

Additional Supports

Taking on the role of informal caregiver has been found to increase the risk of elevated stress hormones (Kiecolt-Glaser et al., 2003; Vitaliano et al., 2003), make physical illness and psychological distress more likely (Emanuel et al., 2000; Pinquart and Sorensen, 2003), and raise mortality rates (Christakis and Allison, 2006). Caregivers may have to provide constant care day and night, may be unable to leave the recipient alone, and may even have to provide assistance despite their own physical illness or impairments; such requirements can affect the caregiver in various ways, including causing interrupted sleep, physical strain, and emotional and financial difficulties (Wolff et al., 2007). Longitudinal studies of spouses find that both the assumption of the role of informal caregiver and the continuing long-term provision of high-intensity care are associated with downward trajectories in terms of depression (Burton et al., 2003; Cannuscio et al., 2002), social participation, and quality of the marital relationship (Seltzer and Li, 2000). In spite of this, many informal caregivers are able to adapt and derive personal benefits from their role (Kramer, 1997; Stuckey et al., 1996).

Given the demonstrated importance of informal caregivers to older adults and to society, and given the personal costs that may accompany the role, there has been considerable interest in how it might be possible to improve informal caregivers' experiences and outcomes. A large number of caregiver interventions have been developed, with a large range of strategies, services, and target populations. Programs have been established to provide caregivers with greater education and training, strengthened partnerships with the medical community, and a number of other types of aid including respite care, web-based monitoring systems, technologies that reduce physical strain, and financial supports. Several health services interventions targeted specifically at older caregivers have proven to benefit both their health (Silliman et al., 1990) and their well-being (Hughes et al., 2000; Weuve et al., 2000).

In recent years there has been a significant amount of legislation at the state and federal levels aimed at providing various types of aid to family caregivers. According to one accounting, between 2004 and 2006 over 100 bills to assist informal caregivers were introduced in 32 states and at the federal level, typically focusing on increased tax incentives, family and medical leave provisions, and respite care supports. Of those, 21 were passed—16 bills in 13 states and 5 in the U.S. Congress (FCA, 2007).

The National Family Caregiver Support Program (NFCSP), initiated under the Older Americans Act Amendments of 2000, is the first—and so far only—federally funded program intended specifically to assist informal caregivers of older adults. The program funds state initiatives for such things as information dissemination, organization of support groups, and the provision of individual counseling, training, respite care, and other supplemental services. The NFCSP is implemented at the state level in partnership with area agencies on aging and local-area service providers. States have considerable discretion in the design and delivery of the program, and eligibility, service offerings, methods of compensation, and approaches to accessing services vary widely across states, and in some cases, within states (Feinberg and Newman, 2004, 2006). The program expanded the range of service offerings to family caregivers, but its modest funding ($162 million in 2007) has resulted in geographic disparities and gaps in service availability (AOA, 2007).

The Lifespan Respite Care Bill[4] was passed by both branches of the Congress and signed into law by President Bush in December 2006, but it has not yet received federal appropriations. The objective of the program is to allow states to develop a network of respite care providers that will provide family caregivers with high-quality planned and emergency respite services. There have been discussions of an appropriation of $10 million for fiscal year 2008, which would be substantially more limited in scale and scope than the $289 million authorized over 5 years.

Under Medicaid, the movement toward patient-directed care—in which decision-making responsibility shifts from health professionals to patients— is a trend that has implications for informal caregivers. State Cash and Counseling programs (see Chapter 3) give Medicaid recipients a monthly allowance to hire the providers of their choice and provide counseling and financial assistance to help them in planning and managing these responsibilities. Many of these state programs permit Medicaid recipients to hire

---

[4]*Lifespan Respite Care Act of 2006.* Public Law 442. 109th Congress. December 21, 2006.

immediate family members to perform caregiving services for pay, as well as the option to use that money to hire direct-care workers.

These types of consumer-directed programs raise a number of issues, such as their potential impact on direct-care workers, who typically receive even lower pay, fewer benefits, and little or no training or supervision relative to workers hired through an agency (Benjamin and Matthias, 2004). Overall, though, differences in the levels of job stress and satisfaction are thought to be minor, the experiences of patient-directed workers tended to more positive (Benjamin and Matthias, 2004; Foster et al., 2007). Moreover, informal caregivers were shown in one study to be more satisfied with the Medicaid recipients' overall care and their own lives, as compared to a control group, and, that they experienced less financial and physical strain (Foster et al., 2007). In addition, states have put in place a number of measures to improve the basic functioning of the program, such as processing payroll for directly-hired workers in accordance with tax laws and providing training and assistance to Medicaid recipients, or their designees, in recruiting, hiring, training, managing, evaluating, and dismissing workers (Cash & Counseling, 2006).

While a number of programs and policies either directly target, or indirectly influence, the well-being of informal caregivers, the supportive programs that exist are generally small, poorly funded, and fragmented across the federal, state, and local levels. The sections below highlight the three areas in which caregivers frequently request additional support: training, respite, and financial assistance.

Training

Informal caregivers are often required to perform a number of functions for which they may feel inadequately prepared. As described previously, this can include basic tasks such as lifting and turning, medical tasks such as administering medications and injections, and the use of technologies such as mechanical ventilation. Instruction in how to perform these types of tasks would not only improve patient care, but it would also reduce the stress and burden placed on caregivers.

Medicare does not currently include any provisions to help informal caregivers get the education and training they need to competently assist beneficiaries in the post-discharge period. Direct-care workers might be able to perform this function, for instance, but they do not currently receive reimbursement for it. Some have proposed establishing a national training center that would identify and disseminate best practices, provide training, and evaluate approaches to improving caregiver competence. Such an effort would combine the available research with current practices in caregiver assessment and education.

To the extent that an older adult is dependent on an informal caregiver—for example, in transitioning from hospital to home—clinicians need to explicitly assess the caregiver's abilities, needs, and competence to perform the required tasks. Thus developing methodologically rigorous caregiver assessment tools is a necessary first step toward the routine use of these tools in clinical practice and, eventually, toward developing effective programs to prepare caregivers for their roles.

Respite

Respite is among the most common requests of informal caregivers (Jenson and Jacobzone, 2000), and ensuring that it becomes more widely available is one of the goals of the National Family Caregiver Support Program and Lifespan Respite Care Bill. At present, support services for informal caregivers, including respite care, are delivered mainly by state and local agencies. This approach has the advantage that it makes it easier to customize services to accommodate various characteristics of geographic and cultural subgroups, but the resulting variation creates complexity in the system overall (Feinberg and Newman, 2006; Stone and Keigher, 1994).

Policy makers have considered establishing a defined, national respite care benefit program for informal caregivers. A number of decisions would have to be made about the design of such a national program, including the size and the structure of the benefits (e.g., service voucher versus cash allowance, and whether the benefit needs to be uniform or needs to vary according to the severity of the recipient's disability) and the particulars of the eligibility criteria (e.g., whether the benefit needs to be means-tested and whether it needs to be restricted to certain categories of caregivers). Although the specific provisions vary widely, a number of other countries have adopted formal respite-care programs for informal caregivers, either as part of comprehensive long-term care reform (e.g., Germany and Japan) or as freestanding caregiver programs (e.g., Canada and Australia) (Jenson and Jacobzone, 2000).

As the predominant health insurance program of older Americans, Medicare is relevant to—and, in many ways, reliant upon—informal caregivers. Yet aside from covering respite care through the hospice benefit, the Medicare program does not currently consider informal caregivers in formal policy.

Financial Assistance

Providing financial assistance to family members acting as caregivers could have a negative effect on employment and may also have financial ramifications for the caregivers themselves. Studies indicate that some family members acting as caregivers quit their jobs or take time off work, are forced to take out loans or mortgages, or make other life changes in order to be able to provide assistance (Covinsky et al., 2001; Emanuel et al., 2000). In one study of severely ill patients of all ages, 31 percent of families reported that most of their family savings were lost; smaller numbers of families reported having to move to a less expensive home (6 percent), delay medical care (6 percent), or alter educational plans for another family member (4 percent) because of the cost of patients' illness (Covinsky et al., 1994). Adult daughter caregivers have been shown to reduce their own labor participation or leave the workforce entirely (Ettner, 1995; Johnson and Lo Sasso, 2006). And the opportunity costs related to caregiving, including foregone earnings, retirement savings, and employer-sponsored benefits, may actually exceed the direct costs, such as the time spent in direct care, out-of-pocket expenses, and costs associated with adverse health effects (Moore et al., 2001).

The existence of these opportunity costs makes it even more important to come up with effective policies to promote financial, retirement, and health care security for informal caregivers who leave the workforce to care for an older adult. Among the strategies that have been considered are tax incentives (including credits, deductions, or exemptions), cash allowances, and provisions that allow an accumulation of Social Security credits for caregivers. Employer-based approaches have focused, among other things, on restructuring the workplace to facilitate greater flexibility, the provision of family and medical leave, access to supportive services such as adult day care, and the availability of tax-deductible dependent-care assistance programs. And given the high costs and difficulty that individuals face in getting health insurance outside of the workplace, some have suggested providing caregivers with government-assured access to coverage through measures such as broadening Medicare eligibility to include informal caregivers for older adults.

There are limited data with which to assess the relative merits of these options. One report examined how several countries' informal caregiver programs affected women and found that caregiver allowances as typically implemented did not approach a labor market wage (Jenson and Jacobzone, 2000). Instead of focusing on short-term strategies such as tax credits or allowances, that report advocated greater emphasis on longer-term compensatory strategies such as pension rights. Several states offer tax incentives for family caregiving (Stone and Keigher, 1994), which may be structured in a variety of ways. As some tax incentives may benefit higher-income families (Keefe and Fancey, 1999; Stone and Keigher, 1994), the establishment of any federal policy requires careful deliberation. While the evidence is far from definitive, the limited empirical data indicate that the magnitude of relief afforded to informal caregivers through existing programs and policies is largely symbolic rather than meaningful (Jenson and Jacobzone, 2000). Research in this area is critically important and is a task that could be undertaken by a national center spanning multiple disciplines and federal agencies.

As described in Chapter 3, the committee recommends that the Congress and private foundations increase support for research that promotes the effective use of the workforce to care for older persons. One important topic that needs to be investigated through research is the effect of financial incentives on informal caregiving.

CONCLUSION

Patients and informal caregivers play a substantial, but often underappreciated, role in the health care delivery process. Their roles will be even more substantial in the future, given the rising incidence of chronic disease, which requires greater self-monitoring on the part of patients, and the rapidly increasing number of older Americans, which will place greater responsibilities on family and friends to provide care assistance. Informal, unpaid caregiving is an essential component of an optimal health care workforce for an aging population. However, the trend toward fewer informal caregivers at a time when the number of older persons is expanding underscores the importance of identifying effective strategies to support informal caregivers, such as offering them increased training opportunities. It will also be important to develop and distribute technologies that promote greater independent functioning among older adults and reduce their reliance on the direct-care workforce and on informal caregivers.

REFERENCES

AARP. 2007. *Valuing the invaluable: A new look at the economic value of family caregiving.* Washington, DC: AARP.

Agree, E. M. 1999. The influence of personal care and assistive devices on the measurement of disability. *Social Science and Medicine* 48(4):427-443.

Allen, S. M., and V. Mor. 1997. The prevalence and consequences of unmet need. Contrasts between older and younger adults with disability. *Medical Care* 35(11):1132-1148.

AOA (Administration on Aging). 2007. *The national family caregiver support program.* http://www.aoa.gov/prof/aoaprog/caregiver/careprof/progguidance/research/NFCSP_BROCHURE.pdf (accessed October 10, 2007).

Arno, P. S. 2006. *Economic value of informal caregiving: 2004.* Presented at the Care Coordination & the Caregiver Forum, Bethesda, MD. January 25-27.

ASPE and AOA (The Office of the Assistant Secretary for Planning and Evaluation and the Administration on Aging). 1998. *Informal caregiving: Compassion in action.* Washington, DC: Department of Health and Human Services (HHS) and AOA.

Baker, D. W., R. M. Parker, M. V. Williams, W. S. Clark, and J. Nurss. 1997. The relationship of patient reading ability to self-reported health and use of health services. *American Journal of Public Health* 87(6):1027-1030.

Ball, M. M., M. M. Perkins, F. J. Whittington, B. R. Connell, C. Hollingsworth, S. V. King, C. L. Elrod, and B. L. Combs. 2004. Managing decline in assisted living: The key to aging in place. *Journals of Gerontology, Series B: Psychological Sciences and Social Sciences* 59(4):S202-S212.

Baptiste, A. 2007. Technology solutions for high-risk tasks in critical care. *Critical Care Nursing Clinics of North America* 19(2):177-186.

Barrett, A. E., and S. M. Lynch. 1999. Caregiving networks of elderly persons: Variation by marital status. *Gerontologist* 39(6):695-704.

Belle, S. H., L. Burgio, R. Burns, D. Coon, S. J. Czaja, D. Gallagher-Thompson, L. N. Gitlin, J. Klinger, K. M. Koepke, C. C. Lee, J. Martindale-Adams, L. Nichols, R. Schulz, S. Stahl, A. Stevens, L. Winter, and S. Zhang. 2006. Enhancing the quality of life of dementia caregivers from different ethnic or racial groups: A randomized, controlled trial. *Annals of Internal Medicine* 145(10):727-738.

Benjamin, A. E., and R. E. Matthias. 2004. Work-life differences and outcomes for agency and consumer-directed home-care workers. *Gerontologist* 44(4):479-488.

Bertrand, R. M., L. Fredman, and J. Saczynski. 2006. Are all caregivers created equal? Stress in caregivers to adults with and without dementia. *Journal of Aging and Health* 18(4):534-551.

Bodenheimer, T., K. Lorig, H. Holman, and K. Grumbach. 2002. Patient self-management of chronic disease in primary care. *Journal of the American Medical Association* 288(19): 2469-2475.

Brodaty, H., A. Green, and A. Koschera. 2003. Meta-analysis of psychosocial interventions for caregivers of people with dementia. *Journal of the American Geriatrics Society* 51(5):657-664.

Burton, L. C., B. Zdaniuk, R. Schulz, S. Jackson, and C. Hirsch. 2003. Transitions in spousal caregiving. *Gerontologist* 43(2):230-241.

Cannuscio, C. C., C. Jones, I. Kawachi, G. A. Colditz, L. Berkman, and E. Rimm. 2002. Reverberations of family illness: A longitudinal assessment of informal caregiving and mental health status in the nurses' health study. *American Journal of Public Health* 92(8):1305-1311.

Cash & Counseling. 2006. *The "Cash & Counseling Model" vision statement.* http://www.cashandcounseling.org/resources/20060807-100150/CCvisionstatement.doc (accessed February 1, 2008).

CBO (Congressional Budget Office). 1993. *Baby boomers in retirement: An early perspective.* Washington, DC: CBO.

Chodosh, J., S. C. Morton, W. Mojica, M. Maglione, M. J. Suttorp, L. Hilton, S. Rhodes, and P. Shekelle. 2005. Meta-analysis: Chronic disease self-management programs for older adults. *Annals of Internal Medicine* 143(6):427-438.

Christakis, N. A., and P. D. Allison. 2006. Mortality after the hospitalization of a spouse. *New England Journal of Medicine* 354(7):719-730.

Coleman, E. A. 2003. Falling through the cracks: Challenges and opportunities for improving transitional care for persons with continuous complex care needs. *Journal of the American Geriatrics Society* 51(4):549-555.

Covinsky, K. E., C. Eng, L.-Y. Lui, L. P. Sands, A. R. Sehgal, L. C. Walter, D. Wieland, G. P. Eleazer, and K. Yaffe. 2001. Reduced employment in caregivers of frail elders: Impact of ethnicity, patient clinical characteristics, and caregiver characteristics. *Journals of Gerontology, Series A: Biological Sciences and Medical Sciences* 56(11):M707-M713.

Cutilli, C. C. 2007. Health literacy in geriatric patients: An integrative review of the literature. *Orthopaedic Nursing* 26(1):43-48.

Deimling, G. T., V. L. Smerglia, and C. M. Barresi. 1990. Health care professionals and family involvement in care-related decisions concerning older patients. *Journal of Aging and Health* 2(3):310-325.

DesRoches, C., R. Blendon, J. Young, K. Scoles, and M. Kim. 2002. Caregiving in the post-hospitalization period: Findings from a national survey. *Nursing Economics* 20(5):216-221, 224.

DiMatteo, M. R. 2004. Social support and patient adherence to medical treatment: A meta-analysis. *Health Psychology* 23(2):207-218.

Donelan, K., C. A. Hill, C. Hoffman, K. Scoles, P. H. Feldman, C. Levine, and D. Gould. 2002. Challenged to care: Informal caregivers in a changing health system. *Health Affairs* 21(4):222-231.

Emanuel, E. J., D. L. Fairclough, J. Slutsman, and L. L. Emanuel. 2000. Understanding economic and other burdens of terminal illness: The experience of patients and their caregivers. *Annals of Internal Medicine* 132:451-459.

Ende, J., L. Kazis, A. Ash, and M. A. Moskowitz. 1989. Measuring patients' desire for autonomy: Decision making and information-seeking preferences among medical patients. *Journal of General Internal Medicine* 4(1):23-30.

Ersek, M., J. A. Turner, S. M. McCurry, L. Gibbons, and B. M. Kraybill. 2003. Efficacy of a self-management group intervention for elderly persons with chronic pain. *Clinical Journal of Pain* 19(3):156-167.

Ettner, S. L. 1995. The impact of "parent care" on female labor supply decisions. *Demography* 32(1):63-80.

FCA (Family Caregiver Alliance). 2007. *Federal and state family caregiving legislation: A summary of bills from 2004-2006.* http://www.caregiver.org/caregiver/jsp/content/pdfs/Fed_and_State_CG_Leg_final_summ.02.21.07.pdf (accessed August 2, 2007).

Feinberg, L. F., and S. L. Newman. 2004. A study of 10 states since passage of the National Family Caregiver Support Program: Policies, perceptions, and program development. *Gerontologist* 44(6):760-769.

Feinberg, L., and S. Newman. 2006. Preliminary experiences of the states in implementing the National Family Caregiver Support Program: A 50-state study. *Journal of Aging and Social Policy* 18(3-4):95-113.

Fisher, L., and K. L. Weihs. 2000. Can addressing family relationships improve outcomes in chronic disease? Report of the National Working Group on Family-Based Interventions in Chronic Disease. *Journal of Family Practice* 49(6):561-566.

Fleming, K. C., J. M. Evans, and D. S. Chutka. 2003. Caregiver and clinician shortages in an aging nation. *Mayo Clinic Proceedings* 78(8):1026-1040.

Foster, L., S. B. Dale, and R. Brown. 2007. How caregivers and workers fared in cash and counseling. *Health Services Research* 42(1):510-532.

Freedman, V. A., E. M. Agree, L. G. Martin, and J. C. Cornman. 2006. Trends in the use of assistive technology and personal care for late-life disability, 1992-2001. *Gerontologist* 46(1):124-127.

Funnell, M. M. 2000. Helping patients take charge of their chronic illnesses. *Family Practice Management* 7(3):47-51.

Gallagher-Thompson, D., and D. W. Coon. 2007. Evidence-based psychological treatments for distress in family caregivers of older adults. *Psychology and Aging* 22(1):37-51.

Gitlin, L. N., L. D. Burgio, D. Mahoney, R. Burns, S. Zhang, R. Schulz, S. H. Belle, S. J. Czaja, D. Gallagher-Thompson, W. W. Hauck, and M. G. Ory. 2003. Effect of multicomponent interventions on caregiver burden and depression: The REACH multisite initiative at 6-month follow-up. *Psychology and Aging* 18(3):361-374.

Given, B. A., C. W. Given, and S. Kozachik. 2001. Family support in advanced cancer. *CA: A Cancer Journal for Clinicians* 51(4):213-231.

Glynn, S. M., A. N. Cohen, L. B. Dixon, and N. Niv. 2006. The potential impact of the recovery movement on family interventions for schizophrenia: Opportunities and obstacles. *Schizophrenia Bulletin* 32(3):451-463.

Gordon, H. S., and G. E. Rosenthal. 1995. Impact of marital status on outcomes in hospitalized patients. *Archives of Internal Medicine* 155(22):2465-2471.

Greene, J., J. Hibbard, and M. Tusler. 2005. *How much do health literacy and patient activation contribute to older adults' ability to manage their health?* Washington, DC: AARP.

Greene, V. L. 1983. Substitution between formally and informally provided care for the impaired elderly in the community. *Medical Care* 21(6):609-619.

Gurwitz, J. H., T. S. Field, L. R. Harrold, J. Rothschild, K. Debellis, A. C. Seger, C. Cadoret, L. S. Fish, L. Garber, M. Kelleher, and D. W. Bates. 2003. Incidence and preventability of adverse drug events among older persons in the ambulatory setting. *Journal of the American Medical Association* 289(9):1107-1116.

Haigh, K. Z., L. M. Kiff, and G. Ho. 2006. The independent lifestyle assistant: Lessons learned. *Assistive Technology* 18(1):87-106.

Harding, R., and I. J. Higginson. 2003. What is the best way to help caregivers in cancer and palliative care? A systematic literature review of interventions and their effectiveness. *Palliative Medicine* 17(1):63-74.

Hibbard, J. H. 2003. Engaging health care consumers to improve the quality of care. *Medical Care* 41(1 Suppl):I61-I70.

Hickey, M. 1990. What are the needs of families of critically ill patients? A review of the literature since 1976. *Heart & Lung* 19(4):401-415.

Hoenig, H., L. Lundberg, and D. Lansdale. 2002. *Assistive and smart technologies: Improving older adults' quality of life.* http://www.annalsoflongtermcare.com/altc/attachments/Assistive_8_02.pdf (accessed March 11, 2008).

Hoenig, H., D. H. Taylor, Jr., and F. A. Sloan. 2003. Does assistive technology substitute for personal assistance among the disabled elderly? *American Journal of Public Health* 93(2):330-337.

Hughes, S. L., F. M. Weaver, A. Giobbie-Hurder, L. Manheim, W. Henderson, J. D. Kubal, A. Ulasevich, and J. Cummings. 2000. Effectiveness of team-managed home-based primary care: A randomized multicenter trial. *Journal of the American Medical Association* 284(22): 2877-2885.

ILC-SCSHE Taskforce. 2007. *Caregiving in America.* The Caregiving Project for Older Americans. http://www.agingtech.org/documents/ilc_caregiving_report.pdf (accessed March 5, 2008).

IOM (Institute of Medicine). 2001. *Crossing the quality chasm: A new health system for the 21st century.* Washington, DC: National Academy Press.

IOM. 2004. *Health literacy: A prescription to end confusion.* Washington, DC: The National Academies Press.

IOM. 2007. *The future of disability in America.* Washington, DC: The National Academies Press.

Ishikawa, H., D. L. Roter, Y. Yamazaki, and T. Takayama. 2005. Physician-elderly patient-companion communication and roles of companions in Japanese geriatric encounters. *Social Science and Medicine* 60(10):2307-2320.

Jenson, J., and S. Jacobzone. 2000. *Occasional papers no. 41. Care allowances for the frail elderly and their impact on women care-givers.* http://www.cprn.org/documents/24968_en.pdf (accessed January 8, 2008).

Johnson, R. W., and A. T. Lo Sasso. 2006. The impact of elder care on women's labor supply. *Inquiry* 43(3):195-210.

Johnson, R. W., and S. G. Schaner. 2005. *Many older Americans engage in caregiving activities.* Perspectives on Productive Aging, No. 3. Washington, DC: The Urban Institute.

Johnson, R. W., and J. M. Wiener. 2006. *A profile of frail older Americans and their caregivers.* The Retirement Project, Occasional Paper No. 8. Washington, DC: The Urban Institute.

Kalra, L., A. Evans, I. Perez, A. Melbourn, A. Patel, M. Knapp, and N. Donaldson. 2004. Training care givers of stroke patients: Randomised controlled trial. *British Medical Journal* 328(7448):1099-1101.

Kane, R. L., Q. Chen, M. Finch, L. Blewett, R. Burns, and M. Moskowitz. 2000. The optimal outcomes of post-hospital care under Medicare. *Health Services Research* 35(3): 615-661.

Kapp, M. B. 1991. Health care decision making by the elderly: I get by with a little help from my family. *Gerontologist* 31(5):619-623.

Kasper, J. D., A. Shore, and B. W. J. H. Penninx. 2000. Caregiving arrangements of older disabled women, caregiving preferences, and views on adequacy of care. *Aging (Milano)* 12(2):141-153.

Keefe, J., and P. Fancey. 1999. Compensating family caregivers: An analysis of tax initiatives and pension schemes. *Health Law Journal* 7:193-204.

Kennedy, J. 2001. Unmet and undermet need for activities of daily living and instrumental activities of daily living assistance among adults with disabilities: Estimates from the 1994 and 1995 disability follow-back surveys. *Medical Care* 39(12):1305-1312.

Kiecolt-Glaser, J. K., K. J. Preacher, R. C. MacCallum, C. Atkinson, W. B. Malarkey, and R. Glaser. 2003. Chronic stress and age-related increases in the proinflammatory cytokine IL-6. *Proceedings of the National Academy of Sciences of the United States of America* 100(15):9090-9095.

Kirchhoff, K. T., L. Walker, A. Hutton, V. Spuhler, B. V. Cole, and T. Clemmer. 2002. The vortex: Families' experiences with death in the intensive care unit. *American Journal of Critical Care* 11(3):200-209.

Kramer, B. J. 1997. Gain in the caregiving experience: Where are we? What next? *Gerontologist* 37(2):218-232.

Lee, J., K. Soeken, and S. J. Picot. 2007. A meta-analysis of interventions for informal stroke caregivers. *Western Journal of Nursing Research* 29(3):344-356, 357-364.

Levine, C., S. M. Albert, A. Hokenstad, D. E. Halper, A. Y. Hart, and D. A. Gould. 2006. "This case is closed": Family caregivers and the termination of home health care services for stroke patients. *Milbank Quarterly* 84(2):305-331.

Lima, J. C., and S. M. Allen. 2001. Targeting risk for unmet need: Not enough help versus no help at all. *Journals of Gerontology, Series B: Psychological Sciences and Social Sciences* 56B(5):S302-S310.

Liu, K., K. G. Manton, and C. Aragon. 2000. Changes in home care use by disabled elderly persons: 1982-1994. *Journals of Gerontology, Series B: Psychological Sciences and Social Sciences* 55(4):S245-S253.

Lotus Shyu, Y., M. Chen, and H. Lee. 2004. Caregiver's needs as predictors of hospital readmission for the elderly in Taiwan. *Social Science & Medicine* 58(7):1395-1403.

Mackenzie, A., L. Perry, E. Lockhart, M. Cottee, G. Cloud, and H. Mann. 2007. Family carers of stroke survivors: Needs, knowledge, satisfaction and competence in caring. *Disability and Rehabilitation* 29(2):111-121.

Mann, W. C., K. J. Ottenbacher, L. Fraas, M. Tomita, and C. V. Granger. 1999. Effectiveness of assistive technology and environmental interventions in maintaining independence and reducing home care costs for the frail elderly. A randomized controlled trial. *Archives of Family Medicine* 8(3):210-217.

Mann, W. C., T. Marchant, M. Tomita, L. Fraas, and K. Stanton. 2001. Elder acceptance of health monitoring devices in the home. *Care Management Journals* 3(2):91-98.

Mattimore, T. J., N. S. Wenger, N. A. Desbiens, J. M. Teno, M. B. Hamel, H. Liu, R. Califf, A. F. Connors, J. Lynn, and R. K. Oye. 1997. Surrogate and physician understanding of patients' preferences for living permanently in a nursing home. *Journal of the American Geriatrics Society* 45(7):818-824.

McCann, S., and D. S. Evans. 2002. Informal care: The views of people receiving care. *Health & Social Care in the Community* 10(4):221-228.

McClaran, J., R. T. Berglas, and E. D. Franco. 1996. Long hospital stays and need for alternate level of care at discharge. *Canadian Family Physician* 42:449-461.

McKune, S. L., E. M. Andresen, J. Zhang, and B. Neugaard. 2006. *Caregiving: A national profile and assessment of caregiver services and needs.* Rosalyn Carter Institute and the University of Florida. http://www.rosalynncarter.org/UserFiles/File/UFL_RCI_Final CaregiverReport.pdf (accessed January 18, 2008).

Miller, E. A., and W. G. Weissert. 2000. Predicting elderly people's risk for nursing home placement, hospitalization, functional impairment, and mortality: A synthesis. *Medical Care Research and Review* 57(3):259-297.

Mittelman, M. S., D. L. Roth, D. W. Coon, and W. E. Haley. 2004. Sustained benefit of sup-portive intervention for depressive symptoms in caregivers of patients with Alzheimer's Disease. *American Journal of Psychiatry* 161(5):850-856.

Mittelman, M. S., W. E. Haley, O. J. Clay, and D. L. Roth. 2006. Improving caregiver well-being delays nursing home placement of patients with Alzheimer Disease. *Neurology* 67(9):1592-1599.

Moore, M. J., C. W. Zhu, and E. C. Clipp. 2001. Informal costs of dementia care: Estimates from the national longitudinal caregiver study. *Journals of Gerontology, Series B: Psy-chological Sciences and Social Sciences* 56(4):S219-S228.

Muramatsu, N., H. Yin, R. T. Campbell, R. L. Hoyem, M. A. Jacob, and C. O. Ross. 2007. Risk of nursing home admission among older Americans: Does states' spending on home- and community-based services matter? *Journals of Gerontology, Series B: Psychological Sciences and Social Sciences* 62(3):S169-S178.

MyhealtheVet. 2008. *Frequently asked questions.* http://www.health-evet.va.gov/faqs.asp (ac-cessed January 31, 2008).

National Alliance for Caregiving and AARP. 2004. *Caregiving in the U.S.* http://www.caregiving.org/data/04finalreport.pdf (accessed January 18, 2008).

National Family Caregivers Association & Family Caregiver Alliance. 2006. *Prevalence, hours, and economic value of family caregiving, Updated state-by-state analysis of 2004 national estimates.* http://www.caregiver.org/caregiver/jsp/content/pdfs/State_Caregiving_Data_Arno_20061107.pdf (accessed January 19, 2007).

Newman, S., L. Steed, and K. Mulligan. 2004. Self-management interventions for chronic illness. *Lancet* 364(9444):1523-1537.

Patel, A., M. Knapp, A. Evans, I. Perez, and L. Kalra. 2004. Training care givers of stroke patients: Economic evaluation. *British Medical Journal* 328(7448):1102.

Picone, G., R. M. Wilson, and S. Chou. 2003. Analysis of hospital length of stay and discharge destination using hazard functions with unmeasured heterogeneity. *Health Economics* 12(12):1021-1034.

Piercy, K. W., and G. J. Dunkley. 2004. What quality paid home care means to family caregiv-ers. *Journal of Applied Gerontology* 23(3):175-192.

Pinquart, M., and S. Sorensen. 2003. Differences between caregivers and noncaregivers in psychological health and physical health: A meta-analysis. *Psychology and Aging* 18(2):250-267.

Pinquart, M., and S. Sorensen. 2006. Helping caregivers of persons with dementia: Which interventions work and how large are their effects? *International Psychogeriatrics* 18(4): 577-595.

Procter, S., J. Wilcockson, P. Pearson, and V. Allgar. 2001. Going home from the hospital: The carer/patient dyad. *Journal of Advanced Nursing* 35(2):206-217.

Quijano, L. M., M. A. Stanley, N. J. Petersen, B. L. Casado, E. H. Steinberg, J. A. Cully, and N. L. Wilson. 2007. Healthy ideas: A depression intervention delivered by community-based case managers serving older adults. *Journal of Applied Gerontology* 26(2):139-156.

Schulz, R., S. H. Belle, L. N. Gitlin, S. J. Czaja, S. R. Wisniewski, and M. G. Ory. 2003a. Introduction to the special section on resources for enhancing Alzheimer's caregiver health (REACH). *Psychology and Aging* 18(3):357-360.

Schulz, R., A. B. Mendelsohn, W. E. Haley, D. Mahoney, R. S. Allen, S. Zhang, L. Thompson, and S. H. Belle. 2003b. End-of-life care and the effects of bereavement on family caregivers of persons with dementia. *The New England Journal of Medicine* 349(20):1936-1942.

Schwarz, K. A., and C. S. Elman. 2003. Identification of factors predictive of hospital readmissions for patients with heart failure. *Heart & Lung* 32(2):88-99.

Scott, T. L., J. A. Gazmararian, M. V. Williams, and D. W. Baker. 2002. Health literacy and preventive health care use among Medicare enrollees in a managed care organization. *Medical Care* 40(5):395-404.

Seavey, D. 2005. *Family care and paid care: Separate worlds or common ground?* http://www.bjbc.org/content/docs/BJBCIssueBriefNo5.pdf (accessed February 11, 2008).

Seltzer, M. M., and L. W. Li. 2000. The dynamics of caregiving: Transitions during a three-year prospective study. *Gerontologist* 40(2):165-178.

Silliman, R. A., S. T. McGarvey, P. M. Raymond, and M. D. Fretwell. 1990. The senior care study. Does inpatient interdisciplinary geriatric assessment help the family caregivers of acutely ill older patients? *Journal of the American Geriatrics Society* 38(4):461-466.

Silver, H. J., N. S. Wellman, D. Galindo-Ciocon, and P. Johnson. 2004. Family caregivers of older adults on home enteral nutrition have multiple unmet task-related training needs and low overall preparedness for caregiving. *Journal of the American Dietetic Association* 104(1):43-50.

Soldo, B. J., D. A. Wolf, and E. M. Agree. 1990. Family, households, and care arrangements of frail older women: A structural analysis. *Journals of Gerontology* 45(6):S238-S249.

Sorensen, S., M. Pinquart, and P. Duberstein. 2002. How effective are interventions with caregivers? An updated meta-analysis. *Gerontologist* 42(3):356-372.

Spillman, B. C., and K. J. Black. 2005. *Staying the course: Trends in family caregiving.* Washington, DC: AARP.

Spillman, B. C., and L. E. Pezzin. 2000. Potential and active family caregivers: Changing networks and the "sandwich generation." *Milbank Quarterly* 78(3):347-374.

Stone, R. I. 2000. *Long-term care for the elderly with disabilities: Current policy, emerging trends, and implications for the twenty-first century.* New York: Milbank Memorial Fund.

Stone, R. I., and S. M. Keigher. 1994. Toward an equitable, universal caregiver policy: The potential of financial supports for family caregivers. *Journal of Aging & Social Policy* 6(1-2):57-75.

Stuckey, J. C., M. M. Neundorfer, and K. A. Smyth. 1996. Burden and well-being: The same coin or related currency. *Gerontologist* 36(5):686-693.

Teno, J. M., B. R. Clarridge, V. Casey, L. C. Welch, T. Wetle, R. Shield, and V. Mor. 2004. Family perspectives on end-of-life care at the last place of care. *Journal of the American Medical Association* 291(1):88-93.

Thielemann, P. 2000. Educational needs of home caregivers of terminally ill patients: Litera-
ture review. *American Journal of Hospice & Palliative Care* 17(4):253-257.
Tomita, M. R., W. C. Mann, L. F. Fraas, and K. M. Stanton. 2004. Predictors of the use of
assistive devices that address physical impairments among community-based frail elders.
Journal of Applied Gerontology 23(2):141-155.
Vickrey, B. G., B. S. Mittman, K. I. Connor, M. L. Pearson, R. D. Della Penna, T. G. Ganiats,
R. W. Demonte, J. Chodosh, X. Cui, S. Vassar, N. Duan, and M. Lee. 2006. The effect of
a disease management intervention on quality and outcomes of dementia care: A random-
ized, controlled trial. *Annals of Internal Medicine* 145(10):713-726.
Vincent, C., D. Reinharz, I. Deaudelin, M. Garceau, and L. R. Talbot. 2006. Public telesur-
veillance service for frail elderly living at home, outcomes and cost evolution: A quasi
experimental design with two follow-ups. *Health and Quality of Life Outcomes* 4:41.
Vitaliano, P. P., J. Zhang, and J. M. Scanlan. 2003. Is caregiving hazardous to one's physical
health? A meta-analysis. *Psychological Bulletin* 129(6):946-972.
Wagner, E. H. 2000. The role of patient care teams in chronic disease management. *British
Medical Journal* 320(7234):569-572.
Weinberg, D. B., R. W. Lusenhop, J. H. Gittell, and C. M. Kautz. 2007. Coordination
between formal providers and informal caregivers. *Health Care Management Review*
32(2):140-149.
Weuve, J. L., C. Boult, and L. Morishita. 2000. The effects of outpatient geriatric evaluation
and management on caregiver burden. *Gerontologist* 40(4):429-436.
Williams, M. V., D. W. Baker, R. M. Parker, and J. R. Nurss. 1998. Relationship of functional
health literacy to patients' knowledge of their chronic disease: A study of patients with
hypertension and diabetes. *Archives of Internal Medicine* 158(2):166-172.
Wilson-Stronks, A., and E. Galvez. 2007. *Hospitals, language, and culture: A snapshot of the
nation.* http://www.jointcommission.org/NR/rdonlyres/E64E5E89-5734-4D1D-BB4D-
C4ACD4BF8BD3/0/hlc_paper.pdf (accessed March 26, 2008).
Winkler, M., V. Ross, U. Piamjariyakul, B. Gajewski, and C. Smith. 2006. Technology depen-
dence in home care: Impact on patients and their family caregivers. *Nutrition in Clinical
Practice* 21(6):544-556.
Wolff, J. L. 2007 (unpublished). *Supporting and sustaining the family caregiver workforce for
older Americans.* Paper commissioned by the IOM Committee on the Future Health Care
Workforce for Older Americans.
Wolff, J. L., and J. D. Kasper. 2006. Caregivers of frail elders: Updating a national profile.
Gerontologist 46(3):344-356.
Wolff, J. L., S. M. Dy, K. D. Frick, and J. D. Kasper. 2007. End of life care: Findings from a
national survey of family caregivers. *Archives of Internal Medicine* 167:40-46.
Yoo, B., J. Bhattacharya, K. McDonald, and A. Garber. 2004. Impacts of informal caregiver
availability on long-term care expenditures in OECD countries. *Health Services Research*
39(6):1971-1992.

APPENDIX
A

Committee Biographies

John W. Rowe, M.D. (*Chair*), is a Professor in the Department of Health Policy and Management at the Columbia University Mailman School of Public Health. From 2000 until late 2006, Dr. Rowe served as Chairman and CEO of Aetna, Inc, one of the nation's leading health care and related benefits organizations. Before his tenure at Aetna, from 1998 to 2000, Dr. Rowe served as President and Chief Executive Officer of Mount Sinai NYU Health, one of the nation's largest academic health care organizations. From 1988 to 1998, prior to the Mount Sinai-NYU Health merger, Dr. Rowe was President of the Mount Sinai Hospital and the Mount Sinai School of Medicine in New York City. Before joining Mount Sinai, Dr. Rowe was a Professor of Medicine and the founding Director of the Division on Aging at the Harvard Medical School, as well as Chief of Gerontology at Boston's Beth Israel Hospital. Dr. Rowe has received many honors and awards for his research and health policy efforts regarding care of the elderly. He was Director of the MacArthur Foundation Research Network on Successful Aging and currently leads the MacArthur Foundation's Research Network on An Aging Society. Dr. Rowe was elected a member of the Institute of Medicine of the National Academies and a Fellow of the American Academy of Arts and Sciences and a Trustee of the Rockefeller Foundation and Lincoln Center Theater.

Paula G. Allen-Meares, B.S., M.S.W., Ph.D., is Dean, Norma Radin Collegiate Professor of Social Work, and Professor of Education at the University of Michigan. Research interests include the tasks and functions of social workers employed in educational settings; psychopathology in children, adolescents, and families; adolescent sexuality; premature parenthood; and various aspects of social work practice. She is the principal investigator of the School's Global Program on Youth, an initiative supported by the W.K. Kellogg Foundation; co-principal investigator of the NIMH Social Work Research Center on Poverty, Risk, and Mental Health; and a co-investigator on an NIMH research grant. Dean Allen-Meares serves on several editorial boards, as well as national professional and scientific committees promoting the intellectual and empirical advancement of the profession. She is a past member of the Institute for Advancement of Social Work Research, Treasurer of the Council on Social Work Education, Chair of the Publication Committee for the National Association of Social Workers, and Vice President for the National Association of Deans and Directors of Social Work. Dean Allen-Meares serves as a member of the Board of Trustees of the William T. Grant Foundation, and has served as President of the Society for Social Work and Research and a University of Michigan Senior Fellow. She is presently appointed to the New York Academy of Medicine's panel on long-term care issues in the United States and is a member of the Institute of Medicine of the National Academies. Dean Allen Meares serves on numerous committees at the University of Michigan that promote interdisciplinary research and instruction, fundraising, and diversity. Other areas of research/scholarly interest include school social work, racial issues, social work practice, and mental health.

Stuart H. Altman, Ph.D., is the Dean and Sol C. Chaikin Professor of National Health Policy at the Heller School for Social Policy and Management, Brandeis University. He served as dean of the Heller School from 1977 to a 1993; and, in August 2005, he again assumed the deanship of the Heller School. Professor Altman has had extensive experience with the federal government, serving as Deputy Assistant Secretary for Planning and Evaluation/Health in the U.S. Department of Health, Education, and Welfare, 1971-1976; as the chairman of the congressionally-mandated Prospective Payment Assessment Commission, 1983-1996; and, as a member of the Bipartisan Commission on the Future of Medicare, 1999-2001. In addition, from 1973 to 1974, he served as Deputy Director for Health of the President's Cost-of-Living Council and was responsible for developing the council's program on health care cost containment. Dean Altman has testified before various congressional committees on the problems of rising health care costs, Medicare reform, and the need to create a national health insurance for the United States. He chaired the Institute of Medicine's Committee on the Changing Market, Managed Care, and the Future Viability of Safety Net Providers. His research activities include several studies concerning the factors causing the recent increases in the use of emergency rooms. He holds a Ph.D. in economics from the University of California, Los Angeles, and has taught at Brown University and the University of California, Berkeley.

Marie A. Bernard, M.D., is the Donald W. Reynolds Chair in Geriatric Medicine, and Professor and Chairman of the Reynolds Department of Geriatrics at the University of Oklahoma College of Medicine. She also serves as the Associate Chief of Staff for Geriatrics and Extended Care at the Oklahoma City Veterans Affairs Medical Center. She is President of the Association of Directors of Geriatric Academic Programs, President of the Association for Gerontology in Higher Education, and Past-Chair of the Clinical Medicine Section of the Gerontological Society of America. Dr. Bernard's research interests include nutrition and function in aging populations, with particular emphasis upon ethnic minorities. She serves on the following national committees: Chair, National Research Advisory Council, Department of Veterans Affairs; Board of Directors, American Geriatrics Society; Board of Directors, Alliance for Aging Research; Board of Directors, International Longevity Center; Editorial Board, *Journal of Gerontology—Medical Sciences*; Editorial Board, Geriatrics. She recently completed a 4-year term on the National Advisory Council on Aging of the National Institute of Aging (2001-2005), during which time she chaired the Minority Task Force (2004-2005).

David Blumenthal, M.D., M.P.P., is Director, Institute for Health Policy and Physician at Massachusetts General Hospital/Partners HealthCare System in Boston, Massachusetts. He is also Samuel O. Thier Professor of Medicine and Professor of Health Care Policy at Harvard Medical School. He is a member of the Institute of Medicine, a National Associate of the National Academy of Sciences, and serves on several editorial boards, including the *American Journal of Medicine* and the *Journal of Health Politics, Policy and Law*. He is also a National Correspondent for the *New England Journal of Medicine*. Dr. Blumenthal was the founding chairman of Academy-Health. He is also Director of the Harvard University Interfaculty Program for Health Systems Improvement. From 1995 to 2002 Dr. Blumenthal served as Executive Director for the Commonwealth Fund Task Force on Academic Health Centers. He has served as a trustee of the University of Chicago Health System and currently serves as a trustee of the University of Pennsylvania Health System (Penn Medicine). His research interests include the dissemination of health information technology, quality and safety management in health care, the determinants of physician behavior, access to health services, and the extent and consequences of academic-industrial relationships in the health sciences.

Susan A. Chapman, Ph.D, R.N., is the Director of the Allied Health Care Workforce Program at the UCSF Center for the Health Professions and Assistant Professor in the Department of Social and Behavioral Sciences, School of Nursing. Her areas of expertise are nursing and allied health workforce research and policy, program development, managed care, mental health, and health system administration. Dr. Chapman's research focuses on studies of the supply, demand, and need for allied health workers. Past research includes a multi-year effort to develop innovative allied health workforce programs in California, an evaluation of California workforce initiatives focused on nursing and long-term caregivers, and national studies of certified nurse assistants, licensed practical nurses, home-care workers, and other allied health occupations. She teaches health policy and research in the UCSF School of Nursing and serves on the advisory committees for several nursing programs and health workforce initiatives.

Terry T. Fulmer, Ph.D., R.N., F.A.A.N., is the Erline Perkins McGriff Professor and Dean of the College of Nursing at New York University. She received her bachelor's degree from Skidmore College, her master's and doctoral degrees from Boston College and her Geriatric Nurse Practitioner Post-Master's Certificate from New York University. Dr. Fulmer's program of research focuses on acute care of the elderly and specifically, elder abuse and neglect. She served on the National Research Council's panel to review risk and prevalence of elder abuse and neglect and has published widely on this topic. She has received the status of Fellow in the American Academy of Nursing, the Gerontological Society of America, and the New York Academy of Medicine. She is a member of the National Committee for Quality Assurance geriatric measurement assessment panel and the Veteran's Administration Geriatrics and Gerontology Advisory Committee. She completed a Brookdale National Fellowship and is a Distinguished Practitioner of the National Academies of Practice. Dr. Fulmer was the first nurse to be elected to the board of the American Geriatrics Society and the first nurse to serve as the president of the Gerontological Society of America.

Tamara B. Harris, M.D., M.S., is Chief of the Geriatric Epidemiology Section in the Laboratory of Epidemiology, Demography, and Biometry, Intramural Research Program, National Institute on Aging. The role of the Geriatric Epidemiology Section is to integrate molecular and genetic epidemiology with interdisciplinary studies of functional outcomes, disease endpoints and mortality in older persons. This includes identification of novel risk factors and design of studies involving biomarkers, selected polymorphisms and exploration of gene/environment interactions. The Section has been particularly active in devising methods to integrate promising molecular or imaging techniques to explore the physiology underlying epidemiologic associations including adaptation of imaging protocols to epidemiologic studies. Dr. Harris received her M.D. from Albert Einstein College of Medicine. She trained in internal medicine at Montefiore Hospital and in geriatric medicine at Harvard University, Division on Aging, where she was a Kaiser Fellow in Geriatric Medicine. She obtained an M.S. in Epidemiology from Harvard School of Public Health and also has an M.S. in Human Nutrition from Columbia University College of Physician's and Surgeons.

Miriam A. Mobley Smith, B.S. Pharm., Pharm.D., is the Associate Dean and Associate Professor at the Chicago State University College of Pharmacy. Before joining Chicago State, she was the Director of Experiential Education at the University of Illinois at Chicago College of Pharmacy. Dr. Mobley Smith is an adjunct faculty member in the Allied Health, Nursing and Human Services Department at South Suburban College, South Holland, Illinois, and served on the curriculum advisory board, "Tech Prep Medical Professional" advisory committee and re-accreditation review team. She was a U.S. Department of Health and Human Services 2005 Primary Healthcare Policy Fellow and an American Association of Colleges of Pharmacy 2006 Academic Leadership Fellow. She has chaired the Pharmacy Technician Certification Examination Standards Setting Committee, 2005 National Practice Analysis and was Past-President of the Pharmacy Technician Certification Board Certification Council. Dr. Mobley Smith was featured in the Aetna 2005 African American History Calendar for her impact in older adult communities, received the Illinois Area Agencies on Aging 2006 Sid Granet Aging Network Achievement Award, the 2005 Illinois Council of Health-System Pharmacists "Pharmacist of the Year," and the 2004 National Pharmaceutical Association's James N. Tyson Award in recognition of outstanding achievement in contributions to the profession of pharmacy. She is a member of the American Society of Health-System Pharmacists' Council on Education and Workforce Development, American Society of Consultant Pharmacists, American College of Clinical Pharmacy, American Pharmacists Association, The Joint Commission Health Care Professional Education Roundtable and Illinois Drug Policy Coalition. Dr. Mobley Smith received her B.S in Pharmacy from the University of Michigan and her Pharm.D. from the University of Illinois. Her research and grants focus on preventive health-related issues affecting older adults, including an Illinois Department on Aging, Title III-D program entitled "Medication Monitoring and Safety in Older Adults," the "Senior Medication Education and Review Program" for the Woodlawn Community Development Corporation and Chicago Housing Authority, and the Chicago Department on

Aging Wellness Program (in collaboration with Area Agencies on Aging). She has delivered over 100 invited local, regional and national presentations and published in areas relative to her areas of focus.

Carol Raphael, M.P.A., is President and Chief Executive Officer of Visiting Nurse Service of New York (VNSNY), the largest nonprofit home health agency in the United States. She oversees VNSNY's comprehensive programs in post-acute care, long-term care, children's and family services, end-of-life care, rehabilitation, mental health and public health, as well as its health plans for dually eligible Medicare and Medicaid beneficiaries. Ms. Raphael developed the Center for Home Care Policy and Research, which conducts policy-relevant research focusing on the management and quality of home and community-based services. Previously, Ms. Raphael held positions as Director of Operations Management at Mt. Sinai Medical Center and Executive Deputy Commissioner of the Human Resources Administration in charge of the Medicaid and Public Assistance programs in New York City. Between 1999 and 2005, Ms. Raphael was a member of MedPAC. She served on the New York State Hospital Review and Planning Council for 12 years (1992-2004) and chaired its Fiscal Policy Committee. She chairs the New York eHealth Collaborative and is a member of the IOM's Committee to Study the Future Health Care Workforce for Older Americans, Harvard School of Public Health's Health Policy Management Executive Council, the Markle Foundation Connecting for Health Steering Group, Atlantic Philanthropies Geriatrics Practice Scholars Program, the Advisory Board for The Jonas Center for Excellence in Nursing, the National Advisory Committee of the Caregiving Project for Older Americans, and the AHA's Health for Life Expert Advisory Group on Chronic Care Management. She is also on the Boards of Barrier Therapeutics, Excellus/Lifetime Healthcare Company, the American Foundation for the Blind, Pace University and the Continuing Care Leadership Coalition. She has authored papers and presentations on post-acute, long-term and end-of-life care and co-edited the book *Home Based Care for a New Century*. Ms. Raphael has an M.P.A. from Harvard University's Kennedy School of Government, and was a Visiting Fellow at the Kings Fund in the United Kingdom. Ms. Raphael was recently listed in *Crain's New York Business* Top 25 Most Influential Businesswomen in New York City.

David B. Reuben, M.D., is the Director of the UCLA Multicampus Program in Geriatric Medicine and Gerontology, Archstone Professor, and Director of the UCLA Claude D. Pepper Older Americans Independence Center. He is a Geriatrician-researcher with expertise in studies linking common geriatric syndromes (e.g., functional impairment, sensory impairment, malnutrition) to health outcomes such as mortality, costs and functional decline. He also has extensive experience with interventional research (e.g., comprehensive geriatric assessment) that has focused on health care delivery to older persons. His most recent work focuses on developing and testing interventions to improve the quality of care that primary care physicians provide for geriatric conditions. In 2000, Dr. Reuben was given the Dennis H. Jahnigen Memorial Award for outstanding contributions to education in the field of geriatrics. He is a past-president of the American Geriatrics Society and the Association of Directors of Geriatric Academic Programs (ADGAP). Dr. Reuben is currently a member of the Board of Directors of the American Board of Internal Medicine and sits on its Executive Committee. He is lead author of the widely distributed book *Geriatrics at Your Fingertips*. Dr. Reuben has served on two previous IOM Committees: Strengthening the Geriatric Content of Medical Training (1993) and Nutrition Services for Medicare Beneficiaries (2000).

Charles F. Reynolds III, M.D., is the UPMC Professor of Geriatric Psychiatry (University of Pittsburgh School of Medicine) and Professor of Behavioral and Community Health Science (University of Pittsburgh Graduate School of Public Health). Dr. Reynolds directs the NIMH-sponsored Advanced Center for Interventions and Services Research in Late-Life Mood Disorders and the John A. Hartford Center of Excellence in Geriatric Psychiatry. He is internationally renowned for his research in the mood and sleep disorders of old age, with a particular focus on mental health services in primary care, preventive interventions, and suicide prevention. He has served as a member of the National Advisory Mental Health Council of the NIMH (2003-2006) and as President of the American College of Psychiatrists (2004-2005) and the International College for Geriatric Psychoneuropharmacology (2004). Dr. Reynolds has served on two previous IOM studies (Reducing Suicide: A National Imperative, 2001-2002; and Sleep Disorders: An Unmet Public Health Problem, 2005-2006). He currently serves as Senior Associate Dean of the University of Pittsburgh School of Medicine and is a graduate of the Yale Medical School (1973).

Joseph E. Scherger, M.D., M.P.H., is Clinical Professor in the Department of Family and Preventive Medicine at the University of California, San Diego, School of Medicine. Dr. Scherger is Medical Director for County Medical Services in San Diego, administered by AmeriChoice, a subsidiary of United Health Group. He is also Consulting Medical Director of Informatics for Lumetra, the Quality Improvement Organization for California. Dr. Scherger's main focus is on the redesign of office practice using the tools of information technology and quality improvement. Dr. Scherger is an IOM member and served on the Committee on the Quality of Health Care in America from 1998-2001. Dr. Scherger has served on the Board of Directors of the American Academy of Family Physicians and the American Board of Family Medicine.

Paul C. Tang, M.D., M.S., is an Internist and Vice President, Chief Medical Information Officer at the Palo Alto Medical Foundation (Palo Alto, California), and is Consulting Associate Professor of Medicine (Biomedical Informatics) at Stanford University. He received his B.S. and M.S. in Electrical Engineering from Stanford University and his M.D. from the University of California, San Francisco. Dr. Tang is a member of the Institute of Medicine (IOM), a member of the IOM Health Care Services Board, and a National Associate of the National Academy of Sciences. He chaired the IOM Committee on Data Standards for Patient Safety, which published: Patient Safety: A New Standard for Care, and Key Capabilities of an Electronic Health Record System. He is the Immediate Past Chair of the Board for the American Medical Informatics Association, a member of the National Committee on Vital and Health Statistics (NCVHS), and a member of the American Health Information Community Consumer Empowerment Workgroup. Dr. Tang chairs the National Quality Forum's (NQF's) Health Information Technology Expert Panel and the Robert Wood Johnson Foundation's National Advisory Council for Project HealthDesign and co-chairs the NCVHS Quality subcommittee and the Measurement Implementation Strategy work group of the Quality Alliance Steering Committee. Dr. Tang's medical informatics research interests involve electronic health record (EHR) systems, personal health record systems, EHR-based quality measurement, clinical decision support, online disease management, and health information technology public policies. He is a Fellow of the American College of Medical Informatics, the American College of Physicians, the College of Healthcare Information Management Executives, and the Healthcare Information and Management Systems Society.

Joshua M. Wiener, Ph.D., is Senior Fellow and program director of the Aging, Disability, and Long-Term Care Program at RTI International; he has more than 30 years of experience as a health care researcher and government official. His specialties are long-term care, Medicaid, and health care for the elderly population. Dr. Wiener has directed projects analyzing changes in state health policies, the long-term care workforce, Medicaid eligibility for the aged, blind, and disabled, and Medicaid home and community-based services. He is the author or editor of eight books and more than 100 articles on long-term care, people with disabilities, health reform, health care rationing, and maternal and child health. In addition to RTI International, Dr. Wiener has done research and policy analysis for the Urban Institute, the Brookings Institution, the Health Care Financing Administration, the Massachusetts Department of Public Health, the New York State Moreland Act Commission on Nursing Homes and Residential Care Facilities, and the New York City Department of Health.

APPENDIX
B

Commissioned Papers

Health Workforce and Future Technologies
Author: The Health Technology Center (HealthTech)

How Will the U.S. Health Care System Meet the Challenge of the Ethnogeriatric Imperative?
Author: Gwen Yeo, Ph.D., with assistance from Wendy King, Stanford
    University School of Medicine

Paraprofessional Health Care Workforce for an Aging Population
Author: R. Tamara Konetzka, Ph.D., University of Chicago

State Profiles of the U.S. Health Care Workforce
Author: Mark Mather, Ph.D., Population Reference Bureau

Successful Models of Comprehensive Health Care for Multi-Morbid Older Persons: A Review of Effects on Health and Health Care
Authors: Chad Boult, M.D., M.P.H., M.B.A., Johns Hopkins University
    Bloomberg School of Public Health
    Ariel Green, M.P.H., Johns Hopkins University School of
    Medicine
    Lisa B. Boult, M.D., M.P.H., M.A., Johns Hopkins University
    School of Medicine
    James T. Pacala, M.D., M.S.P.H., University of Minnesota
    Medical School

279

Claire Snyder, Ph.D., Johns Hopkins University School of
    Medicine
Bruce Leff, M.D., Johns Hopkins University School of Medicine

*Supporting and Sustaining the Family Caregiver Workforce for Older
Americans*
Author: Jennifer L. Wolff, Ph.D., Johns Hopkins Bloomberg School of
        Public Health

NOTE: All commissioned papers have been placed in this project's public
access file.

APPENDIX
C

Workshop Presentations

March 27, 2007: Workshop on the Health Care Needs of Older Americans

David B. Reuben, M.D.
University of California, Los Angeles
"Health Care Needs of Today's Older Americans"

Robyn I. Stone, Dr.P.H.
Institute for the Future of Aging Services (IFAS)
American Association of Homes and Services for the Aging (AAHSA)
"The Demand for Long-Term Care: Implications for Workforce Development"

Dan Zabinski, Ph.D.
MedPAC
"Medicare in the 21st Century: Changing Beneficiary Profile"

Stephen Goss, Social Security Administration
Alice Wade, Social Security Administration
"Population and Future Needs for Health Care Workers"

Federico Girosi, Ph.D.
RAND
"Projections of Health Status and Utilization for Older Americans"

June 28, 2007: Workshop Session I—Models of Care for Older Americans

Jennie Chin Hansen, M.S., R.N., F.A.A.N.
University of California, San Francisco
"The PACE Model: An Overview"

Gwen Yeo, Ph.D., AGSF
Stanford University School of Medicine
"How Will the U.S. Health Care System Meet the Challenge of the Ethnogeriatric Imperative?"

Eric Coleman, M.D., M.P.H.
University of Colorado Health Sciences Center
"Looking Forward: Imagining New Models of Care"

Michèle J. Saunders, D.M.D., M.S., M.P.H.
The University of Texas Health Science Center at San Antonio
"The Future Health Care Workforce for Older Americans—Dentistry"

Bruce Leff, M.D.
Johns Hopkins University Schools of Medicine and Public Health
"Dissemination of Models of Geriatric Care: Facilitators and Barriers"

June 28, 2007: Workshop Lunch Session

Steven DeMello
Barbara Harvath, R.N., B.A.
HealthTech
"Health Care Workforce and Future Technologies"

June 28, 2007: Workshop Session II—Recruitment and Retention

Sharon A. Levine, M.D.
Boston University School of Medicine
"Recruitment and Retention of Physicians"

Charlene Harrington, Ph.D., R.N., F.A.A.N.
University of California, San Francisco
"Nursing Home Labor Market Issues"

Jeanie Kayser-Jones, R.N., Ph.D., F.A.A.N.
University of California, San Francisco
"Building Academic Geriatric Nursing Capacity Initiative"

Steven Dawson
PHI
"PHI: Quality Care Through Quality Jobs"

Marcia K. Brand, Ph.D.
Health Resources and Services Administration, Office of Rural Health Policy
"The Future Healthcare Workforce for Older Americans: Rural Recruitment and Retention"

Index